Poetry
Writers'
YEARBOOK
2007

Edited by Gordon Kerr

A & C Black • London

First edition 2006
A & C Black Publishers Limited
38 Soho Square, London W1D 3HB
www.acblack.com

ISBN-10: 0–7136–7576–4
ISBN 13: 978–0–7136–7576–4

A CIP catalogue record for this book is available from the British Library.

The publishers make no representation, express or implied, with regard to the accuracy of the information contained in this book and cannot accept any legal responsibility for any errors or omissions that may take place.

This book is produced using paper that is made from wood grown in managed, sustainable forests. It is natural, renewable and recyclable. The logging and manufacturing processes conform to the environmental regulations of the country of origin.

Typeset by QPM from David Lewis XML Associates Ltd
Printed and bound in Great Britain by William Clowes Ltd, Beccles, Suffolk

Contents

Foreword

For many years, *Writers' and Artists' Yearbook* has been essential reading for all those beginning their career in print, as well as for those who are comparatively well established. But within its family of interested parties, poetry was always the poor relation: the audience didn't justify much space; the range of publishing opportunities was small; and agents were assumed to be concentrating on lucrative fiction and non-fiction ...

Times have changed. Even before new technology became commonplace, traditional ideas about how poetry could best be published had begun to alter. Specialist publishers like Carcanet and Bloodaxe broke into the poetry-publishing world, which had been dominated for generations by Faber and other mainstream metropolitan concerns (Cape, Chatto). Some of the old-guard (Secker, Oxford) hoisted the white flag. A culture of new magazines flourished while other, long-established outlets (such as *The Listener* and *Outposts*) disappeared. A huge network of public readings at festivals and elsewhere began to establish a larger – and quite different – sort of audience.

These changes were not simply driven by commercial fluctuations; they reflected developments in poetry itself. Between the start of the 20th century and the 1960s, the Establishment had (broadly speaking) protected itself by discovering how to contain the experiments of the modernists and make them part of the mainstream; after the 1960s, the defences started to give way. Successive new generations of poets challenged the old orthodoxies; an increasingly diverse literary culture demanded equally diverse kinds of publishing opportunity; and cracks appeared in the ancient alliance between general readers and the academy. It was a pretty quiet revolution (the wide world continues to pay precious little attention to poetry), but a revolution none the less.

New technology has dramatically extended these changes – for the very simple reason that it is now possible for anyone to publish their work on the Internet and find a readership. What size of readership, what sort of connection it allows with readers, and what kind of difference might be made by marketing are still unclear. But the fact remains that poetry now has a new kind of openness. Not an openness in which the old structures have been entirely destroyed, but an openness in which poets and poetry readers can choose more widely and freely the kind of publishing that suits them best. Once upon a time, such discriminations were accompanied by rigid and hierarchical value-judgements – but not any more. Today we do not so much live in a poetic culture as in a culture of poetries, where we are able to say what we like best and why, without feeling that our decisions necessarily imply a resistance to other kinds of writing.

For all these reasons, *Poetry Writers' Yearbook* is a timely and necessary thing. It maps the marvellous variety of poetry now being written in our islands, gives practical advice about where to submit particular forms of work, and shares information about workshops and educational courses. Best of all, it does these things without suggesting that openness means 'anything goes', and that accessibility matters more than anything. Accessibility is crucial, but as the *Yearbook* implies, its potential can only be fully realised if writers and readers continue to ask the most of themselves, and show a proper curiosity about styles which might not be their own.

Andrew Motion is Poet Laureate. His memoir, entitled *In the Blood*, is published by Faber in autumn 2006.

Introduction
Reading, writing, learning, being

The poet **George Szirtes**, whose first collection was published in 1979, examines what it means to be a poet, and how and why we write poetry. He casts his eye over the poetry world of the early 21st century – noting the opportunities afforded by technology, and finding reasons to be cheerful in the number of writing courses on offer today, as well as the volume of entries for poetry competitions.

To be a poet; is that the same as writing a poem, or maybe a dozen? If so, there are hundreds of thousands of poets in the country, if not more; perhaps millions – people who have at some time or other felt that the appropriate thing to do in respect of this or that experience or memory or desire was to take a piece of paper and try to write it down in a form that had lines, a steady rhythm and, usually, rhyme. This feeling may have come upon them in their youth and perhaps persisted on an intermittent basis; even, in some cases, into old age. They might have liked the lyrics of some song, or sung hymns, or laughed at some particularly adroit piece of wit whose sharpness was provided by rhythm or rhyme. Or maybe they felt that there was some peculiar, ritual, commemorative power in verse; such verses could be seen on gravestones and on monuments. Or it was simply that the emotional power of the experience, memory or desire was such that ordinary talk, ordinary writing, couldn't capture it – and capturing it, or at least representing it in some way, was important. Poetry was that form, and always has been. Poetry is that instinct finding a shape in language. And not only in language, but in action too. It isn't that there are sensitive people who understand poetry (a small minority) and insensitive people who don't (the vast majority), for almost everyone who at some time or other has uttered, "Sheer poetry!" or simply gasped, "Wow!" at a bird soaring, a footballer swerving or any act that seems perfect in itself, understands poetry in the most visceral sense.

The desire to commemorate, celebrate, mourn or gasp "Wow!" is the stuff of poetry. That is why poetry can never die, and why it is at the very beginning of writing and speaking and singing. Unless this is understood as the basis on which the whole structure of poetry stands, we may as well give up. The state of poetry in the country is therefore as it ever was; central, vital, and partly hidden.

A private art

Partly hidden because, as Geoffrey Grigson said, poetry is in some respects a private art. Private not only in the sense that it is written out of keenly personal sensibility – all the arts have their origins in the solitary mind wandering about the unknown world of language and experience – but in that most poetry, even when read by, or read to, or spoken or sung to hundreds or even thousands of people, is addressed to a mind as solitary and ambient as itself. There is communal experience, of course: the cabaret, the slam, the rally, events that act as important public confirmations of communality. And yet, it seems to me that even in those conditions, at some level there is a seeking of what theologian Martin Buber called "the I-Thou communion". Something that moves from depth to depth and implies, as did Rilke's sonnet on the Archaic Torso of Apollo, that you must change your life. Depth needn't be the same as solemnity, of course. It may come as a form of serious existential play, but depth it is, the echo deep and wide.

This is, of course, a personal view, not an attempt to point to a hierarchy among kinds of poetry. It is offered as one possible reason why poetry is a hidden art: it addresses the hidden. It takes concentration. It makes demands but it rewards enormously. The demands are not necessarily those of 'difficulty' but of attention – attention to the true articulation of all those experiences, memories and desires I have already mentioned. Such attention is at a premium everywhere. Often it is at its greatest when most needed, and it tends to be needed more in poverty, in trouble, in discomfort, where truth and the desire for meaning are more pressing. Fat, comfortable societies don't need it; what they want is distraction and entertainment. Words are dirt cheap.

Nevertheless, there are cultural differences even among fat and comfortable societies replete with entertainments. This is not the place to undertake a serious description of British society and its attitudes to art. Art as news, art as personality, art as entertainment, art as a nice big noise has no real problem here. People have no problems with verse either, provided it turns on some of the ready taps and gives us nice, ready, warm feelings. But there is, and has long been, a kind of emotional embarrassment, particularly in English society, which prefers the impersonal to the personal, the non-verbal to the verbal, and is afraid of boring the pants off someone else by betraying something about itself. This is partly a product of the complex class system, the tradition of empiricism and the fear of pretension – or worse still, of being perceived as pretentious – but whatever it is, it does constitute a cultural pattern.

Such ingrained cultural patterns have considerable virtues. People are less liable to being told nonsense, or to fall under the spell of demagogues. There is at some level a great bottom of good sense that rejects cant. On the other hand this mindset can lead to a certain blandness, in turn producing a stylised reaction in which the cult of the rough is turned into a series of approvable gestures. There are also the approved eccentrics, of course – the lovably barking, who eventually become 'national treasures'; but even so these establish a fairly low level of tolerance for the kind of art that poetry can be at its best.

But times and generations change. The poetry I grew up with is different from the poetry I came to some sort of maturity with, and is different again now as I move towards 60. I grew up at the end of post-war romanticism, in the world of the Movement, the Group and of Alvarez's *The New Poetry* on the one hand and the Beats and the Mersey Sound on the other. I came to my first adulthood in writing at the time of the *New Review*, of Lowell, Plath, Berryman, moving towards Hamilton, Heaney, Longley and Harrison. I found myself to some extent in Mahon. I arrived in one boat with the Martians. The kind of approach to formality I found myself using in the 80s is fairly general parlance now: I see it in O'Brien, Paterson, Donaghy, Farley and many others. That's just literary history, and ten years from now it will be different again.

What has changed, and changed greatly, is the interest in learning to write poetry. In the last five years or so more than 50 MAs in Creative Writing have sprung up, all desperate to fill their places and mostly with enough applicants to do just that. And beyond that there are the expanding short courses offered by organisations like the Arvon Foundation, which now has four centres to work from, as well as external courses run from universities and other colleges. Whether this is a result of an aspirational leisured middle-class; of the acceptability of borrowing and living in debt; of the desire to supplement a communal and individual spiritual space; of years of degrees in arts administration; of crafty funding initiatives by central and regional arts bodies; or of a genuine awakening in the art of poetry is hard to say. Probably something of each. Having worked often as a tutor for Arvon, and been both tutor and examiner on MA courses, I am pretty sure that they can be extremely worthwhile and interesting. In teaching through reading they are also serving the broader purpose of creating an intelligent, involved matrix of readers-and-writers which may well bear fruit in the future. It is not simply the egotistical satisfaction of the individual at stake: when a course is properly conducted and understood, it encourages a critical awareness of daily language and the forms it employs.

It is a different story in publishing, reviewing and book-buying. People write more but read less, they say. Few publishers of poetry can get by without grants, and the getting of grants is a long, tortuous, managerial process that may entail filling in forms of 40-odd pages and answering questions driven by different agendas. In return for these grants the publisher can publish a number of volumes that sell in their hundreds rather than their thousands, partly because the big book chains store very little poetry, preferring to pile high and sell cheap, and partly because the books (when they appear) are not always noticed. Not that this is so different from the situation when I started. My first book from Secker and Warburg in 1979, *The Slant Door*, was expected to sell about 700 copies at best. It won the Faber Prize so it might have sold a few more, I don't remember now, but it wouldn't have made a substantial difference. Secker was a mainstream publisher working without funding; its poetry list was supported by the most successful items on the fiction list. No big sales of money then either. However the book was reviewed on the day of its appearance – in the *New Statesman*, if I remember right.

There were many more independent bookshops then. The best of them displayed and sold literary magazines, set up or advertised events and welcomed as much poetry as they could. Poetry at the sales end was better supported. Sales improved still further when books or poets got on to schools' or universities' syllabuses.

It also helped that there were more magazines and periodicals that published poems and reviews. *The Observer*, the *Sunday Times*, the *Sunday Telegraph* and others had a certain amount of regular space for both. Poetry was more a part of the literary conversation. That is not to say it is entirely peripheral now – *The Guardian* does its level best to keep the conversation going – but serious general magazines such as *The Listener* and *Encounter* are gone, and the *TLS* publishes far fewer poems or reviews of poetry than it did.

This represents a serious loss, but there are some gains too. New magazines have appeared and there is the whole Web to play on. The Internet and computer technology generally have made and continue to make a significant contribution to the publication, discussion and sale of poetry. Though vast and formless at first – like an infinitely large tobacconist's window; one that displayed anything anyone cared to put in it – the Web is on the way to developing a proper literary society of its own. Magazines appear, as do newspapers. Bloggers have created a new political space, and the use of links has enabled various meetings of minds in poetry (as in much else). The infinitely large tobacconist's window remains, but sections of it are talking to each other. Nor is it only the young and the geeky driving the process: email is used by people of all ages and needs no great sophistication, so poems circulate by email, from poet to friend to tutor or student to editor and publisher, and may appear on your screen rather than on a piece of paper. News travels fast.

Eventually, though, it is still the book that matters. The new technology allows books to be set and edited quickly, and even printed to order, bypassing the chain-stores of the big book companies. I expect this to expand, and many publishers and literary agents believe that books of poetry and other serious literature will be often produced and made available in this way.

The process is quite exciting at this stage: it is like being at the birth of a new culture that is technological but not impersonal.

Despite the push in the 80s onwards to get poetry, or rather poets, 'out of the poetry ghetto' and into factories, supermarkets, surgeries and oilrigs, the last 20 years have not produced a surge in poetry-buying. The best initiatives have, I suspect, been strictly non-managerial and non-institutional. The most successful individual act of genius has probably been *Poems on the Underground*, of which there have been several series now. The secret, I think, is that this addresses the potential reader in the best one-to-one way, as part of daily life. The tube isn't a social mode of transport: it is often uncomfortable; there may not be enough elbow room to open a newspaper, and the traveller is both physically and psychologically in an in-between state. As a reader, he or she comes across the poem as an object of brief personal contemplation. The poem is caught in a fascinating attention space. There is nothing else to do, there is no communal dynamic. There, among all the advertisements with their commercial language, is this entirely other language addressing another aspect of the human condition. One could well have short poems on bookmarks, serviettes, tickets, tube maps. There is a potential readership for such things.

For ordinary books of poetry, leaving out most bookshops, there is Internet shopping and the Poetry Book Society, a small but important organisation that acts not only like a book club but also as a magazine and a maker of reputations through its Choices, Recommendations and prizes.

And lastly there is the great expansion in prizes, quite wealthy prizes, from £500 to £10,000, for books and for individual poems. These have been instrumental in familiarising the work of a number of writers, some of them little-known before the award of the prize. It is in judging these that one discovers how many people write poetry. The entries come in their hundreds and thousands.

And this takes us back to the beginning, to the reasons why all kinds of people write poetry and think it appropriate to do so. To be a poet, however, is more than writing the occasional poem. The desire is not the deed; the recognition of the possibility of grace is not the achievement of grace. Poetry is a vocation, a delight, a discipline, a kind of necessity, an ache, occasionally a terrible pain. There isn't such a thing as a poet's career with a specific job description, promotion scheme and pension. The one thing certain is that being a poet in the sense of being engaged in the pursuit of writing poetry, trying to embody ever deeper, ever more complex experiences, memories and desires – in fact, ever more of life – in ever better poems is something quite distinct from whatever public success or status the person who is a poet may achieve or fail to achieve as a person. "Poetry begins in delight," said Frost, "and ends in wisdom." There is certainly the hope of wisdom – if nothing else, the wisdom of understanding what it means to articulate life in language.

This is what it is like being alive, says the poem. Speak it, sing it, whisper it.

Sheer poetry.

George Szirtes was born in Budapest in 1948 and came to England as a refugee in 1956. His poems began appearing in national magazines in 1973 and his first book, *The Slant Door*, was published in 1979, winning the Faber Memorial prize the following year – the first of many prizes including the TS Eliot Prize for *Reel* (Bloodaxe) in 2005.

Markets for poetry
A publisher writes

Does poetry ignore its audience? Do poets seeking publication often neglect the great poetic tradition that has gone before them, and pay scant attention to the poetry being written and published around them? **Neil Astley**, Editor at Bloodaxe, is the man who has to sift through all those manuscripts sent in hope. But he accuses the poetry world of often neglecting its duties, and reminds the poet firstly that s/he has an audience, and secondly that the road to publication is, indeed, a rocky one.

While a poet may not write *for* other readers, it's the *readership* that justifies publication. All editors are flooded with submissions of poetry from people whose desire to be published is greater than their desire to write well or to communicate – which must involve reading the work of poets from all periods. Few however seem to grasp that if you don't read poetry, you can't expect to be able to write poetry of any value; poetry that other people will want to read.

I would say that 95 per cent of the submissions I receive are unsuitable for book publication, for one of the following five reasons:

1. The so-called poet does not read poetry

This is the main reason for the rejection of most manuscripts. If you do not read much contemporary poetry, or if you write poetry "as a hobby", I'm unlikely to be interested in your work. You may disagree, but I believe that no one can write poetry of quality unless they read other poets and are in touch with the literary culture. I think you need to read poetry from all periods as well as contemporary poetry, and to have both an awareness and a *love* of English poetry from Shakespeare to Shapcott. If you also read other English-language poetry and poetry in translation or in the original language, so much the better. But if your knowledge of poetry stops at the beginning of the 20th century, don't even bother sending your work to any publisher or magazine. In poetry terms, you are an anachronism. If you don't talk like a person from the 18th or 19th century, why should you write like one?

Likewise, if you think your own work is much better than what today's poets have to offer the reader, and believe that publishers should see this – publishing you regardless of all the problems they have in marketing and disseminating poetry, because you are the real thing – forget it. You are deluded. You are out of touch not only with contemporary poetry, but also with the readers who buy (or don't buy) poetry books and are a truer test than even the poetry editors and reviewers.

2. It's a case of premature ejaculation

Before you even think about putting a book together, you should be submitting poems to magazines and pamphlet presses. Such a 'track record' is not used by publishers as a guarantee of quality, but as an indication that the writer has spent time building up a publishable collection. Trying to publish a book before you have had work taken by magazines is viewed by publishers as thinking you can run before you can walk. In sporting terms it would be like a Sunday afternoon footballer expecting to be picked to play for England. I use the football metaphor deliberately here, because this kind of ignorance – which often borders on arrogance – is displayed more by young male writers than by women.

3. The poet is trying the wrong publisher

Don't submit to publishers unless you've read their books, or to magazines unless you're familiar with the kind of work they publish. Every imprint is different, and you will not be able to publish much unless you research the field and send to the publishers or magazines whose output you like and respect. The books I publish are those I respond to as a reader, and what interests me most is subject matter, breadth of vision and engagement with language. I look for an original voice and poetry showing a lively interplay of intellect and emotion. Technique has to be a *given* if a writer is expecting to publish a book: before I even begin to read and absorb a manuscript, I register immediately whether or not the work is well-crafted. If it's prose chopped into lines, or rhyming verse with no metre or rhythmical sense (the two most common crimes against poetry committed by unpublished writers), it goes straight back into the envelope. I have very wide taste – from traditional to postmodern – but there are publishers whose editors are only interested in certain kinds or schools of poetry.

4. The poet needs help, not publication

I can't offer detailed criticism of poetry submitted for publication. That's not the publisher's 'job'. But there are organisations offering critical services, writers' courses, workshops and mentoring, some of these via the Poetry Society. The Arvon Foundation's residential week-long writers' courses in Britain, based in Yorkshire, Devon, Scotland and now Shropshire, have been tremendously important, as has the Poetry School in London, and there are now postgraduate creative writing programmes at several universities, notably at East Anglia, City University and Goldsmiths College in London, Lancaster, Sheffield Hallam, Newcastle, Warwick, and the Oscar Wilde Centre at Trinity College Dublin. Many poets who have published their first collections over the past two decades have benefited from working with established writers on their manuscripts by one or other of these methods.

5. It's a matter of sheer numbers

At Bloodaxe I receive around a hundred manuscripts, samples or letters offering collections every week. That's 5000 poets a year wanting to be taken on by just one publisher. Bloodaxe publishes 30 or so new books of poetry a year, but only one or two of those will be first collections: we have a stable of more than 200 already-published poets with new books coming out every month, as well as poets from America, Europe and the Commonwealth whose work we want to introduce to our readers. But along with all the other poetry publishers, Bloodaxe has had to reduce its output of new titles because the bookshops have been drastically reducing their ordering and stock range of poetry.

Apart from Bloodaxe, there are now only four other publishers in Britain actively publishing and distributing new books of poetry in significant numbers: Picador, Faber, Cape and Carcanet (including the Oxford/Carcanet list with separate Oxford University editors); in Ireland there is Gallery Press. None of the other commercial publishers has any commitment to new poets; Chatto only publishes Chatto poets and Harvill only publishes Paul Durcan, while Penguin publishes paperback editions of books originated by other publishers, or new books by really famous poets. Of the other small or specialist British poetry presses, only Anvil, Arc, Enitharmon, Flambard, Peterloo and Smith/Doorstop have active poetry lists, but are able to take on very few new poets. Peepal Tree concentrates on Black and Asian writers, and especially poetry (and fiction) from the Caribbean, while Seren has reverted to publishing only poets from Wales. Avant-garde or modernist poets are served by Shearsman and Salt (whose books are produced on a print-on-demand basis).

There are many presses producing pamphlets, including several recent ventures (notably Donut, Flarestack and tall-lighthouse), but other small presses – such as Rockingham, Shoestring, Waywiser and Worple – produce only occasional collections in book form, mostly by writers with some kind of track record of publication. The only new imprints producing poetry in book form are Smokestack in Middlesbrough and a first-collection imprint run by *The Rialto* magazine. There are many poets in Britain who used to publish with commercial and specialist poetry publishers who no longer have their books in print, and who now have no possibility of having their new work taken on by those imprints which are still active. Many of those who rely upon readings or schools or community work for their livelihood have been resorting to self-publication (either getting printers to produce their books and then storing them, or using print-on-demand publishers and selling from a website). The main reason why the poetry publishers have had to cut back is the rationalisation of the UK book trade which followed the demise of the Net Book Agreement, when the bookshops were forced to compete with the supermarkets for their share of the bestseller market. The big chains have been doing what they call 'professionalising' their operations: this means telling publishers they will only stock their books if they give them a minimum of 50 per cent discount, which is unviable for the short print run economies of specialist areas of cultural publishing such as poetry. The main bookshops are stocking less and less poetry, concentrating mainly on better-selling titles such as anthologies and 'selecteds' by big-name authors. As a direct result of this, all the poetry publishers have reduced their output of new titles. But most haven't helped themselves or their poets. Continuing to package their books to appeal only to an intellectual elite has severely disadvantaged them in the marketplace. If readers find a book cover visually unappealing, they won't pick up the book. And if the back cover blurb is a piece of literary criticism more concerned with craft than content, new readers will be put off. Reducing print runs has also meant that many poetry publishers have had to increase their cover prices, which in turn has further affected their sales. But an even more damaging cause of the downturn in poetry sales has been the huge gulf which exists between poetry publishing and the grassroots readership.

Readers don't have access to the diverse range of poetry being written, not just in Britain, but from around in the world, because much of the poetry establishment – including many publishers and reviewers – has become narrowly based, male-dominated, white, Anglocentric and skewed by factions and vested interests. Too often, poetry editors think of themselves and their poet friends as the only arbiters of taste, only publishing writers whom they think people *ought* to read and de-priving readers of other kinds of poetry which many people would find more rewarding. Publishers and writers who address a broader readership are attacked by elitist critics for 'dumbing down', but receive overwhelming support from read-ers as well as from the more intelligent poets. Publishers have also been unre-sponsive to much poetry by women (who comprise over two-thirds of poetry's readership) as well as to writing from Britain's rapidly growing ethnic population. Ignoring the readership would be commercial suicide in any other field, but this malpractice in poetry publishing and reviewing has survived into the 21st century because of what one might call 'academic protectionism'.

A recent report in *The Observer* quoted the latest statistics: sales of poetry in Britain last year sank to 890,000 books, the worst performance in years, while sales of fiction soared to nearly 46 million books. The only British poetry publisher whose sales have been increasing (and that's because we've been reaching a broader readership through imaginative, anti-elitist marketing which ensures that we are connecting with the readership at grassroots level) is Bloodaxe. And as if to show how inept the poetry community is in reaching a wider audience, the bookshop statistics for sales during the week of National Poetry Day in October over the past five years show that sales of poetry books actually go *down* in that week, when the media are giving contemporary poetry its biggest publicity boost of the whole year. Whatever interest in poetry that activity creates, it isn't something that's making people want to *read* more poetry books. While poetry has been receiving more feature coverage in the press, the amount and quality of serious review coverage has declined. And because it's often three or four months before the reviews start appearing in the papers, by the time you see the reviews and are prompted to go and look for the book in the shop, many titles may have been returned because without the publicity they haven't sold any copies.

Too many poetry reviews in national newspapers are written by poets or critics who don't review the books for the reader of the newspaper, but instead discuss their content in minute and acutely critical detail in terms which are only comprehensible or of interest to academics or other poets. They use the same critical language and terms of reference when reviewing for a newspaper as for a specialist poetry magazine, weaving strings of quotations broken up by slashes into a text-linked commentary which means nothing to anyone who hasn't already read the book. Many of these reviews read like potted academic essays. Even dedicated poetry-readers find them difficult to follow. Positive reviews written in this inappropriate critical jargon don't encourage potential readers to seek out the books; they put them off.

But few people seem to care about the poor reader now, or about choice and range of titles. The monster of Thatcherism may have been vanquished in Britain but the dragon's curse has paralysed many areas of our culture, from supermarket-style bookselling to the performance-related criteria of university management (the poets of Oxford University Press's former poetry list being just the latest casualties: their books didn't make a loss, but they didn't make enough profit).

Poets write poetry. Publishers sell it. Readers buy the books and read them. Poetry doesn't sell purely on merit, especially in the current commercial climate – it has to be marketed to reach its potential readership. While a poet may not write *for* other readers, it's the *readership* which justifies publication. Any poet who thinks otherwise is a deluded egotist, and most readers aren't actually interested in reading poetry written out of such an arrogant mindset. All of which brings me full circle back to where I started this piece: that publishers publish for readers, not to serve the vanities of poets or to follow poetical orthodoxies and fashions. But if you are a passionate *reader* of poetry – and don't just want to write the stuff – and even more importantly, if you really do have something to *say* in your work, and a distinctively original way of saying it, your conviction and persistence may eventually result in you having a book published. Wanting to write must come before wanting to be a writer. But don't underestimate the difficulties. It is a very difficult field to break into.

Neil Astley is Editor of Bloodaxe Books, a not-for-profit limited liability company supported by Arts Council England, specialising in publishing the best contemporary poetry.

The long and winding road to publication

Publisher **Alex Macmillan** explains the difficulties that await the poet attempting to get published. All is not lost, however; he explains the different outlets that do exist for poets.

Dozens of independent presses scattered across the British Isles publish hundreds of poets and broadly represent the range of contemporary poetry being written, as well as reflecting the poetic tastes of editors. The publishing activities of these presses are diverse; many specialise in publishing periodic magazines featuring several poets; some publish magazines and individual collections; others publish pamphlets and magazines; a few publish pamphlets; many publish on the Internet, and so on. Most of the printed magazine presses are available mainly through subscription, and if they are displayed in bookshops, their availability in retail outlets is limited. The publishing landscape for aspiring and established poets is as confusing as it is diverse. Numerous publishing opportunities appear to beckon, yet it is difficult to get work published even in magazines, and the process – even after acceptance of work – is often time-consuming. And post-publication, a poet's life may not change radically.

On high-street retail bookshelves, poetry collections and pamphlets from independent presses are rarely available. Most are easier to find through publishers' dedicated websites or consortia of small presses like Inpress or Independent Northern Publishers.

Templar Poetry has established a poetry press in response to the often difficult publishing and working environment that poets encounter when they seek wider exposure of their work. Although it may seem perverse, this is an appropriate moment at which to establish an independent press with innovative approaches to publishing poetry. Revolutions in print and communication technologies enable small publishing organisations to operate alongside larger ones in publishing new authors into wide markets, and reach their readers and audiences effectively. Furthermore, the new technologies provide independent publishers with exciting opportunities to transmit the best new writing, in diverse styles and new formats. Templar Poetry, for example, will be publishing its first pamphlet with a CD audio insert in October, and plans to offer the option of simultaneous text and audio publication to all its authors from 2007.

For most aspiring poets seeking publication of their work, there are a range of pressures (some perceived, others imagined) from within poetry's celestial circles and academies, collectively defining who is the 'real thing' and who is not. Some of these camps hold on to an elitist position that emerged from modernism and several modernist poets, whose influence and power is still assiduously maintained, often with a chilling and overbearing 'authority'. Some would argue that it is like a poison preventing poetry from developing a much wider and more popular following. The elitists are often linked to various academies and groups of one persuasion or another, and can hold specific and sometimes narrow views of what 'ought' to be regarded as 'real' poetry. Unfortunately for writers of poetry, poetry is not a broad church exercising wide tolerance for the range of 'poetries' that are written and published, which collectively represent the genre. Aspiring new poets find themselves writing and submitting their work in a fraught environment where they struggle through a labyrinthine critical system dependent on extensive peer review, in the quest to seek the 'validity' (or otherwise) of their work.

Sadly, the journey rarely encourages hope and aspiration. One high-profile annual national competition aimed at young new poets explicitly tells winners to dumb down any poetic career expectations, and expect to maintain a day job as well – as TS Eliot did for most of his career. However, in a world where sports practitioners are paid handsomely for playing even the most obscure sports badly, it is not unreasonable to advocate that good new poets be offered the opportunity to earn a reasonable income as working poets. It is also true that the most substantial poetry market (with a handful of high-profile exceptions) in published poetry comes from the work of poets whose poetry has apparently becomes more important after their death. There is much work to be done by poets, publishers, and both the published and the broadcast media to work together in raising the public profile and recognition of the best contemporary poetry – bringing more poetry back into the living language of our culture, and enabling poets to earn a fair and appropriate reward for their work.

Conventional wisdom suggests several routes to publication. The most commonly held is the road taken by developing a track record of magazine publication, perhaps achieving some success in major open competitions, and pamphlet publication – leading finally to the publication of a full collection. Another possible route to publication is through attending creative writing courses or workshops, which are now widely offered by universities and colleges as well as by dedicated poetry writing organisations like the Arvon Foundation and The Poetry School. Information on poetry writing courses and workshops is widely available on the Internet and is also often advertised in public libraries. The Poetry Society, The Poetry Library in London, and the Scottish Poetry Library provide extensive information with links on their respective websites for practising poets.

Most magazine publishers recommend that poets read their magazines prior to submission, to establish whether or not their style of poetry is likely to fit in with the published poets. Submissions to some magazines gain almost instant responses one way or the other; others take months or even longer to respond, and some expect writers to submit several times before serious consideration is given to their work. It is hard work submitting to magazines and it is best to keep a record. Many will be upset if you submit the same poem or poems simultaneously to other magazines or competitions and then receive simultaneous offers of publication. Poets should do their homework on their submission strategies and appreciate that magazines are often keen to discover new writers first. They should also temper their judgement in the knowledge that it is difficult to get accepted in the first instance. Some magazines have single editors; others have several readers who will decide which poetry to accept and publish. Some pay nominal amounts for publication; others not at all – however, poets should always retain copyright of their work. Most magazines indicate reading times for submissions, but a realistic strategy is probably to choose a few magazines and send poems to them on several occasions. Do not expect a critique of your work on its return; a brief pithy remark expressing some level of interest may occasionally encourage you to submit again.

Poetry competitions run all year round, and single poem competitions are numerous; details are readily available from Internet search engines. There are several dedicated poetry websites, such as Poetrykit, which list most of the competitions with closing dates, and give links to appropriate websites which provide access to entry forms and competion rules. These competitions do not usually lead to wider publication, but some single-poem competitions have substantial cash prizes and are widely 'respected' in the poetry world. The biggest of these competitions include the National Poetry Prize, The Arvon Prize (biennial), The Academi Cardiff International Competition, and the Bridport Prize.

Poets who have accumulated a body of work may opt to submit to pamphlet competitions, where their work will usually be read by poets with significant national or international reputations. If judged to be of sufficient quality, their work may be put forward for publication as a small collection or pamphlet. This is often regarded as a first step towards publishing a full collection. The entry fees to these competitions tend to be higher than single-poem competitions, but the potential outcomes in terms of publication and career development are more extensive.

Writers who have arrived at a point where they are confident that they have a substantial body of work which merits consideration for publication as a full collection should research the publication opportunities available and consider which publishing house might look at their work. This should involve an awareness of the published poets of any given publishing house: too many writers do not appear to read contemporary poetry. Individual publishers, large and small, usually post submission guidelines and information on their websites, but these tend to vary and writers should always check the current submission situation with any preferred publishers. Larger poetry publishers such as Faber, Cape, Picador and the large independents like Bloodaxe and Carcanet vary in their submission policies, and writers should look at their websites or contact the relevant poetry editor when they are considering submission (do not always expect rapid responses, even to minor questions). One poet I am aware of with an impressive 'track record' submitted work to one of the larger independents and waited for almost three years for a negative response. This poet has subsequently been published elsewhere, but such a response timescale is not unusual, and is certainly detrimental to the development of new poets and public access to their work. Their work may be several years 'out of date' by the time it is published. Poets, even if they are very very good indeed, need to take the view that if you can't go through an obstacle, go around it – water does.

Alex Macmillan is Managing Editor of Templar Poetry, a new independent press which publishes contemporary poetry and facilitates and promotes wider access to poetry in the community. Templar Poetry aims to bring a refreshing and unfettered approach to publishing poetry, and is committed to ensuring that poetry engages with new readers. To find out more, or to submit your work, visit www.templarpoetry.co.uk.

Publishers UK and Ireland

The poetry publishing world is like an iceberg: seven-eighths of it takes place beneath the surface, with dozens of small presses publishing sometimes only a handful of books a year. It has to be said that the few major publishers showing above the surface still do not publish a huge number of new poets. Therefore, it pays to carry out some research before sending off the manuscript you have been sweating over for years. Investigate what kind of poetry a publisher is interested in, and ensure that they are happy to receive material. An email or a letter in advance could save everyone time and prevent you from having any misplaced optimism about being published. Submissions should *always* be accompanied by a stamped, addressed envelope if a response is required.

Abbey Press

Courtenay Hill, Newry, Co Down, Northern Ireland BT34 2ED
tel 028-3026 3142 *fax* 028-3026 2514
email adrianrice@earthlink.net
website www.geocities.com/abbeypress
Editor Adrian Rice

A fast-growing literary publisher with a strong poetry list. It also publishes biography, memoirs, fiction, history, politics and academic titles. Since 1997, it has published 15 poetry books, including works from major Irish poets like Michael Longley and Brendan Kennelly.

Acair

7 James Street, Stornoway, Isle of Lewis HS1 2QN
tel (01851) 703020
email info@acairbooks.com
website www.acairbooks.com
Contact Norma Macleod

Publishes all categories of fiction and non-fiction for children in the Gaelic language. Adult books relating to the Gaidhealtachd, history, music, poetry, biography, environmental studies, Gaelic language.

Acorn Book Company

PO Box 191, Tadworth, Surrey KT20 5YQ
email info@acornbook.co.uk
website www.acornbook.co.uk

An independent publisher specialising in small, high-quality editions. Publishes haiku and minimalist poetry and literature in translation.

Agenda Editions

The Wheelwrights, Fletching Street, Mayfield, East Sussex TN20 6TL
tel (01435) 873703
email editor@agendapoetry.co.uk
website www.agendapoetry.co.uk
Editor Patricia McCarthy

A small independent poetry publishing press run in tandem with *Agenda Poetry Journal*. It publishes small, individual collections by poets considered by the editor to be worthy of promoting.
   Submission details Send hard copies in a folder, each page numbered and with name, address and email clearly marked.

Akros Publications

33 Lady Nairn Avenue, Kirkcaldy, Fife KY1 2AW
website www.scottish-pamphlet-poetry.com
A Scottish pamphlet publisher.

Alison Allison

Double Dykes, Elm Row, Galashiels TD1 3HT

tel (01896) 753728
email alisonallisondouble@yahoo.co.uk
website www.scottish-pamphlet-poetry.com
Contact Alison Allison

A Scottish pamphlet publisher.

Angel Books

3 Kelross Road, London N5 2QS
tel 020-7359 3143
email woodangel@ukonline.co.uk
Contact Anthony Wood

Anvil Press Poetry

Neptune House, 70 Royal Hill, London
SE10 8RF
tel 020-8469 3033 *fax* 020-8469 3363
email anvil@anvilpresspoetry.com
website www.anvilpresspoetry.com
Director Peter Jay

Founded by Peter Jay in 1968. Anvil Press
Poetry is England's longest-standing
independent poetry publisher. It publishes
the best of English-language poets:
Martina Evans, AB Jackson, Dennis
O'Driscoll, Greta Stoddart, Dick Davis,
James Harpur, Michael Hamburger and
others. In addition, Anvil boasts a backlist
containing 4 Nobel prize laureates and has
a deserved reputation for the finest
translations of the finest poets in the
international canon (Apollinaire,
Baudelaire, Bei Dao, Goethe Hikmet,
Lorca, Neruda, Seferis, Tagore, etc.).
Publishes about 12 new titles annually. For
those who wish to familiarise themselves
with the flavour of the list, Anvil's 30th
anniversary anthology, *The Spaces of Hope*,
gives a perfect starting point.

Arc Publications

Nanhome Hill, Shaw Wood Road,
Todmorden, Lancashire OL14 6DA
tel (01706) 812338 *fax* (01706) 818948
email arc.publications@btconnect.com

website www.arcpublications.co.uk
Editor Tony Ward

Publishes new and established writers
from the UK, English-speaking,
international poets, and bilingual
translation editions.

Submission details Submissions are not
encouraged, but all must include
publishing history and be familiar with
type of work normally published. No
electronic communication and no
response unless an sae is included.

Arehouse

72 Sedgwick Street, Cambridge CB1 3AL
email arehouse@cambridgepoetry.org
website www.cambridgepoetry.org/
arehouse.htm
Editor Neil Pattison, Sam Ladkin

Argyll Publishing

Glendaruel, Argyll PA22 3AE
tel (01369) 820229
email info@argyllpublishing.co.uk
website www.argyllpublishing.com
Contact Sean Bradley

Argyll Publishing was established in 1992;
from its base in Glendaruel it produces a
general list of titles. It has a fiction/poetry
imprint, Thirsty Books.

Arrowhead Press

70 Clifton Road, Darlington, Co Durham
DL1 5DX
website www.arrowheadpress.co.uk
Poetry Editor Joanna Boulter

A small press specialising in the
publication of quality books and
pamphlets of contemporary poetry. Aims
to provide a platform for poets to cross
the difficult gap between magazine
publication and first pamphlet or full
collection. This does not, however,
preclude publication of more established
authors.

Submission details Submit by post, including a brief biography and publishing history. You must already have been published in reputable magazines or have had a pamphlet published.

Atlantean Publishing

38 Pierrot Steps, 71 Kursaal Way, Southend-on-Sea, Essex SS1 2UY
email atlantean publishing@hotmail.com
website www.geocities.com/dj-tyrer/atlantean_pub.html
Editor DJ Tyrer

A non-profit small press seeking poetry in all styles, lengths and genres for inclusion in its magazines and collections. It also produces solo-poet broadsheets and chapbooks.

Submission details Unsolicited submissions accepted via post (with sae) or email. Poet receives complimentary copies as payment.

Avalanche Books

130 Oxford Street, Totterdown, Bristol BS3 4RH
tel 0117-377 0007
email deborahgaye@blueyonder.co.uk

Specialises in cutting-edge, high-quality poetry.

Bad Press

email badpress@gmail.com
website http://badpress.infinology.net

Publishes conceptually uncompromising, linguistically innovative, and politically informed poetry.

Barque Press

c/o Andrea Brady, 70a Cranwich Road, London N16 5JD
email info@barquepress.com
website www.barquepress.com
Contacts Andrea Brady, Dr Keston Sutherland

Founded by Andrea Brady and Keston Sutherland in 1995; since then, has published more than 30 chapbooks and four perfect-bound books. Published poets are from the UK, the US, France and Canada. In addition to these text-based publications, it has produced four CDs, which include spoken-word performances by a variety of artists alongside improvisational music.

Submission details Not currently accepting submissions.

Between the Lines

9 Woodstock Road, London N4 3ET
tel 020-8374 5526 *fax* 020-8374 5736
email btluk@aol.com
website www.interviews-with-poets.com
Contact Philip Hoy

Produces book-length interviews with established poets of note, chosen by an editorial board. Has published 13 volumes to date, including in each not just the interview, but also a career sketch, a comprehensive bibliography, career-spanning critical quotations and, in more recent volumes, a gallery of photos.

Bewrite Books

32 Bryn Road South, Ashton in Makerfield, Wigan, Lancashire WN4 8QR
website www.bewrite.net

Founded in 2004. Since its inception, this editorially driven publishing house has released more than 20 paperback titles a year, in several genres (each backed by eBook versions).

Birlinn Ltd

West Newington House, 10 Newington Road, Edinburgh EH9 1QS
tel 0131-668 4371 *fax* 0131-668 4466
email info@birlinn.co.uk
website www.birlinn.co.uk
Managing Director Hugh Andrew

Publishes a wide range of books of Scottish interest. Its Polygon imprint publishes modern and classic Scottish poetry, including Liz Lochead and Norman MacCaig, in addition to anthologies.

Biscuit Publishing

email info@biscuitpublishing.com
website www.biscuitpublishing.com
Contact Brian Lister

Founded in 2000 by the Lister family. Publishes mainly fiction, some non-fiction, and very occasionally poetry.

Submission details All publications are by Biscuit prize winners, or by selected authors approached and commissioned by Biscuit. See website for details.

Black Spring Press

Curtain House, 134-146 Curtain Road, London EC2A 3AR
tel 020-7613 3066 *fax* 020-7613 0028
email enquiries@blackspringpress.co.uk
website www.blackspringpress.co.uk

Black Spring specialises in the contemporary, as well as breathing new life into neglected classics. Since 1985 it has produced work by Nick Cave, Anaïs Nin, Charles Baudelaire, Kyril Bonfiglioli, Carolyn Cassady and Leonard Cohen, among many others.

Blackstaff Press

4c Heron Wharf, Sydenham Business Park, Belfast BT3 9LE
email info@blackstaff.com
website www.blackstaffpress.com
Contact Stefan Baxter

Launched in Belfast in 1971, Blackstaff Press is now regarded as one of Ireland's foremost publishers. Over 750 titles have been published, covering a wide range of subjects. The Press provides an important platform for creative writers and artists; its contribution to cultural life is recognised in the generous assistance it receives from the Arts Council of Northern Ireland. Blackstaff books are produced to the highest standards by a prize-winning team of editors and designers, and professional in-house marketing staff ensure effective sales distribution throughout the world.

Submission details Submit 10-12 poems with covering letter and short biography. See website for more details.

Bloodaxe Books Ltd

Highgreen, Tarset, Northumberland NE48 1RP
tel (01434) 240500 *fax* (01434) 240505
email editor@bloodaxebooks.com
website www.bloodaxebooks.com
Directors Neil Astley, Simon Thirsk

Poetry, literary criticism. No submissions from new authors this year. Founded 1978.

Bluechrome Publishing

PO Box 109, Portishead, Bristol BS20 7ZJ
tel (07092) 273360
email anthony@bluechrome.co.uk
website www.bluechrome.co.uk
Editor Anthony Delgrado

Established in 2002 as an independent publisher of poetry and some fiction. Has published a wide range of styles. Poets include: DM Thomas, James Kirkup, Alexis Lykiard, Rupert Loydell and Kevin Bailey.

Submission details Submission guidelines can be found on the website, although submissions by email are preferred.

Bogle L'Ouverture Press

PO Box 2186, London W13 9QZ
tel 020-8579 4920
email bogle.louverture@btinternet.com

Contact EL Huntley

Mainly interested in work giving a positive stance to the African diaspora.

Bradshaw Books (Tigh Fili)

tel 353 21 4509274
email info@tighfili.com
website www.tighfili.com
Contact Máire Bradshaw

Bradshaw Books provides an outlet in publishing for new names in poetry. It has published many previously unknown writers who have gone on to greater success.

Brindin Press

Drake Wood, Devonshire Avenue, Amersham, Buckinghamshire HP6 5JF
tel (01494) 726214 *fax* (01494) 432281
email brindinpress@aol.com
website www.brindin.com

A specialist publisher of poetry in translation.

The Brodie Press

c/o Department of English, University of Bristol, 3/5 Woodland Road, Bristol BS8 1TB
email thebrodiepress@hotmail.com
website www.brodiepress.co.uk
Contact Tom Sperlinger

A small independent press, which publishes individual volumes of poetry and anthologies. Aims to give new writers a voice and to allow established writers the opportunity to undertake unusual or experimental projects.

Jonathan Cape

The Random House Group, 20 Vauxhall Bridge Road, London SW1V 2SA
tel 020-7840 8400 *fax* 020-7828 6681
website www.randomhouse.co.uk
Editor Robin Robertson

Robin Robertson presides over one of the UK's most exciting poetry lists, including Anne Carson, John Burnside, Michael Symmons Roberts, Sharon Olds, Michael Longley and Peter Redgrave.

Carcanet Press Ltd

4th Floor, Alliance House, 28-34 Cross Street, Manchester M2 7AQ
tel 0161-834 8730 *fax* 0161-832 0084
email info@carcanet.co.uk
website www.carcanet.co.uk
Director Michael Schmidt

Poetry, *Fyfield* series, Oxford Poets, translations. Founded 1969.

Cargo Press

The Annex, Penhaver House, Cliff Road, Gorran Haven PL26 6JN
tel (07813) 930827
email info@cargo-press.co.uk
website www.cargo-press.co.uk
Contact Derek Hines

Cargo Press is a small press based in Cornwall. It publishes limited editions of poetry and *belles-lettres* to a very high standard.

The Celtic Cross Press

Ovins Well House, Lastingham, York YO62 6TJ
tel (01751) 417298
email info@celticcrosspress.com
website www.celticcrosspress.com

Prints and publishes limited editions of fine books. Publishes poetry and short works of prose, hand-printed by letterpress, on fine paper and bound in full cloth covered boards. Each copy is numbered and signed.

Chapman Publishing

4 Broughton Place, Edinburgh EH1 3RX
tel 0131-557 2207

email chapman-pub@blueyonder.co.uk
website www.chapman-pub.co.uk
Contact Joy Hendry

Founded in 1986, Chapman Publishing sprang from the idea that poets published in *Chapman Magazine* were not getting a voice in poetry collections. Poetry remains at the heart of the company, with books by Dylis Rose, George Gunn, Magi Gibson and Janet Paisley among recent titles.

Submission details Priority is given to poets published in *Chapman Magazine*. Other writers are unlikely to be considered.

Cinnamon Press

Meirion House, Glanyrafon, Tanygrrsiau, Blawnau Ffestiniog LL41 3SU
tel (01766) 832 2112
email jan@cinnamonpress.com
website www.cinnamonppress.com
Contact Jan Fortune-Wood

Small press publishing mainly poetry, including first collections. Holds annual competitions to select first collections for publication. Also publishes *Coffee House Poetry Magazine*.

Submission details Submit 10 poems with covering letter and writing credits, initially.

Clo Iar-Chonnachta

Indrebhan, Co Galway, Ireland
tel 353 91 593 307
email cic@iol.ie
website www.cic.ie

A publishing company located in Connemara, Galway, publishing books primarily in Irish.

Clutag Press

Clutag Press, PO Box 154, Thame OX9 3RQ
email mervynlinford@aol.com
website www.clutagpress.com
Contact Andrew McNeillie

Established in 2000 to issue Clutag Poetry Leaflets, by established and emerging poets.

Cois Life

62 Páirc na Rós, Ascaill na Cille, Dún Laoghaire, Co Bhaile Átha Cliath, Éire
tel (01) 2807 951
email eolas@coislife.ie
Contact Dr Caoilfhionn Nic Pháidín

Cois Life was established in 1995 to publish literary and research works in the Irish language. Publishes books for learners of Irish, for young people and also plays, fiction and poetry.

The Collective Press

c/o Penlanas Farm, Llantilio, Y-fenni, Gwent NP7 7HN
tel (01873) 859559
email through website
website www.welshwriters.com
Coordinator John Jones *Editor* Frank Olding

A not-for-profit organisation supported by the Welsh Arts Council and staffed by volunteers. Main aim is to promote and publish contemporary poetry without regard to race, religion or profit.

Submission details Postal submissions only.

Comma Poetry Press

3 Vale Bower, Mytholmroyd, West Yorkshire HX7 5EP
tel (07792) 564747
website www.commapress.co.uk/poetry
Contact Ra Page

Set up to discover and promote the best in new British poetry, as well as to support established poets, through anthologies and single poet collections.

Community of Poets & Artists Press

26 St Mildred's Avenue, Minnis Bay, Kent CT7 9LD
tel (01843) 842780
email bennetta.artco@virgin.net
website www.artistspress.co.uk

Printmakers and publishers with an increasing focus on printing and publishing original artwork and poetry/text. The press is based in Kent, and produces special-edition fine books, artists' books and hand-sewn collections. Has an online poetry magazine and exhibition space. Produces a poetry journal, *Community of Poets*.

Crescent Moon Publishing

PO Box 393, Maidstone, Kent ME14 5XU
tel (01622) 729593
email cresmopub@yahoo.co.uk
website www.crescentmoon.org.uk
Director Jeremy Robinson *Editors* C Hughes, BD Barnacle

Literature, poetry, arts, cultural studies, media, cinema, feminism.

Submission details Submit sample chapters or 6 poems plus sae, not complete MSS.

Crocus Books

Commonword, 6 Mount Street, Manchester M2 5NS
tel 0161-832 3777
website www.commonword.org.uk

The publishing imprint of Commonword and Cultureword. Publishes paperback poetry and fiction reflecting the diverse talents of North West writers, and bringing those talents to a national audience.

Dark Diamonds Publications

PO Box HK 31, Leeds, West Yorks LS11 9XN

Contact Andrew Cocker

A small press that also publishes *A Riot of Emotions*, an art/poetry fanzine.

David Paul Books

25 Methuen Park, London N10 2JR
tel (07958) 991121 *fax* 020-8444 8698
email info@davidpaulbooks.com
website www.davidpaulbooks.com

Publishes books and translations of Jewish and international interest, including fiction, history, memoir and poetry.

Day Dream Press

39 Exmouth Street, Swindon, Wiltshire SN1
tel (01793) 523927 *Editor* Kevin Bailey

Publisher of *HQ* magazine.

Dedalus Poetry Press

13 Moyclare Road, Baldoyle, Dublin 13, Ireland
email editor@dedaluspress.com
website www.dedaluspress.com
Contact John Deane

Poetry from Ireland and around the world.

Submission details Always include sufficient return postage and a self-addressed envelope with your work, together with a short covering letter giving details of previous publications. Expect a response time of approximately 3 months.

Deliberately Thirsty

Argyll Publishing, Glendaruel, Argyll
email thirstybooks@hotmail.com
website www.deliberatelythirsty.co.uk

Poetry imprint of Argyll Publishing.

Diamond Twig

PO Box 279, Newcastle upon Tyne NE6 5ZE

tel (0191) 276 3770
email diamond.twig@virgin.net
website www.diamondtwig.co.uk
Contact Ellen Phethean

A women's press based in North East England. Publishes poetry and short stories for new women writers with a Northern connection.

Submission details Always write or email before submitting. Does not accept unsolicited material.

diehard

91–93 Main Street, Callander FK17 8BQ
tel (01877) 339449
website www.poetryscotland.co.uk
Directors Ian William King (managing), Sally Evans (marketing)

Scottish poetry. Founded 1993.

Dionysia Press

127 Milton Road West, 7 Duddingston House Courtyard, Edinburgh EH15 1JG
tel 0131-661 1156
Contact Denise Smith

Submission details Submit MSS of circa 100 pages.

Doghouse

PO Box 312, Tralee GPO, Tralee Co Kerry, Ireland
tel (066) 713 7547
email doghouse312@circom.net
website www.doghousebooks.ie
Contact Noel King

Founded in 2003 to publish Irish-born poets and short-story writers with established records in the small presses, journals, magazines, etc.

Submission details Send 4 hard copies of full manuscript (40-60 poems) with CV and publishing credits.

Donut Press

PO Box 45093, London N4 1UZ
email donutpress@hotmail.co.uk

website www.donutpress.co.uk
Editorial/Sales Andy Ching

Small poetry press publishing 2 pocketbooks per year and occasional full collections.

Submission details Submissions by post, accompanied by an sae.

Dreadful Night Press

82 Kelvin Court, Glasgow G12 0AQ
tel 0141-339 9150
email dreadfulnight1@aol.com
website www.scottish-pamphlet-poetry.com

A Scottish pamphlet publisher.

Driftwood Publications

5 Timms Lane, Freshfield, Merseyside L37 7DW
tel 0151-525 0417 *fax* 0151-524 0216
email janet.speedy@tesco.net
Contact Janet Speedy

Attempts to provide outlets (books, readings, etc.) for poets whose work has been hitherto neglected – new or established poets who are no longer on the lists of larger presses. "Poetry for the page more than for the stage."

Submission details Unsolicited manuscripts welcome.

Earlyworks

45 Robertson Street, Hastings, Sussex TN34 1HL
website www.earlyworkspress.co.uk

Produces at least 3 anthologies a year, based on its Open Competitions. Altogether, this gives an opportunity for 50-100 writers and illustrators to publish in book form.

Egg Box Publishing

25 Brian Avenue, Norwich NR1 2PH
tel (01603) 470191
email mail@eggboxpublishing.com

website www.eggboxpublishing.com
Editor Alexander Gordon Smith, Nathan Hamilton

Publishes first collections by some of the best new poets around the country. Also runs *Eggbox* magazine.

Submission details Submissions should be accompanied by a brief biography. No email submissions.

Enitharmon Press
26b Caversham Road, London NW5 2DU
tel 020-7482 5967 *fax* 020-7284 1787
email books@enitharmon.co.uk
website www.enitharmon.co.uk
Director Stephen Stuart-Smith

Poetry, literary criticism, fiction, translations, artists' books. Founded 1967.

Submission details No unsolicited MSS. No freelance editors or proofreaders required.

Equipage
Jesus College, Cambridge CB5 8BL
email equipage@cambridgepoetry.org
website www.cambridgepoetry.org/equipage.htm
Editor Rod Mengham

Small press operating out of Cambridge.

Etruscan Books
28 Fowler's Court, Fore Street, Buckfastleigh, Devon TQ11 0AA
email etruscan@macunlimited.net
website www.seaham.i12.com/etruscan
Contact Nicholas Johnson

Poetry publisher with a book club.

Faber and Faber Ltd
3 Queen Square, London WC1N 3AU
tel 020-7465 0045 *fax* 020-7465 0034
website www.faber.co.uk
Editor Paul Keegan

High-quality general fiction and non-fiction, children's fiction and non-fiction, drama, film, music, poetry. Unsolicited submissions accepted for poetry only. For information on poetry submission procedures, ring 020-7465 0189, or consult the website.

Fal Publications
PO Box 74, Truro, Cornwall TR1 1XS
tel (07887) 560018
email info@falpublications.co.uk
website www.falpublications.co.uk
Editor Victoria Field

An award-winning small press based in Cornwall, focusing on Cornish writers.

Submission details No unsolicited submissions. Enquire by email first.

Feather Books
PO Box 438, Shrewesbury, Shropshire SY3 0WN
tel (01743) 872177
email john@waddysweb.freeuk.com
website www.waddysweb.freeuk.com/
Contact Rev John Waddington-Feather

Publisher of Christian poetry, music and drama. With its associate company, Moorside Words and Music, it also produces CDs/cassettes and audio-books.

Fighting Cock Press
45 Middlethorpe Drive, York YO24 1NA
Editor Pauline Kirk

Very small non-profit-making press, specialising in high-quality poetry and short prose from the north of England.

Five Leaves Publishing
PO Box 81, Nottingham NG5 4ER
tel 0115-969 3597
email info@fiveleaves.co.uk
website www.fiveleaves.co.uk
Contact Ross Bradshaw

Small publisher, specialising in social history, regional writers and Jewish secular culture. Collections include: *Red Sky at Night: An Anthology Of Socialist Poetry.*

Submission details All work is commissioned. No unsolicited submissions.

Five Seasons Press

41 Green Street, Hereford HR1 2QH
tel (01432) 261100
email books@fiveseasonspress.com
website www.fiveseasonspress.com
Contact Glenn Storhaug

Publishes a few carefully produced titles each year, in collaboration with poets who fuss over the sound and etymology of every word. Parallel-text translations are always of interest.

Submission details Send letter (not email) with an account of the proposed book's structure, and no more than 6 sample poems/pages. See the website for further guidelines.

Flambard Press

Stable Cottage, East Fourstones, Hexham, Northumberland NE47 5DX
tel (01434) 674360 *fax* (01434) 674178
email flambardpress@btinternet.com
website www.flambardpress.co.uk
Managing Editor Peter Lewis *Deputy Editor* Will Mackie

Publishes poetry and literary fiction, but only 4 books of poetry a year. Consider proposals from everywhere, but has a particular interest in writers living in the north of England. Good track record of magazine and/or pamphlet publication normally required. Founded 1990.

Submission details Only hard-copy submissions of 10-15 poems with sae will be considered; these should be accompanied by a short biographical note and list of previous publications. Preliminary letter required. No phone calls, emails or faxes. See website for further information.

Flarestack Publishing

41 Buckley's Green, Alvechurch, Birmingham B48 7NG
tel 0121-445 2110
Editor Charles Johnson

Flarestack has been publishing stapled A5 pamphlet collections by new poets since 1995. Poetic excellence and coherence override commercial viability and the whims of poetic fashion. Combining simple production methods with an eye for colour and style, each pamphlet is carefully designed as an individual hand-crafted object with its own look.

Flax Books

PO Box 751, Lancaster LA1 9AJ
tel (01524) 62166
website www.litfest.org

A digital and print publishing programme showcasing talented yet under-exposed writers from Lancashire and Cumbria. Launched by Litfest. Aims to highlight the contemporary voices of this diverse region of England.

Flipped Eye Publishing Ltd

tel 0845-430 9517 *fax* 0845-430 9518
email books@ flippedeye.net
website www.flippedeye.net

Formed in Ghana by a group of schoolfriends in a bid to start a literature revival in the country. The UK company was established in 2001. Aims to produce consistently high-quality fiction, non-fiction and related products, with a focus on poetry; also, to raise the profile of performance and oral literature as legitimate and viable forms of artistic interpretation and learning.

Forward Press

Forward Press Ltd, Remus House, Coltsfoot Drive, Woodston, Peterborough PE2 9JX

tel (01733) 898105
email info@forwardpress.co.uk
website www.forwardpress.co.uk
Head of Imprints Steve Twelvetree

Founded in 1989 by poet Ian Walton, the company has published more than 900,000 original poems. Sees itself as a bridge to publication, rather than a barrier, giving everyone the opportunity to see their work in print. Writing initiatives include: Anchor Books; Poetry Now; Strong Word; WomensWords; Triumph House; Spotlight Poets; New Fiction; Young Writers; Need2Know; Writers' Bookshop; and Pond View.

Submission details Submit a maximum of 3 poems per theme, each no more than 30 lines in length. Write name and address on each piece of work. Alternatively, email to inbox@forwardpress.co.uk.

Four Quarters Press

7 The Towers, Stevenage, Hertfordshire SG1 1HE
email octillion@ntlworld.com
website www.fourquarterspress.co.uk
Editor Eric Ratcliffe

Non-profit and charity booklets, including poetry.

The Frogmore Press

42 Morehall Avenue, Folkestone, Kent CT19 4EF
tel (07751) 251689
website www.frogmorepress.co.uk
Contact Jeremy Page

The Frogmore Press was founded in 1983 and publishes poetry and prose by new and established writers. *The Frogmore Papers* appears biannually in March and September, and the Frogmore Poetry Prize (est. 1987) is awarded annually and paid in guineas.

Submission details Submissions should be made by post with sae. No more than 6 poems.

Frontier Publishing

Windetts, Kirstead, Norwich NR15 1EG
website www.frontierpublishing.co.uk
Contact J Black

Publishes *The Green Book of Poetry*, established in 1986. Occasional poetry publishers with interests in other subjects, such as Art History.

Submission details Submit by post, with sae.

The Galdragon Press

2B Church Road, Stromness, Orkney KW16 3BT
email galdragonpress@ntlworld.com
website http://homepage.ntlworld.com/galdragonpress
Contact Anne Thompson

A Scottish pamphlet publisher.

The Gallery Press

Loughcrew, Oldcastle, Co Meath, Republic of Ireland
tel 049-854 1779 *fax* 049-854 1779
email gallery@indigo.ie
website www.gallerypress.com
Editor/Publisher Peter Fallon

Poetry, drama, and occasionally fiction – by Irish authors only at this time. Founded 1970.

Godstow Press

60 Godstow Road, Wolvercote, Oxford OX2 8NY UK
tel (01865) 556215 *fax* (01865) 552900
email info@godstowpress.co.uk
website www.godstowpress.co.uk

The aim of Godstow Press is to sing the Orphic song, through books of fiction, poetry and non-fiction, as well as through CDs.

The Goldsmith Press

Newbridge, Co. Kildare, Republic of Ireland

tel (045) 433613 *fax* (045) 434648
email viv1@iol.ie
website www.gerardmanleyhopkins.org
Directors V. Abbott, D. Egan, *Secretary* B. Ennis

Literature, art, Irish interest, poetry. Unsolicited MSS not returned. Founded 1972.

Gomer Books

Gwasg Gomer, Llandysul, Ceredigion SA44 4JL
tel (01559) 362371 *fax* (01559) 363758
email gwasg@gomer.co.uk
website www.gomer.co.uk

Wales's largest independent publisher, publishing books from Wales, about Wales, in Welsh and in English. Produces more than 120 new titles every year, for children and adults, in both languages.

Greville Press

6 Mellors Court, The Butts, Warwick CV34 4ST
website www.haroldpinter.org/poetry/poetry_greville.shtml

Publishes well-designed pamphlets and, over the years, some very big names including Harold Pinter, George Barker, WS Graham and many others.

HappenStance

21 Hatton Green, Glenrothes, Fife KY7 4SD
email nell@happenstancepress.com
website www.happenstancepress.com
Contact Helena Nelson

A pamphlet and chapbook imprint originated in 2005 and run by Helena Nelson. Initial publications were first collections, mainly (but not exclusively) poets based in Scotland. Happenstance will continue to feature first collections and is interested in poets from across the UK, while maintaining a particular emphasis on those based in Scotland, or with Scottish connections.

Submission details Welcomes unsolicited submissions. Send at least 8 (but no more than 20) poems.

Hard Pressed Poetry

37 Grosvenor Court, Templeville Road, Templeogue, Dublin 6, Eire
website http://gofree.indigo.ie/~hpp/frame.html
Contact Billy Mills

A small press which publishes poetry that you won't often find in your local bookshop.

Headland Publications

38 York Avenue, West Kirby, Wirral, Merseyside L48 3JF and Ty Coch, Llansfwrog, Ruthin, Denbighshire LL12 2AR
tel 0151-625 9128
email gladysmarycoles@talk21.com
Contact Gladys-Mary Coles

A quality literary press with high production standards, publishing individual collections of poetry and anthologies.

Submission details Send a preliminary letter of enquiry before submitting.

Hearing Eye

Box 1, 99 Torriano Avenue, London NW5 2RX
email hearing_eye@torriano.org
website www.torriano.org/hearing_eye/

Publishes poetry and also hosts poetry readings in London.

Heaventree Press

PO Box 3342, Coventry CV1 5YB
email info@heaventreepress.co.uk
website www.heaventreepress.co.uk

Contact Jonathan Morley

A not-for-profit West Midlands-based independent publisher, dedicated to promoting the arts in Coventry and the surrounding area and specialising in anthologies and pamphlets of new literature. Set up by local young poets as a community venture.

Hilltop Press

4 Nowell Place, Almondbury, Huddersfield, West Yorkshire HD5 8PB
Contact Steve Sneyd

Founded in 1966, Hilltop Press is a specialist publisher of science fiction and dark fantasy poetry collections and anthologies, including some reprinting of significant past work in the field along with texts about it. Does not have a website, but Hilltop Press publications are listed and can be purchased at www.bbr-online.com/catalogue.

Submission details Submit a small selection of relevant work or an extract, if a long poem. Must be accompanied by an sae.

Hippopotamus Press

22 Whitewell Road, Frome, Somerset BA11 4EL
tel (01373) 466653 *fax* (01373) 466653
email rjhippopress@aol.com
Editors Roland John, Anna Martin

Poetry, essays and criticism. Publishes *Outposts Poetry Quarterly*. Welcomes poetry submissions from new writers; work should be sent by post. Specialises in first full collections by poets who have established a reputation in mainstream poetry magazines. Founded 1974.

Honno Welsh Women's Press

Canolfan Merched y Wawr, Vulcan Street, Aberystwyth SY23 1JH

tel (01970) 623150 *fax* (01970) 623150
email post@honno.co.uk
website www.honno.co.uk
Editor Caroline Oakley

An independent co-operative press run by women and committed to publishing the best in Welsh women's writing.

Submission details Only considers for publication the work of women who are Welsh, living in Wales, or have a significant Welsh connection. Not actively seeking poetry submissions.

Hub Editions

Longholm, East Bank, Wingland, Sutton Bridge, Spalding, Lincolnshire PE12 9YS
Contact Colin Blundell

Small poetry publisher.

Hutchinson

The Random House Group, 20 Vauxhall Bridge Road, London SW1V 2SA
tel 020-7840 8400 *fax* 020-7828 6681
website www.randomhouse.co.uk

A very occasional publisher of poetry.

Independent Northern Publishers

Aidan House, Sunderland Road, Gateshead NE8 3HU
tel 0191-212 0354
email cristae@zoom.co.uk
website www.northernpublishers.co.uk
Contact Crista Ermiya

A group of book and magazine publishers based in North East England. The group includes: *Mslexia*, *Liar Inc*, *Other Poetry*, Flambard, Iron Press, *Diamond Twig*, Vane Women, The Word Foundation, Mudfog, Arrowhead, and Biscuit Publishing

Iron Press

5 Marden Terrace, Cullercoats, North Shields, Northumberland NE30 4PD

tel 0191-253 1901
email seaboy@freenetname.co.uk
website www.ironpress.co.uk
Contact Peter Mortimer

Iron Press was established in 1973, since when it has brought out a regular programme of new poetry, fiction and drama.

Submission details Does not welcome unsolicited submissions; please make telephone contact first.

Katabasis Press
10 St Martin's Close, London NW1 0HR
tel 020-7485 3830
website www.katabasis.co.uk
Contact Dinah Livingstone

Publishes down-to-earth and utopian poetry and prose from home and abroad.

Submission details No unsolicited manuscripts.

Kernow Press
Bude Haven, 18 Frankfield Rise, Tunbridge Wells, Kent TN2 5LF
Contact Bill Headon

Publishes limited small editions.

Kettilonia
24 South Street, Newtyle, Angus PH12 8UQ
tel (01828) 650615
email james@kettilonia.co.uk
website www.kettilonia.co.uk
Contact James Robertson

Set up in 1999, Kettilonia publishes 3 new publications per year, in pamphlet form only (no full-length books). Specialises in new, original, Scottish work.

Submission details No unsolicited submissions; send initial letter or email before submitting.

King of Hearts Publications
7-15 Fye Bridge Street, Norwich NR3 1LJ
tel (01603) 766129

email enquiries@kingofhearts.org.uk
website www.kingofhearts.org.uk
Director & Artistic Manager Aude Gotto

Has published poetry on a variety of subjects and in diverse styles. As part of the King of Hearts Centre for People and the Arts, the press aims to bring to its publications artistic quality, attention to detail in design and production, and an underlying commitment to the human journey and the path of the heart.

King's England Press
Cambertown House, Commercial Road, Goldthorpe Industrial Estate, Rotherham, South Yorkshire S63 9BL
tel (01226) 270258
email Steve@kingsengland.com
website www.kingsengland.com
Contact Steve Rudd

Only publishes children's poetry.

Submission details Hard copy only. See website for detailed submission guidelines.

Koo Press Poetry
19 Lochinch Park, Aberdeen AB12 3RF
email koopoetry@btinternet.com

An independent small press based in Aberdeen, and primarily publishing poetry chapbooks. Its main objective is to provide the poet with a bridge between magazine publication and a full-length poetry collection.

KT Publications
16 Fane Close, Stamford, Lincolnshire PE9 1HG
tel (01780) 754193
Editor Kevin Troop

Looking for *new* material for publication. Copies are sold to authors at a reduced price. Founded 1989.

Submission details Submit by post with sae and covering letter.

Landfill Press

17 Waldeck Road, Norwich NR4 7PG
email sales@landfillpress.co.uk
website www.landfillpress.co.uk

Publishes pocket-sized poem sequences.

Lapwing Productions

1 Balysillan Drive, Belfast BT14 8HQ
Contact Dennis Greig/Catherine Greig

In business for 15 years, an independent, non-grant-aided publisher, specialising in small first collections. Produces a saddle-stitched pamphlet format of up to 44 pages; 'book' format is 48 pages upwards. All work hand-printed and hand-bound. Writers get 20 complimentary copies and extra copies at 50% of cover price.

Submission details Send an introductory letter plus 6 sample poems as well as a brief biography. For books, as above, but send a larger selection of poems.

The Lichfield Press

James Redshaw Ltd, City House, 2 Dam Street, Lichfield, Staffordshire WS13 6AA
tel (01543) 254825
email rj@jrltd.freeserve.co.uk
website www.jamesredshaw.co.uk
Contact Ralph James

A bookshop that not only sells a good selection of poetry books, but also publishes short-run volumes of poetry for both adults and children, by local and internationally published poets, under its imprint The Lichfield Press.

The Lilliput Press

62-63 Sitric Road, Arbour Hill, Dublin 7, Ireland
tel (01) 671 16 47
website www.lilliputpress.ie
Contact Antony Farrell

Has some 250 titles under its imprint; these encompass art and architecture, autobiography and memoir, biography and history, ecology and environmentalism, essays and literary criticism, philosophy, current affairs and popular culture, fiction, drama and poetry– all broadly focused on Irish themes.

The Littoral Press

38 Barringtons, 10 Sutton Road, Southend-On-Sea, Essex SS2 5NA
tel (01702) 473999 *fax* (01702) 617199
website http://mysite.wannado-members.co.uk/mervyn_linford/press.htm
Contact Mervyn Linford

Publishes a limited number of poetry collections, all of which have to be on the theme of 'Nature and the Spirit'. Publication is a partnership deal. All profits (if any) go to the funds of the Littoral Press and *Littoral* magazine. Littoral is a not-for-profit organisation; all work is voluntary and unpaid.

Submission details Hard copy by post accompanied by an sae, or by email attachment.

Loki Books

38 Chalcot Crescent, London NW1 8YD
tel 020-7722 6718 *email* all@lokibooks.u-net.com
website www.lokibooks.com
Contact Ann White

Specialist publishers of translations from modern Hebrew.

Luath Press

543/2 Castlehill, The Royal Mile, Edinburgh EH1 2ND
tel 0131-225 4326 *fax* 0131-225 4324
email gavin.macdougall@luath.co.uk
website www.luath.co.uk
Contact Gavin MacDougall

Committed to publishing well-written work worth reading. More than 150 books in print, including fiction and poetry.

Submission details Send hard copy by post, plus anything else of relevance.

Ludovic Press
Dunadd, Lewis Crescent, Kilbarchan PA10 2HB
tel (01505) 702906

Scottish pamphlet publisher.

Marion Boyars
24 Lacy Road, London SW15 1NL
tel 020-8788 9522 *fax* 020-8789 8122
email catheryn@marionboyars.com
website www.marionboyars.co.uk

A publishing house committed to the new, the unusual and the unexpected.

Mariscat
10 Bell Place, Stockbridge, Edinburgh EH3 5HT
tel 0131-343 1070 *fax* 0131-332 3451
email hamish.whyte@virgin.net
website www.scottish-pamphlet-poetry.com
Contacts Hamish Whyte, Diana Hendry

Publisher of poetry pamphlets.
Submission details Send hard copy with sae.

Masque Publishing
PO Box 3257, Littlehampton BN16 9AF
email masque_pub@tiscali.co.uk
website myweb.tiscali.co.uk/masquepublishing
Contact Lisa Stewart

Publisher of poetry books and *Decanto* magazine.

Maypole Editions Biennial Anthology
65 Mayfair Avenue, Ilford, Essex IG1 3DQ
Contact Barry Taylor

A small press platform for first-time poets who might not otherwise get into print,
and a permanent showcase for those already published who want to break into the mainstream. Most editions come on CD, from which hard copy (including full-colour cover) can be printed without infringing copyright.

Menard Press
8 The Oaks, Woodside Avenue, London N12 8AR
tel 020-8446 5571 *fax* 020-8445 2990
email rudolf@menardpress.co.uk
website www.menardpress.co.uk
Contact Anthony Rudolf

Has been publishing poetry (original and translated) since 1969. Has also published literary criticism and political studies.
Submission details No new submissions for the time being.

Mercier Press
Douglas Village, Cork, Ireland
email pr@mercierpress.ie
website www.mercierpress.ie

Publishes a wide range of books, including poetry.

Mermaid Turbulence
Annaghmaconway, Clone, Leitrim, Ireland
website www.mermaidturbulence.com
Contact Mari-Aymone Djeribi

An independent publisher of books, artistbooks and 'multiples'.

Mews Press
English Department, Sheffield Hallam University, Collegiate Crescent, Sheffield S10 2BP
email s.l.earnshaw@shu.ac.uk
website http://extra.shu.ac.uk/mews-press
Editor Dr Steven Earnshaw

Publishes work connected with the MA in Creative Writing at Sheffield Hallam University. Each year, in *Matter*, it features the work of students alongside that of guest authors.

Mucusart

6 Chatsworth Road, Radcliffe, Manchester M26 4NT
tel 0161-795 5235
email squire@hotmail.com
website www.mucusart.co.uk
Contact Paul Neads

Mucusart publishes small collections by stranded writers.

Submission details Submit by post.

Mudfog

c/o Arts Development, The Stables, Stewart Park, The Grove, Marton, Middlesborough, Tees Valley TS7 8AR
email mudfog@hodgcon.demon.co.uk
website www.mudfog.co.uk

A voluntary cooperative community press dedicated to publication of new writers from the Tees Valley area. Funded by ACE. Published writers receive a fee and retain copyright.

Submission details Send samples of 15-20 poems or 2-3 short stories with sae. Consult the website for more details.

New Beacon Books

76 Stroud Green Road, London N4 3EN
tel 020-7272 4889 *fax* 020-7281 4662
email newbeaconbooks@btconnect.com
Directors Sarah White, Michael La Rose, Janice Durham

Small specialist publishers: general non-fiction, fiction, poetry, critical writings, concerning the Caribbean, Africa, African–America and Black Britain. No unsolicited MSS. Founded 1966.

New Departures

PO Box 9819, London W11 2GQ
email www.connectotel.com/
PoetryOlympics/index.htm

Editor Michael Horovitz

Michael Horovitz founded New Departures publications and Live New Departures road shows while still a student in 1959. He also runs the Poetry Olympics.

New Island New Poetry

2 Brookside, Dundrum Road, Dublin 14
tel ++353 1 298 9937/298 3411
fax ++353 1 298 2783
email editor@newisland.ie
website www.newisland.ie
Editor Deirdre Nolan

New Island New Poetry has grown out of New Island's vibrant poetry list – a list which, over the last few years, has concentrated on publishing the finest new voices in Irish poetry. It took its spirit from Dermot Bolger's legendary Raven Arts Press, and, indeed, Dermot Bolger remains New Island's executive poetry and drama editor.

Norfolk Poets and Writers

Wendy Webb Books, 9 Walnut Close, Norwich NR8 6YN
email ww@webbw.freeserve.co.uk
Contact Wendy Webb

Publishes traditional and new forms. Anthologies with form rules.

Northern Sky Press

PO Box 21548, Stirling FK8 1YY
tel (07981) 173819
email northernsky@hush.com
website www.northernskypress.co.uk

A radical, independent publisher producing politics and poetry pamphlets.

Object Permanence

email undigest@hotmail.com
website www.objectpermanence.co.uk
Editor Pater Manson

Once a magazine, now a small publisher based in Glasgow.

O'Brien Press

12 Terenure Road East, Dublin 6, Ireland
tel ++353 1 492 3333
email books@obrien.ie
website www.obrien.ie

Ireland's leading general publisher of both adult and children's books, with some poetry.

Odyssey Poets

Coleridge Cottage, Nether Stowey, Somerset TA5 1NQ
tel (01278) 732662
email pqr.rev@virgin.net
Contacts Tilla Brading, Derrick Woolf

A small press that will be relaunched in 2007, publishing innovative work and a regular review magazine.

Oleander Press

16 Orchard Street, Cambridge CB1 1JT
tel (01223) 357768
email editor@oleanderpress.com
website www.oleanderpress.com
Contacts Dr Jeremy Toner, Mrs Jane Doyle

A small press founded more than 40 years ago. Typically publishes 1 poetry title each year.
    Submission details No unsolicited manuscripts. Please send letter and sample in the first instance.

Onlywomen Press Ltd

40 St Lawrence Terrace, London W10 5ST
tel 020-8354 0796 *fax* 020-8960 2817
email onlywomenpress@btconnect.com
website www.onlywomenpress.com
Managing Director Lilian Mohin

Lesbian feminist: theory, fiction, poetry, crime fiction and cultural criticism. Founded 1974.

The Oscars Press

BM Oscars, London WC1N 3XX
email pdaniels@easynet.co.uk
website http://easyweb.easynet.co.uk/
pdaniels/oscars.html
Contact Peter Daniels

Publishes top-quality poetry anthologies by lesbians, gay men, and women from both sides of the Atlantic.

The Other Press

19 Marriott Road, London N4 3QN
tel 020-7272 9023
Contact Frances Presley

A very small press that publishes experimental work, usually by women.
    Submission details Submit a short sample of work on A4 paper, enclosing sae.

Oversteps Books

Froude Road, Salcombe, South Devon TQ8 8LH
tel (01548) 843713 *fax* (01548) 844384
email anne@oversteps.fsnet.co.uk
Contact Anne Born

Publishes good, modern poets ready for a first collection who have appeared in magazines and won prizes.
    Submission details No unsolicited submissions.

Parthian Books

The Old Surgery, Napier Street, Aberteifi, Wales SA43 1ED
tel (01239) 612059 *fax* (01239) 612059
email parthianbooks@yahoo.co.uk
website www.parthianbooks.co.uk

An independent publisher, publishing innovative fiction, drama and poetry in Wales for 10 years. It aims to promote new talent and bring exciting new authors to as wide an audience as possible.

Partners

289 Elmwood Avenue, Feltham, Middlesex TW13 7QB

email partners_writing_group@
hotmail.com
Editor Ian Deal

Magazine publisher. Titles include: *A Bard Hair Day*, *ImageNation* and *The Poet Tree*.

Paula Brown Publishing

26 Uplands Road, Drayton, Portsmouth
PO6 1HS
tel (07796) 530826
website www.thepeoplespoet.com/
paulabrownpublishing
Editor Paula Brown

Publishes at least 6 poetry collections each year – the Spring, Summer, Autumn and Winter single author collections, the Christmas Special edition, and the annual anthology. Occasionally undertakes separate funded community projects.

Peace & Freedom Press

17 Farrow Road, Whaplode Drove,
Spalding, Lincs PE12 0TS
email p_rance@yahoo.co.uk
website http://uk.geocities.com/p_rance/
pandf.htm
Contact Paul Rance

A small press founded in 1985. In 1995 it began to publish paperback anthologies of poetry, among other things.

Peepal Tree Press

17 King's Avenue, Leeds LS6 1QS
tel 0113-245 1703
email contact@peepaltreepress.com
website www.peepaltreepress.com

Publishes the very best in Caribbean, Black British and South Asian literature, fiction, poetry and academic books.

Peer Poetry

26 Arlington House, Bath Street, Bath
BA1 1QN
tel (01225) 445298

email peerpoetry@msn.com
website www.publish-your-poetry.co.uk
Contact Paul Amphlett

A not-for-profit enterprise interested in all forms of well-written poetry, including the haiku genre. 3 winners voted for by readers and contributing poets will have a book of their poetry published, but not marketed.

Submission details Submit 3 poems by email, to determine whether they can be entered for the competition (no charge).

Penguin

80 The Strand, London WC2R 0RL
tel 020-7010 3000
website www.penguin.co.uk

Occasional publisher nowadays of new poetry by poets such as Tony Harrison, as well as anthologies and classics.

Pennine Pens

32 Windsor Road, Hebden Bridge, West
Yorkshire HX7 8LF
tel (01422) 843724
email info@penninepens.co.uk
website www.penninepens.co.uk
Contact Elaine Connell

A small publisher working from its home office in Hebden Bridge in the Yorkshire Pennines.

Perdika Press

16b St Andrew's Road, Enfield, Middlesex
EN1 3UB
email editions@perdikapress.com
website www.perdikapress.com

Publishes original and translated works by contemporary poets.

Peterloo Poets

The Old Chapel, Sand Lane, Calstock,
Cornwall PL18 9QX
tel (01822) 833473 *fax* (01822) 833989
email info@peterloopoets.com

website www.peterloopoets.com
Publishing Director Harry Chambers
Trustees Brian Perman, Hannah Elliott,
Rose Taw *Honorary President* Michael
Longley

Well-respected small publisher. Founded
1976.

Photon Press

37 The Meadows, Berwick-upon-Tweed,
Northumberland TD15 1N
tel (01289) 306523
email photon.press@virgin.net
website www.photonpress.co.uk
Contact John Light

Small independent publishing house.
Founded 1986.

Picador

Macmillan Publishers Ltd, 4 Crinan St.
London N1 9XW
tel 020-7833 4000 *fax* 020-7843 4640
website www.panmacmillan.com
Editor Don Paterson

Under the stewardship of Don Paterson,
Picador has established a formidable
poetry list, including work by Paul Farley,
Colette Bryce, Robin Robertson and Kate
Clanchy, amongst others.

Pigasus Press

13 Hazely Combe, Arreton, Isle of Wight
PO30 3AJ
tel (01983) 865668
email mail@pigasuspress.co.uk
website http://freespace.virgin.net/
pigasus.press

Publisher of genre poetry.

Pighog Press

PO Box 145, Brighton BN1 6YU
email info@pighog.co.uk
website www.pighog.co.uk

A small press committed to the
publication of unique voices.

Piper's Ash

Church Road, Christian Malford,
Chippenham, Wiltshire SN15 4BW
tel (01249) 720563 *fax* 0870-568916
email pipersash@supamasu.com
website www.supamasu.com
Contact A Tyson

Small press publisher set up to discover
new authors, writers and poets with talent
and potential.

Submission details Telephone first, or
email proposal.

Piscean Press

6 Guernsey Street, Portland, Dorset
DT5 1JR
tel (01306) 823709
email pisceanpressport@aol.com
Editor Frank Alcock

Publishes the true poet who can be equal
to the rigour of value judgements and
sensitive to the power of every word.

Submission details Submissions should
be typed on A4, loose in a wallet file, and
accompanied by a 30-word CV.

The Poetry Business

The Studio, Byram Arcade, Westgate,
Huddersfield, West Yorkshire HD1 1N
tel (01484) 434840 *fax* (01484) 426566
email editor@poetrybusiness.co.uk
website www.poetrybusiness.co.uk
Editor Peter Sansom

Publishes books and pamphlets under the
Smith/Doorstop imprint; also a poetry
journal, *The North*. Runs an annual book
and pamphlet competition.

Submission details Send a sample
manuscript of 20-25 poems accompanied
by an sae. No email submissions.

Poetry Salzburg

email editor@poetrysalzburg.com
website www.poetrysalzburg.com

Contact Dr Wolfgang Görtschacher

In 1971, James Hogg founded the University of Salzburg Press, publishing books of literary criticism in the fields of Jacobean Drama, Romantic Studies, Elizabethan & Jacobean Studies, and Poetic Drama & Poetic Theory. In the early 1980s he started to publish collections of poetry. Relaunched in 1999 as Poetry Salzburg, the company now publishes 6-8 books per year: poetry, literary criticism, anthologies, annotated bibliographies, and plays.

Polygon – see Birlinn Ltd

Poor Tom's Press
89a Winchester Avenue, Leicester LE3 1AY
tel 0116-289 5400

A poetry pamphlet publisher.

Prest Roots Press
34 Alpine Court, Kenilworth CV8 2GP
Publisher PE Larkin

Begun in 1987 to bring together innovative poetry and fine, hot-metal printing on good papers at prices suitable for readers rather than collectors. There is also a sub-series, *Prest Roots 2*, printed by offset.

Protean Publications
4 Milton Road, Bentley Heath, West Midlands B93 8AA
email versifierlester@yahoo.co.uk
website www.indigogroup.co.uk/llpp/protean.html
Contact Paul Lester

Founded in 1980. Has published around 60 titles, including works by Roy Fisher, Les Roadhouse, and Adrian de Redman.

PS Avalon Press
PO Box 1865, Glastonbury BA6 8YR
tel (01458) 833864
email info@psavalon.com
website www.psavalon.com
Contact Will Parfitt

Publishes books of poetry with a psychospiritual content; contemplative and inspirational poetry with a dark, challenging edge.

Submission details Up to 100 lines should be sent in the body of an email (not as an attachment), or via post accompanied by an sae.

Rack Press
The Rack, Kinnerton, Presteigne, Powys, Wales LD8 2PF
tel (01547) 560411 *mobile* (07817) 424560
email rackpress@britishlibrary.net
website http://pages.britishlibrary.net/nicholas.murray/RackPress.htm

Welsh poetry pamphlet imprint. Relaunched in January 2006; hopes to publish 2-3 short poetry pamphlets a year.

Ragged Raven Press
1 Lodge Farm, Snitterfield, Warwickshire CV37 0LR
tel (01789) 730358
email raggedravenpress@aol.com
website www.raggedraven.co.uk
Contacts Janet Murch, Bob Mee

Small press publishing 1-2 individual collections a year and an anthology linked to an annual competition. Also publishes *Iota*, a quarterly poetry magazine.

Reality Street Editions
63 All Saints Street, Hastings, East Sussex TN34 3BN
tel (01424) 431271
email info@realitystreet.co.uk
website http://freespace.virgin.net/reality.street
Editor Ken Edwards

Formed in 1993. Publishes contemporary writing in English and in translation from other languages. Committed to producing well-designed and well-printed trade paperback editions, in limited runs but at affordable prices.

Redbeck Press

24 Aireville Road, Fritzinghall, Bradford BD9 4HH
tel (01274) 498135
Contact David Tipton

Has published more than 130 books during the 20 years of its existence, including several anthologies, many collections of poetry and some short fiction.
Submission details Enquiry by letter before submission.

The Rialto

PO Box 309, Aylsham, Norwich NR11 6LN
website www.therialto.co.uk
Editor Michael Mackmin

Began in 1964 and has been publishing a magazine since then. Now also publishing first collections and pamphlets.
Submission details Send 6 poems and an sae or IRC. Response time is about 3 months.

The Rockingham Press

11 Musley Lane, Ware, Herts SG12 7EN
tel (01920) 467868 *fax* (01920) 467868
email david@rockpress.freeserve.co.uk
website www.rockingham-press.co.uk
Contact David Perman

David Perman set up the Rockingham Press in 1991, to champion new and neglected poets and also Middle Eastern poetry in translation. Since then it has published, on average each year, 5 paperback collections (always including a first collection) and 1-2 pamphlets.
Submission details Unable to accept submissions at present.

Rough Winds

56 Lady Somerset Road, London NW5 1TU
tel 020-7485 7703 *fax* 020-7485 1525
email info@roughwinds.co.uk
website www.roughwinds.co.uk

Aims to promote poetry in an exciting and original way that brings out the heart of the meaning in a clear and enjoyable manner. Rough Wind's primary interest lies with audio cassettes; however, from time to time poetry pamphlets and posters are published.

Route Books

PO Box 167, Pontefract, Yorkshire WF8 4WW
tel 0845-158 1565
email info@route-online.com
website www.route-online.com
Contact Ian Daley

Publisher of contemporary fiction and performance poetry.
Submission details By audio CD. Details can be found on www.id-publishing.com.

SAF Publishing

149 Wakeman Road, London NW10 5BH
tel 020-8969 6099 *fax* 020-8354 3132
email info@safpublishing.com
website www.safpublishing.com

Poetry and rock music book publisher.

Sahitya Press

1 Donnington Road, Sheffield S2 2RF
email debjani@chatterjee.freeserve.co.uk
website http://sahityapress.mysite.wanadoo-members.co.uk
Contact Debjani Chatterjee

An independent community writing and publishing press based in Sheffield. Run by 2 friends who were also founder-members of the Bengali Women's Support

Group: Indian-born Debjani Chatterjee, and Bangladeshi-born Safuran Ara.

Salmon Publishing

Knockeven, Cliffs of Moher, Co Clare, Ireland
tel (06) 5708 1941
email info@salmonpoetry.com
website www.salmonpoetry.com

Taking its name from the Salmon of Knowledge in Celtic mythology, Salmon was established in 1981 with the publication of *The Salmon*, a journal of poetry and prose, as an alternative voice in Irish literature. Since then more than 200 volumes of poetry have been produced, and Salmon has become one of the most important publishers in the Irish literary world. By specialising in the promotion of new poets, Salmon has enriched Irish literary publishing and now has the most representative list of women poets in Ireland.

Salt Publishing

PO Box 937, Great Wilbraham, Cambridge CB1 5JX
tel (01223) 882220 *fax* (01223) 882260
website www.saltpublishing.com
Publishing Director Christopher Hamilton-Emery

Salt publishes ground-breaking poetry, literary criticism, essays and biography for an international market. The management team, drawn from blue-chip companies, has successfully consolidated the operations of the Australian-born business in the UK. Salt is a class leader in the implementation of new publishing technologies and standards. Sales revenues from the rapidly expanding catalogue are growing at 40% per year. Stocks of award-winning titles are held with major distributors in the UK, USA and Australia, and sold in bookstores around the world.

Salty Press

Mains of Airlie, Kirriemuir, Angus
website www.scottish-pamphlet-poetry.com

A Scottish pamphlet publisher.

Saqi Books

26 Westbourne Grove, London W2 5RH
tel 020-7221 9347
website www.saqibooks.com

Founded in 1984 to bridge the divide between Middle Eastern and Western cultures. Since then Saqi has expanded its network to include writers from the Balkans, Afghanistan, Pakistan and France as well as from the UK.

The Seer Press

PO Box 29313, Glasgow G20 2AE
email admin@theseerpress.com
website www.theseerpress.com

A small pamphlet press publishing contemporary Scottish poetry. Aims to provide a viable outlet for the poetry pamphlet as a grassroots alternative to the publishing industry.

Selkirk Lapwing Press

Lower Kirklands, The Glebe, Selkirk TD7 5AB
email selkirklapwing@freeuk.com
website www.selkirklapwingpress.co.uk
Editor Robert Leach

A not-for-profit outfit, interested in poetry produced in the region either side of Hadrian's Wall – Cumbria, Dumfries and Galloway, Scottish Borders and Northumberland, plus perhaps Lothian, Tyne and Wear and County Durham.

Submission details Submit by post accompanied by sae, or by email. See website for details.

Seren

57 Nolton Street, Bridgend CF31 3AE
tel (01656) 663018 *fax* (01656) 649226
email general@seren-books.com

Publisher Mick Felton

Poetry, fiction, drama, history, film, literary criticism, biography, art – mostly with relevance to Wales. Has published poetry for twenty-five years. Founded 1981.

Submission details Hard copy with S.A.E.

Shearsman Books

58 Velwell Road, Exeter, Devon EX4 4LD
tel (01392) 434511
email editor@shearsman.com
website www.shearsman.com
Contact Tony Frazer

Publisher devoted to contemporary poetry in English and in translation. Interested mainly in work that shows knowledge of the Modernist tradition.

Submission details Postal submissions must be accompanied by sae. If work is sent by email, no attachments other than PDFs will be opened.

Shepheard-Walwyn Publishers Ltd

Suite 604, The Chandlery, 50 Westminster Bridge, London SE1 7QY
tel 020-7721 7666
email books@shepheard-walwyn.co.uk
website www.shepheard-walwyn.co.uk
Managing Director Anthony Werner

An independent publisher that has been publishing books for over 30 years.

Shoestring Press

19 Devonshire Avenue, Beeston, Nottingham NG9 1BS
tel 0115-925 1827
website www.shoestringpress.co.uk
Editor John Lucas

Publishes work by good contemporary poets, in full collection and pamphlet form. Also publishes poetry in translation, especially from the Greeks, and very occasionally works in prose.

Submission details No more than 6 poems should be submitted, and only after a letter of enquiry.

Sixties Press

89 Connaught Road, Sutton, Surrey SM1 3PJ
tel 020-8286 0419
email sixtiespress@blueyonder.co.uk
website www.sixtiespress.co.uk or www.barrytebb.co.uk or www.criticalobs.co.uk
Editor Barry Tebb

A writers' cooperative, which began as a literary press but increasingly concentrates on work by survivors of mental-health disorders.

Submission details Poet pays for individual collection, but not for inclusion in an anthology.

Skoob Books

Woodhill Farm, Willow Marsh Lane, Yoxford, Suffolk IP17 3JR
email skoobrussellsquare@hotmail.com
website www.skoob.com
Contact M Lovell

Former bookshop that publishes some poetry.

Smaller Sky Books

1st Floor, Llwyn Eilian, Rhosgadfan Gwynedd LL54 7HE
mobile (07050) 632277
email editor@smallersky.com
website www.smallersky.com

An independent paperback publishing house, specialising in poetry and fiction. Committed to a supportive and nurturing relationship with authors, offering strong editorial support. Smallersky.com also offers a showcase of new writing.

Smith/Doorstop Books

The Poetry Business, The Studio, Byram Arcade, Westgate, Huddersfield, West Yorkshire HD1 1N

tel (01484) 434840 *fax* (01484) 426566
website www.poetrybusiness.co.uk/
smithdoorstop.aspx
Contact Janet Fisher

A small independent publisher of
contemporary poetry, publishing books,
pamphlets and audio-cassettes.

Smokestack Books

PO Box 408, Middlesbrough TS5 6WA
tel (01642) 813997
email info@smokestack-books.co.uk
website www.smokestack-books.co.uk
Contact Andy Croft

Champions poets who are unfashionable,
unconventional, radical or left-field, and
who work a long way from the centres of
cultural authority. Is interested in the
world as well as the word, and believes
that poetry is a part of and not apart from
society.

Submission details See submission
guidelines on the website.

Snapshot Press

PO Box 132, Crosby, Liverpool L23 8XS
email info@snapshotpress.co.uk
website www.snapshotpress.co.uk

Publishes tanka and related poetic forms.

Snapshot Press

PO Box 132, Waterloo, Liverpool
L22 8WZ
email info@snapshotpress.co.uk
Editor www.snapshotpress.co.uk
Contact John Barlow

Publishers of haiku, tanka and other short
poetry.

Spike

c/o 96 Bold Street, Liverpool L1 4HY
tel 0151-709 3688
Contact Dave Ward

Publishes first collections from Merseyside
and the North West.

Submission details No unsolicited
manuscripts.

Steve Savage Publishers

The Old Truman Brewery, 91 Brick Lane,
London E1 6QL or 6 Hillview, Edinburgh
EH4 2AB
tel 020-7770 6083
email mail@savagepublishers.com
website www.savagepublishers.com

Publishes books on Scottish history,
literature, languages and folklore, as well
poetry, guidebooks, humorous titles, and
new and classic writing from Scotland and
elsewhere.

Stride Publications

11 Sylvan Road, Exeter EX4 6EW
email editor@stridebooks.co.uk
website www.stridebooks.co.uk
Managing Editor Rupert M Loydell

Poetry, prose poetry, contemporary music
and visual arts, and interviews. Inhabits
the divide between the avant-garde and
the traditional, the secular and the sacred,
the mysterious and the everyday, the
modern and the postmodern. Committed
to innovative poetry and fiction by both
known and unknown authors. Founded
1980.

Submission details No submissions are
currently being sought.

the tall-lighthouse

33 Longhurst Road, Hither Green,
London SE13 5LR
tel 020-8297 8279
email info@tall-lighthouse.co.uk
website www.tall-lighthouse.co.uk
Contact LK Robinson

An independent publisher, producing full
collections and pamphlets and organising
poetry readings, events and workshops in
London and around the UK.

Submission details Submit 6 poems by post, accompanied by an sae. Please check website before submitting.

Templar Poetry

Box No 7082, Bakewell DE45 9AF
tel (01629) 810085
email info@templarpoetry.co.uk
website www.templarpoetry.co.uk
Managing Editor Alex Macmillan

An independent publishing house based in Derbyshire, publishing new poetry and committed to promoting emerging poets.

Submission details Submit via the annual Pamphlet and First Collection Competition, and by commission only. No unsolicited manuscripts will be considered.

Terra Firma Press

11 Sinclair Drive, Glasgow G42 9PR
Editor A Murray

A Scottish pamphlet publisher.

Two Rivers Press

35-39 London Street, Reading, Berkshire RG1 4PS
tel 0118-966 2345
email enquiries@tworiverspress.com
website www.tworiverspress.com

A cooperative, with a growing reputation for bold design and illustration combined with distinctive new writing. The press is developing a strong line in illustrated poetry and prose from local writers, exemplified by *The Waterlog*, a journal of poetry, prose and visual arts featuring a range of writers from the well known (Peter Redgrove, Mario Petrucci, etc.) to the previously unknown.

Vane Women Press

19a Vane Terrace, Darlington DL3 7AT
website www.vanewomen.co.uk

Contact Dorothy Long

A writers' collective from the North of England; runs a press and workshops.

Vennel Press

8 Richmond Road, Staines, Middlesex TW18 2AB
email vennel@hotmail.com
website www.indigogroup.co.uk/llpp/vennel.html
Contact Leona Medlin

A small press founded by Leona Medlin and Richard Price in 1990. Publishes modern Scottish poetry, poetry associated with 'The Poetry Workshop' (London), and modernist poetry in translation.

Waterways Publishing

PO Box 43771, Suite 13, London W14 8ZY
tel 0845-430 9517
email editor@waterways-publishing.com
website www.waterways-publishing.com
Editor Stuart Strong

Launched in 2001. Publishes outstanding poetry with a focus on writers who read well in public.

Submission details Submit 6 poems by email in the first instance. Editor will respond if interested.

The Waywiser Press

9 Woodstock Road, London N4 3ET
tel 020-8374 5526 *fax* 020-8374 5736
email waywiserpress@aol.com
website www.waywiser-press.com
Editor Philip Hoy

A small independent company, with its main office in London and a subsidiary in Baltimore. Founded in late 2001; started publishing in 2002. The press specialises in the publication of modern poetry in English, and is keen to promote the work of new as well as established authors.

Wendy Webb Books

9 Walnut Close, Taverham, Norwich
NR8 6YN
email tipsforwriters@yahoo.co.uk
Contact Wendy Webb

New and traditional rules of poetry forms;
Tips newsletter; Challenges: Davidian
Open Poetry Competition.

    Submission details Send sae for sample
of *Tips* before submitting. Publishes short
poems, a maximum of 3 in any form.

West House Books

40 Crescent Road, Sheffield S7 1HN
tel 0114-258 6035
email info@westhousebooks.co.uk
website www.westhousebooks.co.uk
Contact Alan Halsey

Publishers of poetry and poetry-related
work, mainly contemporary and in the
Modernist tradition.

White Adder Press

Lynn Cottage, East Linton, East Lothian
EH40 3DA
email bates_martin@yahoo.co.uk
website www.scottish-pamphlet-
poetry.com
Editor Martin Bates

Publisher of beautifully produced
pamphlets.

White Leaf Press

PO Box 734, Aylesbury HP20 9AL
email editor@whiteleafpress.co.uk
website www.whiteleafpress.co.uk
Contact Stephen Brown

An independent press dedicated to
publishing exciting new work by poets and
writers who aim to stretch boundaries and
challenge preconceptions.

    Submission details Send 10-12 poems
initially by post or email, with a short
biographical note. State which poems have

already been published and where, if
possible. For electronic submissions, work
should be included in the body of the
email (no attachments). Send
to editor@whiteleafpress.co.uk with
'submissions' in the subject line.

Wild Honey Press

16a Ballyman Road, Bray, County
Wicklow, Ireland
email poetry@wildhoneypress.com
website www.wildhoneypress.com

Publishes poetry books and CDs featuring
Irish and international poets.

Wild Women Press

10 The Common, Windermere, Cumbria
LA23 1JH
website www.wildwomenpress.com
Contact Vik Bennett

A not-for-profit press and poets' collective
with a DIY ethic and a mission to
celebrate life creatively.

    Submission details View website for up-
to-date news on submissions.
Announcements are made on the site.
At present only accepting online
submissions.

Wolfhound Press

68 Mountjoy Square, Dublin 1, Republic
of Ireland
tel (01) 874 0354

Publisher of Irish poetry.

Worple Press

2 Havelock Road, Tonbridge, Kent
TN9 1JE
tel (01732) 367466 *fax* (01732) 352057
email TheWorpleCo@aol.com
website www.worplepress.co.uk
Co-director Peter Carpenter

Publishes mainly collections of poetry, but
also produces arts titles. Showcases new

writing and welcomes diversity of format and approach (anthologies, translations, interviews, dictionaries) and has an international outlook.

Wrecking Ball Press

email editor@wreckingballpress.com
website www.wreckingballpress.com
Editor Shane Rhodes

A magazine produced with a real passion for poetry.

Zum Zum Books

Goshem, Bunlight, Drumnadrochit, Inverness-shire IV3 6AH
tel (01456) 459368, (01456) 459370 *email* oramneil@yahoo.com
website www.warp-experience.com
Contact Neil Oram

Publisher of erotic/philosophic poetry.

Making a living as a poet

How do you reconcile the writing of poetry with the need to pay a mortgage and feed yourself? Especially as we are no longer content to starve in a garret – and why should we be? – to make our art. Poet **Michael Symmons Roberts** lays out the options open to poets as they strive for a decent lifestyle that also allows them to practise their craft.

The composer Jean Sibelius once moaned that "it is difficult to keep company with artists. You have to choose businessmen if you want to converse, because artists only talk about money". This rings true for many poets, and with good reason. Businessmen generally know where the money is coming from. Poets can be lauded by critics and admired by readers, but still struggle to make ends meet. Ends can be made to meet by poets in various ways, but most of them have little to do with the writing of poems.

Option one is to give up the day job, to go fully freelance as a poet. This is the purist's path, the route of no compromise. It is also virtually impossible. How many poets in the UK make a living solely from the writing and publishing of their poems? A handful at most. Giving readings can help, but many are not well paid, and they are better seen as a way of meeting readers than a way of earning a living. Short bursts of writing time can be funded by grants and awards. The Society of Authors' Gregory Awards for UK poets aged under 30 are a huge encouragement to poets as they begin to develop their work. There are other grants and awards – from the Arts Council and similar bodies – but they are not replacement salaries. They may allow you to take time out from a day job to write some poems, but they won't replace your salary long-term. In the last few years, more fixed-tenure residencies and placements have been offered to poets; these usually involve some teaching or lecturing, and can provide considerable writing time. For poets with a track record, there are opportunities to teach short courses in libraries or schools, or with specialist organisations like the Arvon Foundation. However, even the hardest-working poet would struggle to keep the wolf from the door on a freelance mixture of writing poems, teaching courses, giving readings, and receiving grants. And the round of travel and form-filling could be a distraction from the writing of the poems themselves. You could find yourself living 'as a poet', but writing fewer poems than you did when you had a day job.

Option two is to give up the day job, and to go fully freelance as a writer, but not just as a poet. This freelance life could include all of option one, but also writing in more lucrative forms such as journalism, fiction, script writing. The advantage of this is that you stand a chance of earning a living, but only if you make a success of these other forms of writing, and you will only do that if you genuinely enjoy them. As with option one, there is a danger of the poems being edged out of the picture by the more pressing deadlines and financial imperatives of the other writing. This is fine – and can be very rewarding – if you love writing fiction, journalism or scripts, but it can be just another form of day job if you don't.

Option three is to give up half the day job. This has become a better option in recent years, as employment legislation has begun to enhance and protect the status of part-time work. The advantage of this is that it gives a taste of freelance life, and a clear time in the week to focus on poetry, whilst maintaining a bedrock of income and security. Whether it works depends on the day job, and on the employer. There may be a price to pay in terms of career development in the day job, as many employers – wrongly – still regard part-time staff as under motivated or lacking focus. But that price may be worth paying for the gains in time and mental space.

Option four is don't give up the day job. All kinds of day jobs have been tried and tested by poets over the years. Traditional favourites have included arts administration, broadcasting, teaching creative writing, teaching English in a school or university, working in publishing or in libraries. How well this combination works depends on the poet and the job. For some poets, it's a perfect long-term solution, especially in education where (despite long hours in term-time) holidays are long and often free for writing. The frustration with so-called 'creative' jobs, or jobs close to writing, is that they often draw on the same energies that make the poems. You may be dealing with poetry or poets every day. But if you stop writing poems yourself, that may be scant compensation. Many poets have written (and still do) productively and well whilst holding down jobs completely unconnected with the arts or writing. When Ezra Pound famously attempted to 'liberate' TS Eliot from his day job at a bank in London, setting up a fund to allow the great poet to write full-time, Eliot was embarrassed and worried. He wasn't at all sure that the insecurity of the freelance life would benefit his writing. And of course, you don't have to be liberated from day jobs, even apparently un-creative day jobs, to fire the imagination. Wallace Stevens trained as a lawyer and pursued a career in insurance, ending up as Vice-President of the firm. On his way to work, this be-suited bureaucrat wrote some of the most expansive and groundbreaking poetry of the 20th Century.

So how can a poet make a living? There is no single answer. What helps one will hinder another. Most poets have tried various options in their writing lives. It's a balancing act between putting bread on the table and securing time to write. And there is another gamble too; by becoming a full-time poet – even if you can make ends meet – you risk writing poems that don't need writing. Poems (unlike fiction) don't respond to you sitting at the desk at 9am daily, expecting them to show up. After all, poetry was never meant to function as a job, which is why poets end up talking about money.

Michael Symmons Roberts is the author of four collections of poetry, and won the Whitbread Prize for Poetry for his most recent book, *Corpus* (Jonathan Cape). His novel, *Patrick's Alphabet* (Jonathan Cape), was published in 2006.

Pamphlet power, poet power

Pamphlet publishing is increasingly popular for two reasons: you can do it yourself; and it does not involve the kind of financial issues that book publishing does. **Hazel Cameron** explains where to look for help and inspiration, and gives some handy tips for the prospective pamphleteer.

From Jonathan Swift in the 1730s to Seamus Heaney, Philip Larkin and Liz Lochhead in modern times, poets have published their work in pamphlet form. Now the millennium has seen a revival in poetry pamphlets. New technology and access to desktop publishing methods have helped poets use their creativity and ingenuity to reach their readers, gaining independence from commerce and subsidy. The poetry pamphlet is flourishing and finding its way to new readers through quite different channels from the usual high street bookshop. Instead, independent bookshops, local retailers, pamphlet fairs and the Internet can all accommodate the pamphlet and help poets reach their audience. If people write poetry and are serious about it, they should make it available to the public, who can then decide what they want to read. The pamphlet offers poets an opportunity to find their readership – something that has become almost impossible through the established methods of commercial publication.

In 2001, Tessa Ransford, founder of the Scottish Poetry Library, set up the Callum Macdonald Memorial Award in memory of her late husband Callum Macdonald, literary publisher and founder of Macdonald Publishers and Printers. The award recognises publishing skill and effort, and validates the practice of poetry publication in pamphlet form. It is supported by the Michael Marks Charitable Trust and many individuals, and is administered by the National Library of Scotland. Since its inception it has not only grown in itself, peaking with 53 entries in 2005, but has encouraged the confidence and development of pamphlet poetry.

Tessa also set up the pamphlet website www.scottish-pamphlet-poetry.com, which allows poets and publishers of pamphlets with a Scottish connection to list and sell their pamphlets on the Web. It helps pamphlet poetry to reach a wider audience, and many of the buyers are from abroad – from individuals, to English departments within overseas universities.

In 2004 the Edinburgh International Book Festival began taking a stand of independently published pamphlets for sale under the Scottish Pamphlet Poetry (SPP) umbrella. Sales increase annually, and last year more than 30 independent publishers were represented among the 200 pamphlets sold. This was a surprising achievement, and shows that the public enjoy the opportunity to discover and decide for themselves what they want to read in terms of poetry.

Pamphlet publishers were further encouraged in 2005 by the launch of *Sphinx* magazine, a magazine set up by the small press HappenStance specifically to review poetry pamphlets. Then in March 2006 the StAnza International Poetry Festival focused for the first time on the category of pamphlet poetry among its other international attractions. It held a successful pamphlet fair during the festival, allowing publishers to sell and display their pamphlets as well as giving poets and publishers the chance to meet and mix. The pamphlet fair is becoming a popular way of distributing poetry; it seems likely that 'market style' fairs will be seen on a regular basis at literary festivals.

There are many benefits to publishing in pamphlet form, as well as a few pitfalls. Generally, if you publish the pamphlet yourself, you can have full control over the contents, layout and cover. However, having your work checked and edited by an independent person before going to print is recommended. Unless you have experience in the printing industry, it is advisable to speak to and probably use a professional printer to produce your final work.

There are a growing number of small presses that produce poetry pamphlets on behalf of poets. Often they will approach a poet whose work they have seen published in poetry magazines, or heard at readings, but many are still happy to be approached by poets with a view to publication. This removes the production and some of the marketing from the poet, yet allows them to remain involved in the content and design of the pamphlet.

With the growing interest in poetry readings and performances, a pamphlet is an excellent way of having your work for sale if you do not have a book. It seems that the public are less likely to buy a book of poetry than to buy a pamphlet; often, they may purchase one to give as a gift or instead of a card. When it comes to distribution, this is usually cheaper and easier to do with pamphlets than with books. Local library shops and other small retailers are more likely to take a few for display on a sale-or-return basis.

If you decide to try the independent approach, please take into consideration the following points:

- It still takes time to produce a pamphlet – usually twice as long as you imagine; design especially is important and should not be rushed. Give yourself sufficient time to make the best of your work.
- Do not start with too many copies: 100 is a good first run.
- Look at other pamphlets; there are lots around. Collaborative projects can take longer, but can be more fun and very satisfying.
- Try to design an attractive cover and have a good title. Take care too with the quality of paper used and the size and style of font (typeface).
- Include a contact number or address in the pamphlet. An ISBN is not essential, but is helpful to shops and festivals – and *always* show a publication date.
- Send your pamphlet to local newspapers and poetry magazines for review.
- Arrange your own readings, or collaborate with others in order to publicise your work.

The best thing about producing a pamphlet yourself is that it is fun. So enjoy it.

Hazel B Cameron is a poet who has published a number of pamphlets. Her work can currently be found on the *Lippy Bissoms* pamphlet, which can be purchased from the Scottish pamphlet website, www.scottish-pamphlet-poetry.com.

An education in everything

Carol Ann Duffy, Sylvia Plath and the Arvon Foundation were instrumental in shaping the life of poet, **Colette Bryce**. Here, she tells us about her journey to becoming a poet.

Being a sorry excuse for a degree student, I was overcome with guilt every time I skulked into the English department to beg an extension on an essay deadline or to daydream my way through another seminar on a novel I had only half read. One of the last flowers of the welfare state, there I was squandering my big chance at an education. My lowest point was writing an essay, in the wee small hours, fuelled on ProPlus and cigarettes, on Tennyson's *Maud* which I hadn't read. I actually passed, which only goes to show that university lecturers have their own problems.

Then two things happened. Firstly, a tutor, Marion Lomax (now the poet Robyn Bolam) had organised a poetry event and appealed to us to attend. "Where's the harm," I said to my friends, sure it would be only a short hop to the pub afterwards; besides, a living poet was quite an exotic concept. The poet turned out to be Carol Ann Duffy and we thought she was rather good. Surprisingly, her poems seemed relevant to our lives. But for me, who secretly wanted to write, the knowledge that a young woman could work as a poet – that this was somehow possible – was a revelation, and a door very quietly opened somewhere in my mind.

The second thing was the appearance on the syllabus of the poetry of Sylvia Plath, closely followed by that of Philip Larkin, both of whom, in near opposite ways, seemed to wake me up with a jolt.

After finishing my degree I revisited the department for some reason and spotted a brochure for the Arvon Foundation's writing courses pinned to the noticeboard. I found myself extremely interested. I was aware, by then, that I had a huge need to write ... but a great fear of it too. I examined the brochure for a long time, and then stole it. That was the first move in my writing life.

But I had no money for an Arvon course. The Foundation offered part-bursaries but still I needed a couple of hundred pounds. I asked my landlord for an extension on the rent (I was an expert at securing extensions by then) and he agreed. I booked a week off work, which was stacking supermarket shelves on the night shift. I chose a beginners' course that was to be tutored by the only living poet I had ever met – the very same Carol Ann Duffy – along with the poet and crime novelist John Harvey. And off I went to Yorkshire with no idea what to expect.

I was very nervous. The other students seemed older and wiser and some had even had poems published in magazines. There was nothing for it but to come clean to the tutors. "I'm a beginner," I told them, "literally. Where do I begin?" And they set me on a path of contemporary reading that opened my eyes to poetry as a vital, relevant art form, full of possibilities. That changed everything: I haven't stopped reading, or writing, since.

I gave up the nocturnal shelf-stacking and took up daylight bookselling, ending up in Waterstone's on Hampstead High Street for a number of years. These were the good old days of bookselling: independents could still make a living; Bernard Stone was in Covent Garden; and Waterstone's was still owned by Dan Dare lookalike, Tim Waterstone and employed people with a passion for books and with capacious brains to memorise stock (and the legendary overstocks). There were no computers, *imagine*. We would hand-write stock lists; phone through orders for hundreds of ISBNs, straight-faced; spend hours chasing the most obscure title for a customer; and squint at microfiche hieroglyphics to see if there just might be an American edition.

We prided ourselves on our sections. There seemed to be nothing the art buyer, the brilliant Mike Payne, didn't know about his subject, or the fiction buyer about hers. With the blessing of the manager and a seemingly limitless budget, I set about constructing my dream poetry section, a situation unthinkable today. Everything I had ever read or wanted to read was there. Everything I should have read and would one day get around to reading was there. All the classics. All the key translations. The Europeans. The Americans. When I discovered a new poet from the States (for example when Sharon Olds' *The Father* was published here) I would import their entire American backlist and pile them high on the table. And they sold.

Receiving poetry deliveries felt like Christmas. Michael Horovitz would appear at the desk bearing quantities of *Grandchildren of Albion*. I had a network of regular poetry readers who would drop in for a chat and to check out what was new. The New-Gen poets were making a splash. Bloodaxe was publishing wonderful anthologies and we stocked them all in generous quantities. Customers would wander in with a half-remembered poem in their heads, could I tell them who wrote it? (Yeats, nearly always.) I was developing a serious poetry habit and the considerable staff discount was keeping me in supplies. I was reading poetry on the bus, on the tube, in the staffroom, on the roof, and behind the till in the twilight zone of the late shift, when only the odd drunk or Bronco John would venture into the store.

Meanwhile, I was writing at night and learning. I would meet up once-weekly in Whitechapel with my friend and fellow poetry nut Kate Clanchy, then a schoolteacher, and swap poems and feedback over a glass of red. I attended a few more courses, and many readings around town, at bookshops and cafés. On days off I would write at a booth in the Poetry Library on the South Bank. This was my kind of education; one thing leading organically to another, a journey of discoveries. And the education was not only in poetry. Poetry, being about everything, is an education in everything.

In 1995, I had my first poems published in a new poets anthology, and I applied for and received an Eric Gregory award from the Society of Authors. It was a good year for me all round because I also fell in love. I was 25. But I was nowhere near ready to publish a collection. In a strange way, being published was beside the point. I had a sense, and still do, that poetry is a life's work and there should be no big rush to publish. Even five years later, when my first book came out, it felt very soon – but that's another story.

My advice? Read; it's as simple as that. And only those who need to will heed it.

Colette Bryce was born in Derry in 1970. Her first collection was *The Heel of Bernadette* (Picador), which won the Aldeburgh Poetry Festival Prize for Best First Collection; her second, *The Full Indian Rope Trick* was published by Picador in 2004.

Magazines, a brief overview: poetry in a matchbox

There is a veritable mountain of poetry magazines published every year. Magazine editor **James Byrne** takes us through some history, and provides useful guidelines for submitting material to magazines.

Tracking the number of poetry magazines in the UK is an impossible task. The Poetry Library website (www.poetrylibrary.org.uk) puts the list at 182, while freely acknowledging that there are "obviously more" in circulation. The figure is more likely to be over 250.

Since its inception in 1964, the Poetry Store Collection (a UCL library initiative) has acquired more than 7000 titles. It also concedes that this figure does not account for every poetry publication available today. One of the reasons for this is that, while some poetry magazines might suddenly disappear, replacements steadily arrive. As this article is being written, a new publication from Manchester called *Matchbox* – a magazine that quite literally fits the size of a matchbox – is being prepared, along with countless others.

Old journals too are being pulled back from extinction. The exciting left-wing experimental magazine *Fragmente*, which fell away in the 1990s, is due for re-issue. But perhaps a more quirky example is *St Botolph's Review*, which has finally produced its second offering some 50 years after Sylvia Plath and Ted Hughes first met during its auspicious launch in Cambridge.

When I moved to London as an aspiring young poet, the Poetry Library, with its bulging stock of poetry magazines, was a crucial find. It has been difficult this past year seeing it wrapped under tarpaulin as part of the Royal Festival Hall's extensive renovations. However, almost as if to compensate for this, the PL now provides a digital library of poetry magazines (www.poetrymagazines.org.uk) which offers some delightful archive material and the digitisation of more than 30 poetry magazines. Each issue reads as closely as possible to original print formatting and celebrates a diversity of poetry that has the potential to reach new audiences. An "independent and free-standing" website, poetrymagazines already has a strong cast list, including many of the leading poetry journals in Britain. There are some real gems to be found, from *Poetry Review*'s inaugural issue in 1912, to the final editorial of the much-missed *Thumbscrew*. An eventual aim of the PL is to digitise its entire collection of magazines – a massive task, but one that would increase the readership of contemporary poetry and make the poet's job far easier in choosing where to submit their own writing.

Another important project for the preservation of poetry journals is provisionally entitled *The Little Magazine's Compendium*, due for publication in the autumn as this *Yearbook* goes to press. It documents thousands of poetry magazines from 1914 to 2000, and tells us where more than 5000 poets sent their work. Here we can find where poetry giants like Ezra Pound, TS Eliot and John Berryman first began to publish their poems as relative unknowns. Excitingly, we can also discover developing trends of writing and exactly where groups of writers made allegiances to particular schools or movements, such as Imagism and Surrealism.

Many of the magazines featured had short print runs or short lives and are now extremely rare. The *Compendium* lists the key libraries where these publications can still be found as well as mapping the birthplaces of magazines across the British Isles. Nearly ten years in the making, it's a book not just for the literary anorak or historian, but for poets of all abilities.

Perhaps you are a reader who is relatively new to poetry but with ambitions to publish. As editor of *The Wolf*, I'll finish by offering a few simple do's and don'ts regarding the presentation of your work.

Firstly – and this has been hammered home by poetry editors for years now – read up on the journals before you lick that stamp. There will be poetry magazines which may not suit your style of writing, however original your submission may be. Indeed, certain poetry magazines publish only love poems; others (like *Mslexia*) will only accept work from female poets. What use would your epic poem on Norse mythology be to a poetry publication that tends only to publish cyberpunk poems?

For those about to send off work to poetry magazines for the first time, you should of course possess a current copy of *Poetry Writers' Yearbook*! – and you may also benefit from *Light's List*, now in its 21st year of publication. It's cheap at £4 and includes names, addresses, prices, page counts and the frequency of more than 1500 UK, US, Canadian, Australian, European, African and Asian small press magazines publishing creative writing in English.

However, most serious poetry magazines will have their own website. Skim through internal guidelines regarding submission. In many cases you will be required to send a short biography or covering letter. Know who it is you are addressing: finding out the editor's name shows good table manners. If you are sending poems via the Web, make sure that attachments can be opened and that you write a subject title in the email. Countless submissions come into *The Wolf*'s email account with 'no subject'; sadly many of these, if unrecognised, get deleted without ever having been read. For postal submissions you should send a stamped-addressed envelope. Furthermore, always write your name and contact details at the end of each poem. If you are sending a long poem you may wish to staple pages together: an editor going through 1000 poems for an issue might get the odd one jumbled up, and it would be terrible for the poem that you've slaved over to be misplaced or even attributed to someone else!

There are a host of other small measures I could suggest, but my last pinch of advice is to aim high and to keep writing better poems. If you think your own poetry good enough to be published, perhaps work out a sliding scale of exactly where you'd like to see yourself in print. Start at the top and work your way through. Inevitably rejection will come along, but it should be rationalised. If your poetry is rich and original it will be published eventually. Certain journals, particularly those which claim to be inundated with reams of submissions, might take an eternity to reply. I remember once having to wait a whole year only to be rejected by a magazine! After smouldering for days, I took comfort in learning that Ted Hughes was repeatedly refused by Faber in his early career, before *The Hawk in the Rain* appeared: a book that fast-tracked him to becoming a leading poet of the 20th century.

James Byrne is Editor of *The Wolf* poetry magazine. He is also currently editing *Priora* – an anthology of poetry and photography to be published by Phaidon in 2007. He has recently worked for the Poetry Translation Centre at the School of Oriental and African Studies, and is finishing a second collection of poems.

Magazines

The list below is a snapshot of the poetry magazine world as of summer 2006. However, by the time you read this it is likely that some of the magazines will no longer be in existence , and that brand new ones will have emerged. The magazines in this list range from photocopied, stapled sheets of densely typed A4 to perfect-bound, immaculately designed, high-quality glossy publications. What they all have in common, though, are relentless enthusiasm and an unbridled love of poetry. As ever, before you send work off, carry out some research to establish that your poetry is suitable, and always include an sae with submissions.

14 Magazine
PO Box 253, Northwood, Middlesex HA6 2ZF
email mike_loveday@hotmail.com
website www.fourteenmagazine.com
Editor Rudy Gordon
Frequency/price 2 p.a. £2.95 plus 35p postage. £6 for 2 issues

Rhymed, unrhymed, traditional, unconventional; all styles accepted, but must have 14 lines only.

Submission details Up to 6 poems, typed, accompanied by sae. Poems may have already been published (provided poet has obtained permission).

AABYE
email geraldengland@yahoo.com
website www.geraldengland.org.uk
Editor Gerald England
Frequency/price £4.50

Eclectic collection of poetry from the traditional to the avant-garde, from haiku to long poems, including translations. Has ceased publication, but copies still available.

Abraxas
57 Eastbourne Road, St Austell, Cornwall PL25 4SU
Editor Paul Newman

Publishes contemporary poetry, with a special emphasis on the lyric mode.

Acorn
Bowes Pub, Fleet Street, Dublin 2, Ireland
email dubwriter@indigo.ie
website www.dublinwriters.org
Frequency/price £3.75

Magazine from Dublin Writers' Workshop.

Submission details Poems and short fiction of any style are considered, in English or French.

Aereings Publications
Dean Head Farm, Scotland Lane, Leeds LS18 5HU
Editor Lesley Quayle, Linda Marshall
Frequency/price £4.50 per issue. Annual UK subscription £11

Areopagus
48 Cornwood Road, Plympton, Plymouth, Devon PL7 1AL
email editor@areopagus.org.uk
website www.areopagus.org.uk
Editor Julian Barritt

A magazine for Christian writers, much of which is poetry, but also publishes articles and fiction. All forms of poetry considered.

Submission details Details sent on subscription. Poet receives free copy.

Aesthetica: A Review of Contemporary Artists
PO Box 371, York YO23 1WL
tel (01904) 674500 *email* info@aestheticamagazine.com

website www.aestheticamagazine.com
Editor Cherie Frederico
Frequency/price Quarterly. £4.50

A contemporary culture magazine that believes in creative expression. Prefers work to reflect issues of contemporary times and to make the reader feel, change or see a new perspective. No bad language and/or overuse of personal pronouns.

Submission details Submit 3-5 poems, via email only. Payment of complimentary copy. See website for guidelines.

Agenda

The Wheelwrights, Fletching Street, Mayfield, East Sussex TN20 6TL
tel (01435) 873703
email editor@agendapoetry.co.uk
website www.agendapoetry.co.uk
Editor Patricia McCarthy
Frequency/price Quarterly. Annual subscription £28 (£35 libraries, institutions and overseas); £22 OAPs/ students

Poetry and criticism. Young poets (and artists), aged 16 to 38, invited to submit work for online Broadsheets Workshop, details online.

Submission details Study the journal before submitting MSS with an sae, or by email. Include email address and a brief biography.

Ambit

17 Priory Gardens, London N6 5QY
tel 020-8340 3566
website www.ambitmagazine.co.uk
Editor Martin Bax *Poetry Editors* Henry Graham, Carol-Ann Duffy *Prose Editors* JG Ballard, Geoff Nicholson *Art Editor* Mike Foreman *Assistant Editor* Kate Pemberton
Frequency/price Quarterly. £6.50 inc. p&p (£25 p.a. UK, £27/€48 Europe, £29/$56 rest of world; £36 p.a., £38/€64 p.a., £40/ $73 p.a. institutions)

Poetry, short fiction, art, poetry reviews. New and established writers and artists. Payment: by arrangement. Illustrations: line, half-tone, colour. Founded 1959.

An Guth

Cruard, Isle Ornsay, Isle of Skye IV43 8QS
tel (01471) 833376
email anguth@onetel.com
Editor Rody Gorman
Frequency/price Annual. £7

Poetry in Scottish or Irish Gaelic.
Submission details Send poems to above address.

Angel Exhaust

35 Stewart's Way, Mannden, Nr Bishop's Stortford, Hertfordshire CM23 1OR
email aduncan@pinko.org
Editor Andrew Duncan, Charles Bainbridge

Recently relaunched poetry magazine.

Anon

67 Learmouth Grove, Edinburgh EH4 1BL
website www.blanko.org.uk/anon
Editor Mike Stocks
Frequency/price As and when. £4 per issue, plus 50p postage

A magazine to which poems are submitted anonymously and assessed blind, using procedures similar to those used by poetry competitions. Poems that are accepted for publication are published under the names of their authors. Payment is 1 free copy.

Submission details Refer to website for submission guidelines.

Aquarius

Flat 4, 116 Sutherland Avenue, London W9 2QP
Editor Eddie Linden
Frequency/price Irregular

An irregularly published but influential magazine.

Areté

8 New College Lane, Oxford OX1 3BN
tel (01865) 289193 *fax* (01865) 289194
email craigraine@aretemagazine.com
website www.aretemagazine.com
Editor Craig Raine
Frequency/price 3 issues p.a.

Fiction, poetry, reportage and reviews.
   Submission details Hard copy only. No international reply coupons. Unsolicited manuscripts should be accompanied by an sae.

Atlantean – see Atlantean on page 12

Avocado

PO Box 3342, Coventry CV1 5YB
email info@heaventreepress.co.uk
website www.heaventreepress.co.uk
Contact Jonathan Morley
Frequency/price Quarterly. £2.50. Annual subscription £10

The in-house journal of Heaventree Press, showcasing poetry, prose, fiction and artwork that is fresh, innovative and culturally aware.

Awen

38 Pierrot Steps, 71 Kursaal Way,
Southend-on-Sea, Essex SS21 2UY
email atlanteanpublishing@hotmail.com
website www.geocities.com/dj-tyrer/
awen.html
Editor DJ Tyrer
Frequency/price Bi-monthly. Free with sae

Open to all styles of poem up to about 50 lines in length. New, unpublished and experienced poets are equally welcome. Payment is 1 complimentary copy.
   Submission details Unsolicited submissions with sae or in the body of an email are welcome.

Bad Poetry Quarterly

PO Box 6319, London E11 2EP
Editor Gordon Smith

Always on the lookout for new poems, poets and illustrations.

Banipal: Magazine of Modern Arab Literature

PO Box 22300, London W13 8ZQ
tel 020-8568 9747
email editor@banipal.co.uk
website www.banipal.co.uk
Editor Margaret Obank
Frequency/price 3 issues p.a. 1 year, £20; 2 years, £30. Rest of Europe, £20/£30. Rest of world, £30/£50

An independent literary magazine publishing contemporary authors and poets from all over the Arab world in English translation. Founded in 1998 by Margaret Obank and Iraqi author Samuel Shimon, the 3 issues a year present established and new authors – most for the first time – through poems, short stories or excerpts of novels. They also feature extensive author interviews, profiles and a series on authors writing about their literary influences. In 7 years of publication *Banipal* has presented works from more than 300 different authors.
   Submission details Submit hard copy only. See website for full guidelines.

Bard

38 Pierrot Steps, 71 Kursaal Way,
Southend-on-Sea SS1 2UY
email atlanteanpublishing@hotmail.com
Editor DJ Tyrer
Frequency/price Monthly. Free for sae

Open to all styles of poetry up to 20 lines (longer poems should be sent to *Monomyth*). New, unpublished and experienced poets welcome.

Submission details Unsolicited submissions with sae or in the body of an email.

A Bard Hair Day

289 Elmwood Avenue, Feltham, Middlesex TW13 7QB
email partners_writing_group@hotmail.com
Editor Ian Deal

A magazine with no rules.

Beat Scene

27 Court Leet, Binley Woods, Coventry CV3 2Q, England
tel (02476) 543604
email kev@beatscene.freeserve.co.uk
website www.beatscene.net
Editor Kevin Ring

Celebrates the work of the Beat Generation, writers, artists, poets, photographers.

The Black Rose

56 Marlescroft Way, Loughton, Essex IG10 3NA
email blackrose@coolvamp.btinternet.co.uk
website www.expage.com/blackrosepoetry
Editor Bonita Hall

Publishes all styles of poetry; new poets welcome.

Black Mountain Review

PO Box 9, Ballyclare BT39 0JW
email info@blackmountainreview.com
website www.blackmountainreview.com
Editor Niall McGrath

A magazine for new writing from Northern Ireland.

Blithe Spirit

12 Eliot Vale, Blackheath, London SE3 0UW
website www.haikusoc.ndo.co.uk/journal.html

Editor Graham High
Frequency/price Quarterly

The journal of the British Haiku Society. Each issue is normally of 64 pages and contains original poems, a diversity of statements about the writing and appreciation of haiku and related forms, book reviews, letters to the editor, and announcements of the winners of major awards, including the Museum of Haiku Literature Award (£50) for the haiku voted best in the previous issue.

Submission details Submissions from members only. Send sae or IRC if you wish a reply. Each issue reflects the season just ended – e.g. March contains winter haiku.

Borderlines

Nant y Brithyll, Llangnyw, Welshpool, Powys SY21 0JS
tel (01938) 810263
Editor Kevin Bamford, Angie Quinn
Frequency/price 2 issues p.a. UK £2.50, £5 annual subscription. Europe, £3, £6 annual subscription. Outside EU, £3.50, £7 annual subscription

Publishes any style or subject. Payment of 1 complimentary copy.

Submission details Submit up to 6 poems, 32 lines maximum preferable, accompanied by sae. Name and address on each poem.

Brittle Star

PO Box 56108, London E17 0AY
email magazine@brittlestar.org.uk
website www.brittlestar.org.uk
Editor Jacqueline Gabbitas, Louisa Hooper, Tina Tse, David Floyd, Martin Parker
Frequency/price 3 issues p.a. £2.50

Focuses on unpublished, original work by new writers, but is not looking for a particular style or subject matter. Read a copy of *Brittle Star* before submitting.

Submission details Submit 1-4 poems by post. Include covering letter and sae. Submissions by email should be sent as a Word or RTF attachment with a covering letter. Do not send work in the main body of the email.

BuzzWords

Calvers Farm, Thelveton, Diss, Norfolk IP21 4NG
website www.buzzwordsmagazine.co.uk
Editor Zoe King

Submission details No more than 6 poems, on any theme and in any style; each should be no longer than 40 lines. All postal submissions must be accompanied by an sae. Email submissions should be via Word or RTF attachments, and should contain the words 'BuzzWords Submission' and either 'Poetry' or 'Fiction' in the subject line. Send to submissions@buzzwordsmagazine.co.uk.

Cadenza

Broadlea House, Heron Way, Hickling, Norfolk NR12 0YQ
website www.cadenza-magazine.co.uk
Editor William Connelly
Frequency/price 2 issues p.a. £15.50, 4 issues

Aims to publish modern, vibrant short stories, articles, poetry and interviews. A5, perfect bound with a glossy cover and around 80-90 pages of content.

Submission details Poems should be a maximum of 40 lines in length. Will accept previously published poems.

Calabash

Centreprise, 136-138 Kingsland High Street, London E8 2NS
tel 020-7249 6572
email literature@centreprisetrust.org.uk

Editor Sharon Duggal
For writers of African and Asian descent.

Candelabrum

1 Chatsworth Court, Outram Road, Southsea PO5 1RA
tel 023-927 5396
email rcp@poetry7.fsnet.co.uk
website www.members.tripod.com/redcandlepress
Editor ML McCarthy
Frequency/price 2 issues p.a. £3 (US $6). £15 (US $30) per volume of 6 numbers

A 40-page, saddle-stitched, formalist magazine. Metrical and rhymed poetry preferred, although good-quality free verse is not excluded. 5/7/5 haiku considered. No room for long poems.

Submission details Submit 3-6 poems, typed on separate sheets. Enclose an sae. No email submissions.

The Cannon's Mouth

22 Margaret Grove, Harborne, Birmingham B17 9JH
email greg@cannonpoets.co.uk
website www.cannonpoets.co.uk
Editor Greg Cox
Frequency/price Quarterly. £2. 4 issues, £8

The Quarterly Journal of Cannon Poets, who have been meeting every month for 21 years at the Midlands Arts Centre, Cannon Hill Park, Birmingham, UK.

Submission details Although *The Cannon's Mouth* is essentially for the benefit of Cannon Poets members and associate members, original poetry articles, reviews and artwork are welcomed from anyone. The standard of poetry published may vary, as the aim is to encourage and improve writing. Submissions by post (must be accompanied by an sae).

Carillon

19 Godric Drive, Brinsworth, Rotherham, South Yorkshire S60 5AN

email editor@carillonmag.org.uk
website www.carillonmag.org.uk
Editor Graham Rippon
Frequency/price 3 issues p.a. £3.20. Annual subscription, £9

Founded in June 2001, aiming to produce an eclectic magazine which gives a forum to talented writers of all shades of publication experience.

Submission details Maximum of 40 lines to submits@carillonmag.org.uk.

Cauldron

10 Glyn Road, Wallasey, Wirral CH44 1AB
tel 0151-200940
email terence.grogan50@ ntlworld.com
website www.thenewcauldron.co.uk
Editor Terence Grogan
Frequency/price Quarterly

A prose and poetry publication for which all genres of poetry are considered. Poems must be no more than 30 lines, in any style and on any subject. Poet receives £2 per published poem.

Submission details Submission in the form of hard copy direct to editor, or via email attachment.

Chanticleer Magazine

6/1 Jamaica Mews, Edinburgh EH3 6HN
email mohard@livermore8304.freeserve.co.uk
Editor Richard Livermore
Frequency/price Varies, but usually every 3 months. £3

Any type or style of poetry considered. A magazine of poetry and ideas – not necessarily in that order.

Submission details Send poems or prose.

Chapman

4 Broughton Place, Edinburgh EH1 3RX
tel 0131-557 2207
email chapman-pub@blueyonder.co.uk
website www.chapman-pub.co.uk
Editor Joy Hendry
Frequency/price 3 p.a. Annual subscription, £20

Poetry, short stories, reviews, criticism, articles on Scottish culture. Illustrations: line, half-tone, cartoons. Payment: £8 per page; illustrations by negotiation. Founded 1969.

Submission details If submitting, bear in mind that the longer you do not hear back, the further along your manuscript has got (in general). Do not try to second-guess editorial policy. Anything stereotypically 'Scottish' will almost certainly be returned.

Chillout

PO Box 3268, Brighton BN1 4FL
Editor Guy Oliver
Frequency/price 4 issues p.a. £1.50. Annual subscription £6 inc. p&p

Prose and poetry on the themes of ghosts, horror, mystery, crime, murder and the supernatural. £25 prize for best poem in each issue as voted by subscribers.

Submission details Direct submissions discouraged. Send sae with 2 x 2nd-class stamps for copy of the magazine and writers' guidelines.

Chimera

118 Nayland Road, Mile End, Colchester CO4 5ET
tel (01206) 751887
email robert@ chimeramagazine.co.uk
website www.chimeramagazine.co.uk
Editor Robert Cole
Frequency/price Biannual. £4.75

Publishes unconventional, experimental work alongside the traditional and, as the title suggests, fantastic or grotesque product(s) of the imagination. Longer poems up to 2 pages.

Submission details Submit by post from the UK and by email from elsewhere (as an attachment).

Chroma

PO Box 44655, London N16 0WQ
email queerchroma@yahoo.co.uk
website www.chromajournal.co.uk
Editor Shaun Levin
Frequency/price 2 issues p.a. £4.95

Poetry and short fiction by lesbian, gay, bisexual and transgendered writers. Each issue has a theme. Welcomes work that is risky and lyrical.

Submission details Check the theme for each issue and submit 3 poems to the Poetry Editor.

Clough Words

Dean Clough Writers, Dean Clough, Halifax HX3 5AZ
Editor Andy J Campbell, Alan Littlewood

A free magazine, but send an sae.

The Coffee House

Charnwood Arts, Loughborough Library, 31 Granby Street, Loughborough, Leicestershire LE11 3DU
email info@charnwood-arts.org.uk
website www.charnwoodarts.com
Editor Deborah Tyler-Bennett
Frequency/price 2 issues p.a. £2.50 (£4.50 for 2, £8.50 for 4)

Publishes poetry and short stories. Quality is the most important factor, irrelevant of type or genre.

Submission details Submit 2-6 poems by post only.

Coffee House Poetry

Ty Meirion, Glan yr Afon, Tanygrisiau, Blaenau Ffestiniog, Gwynedd LL41 3SU
tel (01766) 832112
email jan@ coffeehousepoetry.co.uk

website www.coffeehousepoetry.co.uk
Editor Jan Fortune-Wood
Frequency/price 3 issues p.a., January, May, September. £4 (£10.50 for 3)

Modern poetry with something to say; edge and depth.

Submission details Submit up to 6 poems, maximum 36 lines, by post with sae or in body of an email (no attachments).

Competitions Bulletin

17 Greenhow Avenue, West Kirby, Wirral CH48 5EL
email carolebaldock@hotmail.com
Editor Carole Baldock

Lists details of all current UK writing competitions.

Countryside Tales

Park Publications UK, 14 The Park, Stow on the Wold, Cheltenham, Gloucestershire GL54 1DX
tel (01451) 831053
email parkpub14@hotmail.com
website www.parkpublications.co.uk
Editor David Howarth
Frequency/price Quarterly. £3.50 per issue. Back issues £2 each

Publishes poems with a rural or countryside theme in any style.

Submission details Maximum 40 lines. All work should be sent as hard copy. No email submissions. £10 for the best poem. Free copy to other published poets.

Critical Quarterly

Blackwell Publishing Ltd, Sampson House, Woolpit, Bury St Edmunds IP30 9RN
tel (01359) 242375 *fax* (01359) 242880
website www.blackwellpublishing.com
Editor Colin MacCabe
Frequency/price Quarterly. Annual subscription £26

Fiction, poems, literary criticism. Length: 2000-5000 words. Payment: by arrangement. Founded 1959.

Submission details Study magazine before submitting.

Curlew

Hare Cottage, Kettlesing, Harrogate HG3 2LB
Editor PJ Precious
Frequency/price 2 issues p.a. £2

Anything considered. Payment of complimentary copy.

Submission details Sumission must be accompanied by sae.

Current Accounts

22 Longworth Road, Horwich, Bolton BL6 7BA
tel (01204) 669858
email bswscribe@aol.com
website http://hometown.aol.co.uk/bswscribe/myhomepage/writing.html
Editor Rod Riesco
Frequency/price 2 issues p.a. £2

Publishes any form or subject matter. Prefers poems that avoid clichés, abstract ponderings and sentimentality. Shorter pieces preferred because of limited space.

Submission details Submissions by post or email (in body of message). Sae required for postal submissions. Send maximum of 6 poems, unpublished.

Cutting Teeth

15 Granville Street, Glasgow G3 7EE
email info@cuttingteeth.org
website www.cuttingteeth.org
Contact Lynne Mackenzie
Frequency/price 2 issues p.a. UK £8; Europe £12; Outside Europe £15

A bi-annual small-press publication committed to promoting new Scottish writing.

Submission details Do not send more than 6 poems; each poem on a separate page. State your name and email address clearly on each submission. By post only.

Cyphers

3 Selskar Terrace, Ranelagh, Dublin 6, Republic of Ireland
tel (01) 4978 866 *fax* (01) 4978 866
Frequency/price €12/$25 for 3 issues

Poems, fiction, reviews, translations. Payment: €15 per page. Founded 1975.

Dandelion Arts Magazine

24 Frosty Hollow, East Hunsbury, Northants NN4 0SY
tel (01604) 701730
Editor Jacqueline Gonzalez-Marina

An international publication that is sent to subscribers worldwide. A modern magazine with poetry, articles, stories, art information and illustrations. Non-profit-making.

Submission details It is essential to become a subscriber when expecting to be published. Guidelines available from the editor.

The Dark Horse

c/o 3b Blantyre Mill Road, Bothwell, South Lanarkshire G71 8DD
website www.star.ac.uk/darkhorse.html
Editor Gerry Cambridge

An international literary magazine committed to British and American poetry; published in Scotland.

Dark Horizons

British Fantasy Society, 201 Reddish Road, South Reddish, Stockport SK5 7HR
website www.britishfantasysociety.org.uk
Contact Marie O'Regan

The journal of the British Fantasy Society; welcomes poetry submissions on any subject in the fantasy genre.

Submission details Although space for poetry is limited, *Dark Horizons* is keen to include poems dealing with any aspect of 'fantasy' – interpretation is up to the poet. The maximum number of lines is 50, and any style will be considered (except haiku).

The David Jones Journal

The David Jones Society, 22 Gower Road, Sketty, Swansea SA2 9BY
tel (01792) 206144 *fax* (01792) 470385
email anne.price-owen@sihe.ac.uk
website www.sihe.ac.uk/davidjones
Editor Anne Price-Owen
Frequency/price 1 issue p.a. £7.50

Publishes articles related to the poet/painter, David Jones (1895-1974) or in the spirit of his work – poetry, related criticism, religion, visual arts, 20th-century art, reviews, books, criticism. Poet receives 2 copies of journal in which his/her work is featured.

Submission details Submit by post to editor, accompanied by an sae.

The Dawntreader

Indigo Dreams Press, The Manacles, Predannack, The Lizard, Cornwall TR12 7AU
email dawntreader@indigodreams.plus.com
website www.indigodreamspress.co.uk
Frequency/price 6 issues p.a. £3.50

Specialises in the landscape; myth and legend, nature, spirituality, pre-history, environment, ecology and the mystic.

Submission details Poetry in all forms to 36 lines inc. verse breaks (no more than 3 poems per submission).

Day by Day

Woolacombe House, 141 Woolacombe Road, London SE3 8QP
tel 020-8856 6249

Editor Patrick Richards
Frequency/price Monthly. £1.25

Articles and news on non-violence and social justice. Reviews of art, books, films, plays, musicals and opera. Cricket reports. Payment: £2 per 1000 words. No illustrations required. Founded 1963.

Submission details Short poems and very occasional short stories in keeping with editorial viewpoint.

Decanto

Masque Publishing, PO Box 3257, Littlehampton BN16 9AF
email masque_pub@tiscali.co.uk
website http://myweb.tiscali.co.uk/masquepublishing
Editor Lisa Stewart
Frequency/price 6 issues p.a.

All styles of poetry considered – not just contemporary.

Submission details Submit up to 6 poems by post or email.

Denise Smith

127 Milton Road West, 7 Duddingston House Courtyard, Edinburgh EH15 1JG
tel 0131-661 1156
Editor Denise Smith
Frequency/price 1 issue p.a. £4.50 per copy

Publishes all styles of poetry. Payment is 1 free copy of magazine.

Devil

247 Gray's Inn Road, London WC1X 8JR
tel 020-8994 7767
email steve@thedevilmag.co.uk
website www.thedevilmag.co.uk
Frequency/price Biannual. £6.99 per issue; £18 for 3 issues (UK only)

A journal of fiction, poetry and political essays.

Dial 174

21 Mill Road, Watlington, Norfolk PE33 0HH

email Tallyho-pro1@tiscali.co.uk
Editor Joseph Hemmings
Frequency/price £14 p.a. inc. p&p. Europe
£16 inc. p&p. Rest of world £18 inc. p&p.
£3.50 for a sample copy

Originally a poetry magazine, but now
publishes 60 diversified pages plus a
regular 24-page poetry anthology with
every issue. Experienced and new poets
welcome.

Dream Catcher
4 Church Street, Market Rasen,
Lincolnshire LN8 3ET
tel (01673) 844325
email paulsutherland@hotmail.com
website www.poetrymagazines.org
Editor Paul Sutherland
Frequency/price 2 issues p.a. £6.50

Seeks to publish the very best in
contemporary poetry in English in any
style, including translations, from around
the world. Long poems are welcomed, as is
work from unknown writers.

Submission details Send 5-6 poems
(fewer if long poems) by post in UK.
Email submissions are accepted from
overseas authors.

Dreams That Money Can Buy
35 Mitchell Hey, College Bank, Rochdale,
Lancs OL12 6UL
tel (01706) 648040 *fax* (01706) 648040
email editorial@
dreamsthatmoneycanbuy.co.uk
website
www.dreamsthatmoneycanbuy.co.uk
Contact Poetry Editor

A quarterly journal that explores the
possibilities of contemporary art, poetry,
prose and political satire.

E-Sheaf Magazine
Montgomery House, Sheffield Hallam
University, Sheffield, Yorkshire S24 3TJ

tel (01142) 255555
website www.shu.ac.uk
Contact Gary Kaye

Sheffield Hallam University's celebrated
literary webzine provides a showcase for
both student and local writers.

Earth Love
PO Box 11219, Paisley PA1 2WH
tel 0141-581 9806
email earth.love@ntlworld.com
website homepage.ntlworld.com/
earth.love/earthlove.htm
Editor Tracy Patrick

All submissions should be on a nature
theme, which can be protest or
celebratory. The magazine was set up as a
forum whereby poets can express their
views about our relationship with the
environment; all proceeds go directly to
conservation charities.

Submission details Send poems with sae.
Must be previously unpublished. No email
submissions – will not respond via email.

Eastern Rainbow
17 Farrow Road, Whaplode, Spalding,
Lincolnshire PE12 0TS
email p-rance@yahoo.co.uk
website http://uk.geocities.com/p-rance/
pandf.htm
Editor Paul Rance
Frequency/price 1 issue p.a. £1.75 inc. p&p
(6 issues £10)

Publishes poetry reflecting 21st-century
culture. Poet receives sample copy.

Submission details Send up to 6 poems,
maximum length 32 lines.

Eclipse Poetry Magazine
Everyman Press, 53 West Vale, Neston,
South Wirral L64 9SE
Editor Elizabeth Royd
Frequency/price 6 issues, £18

Edinburgh Review

22a Buccleugh Place, Edinburgh EH8 9LN
tel 0131-651 1415 *fax* 0131-651 1415
website www.edinburghreview.org.uk
Editor Brian McCabe
Frequency/price 3 p.a. Annual subscription
£17 (£34 institutions)

Fiction, poetry, clearly written articles on
Scottish and international cultural and
philosophical ideas. Payment: by
arrangement. Founded 1969.

Eildon Tree

SBC Library Headquarters, St Mary's Mill,
Selkirk TD7 5DG
tel (01750) 724901 Mon-Thu
website www.eildontree.org.uk
Editor Julian Colton, Tom Murray

The *Eildon Tree* magazine was launched in
1999 as a showcase for writing and writers
from the Scottish Borders. It now attracts
submissions from all over Scotland and
beyond. The magazine is published by
Scottish Borders Council with support
from the Scottish Arts Council.
    Submission details Send a maximum of
5 poems accompanied by an sae, to The
Editorial Committee.

English: The Journal of the English Association

The English Association, University of
Leicester, University Road, Leicester LE1
7RH
tel (01162) 523982/2300
email engassoc@le.ac.uk
website www.le.ac.uk./engassoc
Frequency/price 3 issues p.a. Annual
subscription £45

A journal aimed at teachers of English in
universities and colleges of higher
education, with articles on all aspects of
literature and critical theory, a reviews
section, and original poetry.

Envoi

44 Rudyard Road, Biddulph Moor, Stoke-
on-Trent, Staffs ST8 7JN
tel (01782) 517892
Editor Roger Elkin
Frequency/price 3 p.a. Annual subscription
£15

New poetry, including sequences,
collaborative works and translations;
reviews; articles on modern poets and
poetic style; poetry competitions;
adjudicator's reports. Sample copy: £3.
Payment: 1 complimentary copy. Founded
1957.

The Ephemera: A Quarterly Magazine of Ideas and the Arts

c/o London Printing Company, 14-15
Station Parade, Whitchurch Lane,
Middlesex HA8 6RW
email enquiries@theephemera.org
website www.theephemera.org
Frequency/price Quarterly

A journal dedicated to "undermining
those widespread opinions which tacitly
hold that literary magazines, particularly
little literary magazines, are somehow
lesser than their wider-circulating cousins,
that their writing is somewhat worse, that
their opinions are somehow parochial,
that they publish the otherwise
unpublishable, that their mission is one of
charity, and that, despite their best
intentions, they perpetuate the blight of
bad writing."
    Submission details Send work by mail
and, preferably, by post. Enclose an sae if
you want your work to be returned.

Erratica

126 Furze Croft, Furze Hill, Hove
BN3 1PF
tel (01273) 202876 *Editor* Dr Simon
Jenner, Alan Morrison, Dr David Pollard

Frequency/price Annual. £9

Publishes all styles of quality poetry that shows the intelligent avoidance of mainstream blandishment. Creative oddballs – not the ineptly odd!

Submission details Telephone and read your poem, or send 6 poems accompanied by sae.

European Judaism

Leo Baeck College, 80 East End Road, London N3 2SY
tel 020-8349 5600 *fax* 020-8349 5619
email european.judaism@lbc-cje.ac.uk
Editor Dr Jonathan Masonet *Poetry Editor* Ruth Fainlight
Frequency/price 2 issues p.a. Annual subscription £30

Poems should be short and have some relevance to matters of Jewish interest. Poet receives a copy of the magazine.

Submission details Submit 3-4 poems, accompanied by sae.

Eve's Back

c/o The Pankhurst Centre, 60-62 Nelson Street, Manchester M13 9WP
email evesback@yahoo.com
Frequency/price 6 issues p.a. £1.50. Annual subscription £11

Women-only magazine (A4-sized, 32 pages), which features mainly articles, reviews and listings, but also some poetry and short fiction. Women are invited to get involved in the production, or to simply send in stuff they've written.

Exile

1 Armstrong Close, Hundon, Suffolk CO10 8HD
email exile@2from.com
Editor John Marr

A poetry magazine for new poets. Welcomes new poetry in English on any subject.

Submission details Maximum of 30-40 lines per poem, accompanied by sae.

Exiled Ink!

31 Hallswelle Road, London NW11 0DH
tel 020-8458 1910
email jennifer@exiledwriters.fsnet.co.uk
website www.exiledwriters.co.uk
Editor Jennifer Langer
Frequency/price 2 issues p.a. £3, or £3.50 inc. p&p. £7 for 1 year; £13 for 2 years

Poetry, short stories, literature by exiled writers only, worldwide. Articles, essays by exiled writers and others (semi-academic) on issues of literature and cultures of exile. Reviews of books by exiled writers about exiled literature and culture. Worldwide events to do with exile.

Submission details Submit by email or by post.

Federation Magazine: The Magazine of The Federation of Worker Writers & Community Publishers

The FWWCP, Burslem School of Art, Queen Street, Burslem, Stoke-on-Trent, ST6 3EJ
email fwwcp@cwcom.net
website http://www.fwwcp.mcmail.com
Editor Nick Pollard
Frequency/price Quarterly. £1.50

The magazine of the Federation of Worker Writers & Community Publishers, which aims to further working-class writing and community publishing and to make writing and publishing accessible to all. Each issue is accompanied by a Federation Broadsheet featuring poetry and prose by members of the Federation.

Fire Magazine

Field Cottage, Old White Hill, Tackley, Kidlington, Oxon OX5 3AB
Editor Jeremy Hilton

Frequency/price 2 issues p.a. £5. Annual subscription £7

Promotes unpublished, unknown, and unfashionable writers, including young writers and those just starting out.

Submission details Submissions by post only, accompanied by an sae.

The Firing Squad

25 Griffiths Road, West Bromwich B71 2EH
email ppatch66@hotmail.com
website www.purplepatchpoetry.co.uk
Editor Geoff Stevens
Frequency/price 3 issues p.a. £1.80

Publishes all kinds of poetry, but prefers 40 lines maximum. If it rhymes, the rhyme should not intrude excessively.

Submission details Submit at least 2 poems with sae or IRC.

First Offense

Syringa, Stodmarsh, Canterbury, Kent CT3 4BA
email tim@firstoffense.co.uk
website www.firstoffense.co.uk
Editor Tim Fletcher
Frequency/price 1-2 issues p.a.

A magazine for contemporary poetry which is not traditional. Contemporary language and experimental poetry and articles. Prints 300 copies.

Submission details Manuscripts must be typed. No previously published poems and no reply without sae.

The Fix

(formerly Zene)
TTA Press, 5 Martins Lane, Witcham, Ely, Cambs CB6 2LB
email ttapress@aol.com
website www.ttapress.com
Editor Andy Cox
Frequency/price Bi-monthly. 15 p.a. (subscription only)

Reviews of short fiction, in-depth coverage of the world's magazines (both large and small), plus interviews, columns, news and views. Hundreds of markets for writers in every issue. Payment: negotiable. Founded 1995.

Flaming Arrows

Sligo VEC, Riverside, Sligo, Ireland
tel (07) 1914 7304 *fax* (07) 1914 3093
Editor Leo Regan
Frequency/price €7.50 inc. p&p

Publishes coherent, lucid, direct and strong expression grounded in the senses. Contemplative, metaphysical, mystical, spiritual themes expressed in a distinctive, original and mature voice. Work must sustain close and repeated reading, revealing itself through concentration and focus. Where is the sacred in the personal life, and how is it sustained?

Submission details Send printed copy with letter and IRC. Payment is 1 complimentary copy.

Focus

13 Egremont Drive, Sheriff Hill, Gateshead NE9 5SE
email focus.editor@blueyonder.co.uk
website www.avnet.co.uk/home/amaranth/ BSFA/focus1.html
Editor Simon Morden
Frequency/price 2 issues p.a. Annual subscription £21 UK; £26 overseas. Free to members of the British Science Fiction Association

The British Science Fiction Association's magazine for writers. Fiction, poetry, interviews, letters and articles.

Fortnight – An Independent Review of Politics and the Arts

11 University Road, Belfast BT7 1NA
tel 028-9023 2353 *fax* 028-9023 2650
email editor@fortnight.org

website www.fortnight.org
Editor Malachi O'Doherty
Frequency/price Monthly. £2.20

Current affairs analysis, reportage, opinion pieces, cultural criticism, book reviews, poems. Illustrations: line, half-tone, cartoons. Payment: by arrangement. Founded 1970.

Fras

Fras Publications, The Atholl Browse Bookshop, By the station, Blair Atholl PH18 5SG
Editor John Herdman, Walter Perrie
Frequency/price Occasional (approximately 6-monthly). £4

Serious poetry, fiction and literary articles.
Submission details Send a maximum of 10 poems with sae.

The Frogmore Papers

42 Morehall Avenue, Folkestone, Kent CT19 4EF
tel (07751) 251689
website www.frogmorepress.co.uk
Editor Jeremy Page
Frequency/price 2 issues p.a. £3.50. Annual subscription £7; £12 for 2-year subscription

Open to most varieties of poetry although the very traditional and very experimental are unlikely to find favour. No limits on length.
Submission details Send a maximum of 6 poems, accompanied by sae.

From the Horse's Mouth

25 Wyecliffe Street, Ossett, Wakefield, West Yorkshire WF5 9ER
tel (01924) 315324
email blackhorsepoets@hotmail.com; paulncazz@blueyonder.co.uk
Editor Peter Bedford
Frequency/price Quarterly. Free

Publishes all styles and genres of poetry. No payment to poet.
Submission details Submissions by email or post to the editor.

Gabriel: A Christian Poetry Magazine

27 Headingley Court, North Grange Road, Leeds LS6 2QU
Editor Thelma Haycock
Frequency/price Annual (in spring). £5 inc. p&p

Poetry on a Christian theme.
Submission details Submit between November and January each year. Each poem should be on an A4 sheet with name and city underneath poem.

Gairm

29 Waterloo Street, Glasgow G2 6BZ
tel 0141-221 1971
Editor Derick Thomson
Frequency/price Quarterly. Annual UK subscription £9; £11 overseas

An all-Gaelic magazine featuring short stories, poetry and song. Includes articles on historical and contemporary topics, politics, travel features and reviews.

Garbaj

38 Pierrot Steps, Southend-on-Sea, Essex SS21 2UY
email atlanteanpublishing@hotmail.com
website www.geocities.com/dj-tyrer/garbaj.html
Editor DJ Tyrer
Frequency/price Quarterly. Free with sae

Publishes anything satirical, silly or subversive and, sometimes, serious. From 4-liners and limericks to sagas. Payment is 1 complimentary copy.
Submission details Unsolicited submissions with sae, or in the body of an email.

Global Tapestry

Spring Bank, Longsight Road, Copster Green, Blackburn BB1 9EU

tel (01254) 249128
Editor Dave Cunliffe
Frequency/price Irregular. £3

All types of poetry considered. Post-Beat, innovative, trail-blazing, high-energy, bohemian tradition preferred.

Submission details Submit 6 poems by post, accompanied by sae. Long poems considered.

Green Queen

BM Box 5700, London WC1N 3XX
Editor K Bell, E Wallace
Frequency/price 2 issues p.a. 80p per issue, plus postage

Publishes lesbian and gay poetry, or poems on green issues.

Submission details Poems up to 40 lines in length. Submissions by post or email.

Haiku Scotland

2 Elizabeth Gardens, Stoneyburn, West Lothian EH47 8BP
email haiku.scotland@btinternet.com
Editor Frazer Henderson
Frequency/price Quarterly

Original haiku, senryu, epigrams, aphorisms and all short poetry forms. Work by established and unpublished poets considered.

Handshake

5 Cross Farm, Station Road North, Fearnhead, Warrington, Cheshire WA2 0QG
Editor John Francis Haines
Frequency/price Irregular. Send sae/IRC/ stamps/trade/nice letter

Specialises in short genre poems of all styles. Most issues have only a single side of poetry, so there is always a backlog: contributors must be prepared for long waits between acceptance and publication. See a sample copy of magazine before submitting. All rights are returned to author on publication. The other side of the zine is occupied by news and information useful to writers of genre poetry. Print run is currently 80.

Submission details Send up to 3 short genre poems at a time, camera-ready; must be previously unpublished. Send return postage.

Harlequin

PO Box 23392, Edinburgh EH8 7YZ
website www.harlequinmagazine.co.uk
Editor Jim Sinclair
Frequency/price Varies. £3

Publishes high-quality poetry and artwork of beauty, mysticism and wisdom.

Submission details Submit only inspired material accompanied by sae.

HQ Poetry Magazine

(The Haiku Quarterly)
39 Exmouth Street, Swindon SN1 3PU
tel (01793) 523927
Editor Kevin Bailey
Frequency/price 3-4 p.a. £2.80 (4 issues £10 p.a., £13 non-UK)

International in scope, publishes both experimental and traditional work. About one-third of the content is devoted to haikuesque and imagistic poetry. Plus review section and articles. Payment: complimentary copies. Founded 1990.

Submission details No submission guidelines – any amount, any time, but has to be very good to be accepted.

ImageNation

289 Elmwood Avenue, Feltham, Middlesex TW13 7QB
email partners_writing_group@ hotmail.com
Editor Ian Deal

A magazine of poetry and art.

Inclement

White Rose House, 8 Newmarket Road, Fordham, Ely, Cambs CB7 5LL
email inclement-poetry-magazine@hotmail.com
Editor Michelle Foster
Frequency/price Quarterly. £4 (1 year, £15; 2 years, £26, inc p&p)

An independent magazine, funded solely by subscriptions. Subscription is not a condition for publication.

Submission details All forms and lengths of poetry considered. Now accepts work by email as well as by post. Decision within 1 month of submission.

Interlude Magazine

Limehouse Town Hall, 646 Commercial Road, London E14 7HA
email submissions@ interludemagazine.co.uk
website www.interludemagazine.co.uk
Editor Francesca Ricci, Helen Nodding, Becky Philp
Frequency/price £3.50 plus 50p

An arts magazine that includes writings, poetry and visual work.

The Interpreter's House

19 The Paddox, Squitchey Lane, Oxford OX2 7PN
Editor Merryn Williams
Frequency/price 3 issues p.a. £3

Publishes poems and short stories.

Iota

1 Lodge Farm, Snitterfield, Warwickshire CV37 0LR
tel (01789) 730358
email iotapoetry@aol.com
website www.iotapoetry.co.uk
Editor Bob Mee, Janet Murch
Frequency/price Quarterly

Submission details Send up to 6 poems by post with sae, or online in body of email – not as an attachment.

Irish Pages: A Journal of Contemporary Writing

The Linen Hall Library, 17 Donegall Square North, Belfast BT1 5GB
tel 028-9064 1644
email irishpages@yahoo.co.uk
website www.irishpages.org
Editor Chris Agee
Frequency/price Biannual. £10/€14

Poetry, short fiction, essays, creative non-fiction, memoir, essay reviews, nature writing, translated work, literary journalism, and other autobiographical, historical and scientific writing of literary distinction. Publishes in equal measure writing from Ireland and abroad. Payment: only pays for certain commissions and occasional serial rights. Founded 2002.

Island

8 Craiglea Drive, Edinburgh EH10 5PA
email jaj@essencepress.co.uk
website www.essencepress.co.uk
Editor Julie Johnstone
Frequency/price 2 issues p.a. £6/$12. Annual subscription £10/$20

A bi-annual literary magazine providing a distinctive space for new writing inspired by nature and exploring our place within the natural world.

Submission details Unsolicited submissions are welcome, although for most projects poets and writers are now normally approached directly by the editor. Send no more than 5 poems accompanied by an sae.

The Journal

18 Oxford Grove, Ilfracombe, Devon EX34 9HQ
tel (01271) 862708
email smithsssj@aol.com
website http://members.aol.com/smithsssj/index.html

Editor Sam Smith
Frequency/price 3 issues p.a. £2.50

Publishes work written with thought about what it is saying and how it is being said.

Submission details Submit with sae or, if by email, in body of email; no attachments. Payment, complimentary copy.

Keystone

53 Arcadia Court, 45 Old Castle Street, London E1 7NY
email tom_chivers@hotmail.com
website www.pennedinthemargins.co.uk/keystone/
Editor Tom Chivers
Frequency/price Irregular. 3-issue subscription £9

Staunchly eclectic, aims to publish work by young and unknown writers alongside that of better-known names. Accepts poetry, prose, reviews, essays and translations.

Krax

c/o 63 Dixon Lane, Leeds LS12 4RR
Editor Andy Robson
Frequency/price Annual. £3.50 ($7 US)

Light-hearted, amusing or whimsical poetry. Purely descriptive scenes are also accepted. No haiku or smutty limericks.

Submission details Post hard copy, clearly written or typed. The author's name and address should be on the same sheet as the work.

La Reata

48 Bridge Lane, Temple Fortune, London NW11 0E6
email panchromatic@msn.com
Editor Ariel Beller
Frequency/price Variable. £3 per issue

Publishes experimental and classical forms. No political poems. Payment is a free copy.

Submission details Submit 5 poems by post accompanied by sae. Submissions may be by email but there is no guarantee of a reply.

Lallans

Blackford Lodge, Blackford, Perthshire PH4 1QP
tel (01764) 682315
email mail@lallans.co.uk
website www.lallans.co.uk
Editor John Law
Frequency/price £6.50 per issue

Publishes poetry written only in the Scots language. Payment to poet of £10 per published poem.

Lamport Court

63 Lamport Court, Manchester M1 7EG
email adrian.slatcher@gmail.com
website http://lamportcourt.blogspot.com
Editor Adrian Slatcher

A magazine of new poetry, fiction and art published every 4-5 months.

Lapidus Magazine

BM Lapidus, London WC1N 3XX
tel 0845-602 2215
email info@lapidus.org.uk
website www.lapidus.org.uk
Editor Sheelagh Gallagher *Poetry Editor* Miriam Halahmy
Frequency/price Quarterly. £2

Poetry, prose and articles on the use of poetry in the therapeutic environment.
Submission details Email for guidelines.

Laughout

PO Box 3268, Brighton BN1 4AU
Editor Neil Barnett
Frequency/price 4 issues p.a. £1.50

All forms of poetry accepted with a humorous theme or content. £25 cash prize to best poem in each issue, as voted by subscribers.

Submission details Direct submissions discouraged. Send an sae with 2 x 2nd-class stamps for free copy and writers' guidelines.

Leeds Poetry Weekly

89 Connaught Road, Sutton, Surrey SM1 3PJ
website barrytebb.mysite.freeserve.com
Editor Barry Tebb

A magazine notorious for its editor's attacks on the poetry establishment.

Liar Republic

7/8 Trinity Chare, Quayside, Newcastle upon Tyne NE1 3DF
email psummers@liarincltd.fsnet.co.uk
Editor Ian Dowson, Paul Summers
Frequency/price £3.50

Essays and poetry presented in an interesting and eye-catching format. For people who are interested in literature pushed to the limits.

The Liberal

PO Box 42749, London N2 0XX
email editor@theliberal.co.uk
website www.theliberal.co.uk
Editor Ben Ramm
Frequency/price 6 issues, £17

Politics, culture and poetry.

Liminal Pleasures

100 Via Monastero, Cessapalombo, MC62020, Italy
email editors@liminalpleasures.net
website www.liminalpleasures.net
Editor Andrew Nightingale
Frequency/price £3.50/€5

A bi-annual print-based poetry magazine. Poems may be on any subject.
Submission details Send no more than 6 poems at a time. Submissions must be made by email. Poems may be included in the body of the email or in a Word, RTF, PDF or HTML attachment.

Linkway

The Shieling, The Links, Burry Port, Carmarthenshire SA16 0HU
tel (01554) 834486
Editor Fay C Davies
Frequency/price Quarterly. £3.47 inc p&p (1 year, £13.60; EU £3.87 or £15; others £4.25 or £16.50)

A general-interest magazine for all the family, publishing poetry, stories, articles, puzzles and other items. Poetry can be on any subject and in any style.
Submission details Send 4-6 poems, up to 42 lines in length. The poet's name and address should be on the back of his/her work. Send biographical details and a small photo. Submissions must be accompanied by an sae.

The Literary Review

44 Lexington Street, London W1F 0LW
tel 020-7437 9392 *fax* 020-7734 1844
Editor Nancy Sladek
Monthly £3 (£32 p.a.)

Reviews, articles of cultural interest, interviews, profiles, monthly poetry competition. Material mostly commissioned. Length: articles and reviews 800–1500 words. Illustrations: line and b&w photos. Payment: £25 per article; none for illustrations. Founded 1979.

Littoral

38 Barringtons, 10 Sutton Road, Southend-on-Sea, Essex SS2 5NA
tel (01702) 473999 *fax* (01702) 617199
website http://mysite.wannado-members.co.uk/mervyn_linford/comp.htm
Editor Mervyn Linford
Frequency/price Quarterly. £4.50 per issue. £17 for 4 issues. Overseas $12 and $44

respectively. No cheques. Sterling money orders or dollar bills only

Poetry, prose, artwork on the theme of 'Nature and the Spirit'. *Littoral* is a multi-faith and environmental literary magazine devoted to the principle of Unity in Diversity. All contributors receive a free copy.

Submission details Submit by post, accompanied by an sae, or by email.

The Liver Bards

Flat 5, 28 Ullet Road, Liverpool, Merseyside L8 3SR
email thebrodiepress@hotmail.com

Brings together new and imaginative writing from the Merseyside area. Draws on talent that previously hasn't been given a platform, and covers topics as wide-ranging as trombones in Beijing and travels in Pakistan to central heating and local architecture.

The London Magazine: A Review of Literature and the Arts

70 Wargrave Avenue, London N15 6UB
tel 020-8400 5882 *fax* 020-8994 1713
email editorial@thelondonmagazine.net
Administration 32 Addison Grove, London W4 1ER
email admin@thelondonmagazine.net
website www.thelondonmagazine.net
Editor Sebastian Barker *Publisher* Christopher Arkell
Frequency/price Bi-monthly. £6.95 (£32 p.a.)

Poems, stories (2000-5000 words), memoirs, critical articles, features on art, photography, theatre, music, architecture, etc. Also publishes long poems. Payment: by arrangement. First published in 1732.

Submission details Send up to 6 poems, accompanied by a brief covering letter. Sae absolutely essential (3 IRCs from abroad).

Submissions by email are not accepted except when agreed with the editor.

London Review of Books

28 Little Russell Street, London WC1A 2HN
tel 020-7209 1101 *fax* 020-7209 1102
email edit@lrb.co.uk
Editor Mary-Kay Wilmers
Frequency/price Fortnightly. £2.99

Features, essays, poems. Payment: by arrangement.

Submission details Submit by email or by post, accompanied by sae.

Lookout

PO Box 3268, Brighton BN1 4AU
Editor Philip Markham
Frequency/price 4 issues p.a. £1.50. Annual subscription £6 inc. p&p

Publishes all forms of poetry on any topic, theme or subject. Prize of £25 for best poem in each issue, as voted by subscribers.

Submission details Direct submissions not encouraged. Send name, address and sae with 2 x 2nd-class stamps for copy of magazine and writers' guidelines.

Magma

43 Keslake Road, London NW6 6DH
email magmapoetry@ntlworld.com
website www.magmapoetry.com
Editor David Boll and others
Frequency/price 3 issues p.a. £4.95. Annual subscription £14.50 (for 3), inc. postage

Contemporary poetry. Payment of free copy and more at discount.

Submission details Submissions by post or by email to: contributions@magmapoetry.com.

The Magpie's Nest

176 Stoney Lane, Sparkhill, Birmingham B12 8AN

email magpies-nest@tiscali.co.uk
Editor Bal Saini
Frequency/price Quarterly. £2

Poems on any subject.
   Submission details Submit 3-5 poems, each no longer than 40 lines.

Mango Season

Caribbean Women Writers Alliance, Caribbean Centre, Goldsmiths College, University of London, London SE14 6NW
tel 020-7919 7430
Editor Joan Anim-Addo
Frequency/price 3 times p.a. Annual subscription: individuals £21 (UK and Europe), £26 (Rest of the world); institutions £48 (UK and Europe), £65 (Rest of the world).

The journal of the Caribbean Women Writers Alliance. Interviews, poetry, short stories, translations, criticism and articles on the visual arts, criticism, reviews, and events listings.

Manifold

99 Vera Avenue, London N21 1RP
tel 020-8360 3202 *website* www. manifold-poetry.co.uk
Contact Vera Rich
Frequency/price 4 issues p.a. Annual subscription: UK £12; Europe £14; other £15

More than 40 pages of poems, book and exhibition reviews.
   Submission details Welcomes well-crafted poems in any known or innovative style, and on a wide range of subjects, accompanied by an sae. The basic requirement is that the work must succeed as poetry. Considers poems in all variants of English; major European languages (French, German, Italian, Latin, Spanish), usually untranslated; also parallel-text translations from other languages.

Markings

77 High Street, Kirkcudbright DG6 4JW
tel (01557) 331557
email markings@btinternet.com
Editor John Hudson
Frequency/price £5 p.a.
   Submission details Submissions by post should be clearly typed on A4, name and address on each sheet, sae must be included. Submissions by email should be sent in the body of the text if the piece is short, or as an RTF attachment for longer pieces.

Metre

4 Wyndham Avenue, Bray, County Wicklow, Ireland
Editor David Wheatley

Themed magazine.

Modern Poetry in Translation

MPT, The Queen's College, Oxford OX1 4AW
tel (01865) 244701
email editors@mptmagazine.com
website www.mptmagazine.com
Editor David and Helen Constantine
Frequency/price 2 issues p.a. £11

All lively translations into English of poems in any language will be considered. Also original work – poems, essays on the magazine's particular themes, which are announced issue by issue.
   Submission details Send hard copy with return postage. Email submissions only with prior agreement.

Monas Hieroglyphica

649 London Road, Hadleigh, Benfleet, Essex SS7 2EB
email visionarytongue@email.com
website http://myweb.tiscali.co.uk/jamiespracklen/visiontongue/
Editor Jamie Spracklen

Frequency/price 2 issues p.a. £2.50/$5

Publishes dark fantasy fiction and insightful, purposeful verse. Payment: free copies.

Submission details See website for details.

Monkey Kettle

PO Box 5780, Milton Keynes MK10 1AX
email monkeykettle@hotmail.com
website www.monkeykettle.co.uk
Editor Matthew Michael Taylor
Frequency/price 3 issues p.a.

A poetry and creative-writing magazine. 40 pages, A5.

Submission details Submit 5-10 poems at a time.

Monomyth

38 Pierrot Steps, 71 Kursaal Way, Southend-on-Sea, Essex SS21 2UY
email atlanteanpublishing@hotmail.com
website www.geocities.com/dj-tyrer/monomyth.html
Editor DJ Tyrer
Frequency/price Quarterly. £1.95

Publishes longer poems over 50 lines in length, or linked sets of shorter poems. Also publishes articles and news relating to poetry.

Submission details Unsolicited submissions with sae or in the body of emails are welcomed.

Moonstone

CH, Unit 2, Commercial Courtyard, Settle BD24 9RG
email talithaclare@btinternet.com
Editor Talitha Clare, Robin Brooks
Frequency/price 4 issues p.a. £2. Annual subscription £7

A magazine produced in the style of a pamphlet, specialising in pantheistic and ecological poetry.

Moving Worlds

The School of English, University of Leeds, Leeds LS2 9JT
email mworlds@english.novell.leeds.ac.uk
website www.movingworlds.net
Contact Shirley Crew

Biannual international magazine publishing creative work as well as criticism, literary as well as visual texts, scholarly and more personal writing, in English and in translation into English. Open to experimentation and representing work of different kinds from different cultural traditions, it re-appraises acknowledged achievements and promotes fresh talent.

Mslexia

PO Box 656, Newcastle upon Tyne NE99 1PZ
tel 0191-261 6656 *fax* 0191-261 6636
email elizabet@mslexia.demon.co.uk
website www.mslexia.co.uk
Editor Daneet Stephans
Frequency/price 4 p.a. Annual subscription £18.75

Magazine for women writers, which combines features and advice about writing with new fiction and poetry by women. Payment: by negotiation. Founded 1998.

Submission details Considers unsolicited material. Length: up to 3000 words (short stories), articles/features by negotiation, up to 4 poems of no more than 40 lines each in any style which must relate to current themes (or adhere to poetry competition rules).

Naked Punch

email l.marsili@nakedpunch.com
website www.nakedpunch.com
Editor Lorenzo Marsili

Founded by a cultural collective, *Naked Punch* offers the voice of today's most outspoken critics, philosophers, and artists.

Neon Highway
37 Grinshil Close, Liverpool L8 8LD
email poetshideout@yahoo.com
website www.neonhighway.co.uk
Editor Alice Lenkiewcz, Jane Marsh
Frequency/price 1 issue p.a. £5.75

Publishes new and established writers, artists and poets. Looking for visionary, experimental work of a high standard.

Submission details The magazine operates on a commission/subscription basis. The editor commissions poets. Unsolicited material is not accepted.

The Neoteric
43 The Village, Powick, Worcestershire WR2 4QT
Editor Geoffrey Mills
Frequency/price 2 issues p.a. £3. Annual subscription £5

A biannual literary publication intended to identify and disseminate the work of new writers. It is a small press magazine containing quality poetry, short fiction, reviews and essays submitted by writers from the Midlands, England and beyond.

Never Bury Poetry
Bracken Clock, Troutbeck Close, Hawkshaw, Bury BL8 4LJ
tel (01204) 884080
email n.b.poetry@zen.co.uk
website www.nbpoetry.care4free.net/
Editor Jean Tarry
Frequency/price Quarterly. £2.50 (£9.50 for 4 issues) inc. p&p

Each issue is based around a theme. Submissions should demonstrate innovative work, showing lateral thinking around the theme. Humorous poetry is welcomed, as is clever poetry that plays

with words in a natural, unaffected way. A prosaic style, inversions and obvious rhymes are least likely to win favour.

Submission details Send no more than 5 poems of a maximum of 40 lines each.

New London Writers
c/o 38 Groom Place, London SW1X 7BA
tel 0171-249 8717 *fax* 0171-259 5369
email newlonrite@aol.com
Editor Alice Wickham
Frequency/price Subscription £11.80 ($26.50) per 6 issues

New Welsh Review
PO Box 170, Aberystwyth, Ceredigion SY23 1WZ
tel (01970) 628410
email editor@newwelshreview.com
website www.newwelshreview.com
Editor Francesca Rhydderch
Frequency/price Quarterly. £5.40. Annual subscription £20

Literary – critical articles, short stories, poems, book reviews, interviews and profiles. Especially, but not exclusively, concerned with Welsh writing in English. Length: up to 3000 words (articles). Illustrations: colour. Payment: £50 per 1000 words (articles); £25 per poem, £75 per short story, £40 per review, £60 per illustration. Founded 1988.

Submission details Send a hard copy to the editor with an sae bearing sufficient postage for the return of material. Email submissions only with the permission of the editor. Decisions within 3 months of submission.

The New Welsh Review
PO Box 170, Aberystwyth, Ceredigion SY23 1WZ
tel (01970) 628410
email admin@ newwelshreview.com
website www.newwelshreview.com

Editor Francesca Rhydderch
Frequency/price Quarterly. £5.40. Annual subscription £20

All styles of poetry considered.
Submission details Send hard copy with sae for return.

The New Writer

PO Box 60, Cranbrook, Kent TN17 2ZR
tel (01580) 212626
email admin@thenewwriter.com
website www.thenewwriter.com
Editor Suzanne Ruthven
Frequency/price Bimonthly. £4.50

Publishes previously unpublished poems. The editor prefers poems which show a good use of language, and offer challenging imagery, while not forgetting the overall structure.
Submission details No more than 3 poems should be submitted at any one time. Submissions should be typed, single-spaced, on 1 side of white A4 paper, accompanied by an sae.

New Writing Scotland

ASLS, c/o Dept of Scottish History, 9 University Gardens, University of Glasgow, Glasgow G12 8QH
tel/fax 0141-330 5309
email office@asls.org.uk
website www.asls.org.uk
Editor Duncan Jones (Managing Editor)
Frequency/price Annual. £6.95

Accepts previously unpublished short fiction and poetry from writers resident in Scotland, or Scots by birth or upbringing. There are no limits to the type or style of submissions, which may be in English, Scots or Gaelic. Payment of £10 per printed page.
Submission details Submit no more than 6 poems. Author's name and details should not appear on the submission but

should be included in a covering letter. Poems should be typed and submitted on single-sided A4 sheets.

Nightingale

32 Queens Road, Barnetby-le-Wold, North Lincolnshire DN38 6JH
email joe.warner@btinternet.com
Editor Joe Warner
Frequency/price 50p plus postage

A monthly magazine for short poetry (18 lines or fewer) and short fiction (800 words maximum), produced in the UK but with authors and subscribers around the world.

Nomad

Survivors Press, 30 Cranworth Street, Glasgow G12 8AG
tel 0141-357 6838 *fax* 0141-357 6939
email sps@gisp.net
Editor Gerry Loose

Poetry and creative writing by survivors of the mental health system, of abuse or addictions.

Norfolk Poets and Writers

9 Walnut Close, Taverham, Norwich NR8 6YN
email tipsforwriters@yahoo.co.uk
Editor Wendy Webb
Frequency/price 10 issues p.a., variable. £2. Annual subscription £10

Themed challenges and competitions; new forms – Davidian, Magi, Echotain, Andropian, Triptych, Fresco.
Submission details See copy of magazine before submitting.

North

The Poetry Business, The Studio, Byram Arcade, Westgate, Huddersfield HD1 1ND
tel (01484) 434840
email edit@poetrybusiness.co.uk

Editor www.poetrybusiness.co.uk
Frequency/price Biannual. Annual subscription £10

A forum for poetry and critical prose.

Northwords

PO Box 5706, Inverness IV1 9AF
tel (01463) 231758
email rhoda8@btopenworld.com
Frequency/price Quarterly. Annual subscription £6.50

A magazine in a newsprint format, for poets and for fiction writers working in the north.

Obsessed with Pipework

Flarestack Publishing, 8 Abbot's Way, Pilton, Somerset BA4 4BN
tel (01749) 890019
email cannula.dementia@ virgin.net
Editor Charles Johnson (see www.poetrypf.co.uk)
Frequency/price Quarterly: January, April, July, October. £3.50

Does not publish the predictable or the rhyme-led. Must be work that says something about the predicament of being human in the 21st century, and in original language. See poetrymagazines.org.uk.

Submission details Send a maximum of 6 poems. If emailing, send poems in the body of a message. If posting, must be accompanied by sae big enough to send work back.

Once Orange Badge Poetry Supplement

PO Box 184, South Ockendon, Essex RM15 5WT
email onceorangebadge@ poetry.fsworld.co.uk
website http://beehive.thisisessex.co.uk
Editor D Martyn Heath

Poetry supplement for everyone whose life has been touched by illness or disability in some way or at some time throughout their life.

Submission details No preference as to style or length and poems may be on any subject. Submissions must be accompanied by an sae.

Open Wide Magazine

The Flat, Yew Tree Farm, Sealand Road, Chester, Cheshire CH1 6BS
tel (07790) 962317
email contact@openwidemagazine.co.uk
website www.openwidemagazine.co.uk
Editor James Quinton, Liz Roberts, Gary Travis
Frequency/price Quarterly. £3

Punchy poetry and short fiction, contemporary music, art, film and culture reviews. Payment: complimentary copy.

Submission details See website for guidelines.

Orbis

17 Greenhow Avenue, West Kirby, Wirral CH48 5EL
tel 0151-625 1446
email carolebaldock@hotmail.com
Editor Carole Baldock
Frequency/price Quarterly £4 (£15 p.a.); £5/€10/$11 (£20/€30/$36 p.a.) overseas

Poetry, prose (1000 words), news, reviews, views, letters. Payment: £50 for featured writer. £50 Readers' Award: for piece(s) receiving the most votes (4 winners submitted to Forward Poetry Prize, Single Poem Category); £50 split between 4 (or more) runners-up. Founded 1968.

Submission details Up to 4 poems by post; via email, overseas only, up to 2 in body (no attachments). Enclose sae/2 x IRCs with all correspondence.

The Orphan Leaf Review

Flat 4, 2 Zetland Road, Redland, Bristol BS6 7AE

email orphanleaf@jpwallis.co.uk
website www.orphanleaf.co.uk
Editor James Paul Wallis
Frequency/price 3 issues p.a. £4

All styles and genres accepted. Each issue follows a theme; see website for details. Mostly English, but other languages also featured. 'Single lines' also published – works of 70 characters in length.
   Submission details Submit by email. Contributions printed as 'orphan leaves'. See website for details.

Other Poetry

29 Western Hill, Durham DH1 4RL
website www.otherpoetry.com
Editors Michael Standen (Managing), Crista Ermiya, Peter Bennet, JR Burns, Peter Armstrong (consulting)
Frequency/price 3 p.a. £4.50. Annual subscription £13/$30

Payment: £10 per poem. Founded in 1979.
   Submission details Submit up to 4 poems with sae.

Outposts Poetry Quarterly

22 Whitewell Road, Frome, Somerset BA11 4EL
tel (01373) 466653 *fax* (01373) 466653
email rjhippopress@aol.com
Editor Roland John *Founder* Howard Sergeant MBE *Send material to* M Pargitter
Frequency/price Quarterly. £4. Annual subscription £14

Poems, essays and critical articles on poets and their work. Payment: by arrangement. Founded 1943.

Painted, Spoken

24 Sirdar Road, Wood Green, London N22 6RG
website www.hydroho.net
Editor Richard Price
Frequency/price Irregular. Free

A little magazine with a print run of around 100 copies appearing very irregularly. For a copy, send sae (A5) with 2 x 1st-class stamps to cover the postage.
   Submission details Not currently open to submissions.

Panda Poetry

46 First Avenue, Clase, Swansea, West Glamorgan SA6 7LL
tel (01792) 414837
email esmond.j@ntlworld.com
website http://pandawales.tripod.com
Editor Esmond Jones
Quarterly. £3. Annual subscription £10 (Overseas: $5/$15)
   Submission details Submit either by post or email.

The Paper

29 Vickers Road, Firth Park, Sheffield S5 6UY
tel (01142) 441202
email dgk@ kennedyd.fsworld.co.uk
website www.indigogroup.co.uk/llpp/paper.html
Editor David Kennedy
Frequency/price 2 issues p.a. £2.50 or $5. 2 issues £4 or $9 – all inc. p&p

Features new poetry in English with a special emphasis on the work of writers interested in innovation and experimentation. Each issue has a specific theme.
   Submission details No unsolicited submissions.

Parameter

PO Box 220, Wythenshawe, Manchester M23 0WE
email editor@parametermagazine.org
website www.parametermagazine.org
Editor Tom Jenks
Frequency/price 2/3 issues p.a. £3.75.

Focus of magazine is mainly on poetry, but prose pieces, including essays and reviews, are also welcome. No restrictions in terms of style or content; just good work. Payment of complimentary copy.

Submission details Submit a maximum of 6 previously unpublished poems, maximum length 40 lines (prose pieces maximum 2000 words). Email submissions welcome.

Park Publications

14 The Park, Stow on the Wold, Cheltenham, Gloucestershire GL54 1DX
tel (01451) 831053
email parkpub14@hotmail.com
website www.parkpublications.co.uk
Editor David Howard
Frequency/price 4 issues p.a. £3.50 (£2 back copy)

Publishes work with a rural or countryside theme. All poems accepted appear in the quarterly magazine, *Countryside Tales*, which also features articles and short fiction. £10 for best poem in each issue. Free complimentary copy to others.

Submission details Poems in any style, up to 40 lines in length. Submit typed work on single A4 sheets by post.

The PBS Bulletin

Fourth Floor, 2 Tavistock Place, London WC1H 9RA
email info@poetrybooks.co.uk
website www.poetrybooks.co.uk
Editor Chris Holifield
Frequency/price Quarterly. Free to members

A quarterly publication from the Poetry Book Society, offering a definitive review of new poetry books published in the UK.

Peer Poetry International

6 Arlington House, Bath Street, Bath, Somerset BA1 1QN
tel (01225) 445298
email peerpoetry@msn.co.uk

website www.publish-your-poetry.co.uk
Editor Paul Amphlett

PEF Poetry Combination Module

PEF Productions, Poetry Combination Module, 196 High Road, London N22 8HH
email page84direct@yahoo.co.uk
website www.alienonthenet.freehosting.net
Editor Mr Page 84
Frequency/price Late spring, early autumn, mid-winter. Free on request. Also printable from the Internet

Poetry, anti-poetry, artwork and aphorism.

Submission details Submit by post or email. 20-word bio may be published on webfile. Poet receives 3 copies of magazine.

Penniless Press

100 Waterloo Road, Ashton, Preston PR2 1EP
tel (01772) 736421
Editor Alan Dent
Frequency/price Quarterly

Publishes poetry, stories, essays, criticism and reviews. Payment is 1 free copy.

Pennine Ink

The Gallery, Mid Pennine Arts, Yorke Street, Burnley, Lancs BB11 1HD
email sheridansdandl@yahoo.co.uk
Editor Laura Sheridan
Frequency/price 1 issue p.a. £3

Publishes poetry and prose of all kinds.

Submission details Submit by post or email. Poems should be up to 40 lines in length.

Pennine Platform

Frizingley Hall, Frizinghall Road, Bradford BD9 4LD
tel (01274) 541015

website www.pennineplatform.co.uk
Editor Nicholas Bielby
Frequency/price 2 issues p.a., May and November. £4.50 (£8.50 annual subscription) inc. p&p

Publishes original poetry only. Concrete poems, haiku and prose poems are discouraged. Metrical poetry is welcomed and intelligent (even intellectual) poetry is preferred. Sequences are considered. All poems submitted receive constructive comment.
    Submission details Send A4 hard copy by post, printed black for scanning.

Phoenix New Life Poetry
Sea-Dragon, 12 Place Road, Fowey, Cornwall PL23 1DR
tel (01726) 833343
email universalalliance.org@tinyworld.co.uk
website www.universalalliance.org.uk
Editor David Allen Stringer
Frequency/price 4 issues p.a. £3.50/6.25 euros/$7.50 or free as email attachment

All writing styles and genres are considered. Poetry on themes of peace, freedom, social and political justice, social comment, spiritual, psychic and religious experiences, nature, classical myths, legends, etc. No romantic themes.
    Submission details Submissions by email as word attachment or by post with sae or IRC.

Planet: The Welsh Internationalist
PO Box 44, Aberystwyith, Ceredigion, Dyfed SY23 3ZZ
tel (01970) 611255
email planet.enquiries@planetmagazine.org.uk
website www.planetmagazine.org.uk
Editor John Barnie
Frequency/price 6 issues p.a. £3.75. Annual subscription £16

Publishes a wide range of styles and subject matter. Pays a minimum of £30 per poem.
    Submission details Submit 6-8 poems by post, accompanied by sae, or by email.

PN Review
(formerly Poetry Nation)
Carcanet Press Ltd, 4th Floor, Alliance House, 30 Cross Street, Manchester M2 7AQ
tel 0161-834 8730 *fax* 0161-832 0084
email info@carcanet.co.uk
website www.carcanet.co.uk
Editor Michael Schmidt
Frequency/price 6 p.a. £6.99. Annual subscription £29.50

Poems, essays, reviews, translations. Payment: by arrangement. Founded 1973.
    Submission details Submissions by post only.

Poems in the Waiting Room
PO Box 488, Richmond TW9 4SW
email pitwr@blueyonder.co.uk
website www.pitwr.pwp.blueyonder.co.uk
Editor Michael Lee
Frequency/price 4 issues p.a. Free

Any poetic form with content and sentiment suitable for patients to read while waiting for medical consultation when they may be in heightened or anxious mental state.
    Submission details Short poems are preferred and they should be accessible. Submit by email or send typescript by post.

Poet in the Round
18 Blackbridge Lane, Horsham, West Sussex RH12 1RP
Editor Olivia Manning-Daniels
Frequency/price £4.50 (£6 overseas). 4 issues, £17 (£23 overseas)

Glossy, illustrated magazine.

The Poet Tree

289 Elmwood Avenue, Feltham,
Middlesex TW13 7QB
email partners_writing_
group@hotmail.com
Editor Ian Deal

A general poetry magazine.

Poetic Hours

43 Willow Road, Carlton, Nottingham
NG4 3BH
email erranpublishing@hotmail.com
website www.poetichours.homestead.com
Editor Nick Clark
Frequency/price 2 issues p.a., spring and
autumn. £3.75

Submission details By email ideally; 3-4
poems in the body of the text or by post to
the editor. A4 length maximum, any
subject. No gothic, political or extremist.

Poetic Licence

70 Aveling Close, Purley, Surrey CR8
4DW
tel 020-8645 9956
email licence@poetsanon.org.uk
website www.poetsanon.org.uk
Editor Peter Evans (Editorial Coordinator)
Frequency/price 3 issues p.a. £3.50

New poetry.

Submission details By post with sae, or
by email, posted in the body of the email.
No more than 6 poems to be submitted
for any issue.

Poetry and Audience

c/o School of English, University of Leeds,
Leeds LS2 9JT
email panda@leeds.ac.uk
Editor Kamille Stone Stanton
Frequency/price 2 issues p.a. £3

Submission details Submissions are
invited from new and established poets.
Please include sae or IRC.

Poetry and Graphics Monthly

39 Cavendish Road, Long Eaton,
Nottingham NG10 4HY
tel (0115) 9461267
email poetrymonthly@ btinternet.com
website www.poetrymonthly.com
Editor Martin Holroyd
Frequency/price Monthly. £4

Imaginative, but well-controlled work.

Submission details Send 5 poems with
sae, or by email.

The Poetry Church Magazine

Feather Books, PO Box 438, Shrewsbury,
Shropshire SY3 0WN
tel (01743) 872177
email john@ waddysweb.freeuk.com
website www.waddysweb.freeuk.com
Editor Rev John Waddington-Feather
Frequency/price Quarterly. £3.50

Subject matter covers a wide range: from
prisoners' to university academics' verse.
Publishes Christian poems not more than
30 lines in length. Any style; free verse or
rhyme. Also publishes prayers in verse.

Poetry Cornwall

11a Penryn Street, Redruth, Kernow TR15
2SP
tel (01209) 218209
email trycornwal@yahoo.com
website poetrycornwall.freeservers.com
Editor Les Merton
Frequency/price 3 issues p.a. £3.50. Annual
subscription £10

Publishes all types of poetry, plus poems
in original language of poet, plus
translation. Articles on poetry up to 1000
words also considered.

Submission details Submit only 3 poems
at a time. No multiple submission.
Submissions must be accompanied by sae
or IRC. Look at a copy before submitting.

Poetry Ealing

Questors Theatre, Mattock Lane, Ealing
W5 5BQ

tel 020-8567 7234 or 020-8567 0011
email nala.ques@virgin.net or
pitshanger.poets@virgin.net
website pitshangerpoets.co.uk
Frequency/price 1-2 issues p.a. £3

Poetry Ealing started as a community
venture to encourage writers who live,
work and play in Ealing. Now includes the
winners of an annual competition and is
open to a wide range of contributors,
though preference will be given to writers
from West London.

Poetry Express: Quarterly from Survivors' Poetry

Studio 11, Bickerton House, 25-27
Bickerton Road, London N19 5JT
tel 020-7281 4654
website www.survivorspoetry.com
Editor Alan Morrison
Frequency/price Free, but donations
welcome

A magazine promoting the poetry of
survivors of mental illness. Published by
Survivors' Poetry, the national literature
and performance organisation that enables
survivors to participate in writing or
performance training workshops, as well
as publishing and performances
nationwide.

Poetry Fanzine

Unit 3, 5 Durham Yard, London E2 6QF
tel 020-7729 3724
email words@poetryfanzine.org
website www.poetryfanzine.org
Editor Martin McGrath, Jason Skowronek
Frequency/price £6.50

Publishes all sorts of poetry.

Poetry Ireland Review/Éigse Éireann

2 Prouds Lane, off St Stephens Green,
Dublin 2, Repubic of Ireland
tel (01) 478 9974 *fax* (01) 478 0205
email poetry@iol.ie

Editor Peter Sirr
Director Joseph Woods
Frequency/price Quarterly. €7.99. Annual
subscription €30.50/$52

Poetry. Features and articles by
arrangement. Payment: €32 per
contribution or 1 year's subscription; €51
reviews. Founded 1981.

Poetry London

1a Jewel Road, London E17 4QU
tel 020-8521 0776
email admin@poetrylondon.co.uk
website www.poetrylondon.co.uk
Poetry Editor Maurice Riordan *Reviews
Editor* Scott Verner
Frequency/price 3 issues p.a. £5

Publishes the best, most exciting poetry
being written now. Welcomes work from
unpublished as well as established poets.

   Submission details Send a maximum of
6 poems to: Maurice Riordan, 6 Daniels
Road, London SE15 3LR, accompanied by
sae or IRC.

Poetry Monthly

39 Cavendish Road, Long Eaton,
Nottingham NG10 4HY
tel 0115-946 1267
email poetrymonthly@ btinternet.com
website www.poetrymonthly.com
Editor Martin Holroyd
Frequency/price Monthly. £4

Publishes imaginative, well-crafted work.
   Submission details Submit by post with
sae, or by email.

Poetry Nottingham

11 Orkney Close, Stenson Fields, Derby
DE24 3LW
Editor Adrian Buckner
Frequency/price 4 p.a. £3.50. Annual
subscription £12/£18 (UK/overseas)

Poems; reviews; articles. Publishes work
that is philosophical and discursive as well

as the finely wrought lyric. Payment: complimentary copy and occasional payment for articles. Founded 1946.

Submission details Send up to 6 poems. Response within 2 months.

Poetry Now

Remus House, Woodston, Peterborough PE2 9JX
tel (01733) 898105
email info@forwardpress.co.uk
website www.forwardpress.co.uk
Editor Heather Killingray
Frequency/price Quarterly. Annual subscription £12

Poetry features, articles, listings, featured poet.

Poetry Quarterly Review

Odyssey Publications, Coleridge Cottage, Nether Stowey, Somerset TA5 1NQ
Editor Derrick Woolf
Frequency/price Quarterly. £1.75. Annual subscription £6

Mostly reviews and criticism.

Poetry Review

22 Betterton Street, London WC2H 9BX
tel 020-7420 9883 *fax* 020-7240 4818
email poetryreview@poetrysociety.org.uk
website www.poetrysociety.org.uk
Editor Fiona Sampson
Frequency/price Quarterly. Annual subscription £30 (£40 institutions, schools and libraries)

Poems, features and reviews; also cartoons. Payment: £50 per poem.

Submission details Send no more than 6 poems with sae. Preliminary study of magazine essential.

Poetry Scotland

Kings Bookshop, 91-93 Main Street, Callander FK17 8BQ
website www.poetryscotland.co.uk
Editor Sally Evans
Frequency/price 5/6 issues per year

A wide variety of poetry styles. Occasional payment for longer or commissioned work.

Submission details Standard postal submissions with sae. Submission advice on website.

Poetry Wales

38-40 Nolton Street, Bridgend CF31 3BN
tel (01656) 663018 *fax* (01656) 649226
email poetrywales@seren-books.com
website www.seren-books.com, www.poetrywales.co.uk
Editor/Reviews Editor Robert Minhinnick
Frequency/price Quarterly. £4. Annual subscription £16

Poetry, criticism and commentary from Wales and around the world. Payment: by arrangement. Founded 1965.

The Poet's Letter

tel (07931) 357109
email editor@poetsletter.com
website www.poetsletter.com
Frequency/price £2.75

Poetry, politics, literature, philosophy, books, children's literature, book reviews, arts, theatre and music with specific specialist areas of poetry, politics and philosophy.

Premonitions

Pigasus Press, 13 Hazely Combe, Arreton, Isle of Wight PO30 3AJ
tel (01983) 865668
email mail@pigasuspress.co.uk
website http://freespace.virgin.net/pigasus.press/premonitions.html
Frequency/price £4.50

Science fiction, fantasy, horror, genre poetry and fantastic artwork.

Presence

90d Fishergate Hill, Preston PR1 8JD
email martin.lucas2@btinternet.com
website http://freespace.virgin.net/
haiku.presence
Editor Martin Lucas
Frequency/price 3 issues p.a. £3.50

Haiku, haiku-related poetry and essays on topics of haiku interest.

Submission details See website for examples and submission details, or to order a sample copy.

Pretext

School of Literature and Creative Writing, University of East Anglia, Norwich, Norfolk NR4 7TJ
tel (01603) 592783 *fax* (01603) 507728
website www.inpressbooks.co.uk/
penandinc

An international literary magazine that features the best and most exciting new fiction, poetry and essays from around the world.

Submission details Submissions by post only, printed in a plain legible font with your name on each page. Faxes and emails are not accepted. Include a covering letter and a biography of no more than 70 words. Covering letters for poetry submissions must list the titles of all the poems. Enclose sae (or IRCs if you are outside the UK). Indicate (and enclose sufficient postage) if you would like your work returned. Payment of £50 and 1 contributor's copy of publication.

Prop

31 Central Avenue, Farnworth, Bolton BL4 0AU
email chris.hart@dial.pipex.com
Editor Steven Blyth, Chris Hart
Frequency/price Quarterly. £3. Annual subscription £10

A magazine offering 58 A4-sized pages of poetry, reviews, opinion, and prose.

Pulsar

Ligden Publishers, 34 Lineacre, Grange Park, Swindon SN5 6DA
tel (01793) 875941
email pulsar.ed@btinternet.com
website www.pulsarpoetry.com
Editor David Pike
Frequency/price Biannual (every March and September). £4; $7 US

Publishes inspirational, hard-hitting work that has a message and a meaning. No racist or abusive material or deeply religious work. Study the FAQ page of website before submitting. Successful poets receive a free copy of the magazine.

Submission details Submission by email, sending no more than 3 poems. By post, no more than 6 poems accompanied by sae or IRC. Poems must be unpublished and not submitted to another publisher for consideration. Email file attachments will not be read.

Purple Patch

25 Griffiths Road, West Bromwich B71 2EH
email geoff@purplepatchpoetry.co.uk
website www.purplepatchpoetry.co.uk
Editor Geoff Stevens
Frequency/price £2. 3 issues £5

Well-produced and well-established magazine, founded by Geoff Stevens and Olive Hyett in 1976 and still very much alive in 2006, having published its 112th issue.

Submission details Open to submissions of poetry (with sae for reply) at any time on any subject, and from all writers, whether they subscribe or not.

Pussy Poetry

6 Rookery Close, Keddington Park, Louth, Lincolnshire LN11 0GF

A magazine of women's poetry.

Quantum Leap

York House, 15 Argyll Terrace, Rothesay, Isle of Bute P20 0BD
Editor Alan Carter
Frequency/price Quarterly

Welcomes both beginners and old-hands, and pays for all poems published.

Submission details Send sae or 2 x IRCs for guidelines. Maximum 6 poems accompanied by sae or 2 x IRCs.

Quarterly Tadeeb International

14 North View Street, Keighley, West Yorkshire BD20 6AD
tel (01535) 606554
email tadeebuk@hotmail.co.uk
website www.tadeeb.com
Editor Dr Debjani Chatterjee

A dual-language literary and cultural journal devoted not only to established writers of English and Urdu (and other South Asian languages), but also to embracing new, high-quality writing in those languages by previously unpublished writers, particularly the young. It is committed to fostering the art of translation and aims to include translated work to be situated in both the Urdu and English sections.

The Quiet Feather

St Mary's Cottage, Church Street, Dalton-in-Furness, Cumbria LA15 8BA
tel (07901) 522454
email editors@thequietfeather.co.uk
website www.thequietfeather.co.uk
Editor Taissa Csaky, Dominic Hall, Tom Benson, Tim Major
Frequency/price Quarterly. £2.50

Adventurous and intelligent poetry. Entertaining poetry. Fresh and lively poetry. Dark and frightening poetry. Payment 1 free copy.

Submission details Submit poems of 100 lines or fewer. By email or post, but email

submission preferred. See website for further details.

The Radiator

Flat 5, 48 Upper Parliament Street, Liverpool L8 7LF
email scottthurston@btinternet.com
Editor Scott Thurston

Rain Dog

PO Box 68, Manchester M19 2XD
email rd_poetry@yahoo.com
website www.panshinepress.co.uk
Editor Jan Whalen, Suzanne Batty
Frequency/price 2 issues p.a. £3.50. Annual subscription £6

Publishes strong, original voices with something worth saying. Submissions welcomed from new and experienced writers and especially interested in poetry from women.

Submission details Send up to 5 poems with an sae, or email.

Rainbow Poetry News

14 Lewes Crescent, Brighton BN2 1FH
tel (01273) 687053
Editor Hugh Hellicar
Frequency/price Quarterly. £1.50 (postage free)

Preference is given to short poems, under 25 lines, by poets who are members of the Rainbow Poetry Movement. Place poems, nature and love poems preferred.

Submission details Send 2 poems and biographical details by post.

Raw Edge

PO Box 48567, Birmingham B3 3HD
Editor Dave Reeves
Frequency/price 2 issues p.a.

For West Midlands poets only. All styles considered. 16,000 copies distributed per issue. Also publishes a selection of information of interest to readers, including details of opportunities and live events in the region.

Submission details Only writers with a connection to the West Midlands region considered. Send up to 6 poems with A4 sae.

Reach

Indigo Dreams Press at The Manacles, Predannack, The Lizard, Cornwall TR12 7AU
website www.indigodreamspress.co.uk
Editor Ronnie Goodyer
Frequency/price Monthly. £3.50

All welcome, whether established or new to poetry. Join the family feel unique to this publication established for more than 8 years now. Subscribe for as many as you wish and submit your poetry during that period.

Submission details No house style, no age barrier.

Reactions

School of Literature & Creative Writing, University of East Anglia, Norwich, Norfolk NR4 7TJ
tel (01603) 592783 *fax* (01603) 507728
email info@penandinc.co.uk
website www.inpressbooks.co.uk/penandinc
Editor Clare Pollard
Frequency/price 1 issue p.a.. £7.99

An annual anthology of contemporary poetry. Submissions are welcomed from poets who have had a first collection of poetry published, but not a second or who are about to reach that stage. Work must be original and unpublished, although poems due to appear in a collection will be considered. Poems can be of any style and on any subject. Payment to poet of £50.

Submission details Submit a maximum of 10 poems/minimum of 3, by post only;

faxes and emails are not accepted. Include a covering letter that lists all the poems' titles and a biography of no more than 70 words. Enclose S.A.E. or I.R.C. Indicate(and enclose sufficient postage, if you would like your work returned.

The Reader

19 Abercromby Square, Liverpool L69 7ZG
tel 0151-794 2830
email readers@liverpool.ac.uk
website www.thereader.co.uk
Editor Jane Davis
Frequency/price Quarterly. £6

Publishes new poetry as well as short fiction and essays. Payment to poet from £15 to £30 (negotiable).

Submission details Postal submissions only; must include sae.

The Reater

Wrecking Ball Press, 24 Cavendish Square, Hull, East Yorkshire HU3 1SS
tel (01482) 210226
website www.wreckingballpress.com
Editor Shane Rhodes
Frequency/price 2 issues p.a. Price varies

Publishes well-crafted poetry in a well-designed magazine with excellently illustrated covers. Spearheads lesser-known writers.

Submission details Maximum of 6 poems. If possible all submissions should be on a disk as well as hard copy.

Red Lamp

6 Madras Road, Cambridge CB1 3PX
tel (07736) 129694
email evans.baj@yahoo.com
website www.geocities.com/redlamp
Editor Brad Evans
Frequency/price Dependent on quantity of relevant work received. £2.50

Publishes left-wing poetry. Payment of complimentary copy.

Submission details Read submission guidelines on website.

The Red Wheelbarrow
c/o The Poetry House, School of English, University of St Andrews, St Andrews, Fife KY16 9AL
email redwheelbarrow@st-andrews.ac.uk
website www.st-andrews.ac.uk/academic/english/redwheelbarrow/
Frequency/price Biannual. £3

Poems on a theme in each issue which is posted on the website. Also publishes essays, interviews and reviews on contemporary poetry.

Submission details By post (no sae; we respond by email). See website for full details. No email submissions.

Retort
7 Downside Court, Nutfield Road, Merstham, Surrey RH1 3YY
Editor John Lemmon
Frequency/price Quarterly. Annual subscription £19

Reveal
PO Box 184, South Ockendon, Essex RM15 5WT
Editor DM Heath
Frequency/price 3 issues p.a.

Publishes avant-garde and experimental verse.

The Rialto
PO Box 309, Aylsham, Norwich NR11 6LN
email mail@therialto.co.uk
website www.therialto.co.uk
Editor Michael Mackmin
Frequency/price 3 issues p.a.

Started in 1984 aiming to publish work by new poets alongside that of established poets. A 64-page A4 magazine, described by Carol Ann Duffy as "simply the best". Has also published a small number of first collections, 3 of which have won major prizes.

Submission details Read the magazine before submitting. Send no more than 6 poems, plus sae or IRC with sufficient postage to cover return costs. For book publication, please write to the editor before sending poems. Please note, it will be at least 12 weeks before you hear about your work.

A Riot of Emotions
Dark Diamonds Publications, PO Box HK 31, Leeds, West Yorks LS11 9XN
Editor Andrew Cocker

Art/poetry fanzine with small press and music reviews.

Roundyhouse
c/o 3 Crown Street, Port Talbot SA13 1BG
tel (01639) 886186
Editor Editorial board: Byron Beynon, Phil Carradice, Sally R Jones, Brian Smith, Alex Trowbridge-Matthews
Frequency/price 3 issues p.a. £3.50. Annual subscription £9

No limit on subject matter or style, but preferably accessible. Poet receives a free copy of the issue containing his/her work.

Submission details No more than 6 poems should be submitted, accompanied by sae if return required. Poems should be up to 50 lines; longer poems are less likely to be accepted.

Route
PO Box 167, Pontefract, West Yorkshire WF8 4WW
tel (01977) 797695
email info@route-online.com
website www.route-online.com
Contact Ian Daley, Isabel Galan

Contemporary fiction (novels and short stories) and performance poetry, with a commitment to new writing. Imprint of ID Publishing.

Submission details Unsolicited work discouraged. Visit the website for current guidelines. Ring or write for a free catalogue.

The Rue Bella

The Red Lantern Retreat, 41 Grantham Road, Manor Park, London E12 5LZ
Editor Peter Geoffrey Paul Thompson
Frequency/price 2 issues p.a. £5. Annual subscription £10

Traditional, lyrical, spiritual as well as work in broad sympathy with the 18th/19th century Romantic school (e.g. Shelley, Keats Blake, etc.). Rhythm and rhyme are favoured.

Submission details Send typed poems by post only. Must include covering letter and sae. Only considers poetry by subscribers.

Sable

Saks Media, PO Box 33504, London E9 7YE
Frequency/price Quarterly. £5. Annual subscription £16

Literary magazine for writers of colour. Offers professional development for writers through its courses and workshops.

Saccade

93 Green Lane, Dronfield, Sheffield S18 6FG
Editor Robert Gill

Bizarre and fantastic fiction, non-fiction, poetry, artwork (any style), horror, SF, fantasy.

Salopoet

5 Squires Close, Madeley, Telford, Shropshire TF7 5RU
tel (01952) 587487
email rogerhoult@ blueyonder.co.uk
Editor Roger Hoult
Frequency/price Quarterly. £2.50

The magazine of the Salopian Society, founded in 1976. Publishes poetry written by members of the society. *Snippetts* sent with copies of the magazine, contains information of interest to poets generally and runs poetry competitions, both open and for members only. Membership is £10 per year (UK), £12.50 (EU) and $20 elsewhere.

Saw

4 Masefield Avenue, Barnstaple, Devon EX31 1QJ
email sawpoems@btinternet.com
website www.indigogroup.co.uk/llpp/saw.html
Editor Colin Shaddick
Frequency/price 2 issues p.a. £4. 3 issues, £10; 6 issues, £18

Publishes poetry with an edge.

Submission details A maximum of 80 lines per poem, including title and stanza breaks. Email submissions can be sent either as an attachment, or in the body of the email using Microsoft Word if possible. If submitting by post, send an sae.

Scintilla

Little Wentwood Farm, Llantrisant, Usk NP5 1ND
website www.cf.ac.uk/encap/scintilla
Editor Anne Cluysenaar
Frequency/price Annual. £9.50

An annual journal devoted to literature written, and inspired, by the Breconshire writers Henry and Thomas Vaughan. Each volume includes poetry, prose fiction, drama, and essays, which explore themes relevant to the Vaughans, in modern (if not necessarily fashionable) terms. *Scintilla* is published by the Usk Valley Vaughan Association (UVVA), founded in the tercentenary year of Henry Vaughan's death, 23 April 1695, with financial support from the Arts Council of Wales and Cardiff University. The UVVA exists to explore, celebrate, and question the works and lives of Henry Vaughan, poet and doctor, and his twin brother, the famous alchemist Thomas Vaughan, while encouraging the work of modern writers and artists.

Scots Magazine
DC Thomson & Co Ltd, 2 Albert Square, Dundee DD1 9QJ
tel (01382) 223131
email editor@scotsmagazine.com
website www.scotsmagazine.com
Frequency/price Monthly. £1.25

Articles on all subjects of Scottish interest. Scottish short stories and poetry.

The Scottish Review of Books
The Sunday Herald, 9/10 St Andrew Square, Edinburgh EH2 2AF
email media.office@scottisharts.org.uk
Editor Alan Taylor

A quality literary magazine, supported by the Scottish Arts Council and aimed at promoting Scottish literature. Published by Argyll and Birlinn Publishing, it includes articles from leading literary commentators, reviews of recently published books, and poetry.

Scrawl
Questing Beast Distribution, PO Box 1, Blaenau Ffestiniog LL41 3AX
Editor Lucy Neville
Frequency/price Quarterly. £3. Annual subscription £12

Seam
10 Collingwood Road, Woodham Ferrers, Chelmsford CM3 5YB

Editor Frank Dullaghan
Frequency/price 2 issues p.a. £4.50. Annual subscription £8

Publishes strong, fresh poems in any style. Published poets as well as first-timers welcome – it is the quality of the work that counts. Will occasionally accept longer poems, but generally publishes poems under 50 lines.

Submission details Submit 5-6 typed poems with your address on each. Enclose an sae.

Second Light
9 Greendale Close, London SE22 8TG
tel 020-8299 0088
email dyliswood@tiscali.co.uk
Editor Dylis Wood (and guest editors)
Frequency/price 2 issues p.a. £4 to non-members

Second Light is the voice of the Second Light Network of women poets. Membership is by invitation only. It publishes well-honed, exciting poems dealing with all subjects in all styles, including formal.

Sentinel Poetry Quarterly
60 Titmuss Avenue, Thamesmead, London SE28 8DJ
tel (07940) 249812
email info@sentinelpoetry.org.uk
website www.sentinelpoetry.org.uk/quarterlymagazine/
Editor Nnorom Azuonye
Frequency/price Quarterly. £3.95 (UK) or £4.95 (overseas)

A 60-page journal of poems, essays and interviews from the Sentinel Poetry Movement. Payment of complimentary copy.

Submission details Send up to 6 poems (40 lines maximum per poem, includes stanza breaks), any style or theme. Poems must be previously unpublished. Poems posted on Internet discussion boards as part of the writing process are not deemed to have been previously published.

Seshat

PO Box 9313, London E17 8XL
Editor Terence Duquesne (and others)

Cross-cultural perspectives in poetry and philosophy.

The Seventh Quarry – Swansea Poetry Quarterly

Dan-y-bryn, 74 Cwm Level Road, Brynhyfryd, Swansea SA5 9DY
Editor Peter Thabit Jones
Frequency/price 2 issues p.a. £3 ($6)

Serious, quality poems (formal or informal).
   Submission details Submit no more than 6 poems (no very long poems) accompanied by sae or IRC. Payment, complimentary copy.

Shearsman

58 Velwell Road, Exeter EX4 4LD
tel (01392) 434511
email editor@shearsman.com
website www.shearsman.com
Editor Tony Frazer
Frequency/price Biannual. £7.50

Publishes work in the Modernist tradition. Not mainstream British poetry. Payment: 2 copies of magazine.
   Submission details Postal submissions must be accompanied by sae. If by email, no attachments other than PDFs.

Sheffield Thursday

School of Cultural Studies, Sheffield Hallam University, Collegiate Crescent, Sheffield S10 2BP
Editor EA Markham

Published biannually and features a high national standard of poetry, short stories

and reviews, with regular competitions. Editorial and production associates include Margaret Drabble, Mimi Khalvati, Sharon Kivland, Mel McClellan and Sudeep Sen (Asia).
   Submission details Submissions accompanied by an sae or equivalent are welcomed.

The Shop: A Magazine of Poetry

Skeagh, Schull, Co Cork, Republic of Ireland
email wakeman@iolfree.ie (not for submissions)
website www.theshop-poetry-magazine.ie
Editor John Wakeman, Hilary Wakeman
Frequency/price 3 p.a. £7/€8.50

Poems on any subject in any form and occasional essays on poetry, especially Irish poetry. No submissions by email. No illustrations required. Length: 2000-3000 words (essays); any (poems). Payment: by arrangement. Founded 1999.

Smiths Knoll

Goldings, Goldings Lane, Leiston, Suffolk IP16 4EB
tel (01728) 830631
email michael.laskey@ ukonline.co.uk
Editor Joanne Cults, Michael Laskey
Frequency/price 3 issues p.a. £4.50. Annual subscription £12

Publishes poetry that is well-made, linguistically alive, and which makes sense.
   Submission details Submit up to 6 poems by post, accompanied by sae.

Smoke

The Windows Project, First Floor, Liver House, 96 Bold Street, Liverpool L1 4HY
tel 015-1709 3688
email dave@windowsproject.demon.co.uk
website www.windowsproject.demon.co.uk
Editor Dave Calder/Dave Ward

Frequency/price 2 issues p.a. 80p plus p&p (£4 for 5 issues) made payable to 'Windows Project'

New ideas, new ways of using language. Poems with something to say. *Smoke* can introduce you to new writing, poetry and graphics from some of the most established names, alongside new work from Merseyside, as well as from all over the country and around the world.

Submission details Send 6 poems with sae.

Snapshots

Snapshot Press, PO Box 132, Waterloo, Liverpool L22 8WZ
email info@snapshotpress.co.uk
website www.snapshotpress.co.uk
Contact John Barlow
Frequency/price 3 issues p.a. £5.50. Annual subscription £11

A magazine of haiku.

South Poetry Magazine

PO Box 5369, Poole, Dorset BH14 0XN
email south@martinblyth.co.uk
website http://martinblyth.co.uk
Editor Run by management team with different poem selectors for each issue
Frequency/price Twice-yearly (April and October). £5.60 inc. UK postage

Previously unpublished poems in English in any style, but study the magazine before submitting. No translations. Articles on poetry of about 800 words, particularly if related to the southern counties of England. Book reviews. Complimentary copy to successful poets.

Submission details Maximum 3 poems per submission. Poet's name/address or other identifying details must not appear on the manuscript, as poems are selected anonymously. Use the submission form, available (with full guidelines) on the

website, or separate covering letter giving name/address/list of poems. Submissions meeting guidelines get priority. Submit work at any time, but selection process does not begin until after the deadline for each issue (31 November and 31 May). Decision takes about 8 weeks from then. No fax, email or multiple submissions.

Spanner

14 Hopton Road, Hereford HR1 1BE
email kaa45@dial.pipex.com
website www.shadoof.net/spanner/
Editor Alan Fisher

A samizdat magazine which focuses on particular authors or subjects in each issue.

Sphinx

HappenStance, 21 Hatton Green, Glenrothes, Fife KY7 4SD
email nell@happenstancepress.com
website www.happenstancepress.com/Sphinx.htm
Editor Helena Nelson

A magazine which promotes, celebrates and evaluates poetry in chapbook form. It introduces the people behind the poetry imprints: it tells the stories of the publishers and the poets through features and interviews. Prints poems from some of the publications reviewed.

Splizz

4 St Mary's Rise, Burry Port, Carmarthenshire SA16 0SH
email splizzmagazine@yahoo.co.uk
website www.myspace.com/splizz
Editor Amanda Morgan
Frequency/price Quarterly: March, June, September, December. £2

All styles of poetry are considered, provided the work is not racist or homophobic.

Spume

19 Lochinch Park, Aberdeen AB12 3RF
website www.koopress.co.uk/spume.htm
Frequency/price £3

A perfect-bound A5-sized poetry
magazine committed to profiling poetry
with a punch.

Stand Magazine

School of English, University of Leeds,
Leeds LS2 9JT
tel 0113-233 4794 *fax* 0113-233 4791
email stand@leeds.ac.uk
website www.standmagazine.org
Managing Editor Jon Glover
Frequency/price Quarterly £6.50 plus p&p.
Annual subscription £25

Poetry, short stories, translations, literary
criticism. Send sae/IRCs for return.
Payment: £20 per 1000 words (prose); £20
per poem. Founded 1952.

Staple

74 Rangeley Road, Walkley, Sheffield S6
5DW
Editor Elizabeth Barrett, Ann Atkinson
Frequency/price 3 issues p.a. £5. Annual
subscription £15 (£20 overseas)

Contemporary poetry, short fiction,
articles and reviews. Payment: £5 per
poem, £10 fiction/articles. Founded 1982.
Submission details Send up to 6 poems
by post.

The Stinging Fly

PO Box 6016, Dublin 8, Ireland
email stingingfly@hotmail.com
website www.stingingfly.org
Editor Declan Meade
Frequency/price 3 issues p.a. €6/£5

Publishes poetry and fiction by Irish and
international writers, and is particularly
interested in promoting new writers. Each
issue has a 'Featured poet' section,

showcasing the work of a poet yet to
publish his or her first collection.
Submission details Full submission
guidelines can be found on the website.
Submissions are read in February, June
and October.

Submit

3 Bristol Place Edinburgh EH1 1EY
tel 0131-220 4538
email submitmagazine@yahoo.co.uk
website www.theforest.org.uk/

A magazine of prose and poetry available
from the Forest Café and bookshops.

Tandem

13 Stephenson Road, Barbourne,
Worcester WR1 3EB
email tandem@mitt.demon.co.uk
website www.progression.co.uk/tandem
Editor Michael J Woods
Frequency/price 3 issues p.a. Annual
subscription £12

New fiction and poetry.

Tangled Hair (Tanka Journal)

Snapshot Press, PO Box 132, Waterloo,
Liverpool L22 8WZ
email info@snapshotpress.co.uk
website www.snapshotpress.co.uk
Frequency/price 3 issues p.a. £5.50. Annual
subscription £11

A magazine of tanka.

Tears in the Fence

38 Hod View, Stourpaine, Blandford
Forum, Dorset DT11 8TN
tel (01258) 456803 *fax* (01258) 454026
email david@davidcaddy.wanadoo.co.uk
website www.thewordtravels.com
Editor David Caddy
Frequency/price 3 issues p.a. £6

An independent literary journal of
contemporary writing. Appreciates social

and poetic awareness; enjoys what is spontaneous, strong and direct, alongside writing which prompts close and divergent readings.

Submission details Submit by post with short biography and sae.

Temenos Academy Review

PO Box 203, Ashford, Kent TN25 5ZT
email temenosacademy@myfastmail.com
website www.temenosacademy.org
Editor Kathleen Raine

The journal of the Temenos Academy – an organisation that seeks to give space to poets, artists, writers and thinkers who subscribe to the belief that man is firstly a spiritual creature with spiritual needs which have to be nourished if we are to fulfill our potential and be happy. Comprises a mixture of papers given at the Academy, and new work, including poetry, art, and reviews.

Tenth Muse

33 Hartington Road, Southampton SO14 0EW
email andyj@noplace.screaming.net
Editor Andrew Jordan
Frequency/price Occasional. £3.50 (£6 for 2 issues)

Publishes mainly poems written by poets who read poetry. The collision of archaic and modern elements can often create good poetry.

Submission details Submit no more than 6 poems or 2000 words of prose. Sae or IRC essential. Write name and address on each sheet. No multiple submissions or previously published work. Payment by complimentary copy.

The Text

The Word Hoard, Unit 25, The Gatehouse Centre, Albert Street, Lockwood, Huddersfield HD1 3QD

tel (01484) 426626
email hoard@200.co.uk
website www.wordhoard.co.uk
Editor Keith Jafrate
Frequency/price 2 issues p.a. £2.50

Publishes radical and experimental poetry in any form.

Submission details No short poems – only long poems or long poem series considered. See website for submission guidelines. Must include sae/IRC. Email submissions accepted.

The Third Half Literary Magazine

16 Fane Close, Stamford, Lincolnshire PE9 1HG
tel (01780) 754193
Editor Kevin Troop

Publishes new and established writers. 4 writers appear in each issue with a mini-collection from each. Authors can buy their books at a reduced price.

Submission details Send new material only. Up to 8 typed poems with letter and sae.

Time Haiku

Basho-an, 105 King's Head Hill, London E4 7JG
Editor Doreen King
Frequency/price 2 issues p.a. £3

Promotes haiku and haiku-related forms. It aims to increase accessibility through education. *Time Haiku* encourages school and college activities as well as providing a biannual journal and a newsletter. Details can be obtained by writing to the above address. Formed in 1994.

Submission details Submissions must be made on a typed manuscript.

The Times Literary Supplement

Times House, 1 Pennington Street, London E98 1BS

tel 020-7782 5000 *fax* 020-7782 4966
Editor Peter Stothard
Frequency/price Weekly. £2.40

Will consider poems for publication, literary discoveries and articles on literary and cultural affairs. Payment: by arrangement.

Tolling Elves

649 Fulham Road, London SW6 5PU
email tevans21@hotmail.com
website www.onedit.net/tollingelves
Contact Thomas Evans

Tremblestone

Stowford House, 43 Seymour Avenue, St Judes, Plymouth, Devon PL4 8RB
website www.tremblestone.co.uk
Editor Kenny Knight
Frequency/price Annual subscription £4. 3 issues £10; 6 issues £18

A magazine with an international outlook. Has published contemporary poetry from across a broad spectrum of alternative poetries ever since the first issue was launched in November 1999. Perfect bound. 80-96 pages of poetry, including book and magazine reviews.

Submission details Send 5-6 poems with sae or IRCs.

Triumph Herald

Remus House, Coltsfoot Drive, Woodston, Peterborough, Cambs PE2 9JX
tel (01733) 890099
Contact Chris Walton

Christian writers' magazine with poetry, stories and articles written by subscribers.

Twa Dugs Literary Magazine

111 Main Street, West Kilbride, Ayrshire KA23 9AR
email ralf@rgarratt.freeserve.co.uk

Publishes short stories and poetry of 40 lines or fewer, mainly contributed from members of writers groups through which the magazine is promoted and circulated.

The Ugly Tree

Mucusart Publications, 6 Chiffin Way, Trinity, Manchester M3 6AB
tel 0161-833 2738
email paul@mucusart.co.uk
website www.mucusart.co.uk/theuglytree.htm
Editor Paul Neads
Frequency/price 3 issues p.a. (Feb, June, Oct). £3. Annual subscription £8.50

Poetry for performance and the page; poetry, reviews and interviews. Features an eclectic mix of wisdom from around the globe, while retaining its roots with regular contributions from both new and established North West poets. Particularly interested in the translation of performance poetry to the page, although this is not the magazine's prime mover.

Submission details Unsolicited submissions always welcome and no barrier as to style, form or content. Send no more than 5 poems by post or in the body of an email (no attachments). See website for full details.

Understanding

127 Milton Road West, 7 Duddingston House Courtyard, Edinburgh EH18
Editor D Smith
Frequency/price 1 issue p.a. £4.50

Publishes all styles of poetry.
Submission details Submit 5-6 poems.

The Unruly Sun

17 Bay View Terrace, Swansea SA1 4LT
email sales@unrulysun.co.uk
Editor Geoff Sawers
Frequency/price Irregular. £1.50

Poetry magazine based at Reading's Rising Sun Arts Centre. A modest little booklet, aiming to present the best in contemporary poetry from the fringes.

Urthona Magazine

19 Mulberry Close, Cambridge CB4 2AS
tel (01223) 316019
email urthonamag@onetel.com
website www.urtona.com
Editor Ratnagarbha
Frequency/price 2 issues p.a. £3.95

Publishes anything imaginative, alive and down to earth. Vacuous, spiritual uplift, buddhas, etc. not wanted.

Submission details Submissions must be accompanied by an sae.

Various Artists

24 Northwick Road, Bristol BS7 0UG
email tonylj@firewater.fsworld.co.uk
Editor Tony Lewis-Jones

Velvet

PO Box 19, Cambridge CB4 2WZ
email editor@velvet-mag.co.uk
Frequency/price Quarterly. £3. Annual subscription £11

A magazine aimed at lesbian women. A bit more 'intellectual' and issue-based than what's currently on the market, with a bit of fun and humour as well, and some political articles dealing with lesbian-specific issues, along with book and film reviews and a poetry section. Quarterly, glossy, and full colour.

Vigil

2 Rougeront Terrace, Axminster, Devon EX13 5JP
tel (0129) 733959
Editor John Howard-Greaves
Frequency/price 2 issues p.a. £2.25, inc. postage (£1.95 cover price)

Publishes poetry and prose of emotional force or intensity, colour, imagery and appeal to the senses.

Submission details Up to 6 poems of 40 lines maximum.

Voice & Verse

Robooth Publications, Robooth, 7 Pincott Place, London SE4 2ER
tel 020-7277 8831
email robooth@gofornet.co.uk
Editor Ruth Booth
Frequency/price Quarterly. £3

Wasafiri

1-11 Hawley Crescent, Camden Town, London NW1 8NP
tel 020-7556 6110
email wasafiri@open.ac.uk
website www.wasafiri.org
Editor Susheila Nasta
Frequency/price 3 issues p.a. £7. Annual subscription £21

A literary magazine primarily concerned with new and postcolonial writers, with an emphasis on the diversity and range of black and diasporic writers worldwide. It aims to create a definitive forum for the voices of new writers, and to open up lively spaces for serious critical discussion not available elsewhere. Britain's only international magazine for Black British, African, Asian and Caribbean literatures.

Weyfarers

1 Mountside, Guildford, Surrey GU2 4DJ
tel (01252) 702450 *fax* (01252) 703650
email admin@weyfarers.com
website www.weyfarers.com
Editor Martin Junes, Stella Stucker, Jeffrey Wheatley
Frequency/price 3 issues p.a.

An international publication with poetry in English, or in English translation, from many parts of the world. Modern and traditional work published from both new and established poets. Reviews of books and magazines. Submitted work should not have been published or currently submitted elsewhere. Copyright remains with the authors. Payment of a copy of magazine to poets whose work is accepted.

Submission details Manuscripts should be typed with name and address on each poem on separate sheets. Include sae or IRC for the return of unaccepted work.

The Wolf

Fagnal Lane, Winchmore Hill, Amersham HP7 0PG
email editor@thewolfpoetry.org.uk
website www.wolfmagazine.co.uk
Editor James Byrne
Frequency/price 3 issues p.a. £3. Annual subscription £10

Founded in April 2002 by James Byrne and Nicholas Cobic, with a clear emphasis on publishing emerging new poets alongside more established writers. Includes interviews with leading contemporary poets. The poets, however, come purely through submissions.

Submission details Email and postal submissions are both welcome. Send no more than 5 poems, on any style or theme, but originality is a prerequisite. Reviews and essays on any poetry subject are also welcome. Submissions cannot be returned.

Writers' Forum

Writers International Ltd, PO Box 3229, Bournemouth BH1 1NZ
tel (01202) 589828
email editorial@writers-forum.com
website www.writers-forum.com
Editor John Jenkins
Frequency/price Monthly. £3.50

Magazine publishing the winners of the Writers' Forum poetry competition.

Submission details Poems should be a maximum of 40 lines on any subject or style. The deadline is the 15th of every month. There is a first prize of £100 and a

Chambers Dictionary. Entry fee, £5 per poem and £7 for 2.

Writing Magazine

PO Box 168, Wellington Street, Leeds LS1 1RF
tel (01132) 388333
email derek.hudson@ writersnews.co.uk
website www.writersnews.co.uk/main/wm.asp
Editor Derek Hudson
Frequency/price 6 issues p.a. £14.95

Advice on how to break into the writing business, with articles on writing fiction, magazine articles, poetry, short stories, writing for children, screenwriting and other genres. Includes author interviews around the globe.

X-Magazine

Flipped Eye Publishing Ltd, PO Box 43771, London W14 8ZY
email submissions @x-bout.com
website www.flippedeye.net/xmag
Editor Stazja McFadyen, NA Parkes
Frequency/price Quarterly. £4. Annual subscription £15

Publishes poetry and prose of high quality.

Submission details See website for details. Email submission only.

The Yellow Crane

Flat 6, 20 Princes Court, Roath, Cardiff CF24 3AU
Editor J Brookes

Young Writer

Glebe House, Webley, Herefordshire HR4 8SD
tel (01544) 318901 *fax* (01544) 318901
email editor@youngwriter.org
website www.youngwriter.org
Editor Kate Jones
Frequency/price 3 p.a. £3.75 (£10 for 3 issues)

Specialist magazine for young writers under 18 years old: ideas for them and writing by them. Includes interviews by children with famous writers, fiction and non-fiction pieces, poetry; also explores words and grammar, issues related to writing (e.g. dyslexia), plus competitions with prizes. Length: 750 or 1500 words (features), up to 400 words (news), 750 words (short stories – unless specified otherwise in a competition), poetry of any length. Illustrations: colour – drawings by children, snapshots to accompany features. Payment: most children's material is published without payment; £25-£100 (features); £15 (cover cartoon). Free inspection copy. Founded 1995.

Submission details Send by email or, if by post, preferably typed.

E-MAGAZINES

There has been an explosion of poetry e-magazines, and many of the sites are classy, exquisitely designed productions. The list below, comprising poetry e-mags from both the United Kingdom and around the world (mostly US, of course) is by no means comprehensive – that would be almost impossible – but it does demonstrate the breadth of choice that exists, and the kind of quality to which e-magazines can aspire.

2 River View
www.2river.org

3rd Bed
www.3rdBed.com

3rd Muse
www.3rdmuse.com

4Poets.com
admin@4poets.com

42opus
www.42opus.com

A Little Poetry
www.alittlepoetry.com

Abalone Moon – A Journal of Poetry and the Arts
www.abalonemoon.com

Able Muse
www.ablemuse.com

Adagio Verse Quarterly
www.geocities.com/adagioversequarterly

Agnieszka's Dowry
www.asgp.org/agnieszka.html

Alba – A Journal of Short Poetry
www.ravennapress.com/alba

Alt-X
www.altx.com

Amaze – The Cinquain Journal
www.amaze-cinquain.com

Ancient Heart
www.ancientheartmagazine.
pwp.blueyonder.co.uk

Another Sun
www.anothersun.co.uk

Arcanum Cafe
www.arcanumcafe.com

The Argotist Online
www.argotistonline.co.uk

Ariga
http://ariga.com/visions/poetry

The Aurora Review
www.theaurorareview.com

Autumn Leaves
www.sondra.net/al/default.htm

The Beat
www.the-beat.co.uk

Big Bridge
www.bigbridge.org

Birmingham Words
www.birminghamwords.co.uk

Black Medina
www.blackmedina.net

Blackbird
www.blackbird.vcu.edu/

Blaze Vox
www.blazevox.org

The Blue Moon Review
www.thebluemoon.com

Boomerang
www.boomeranguk.com

Born
www.bornmag.com

Caketrain
www.caketrain.org

Centrifugal Forces
www.centrifugalforces.co.uk

The Cortland Review
www.cortlandreview.com

Crossing Borders
www.crossingborders-africanwriting.org/
magazine/

Dash 30 Dash Art and Poetry Magazine
www.dash30dash.com

Dead Drunk in Dublin
www.deaddrunkdublin.com

The Diagram
http://thediagram.com

The Drunken Boat
www.thedrunkenboat.com

Ducky Magazine
www.duckymag.com

Eclectica
www.eclectica.org

Electronic Acorn
www.dublinwriters.org/eacorn

Electronic Poetry Centre
epc.buffalo.edu

Erbacce
www.erbacce.com

Exposed
www.exposweb.net

Facets Magazine
www.facets-magazine.com

Free Verse: a journal of contemporary
poetry & poetics
www.english.chass.ncsu.edu/freeverse

Full Moon
www.fullmoonlm.bravehost.com

Great Works
www.greatworks.org.uk

The Hamilton Stone Review
www.hamiltonstone.org

Ink (&) Ashes
www.inkandashes.com

Interactions Online Jersey
www.interactionspoetry.com

Interpoetry
www.interpoetry.com

Jacket Magazine
www.jacketmagazine.com

Kritya
www.kritya.in

La Petite Zine
www.lapetitezine.org

Limelight
www.thepoem.co.uk/limelight/index.htm

Litter
www.leafepress.com/litter

Living Poets
www.dragonheartpress.com

The MAG
www.muse-apprentice-guild.com

Malleable Jangle
www.malleablejangle.netfirms.com

Man in the Moon
www.maninthemoon.co.uk

Masthead
www.masthead.net.au

Megaera
www.megaera.org

The Melic Review
www.melicreview.com

Memorious
www.memorious.org

Milk
www.milkmag.org

Monsoon Magazine
www.monsoonmag.com

Moria
www.moriapoetry.com

Morpo Review
www.morpo.com

Mot Juste
www.motjustepoetry.com

Mudlark
www.unf.edu/mudlark

Murmurs of a Nobody
www.murmursofanobody.co.uk

Neon Highway
www.neonhighway.co.uk

Nth Position
www.nthposition.com

Onedit
www.onedit.net

Opus
www.sidewalkpress.net

The Page
http://thepage.name

Panic! Brixton Poetry
http://homepages.which.net/
~panic.brixtonpoetry/

Perigee
www.perigee-art.com

Perihelion
http://webdelsol.com/Perihelion/

The Poem: Contemporary British and Irish
Poetry
www.thepoem.co.uk

The Poet's Canvas
www.poetscanvas.org

(the poetry) Worm
www.villarana.freeserve.co.uk

Poetry Daily
www.poems.com

Poetry London
www.poetrylondon.co.uk

Poetry Mine
www.poetrymine.co.uk

Poetry Now
www.poetrynow.org

poetry pf
www.poetrypf.co.uk

Poetry Sz: Demystifying Mental Illness
www.poetrysz.net

Pores
www.pores.bbk.ac.uk

Qualm
www.qualm.co.uk

Quid Magazine
www.jacketmagazine.com/20/quid.html

Red Ink
www.incwriters.com

The Richmond Review
www.richmondreview.co.uk

Rock Salt Plum Review
www.rocksaltplum.com

The Round Table Review
www.roundtablereview.co.uk

Scriberazone
www.scriberazone.co.uk

Sentinel Poetry
www.sentinelpoetry.org.uk

Shadow Train
http://shadowtrain.com

Shampoo Poetry
www.shampoopoetry.com

Signals Magazine
www.signalsmagazine.co.uk

Simply Haiku
www.simplyhaiku.com

Slope
www.slope.org

Snakeskin
http://homepages.nildram.co.uk/
~simmers/

Sol
www.solpubs.freeserve.co.uk/
solmagazine.htm

Soundeye
www.soundeye.org

Southern Ocean Review
www.book.co.nz

Spoken War
www.spokenwar.com

Spokes
www.simegen.com/writers/spokes

Stride
www.stridemagazine.co.uk

This Is It Magazine
www.thisisitmag.co.uk

Three Candles Journal
www.threecandles.org/poetry.html

Triplopia
www.triplopia.org

Underground Window
www.undergroundwindow.com

Vallum Contemporary Poetry
www.vallummag.com

Vending Poetry
www.wearpurple.co.uk/vendingpoetry

Verse Libre Quality
www.vlqpoetry.com

The Verse Marauder
www.theversemarauder.com

Vert Poetry Magazine
www.litvert.com

Voices Literary Magazine
www.1writersway.org

West 47
www.galwayartscentre.ie/west47

Words-Myth
www.words-myth.com

Words Words Words
www.wordswordswords.4t.com

Wordshare – e-magazine for disabled writers
www.lincolnshire.gov.uk

World Haiku Review
www.worldhaikureview.org

writersartists.net
www.writersartists.net

Ygdrasil
www.synapse.net/kgerken/

Young Poets
www.loriswebs.com/youngpoets

Zafusy
www.zafusy.com

Performance poetry: more ear than eye?

Performance poetry venues are springing up the length and breadth of the country, with plenty of opportunities for virgin performers to take advantage of an Open Mic Evening and share their poetry with an unsuspecting world. There is more, however, to performance poetry than just standing in front of an audience and spouting your work. To make performance poetry really work takes technique and considerable restraint, as explained by a master of the art, **Mario Petrucci**.

'Poetry on the page' and 'performance poetry' are kissing cousins rather than differentiable species. A child muttering the line of verse s/he traces with a finger; even poetry metred out in the head while composing – these, too, are 'performative' acts. We're all (to some extent or other) performance poets. And yet, performance poetry – in spite of its remarkable variety – is often instantly recognisable as a genre. What, then, are its hallmarks? Below, I provide a 'pros/cons' paraphrase of some of the more polarised answers to that, selected (and, I admit, somewhat caricaturised) to be provocative. Whether you're gearing up for your first Open Mic slot, launching a book at a poetry festival, or adding a punchy audio clip to your multimedia website, you'll be entering into negotiation with yourself (consciously or otherwise) regarding where you stand among the extremes in this list. I hope you'll contest them vigorously, while allowing yourself to be challenged.

They're so refreshing; not dry or academic.	Half of them haven't even heard of modernism.
There's such physical involvement with the words!	I wish they'd bloody well stand still.
An object lesson in vocal range and dynamism.	Why that silly voice?
The rhythmic motifs really sustain it.	All rhythm – no content.
Wow! Such stage presence.	Where's the poetry?
It's a natural extension of poetry's long oral tradition.	Pap for the masses. It won't last.
It's all about grass roots, difference, individuality.	They all sound much the same.
They're essentially subversive, anti-establishment.	Failed stand-ups, stage-junkies, wannabe celebs.
It's bang on! The future!	It's the end. The whimper.
The key is access: anyone can relate to this stuff.	Not one of them has even heard of modernism.

I'll leave that with you.

Now for some pragmatics and specifics: a few tips and insights regarding poetry performance. The following notes are far from exhaustive, but they're gleaned from performance workshops across a wide range of interests and styles. I'm sure they cover many of the more salient, recurring concerns.

Breath, pace, nerves

You probably won't engage an audience powerfully if you're not prepared, relaxed, breathing. So, develop a simple backstage relaxation ritual. Breathe slowly, right into the pit of your stomach. Sigh. Say a loud doctor's "Ahhh!!" or hum a tune, deeply, changing the notes. Free up the lips, tongue, face. Shake the joints out – especially knees/shoulders/neck/jaw. Wear comfy clothes (shoes in particular). Do some gentle stretches. Hydrate fully. Go onstage beforehand; get a feel for what it's like up there. Most hosts are happy to change something that's genuinely bothering you (being snow-blinded by spotlights is my bugbear).

In the reading itself, speak in a measured way. Slow down till it feels *far* too slow, and it might be about right. Trust those hard-won words – not your stage 'image' or style – to carry you through. Picture words as tiny, unsinkable boats. If you get the shakes, or begin to stall – pause. Are your breaths snatched, shallow? You may be tightening up *because you're forgetting to breathe*. Starving the brain of oxygen deepens anxiety and confusion. Take a solid breath; start again. Become aware of a column of air moving freely through your body. Take good breaths between, as well as during, poems (we often forget). Occupy that wonderful space on stage and hold it. Ask yourself: "Am I enjoying this?" Even if the answer is a resounding *no*, try to find in yourself some shard of a *yes*. Focus on that. It helps you connect with your text, lifting your voice into those subtle variations of pace, tone and emphasis that avoid a flat delivery. As for nerves, they're natural; accept them, then move on. That awful sensation of trembling on the brink is just your body preparing itself for a 'yes' – for flight.

'The position of readiness'

This is a natural, breathing, postural stillness adopted on stage: it keeps the speaking voice central to what's happening, with the body balanced, relaxed and in support. If you're at the mercy of habitual gestures or distorted posture (what I call 'body-noise') then you simply don't have that potent tool of stillness in your performance toolbox. Body-noise can be anything from pacing the stage, audibly playing with the loose change in your pocket, to a slight cocking of the head or constant re-adjusting of specs. By reducing your body-noise, you amplify the effect of any gesture you *do* choose to make. I generally keep such gestures to a minimum because, in the ongoing dialogue between stillness and animation that a poetry performance (and, for that matter, a person) is, I tend to favour the ear over the eye. Ultimately, I suspect that performance poetry tends to work best when the emphasis is on the poetry. Of course, some occasions demand (or tolerate) the opposite, and I'd certainly defend the possibility of a poetry employing the entire body for its delivery; having said that, I rarely gain much from the insistent movements some performers deploy as stock-in-trade. These can descend into predictable mannerism, a kind of running commentary that distracts from the words. If you want to explore this issue further, video yourself performing, or just read to a mirror; but I'd prefer that you address this by collaborating with other writers. If you can, work with people who don't share your propensities or house style. Ask for constructive feedback regarding what you do with voice/body that distracts them from the text. Paradoxically, the detachment achieved in presenting together a *shared* (i.e. co-authored) piece can actually help you towards being more quietly distinctive, more 'yourself', in what you do.

Poems: breath projectiles?

Listen out for it at readings: that faintly precious, slightly mesmerised, dreamy-sweet intonation many poets audibly 'put on' whenever they slip from introduction into poem: like a decaf cappuccino with too much froth. Then there are those performers who go overboard the other way – driving the text too hard in an instinctive attempt to make the poem arrive impressively, moment to moment, as sonic explosions from stage to ear. Alas, too much caffeine! These two extremes invoke that eternal debate between the merits of an 'internalised delivery', which draws the audience into the world of the poem (along Stanislavsky's lines), and an externalised technique or presentation of a 'mask' (as per Brecht, say). Charles Olson offers a third way. In his essay 'Projective Verse', he suggests that poetry proceeds from:

the HEAD, by way of the EAR, to the SYLLABLE

the HEART, by way of the BREATH, to the LINE

Even if you don't agree with that, his idea at least reminds us that words are objects, a series of sonic elements channelled through head and heart, to be sounded in relationship and tension. For Olson, the poet must go "down through the workings of his own throat to that place where breath comes from, where breath has its beginnings, where drama has to come from". You may feel that a stylised delivery (or mask) is a large part of the drama of your performance; but even where a piece is composed entirely for live distribution, Olson's contract between head and heart, between content and delivery, is struck syllable by syllable, line by line. To this, let me add a thought of my own. Whenever we read a poem in a voice that isn't our usual (I hesitate to say 'natural') voice, shouldn't that be done to meet a distinct need in the poem? The greater the departure from your usual voice, the greater and more insistent that need.

The set; the time

The best readings often have a kind of geometry to them. Just as individual poems possess shape and form, so does a reading. Frequently, that shape reveals a variety of pace, tone and content. There are subtle recurrences. There is, in a sense, the larger poem (that 'whole' of the performance set) of which the particular poems are parts. Allowing that larger poem to happen is mostly a case of trusting your instincts, of being alert to the creative possibilities of performance beyond the unit of the single poem. So, choose your poems, and their order, with love and care.

Finally, a word about time. Sorry guys, but 17 poems (plus intros, anecdotes, impromptu observations, dramatic pauses to sip from wineglass) will somewhat exceed the ten minutes you were allotted on stage. And another thing: time running out is not a cue simply to read *faster*. I know we all overrun from time to time.

Occasionally, the audience will not mind. Being enthused by your own work, and wanting others to share that enthusiasm, is spot on. But going on for half an hour when you're booked for ten minutes is – bluntly – rude. Invest in a working watch, take a king-sized egg timer on stage, whatever you need. Please, be one of those who face their audience (as I must now) with the thought, if not the words: 'There's so much more I wanted to get across, to share with you. Alas, I'm out of time. Enough said.'

(For more on voice and collaborative performance ('ShadoWork'), see: http://mariopetrucci.port5.com.)

Mario Petrucci is an ecologist, physicist, voice trainer, songwriter and poetic innovator. Recent residencies at the Imperial War Museum and BBC Radio 3 have confirmed his reputation as one of the country's leading exponents of public/site-specific poetry. Publications include: *Fearnought: poems for Southwell Workhouse* (National Trust, 2006), a unique meeting of poetry, history and photography; and *Catullus* (Perdika Press, 2006), a ribald, but unusual, take on the famous Roman poet. Four times a winner of the London Writers Competition, Petrucci was awarded the *Daily Telegraph/* Arvon Prize for *Heavy Water: a poem for Chernobyl* (Enitharmon, 2004), now the subject of a remarkable new film by Seventh Art commemorating the 20th anniversary of the disaster (www.heavy-water.co.uk).

Poetry venues

Cabarets, spoken-word club nights, music and poetry evenings – there are a wealth of venues where a poet may stand in front of a microphone and perform his or her poetry. It is a fast-moving world, however, and venues move or change all the time. Look out for venues with open-mic. opportunities where novices can climb up on stage alongside more experienced performers. It is advisable, of course, to confirm that the event is actually taking place before turning up.

African Writers
Poetry Café, 22 Betterton Street, London WC2H 9BX
tel 020-7420 9888
website www.poetrysociety.org.uk
Bimonthly evening of African writing hosted by Nii Parkes.

Ambit Writers
Princess Louise, 208 High Holborn, London WC1V AL4
Tuesdays, 7pm. Featured artists with floor spots available after the interval.

Apples & Snakes
Battersea Arts Centre, Lavender Hill, London SW11 5TN
tel 020-7924 3410
email apples@snakes.demon.co.uk
website www.applesandsnakes.org
Fortnightly on the second and and last Friday of each month, 9pm. This is the place to check out the up-and-comers and polished performers.

Aromapoetry
Caffé Nero, 101 Oxford Street, London
website www.x-bout.com/aroma
Every other Sunday hosted by Nii Parkes, from 4.30-6.30pm. Poetry and prose, open mic (6 min each). Very relaxed atmosphere. Always has a fine range of readers. A good place to read for the first time.

Big Word Performance Poetry
The Tron Bar, 9 Hunter Square, Royal Mile, Edinburgh

tel 0131-229 3633
email jemrolls@bigword.fsnet.co.uk
Fortnightly cabaret 9.00-11.00pm.

The Blue Room
Bridge Ho, Newcastle upon Tyne, Tyne and Wear
tel 0191-273 5326
email diamond.twig@virgin.net
website www.diamond.twig.co.uk
Contact Ellen Phethean

A great chance to meet other writers once a month. There are 4 readings of 10 mins each night; perfect length, and great atmosphere with candles and music.

Brel Bar
Ashton Lane, Glasgow G12 8SG.
tel 0141-342 4966

Hosted by Viv Gee and starting at 3.00pm, a great place to hear the latest and best from Glasgow's writers. On the last Sunday of every month.

Brixtongue
Brixton Art Gallery, 35 Brixton Station Road, London SW9
tel (07986) 357156
email brixart@brixtonartgallery.co.uk
website www.brixtonartgallery.co.uk

Second Saturday of the month, 8pm. A monthly blend of poetry, music and humour with MC John Rogers and resident Reggae sound system Zinc Fence. Interested acts and for more info, call.

Buzzwords

The Beehive, Montpellier Villas, Cheltenham
tel (07855) 308122
email cheltpoetry@yahoo.co.uk
website http://www.angelfire.com/poetry/buzzwords/index.html

Cheltenham's poetry café, running the first Sunday of every month. Each event starts with writing time: exercises, themes and tips to get you going, followed by a guest poet. Starts 7pm if wishing to write, otherwise 8pm. There are also open mic slots available on a first come, first served basis.

Cafe Caprice, Clitheroe

6-8 Moor Lane, Clitheroe BB7 1BE
tel (01200) 422034
email cafecaprice@talk21.com

Poetry readings organised by the Clitheroe Bookshop.

Café Frug

Chapel House, Chapel Street, Penzance, Cornwall TR18 4AQ

Every second Thursday, 8pm.

Can Openers

The Poetry Can, Unit 11, Kuumba Project, Hepburn Road, Bristol BS2 8UD
tel (01179) 426976
email info@poetrycan.demon.co.uk
website www.poetrycan.demon.co.uk/canopeners.htm

Events run by the poetry organisation, The Poetry Can, in Bristol and Bath.
  Bristol: Second Thursday of the month. Held at the YHA, Narrow Quay. Starting time 8pm. For more information contact Lucy Hudson on (01179) 245764 or lucy@poetrycan.demon.co.uk.
  Bath: Third Thursday of the month. Held at the Windows Arts Centre, St James Memorial Hall, Lower Borough Walls. Starting time 8pm. For more information contact Richard Carder on (01225) 313531.

Catweazle Club

East Oxford Community Centre, corner of Cowley Road & Princes' Street, Oxford
email mother@catweazleclub.org

Oxford's well-established performing arts club. Thursdays, 8pm.

Caulder Events

Caulder Bookshop, 51 The Cut, London SE1 8LF
tel 020-7620 2900
email info@calderpublications.com
website www.calderpublications.com

Thursdays, at 6.30 pm, featuring high-calibre readings by the author or by actors with expert lecturers.

CB1 Café

32 Mill Road, Cambridge CB1 2AD

Provides a platform for local poets; also attracts widely known poets. Tuesdays, 8.00-9.45pm.

The Cellar

Poetry Café, 22 Betterton Street, London WC2H 9BX
tel 020-7420 9888
website www.poetrysociety.org.uk

Saturday evening event celebrating what is currently brilliant about the poetry scene; brings together written and performance poetry and nurtures new talent. Host Niall O'Sullivan.

The Citadel

Waterloo Street, St Helen's WA10 1PX
tel (01744) 735436
website www.citadel.org.uk

A once-a-month event where you can perform your own songs, your own poems, your own comedy routine.

City Voices

City Bar, 2-3 King Street, Wolverhampton
WV1 1ST
tel (01902) 552061

Regular showcase for local writers, poets, comedians, storytellers and musicians.

Clitheroe Books Open Floor Poetry Readings

New Inn, Parson Lane, Clitheroe,
Lancashire BB7 2JN
tel (01200) 444242
email joharbooks@aol.com
website www.roundstonebooks.co.uk
Contact Jo Harding

Hosts open-floor poetry readings at the New Inn on the last Thursday of each month, starting at 7.30pm. Admission free.

Coffee-house Poetry at the Troubadour

265 Old Brompton Road, Earls Court,
London
tel 020-8354 0660
email CoffPoetry@aol.com
website www.troubadour.co.uk

A year-round programme of poetry readings at the famous café in London.

Colpitt Poets

website www.colpittspoetry.co.uk

Colpitts Poetry was founded in 1975 by 2 poets and academic librarians, David Burnett and Richard Caddel, and a lecturer at Durham University, Diana Collecott. Since then, it has mounted more than 360 live readings in Durham, presenting an enormous range of poets, mainly from the UK but also from the USA, Europe and elsewhere, as well as a number of distinguished prose writers.

Come Strut Your Stuff

The Egg Café, Top Floor, 16-18
Newington Buildings, Liverpool L1 3ED
tel 0151-280 5453
email info@comestrutyourstuff.co.uk

Popular, long-running poetry and acoustic music event that takes place once a month in the intimate and friendly atmosphere of Liverpool's Egg Café.

The Dead Good Poets, Aberdeen

22 Belmont Street, Aberdeen AB10 1JH
email koopoetry@btinternet.com

A reading-for-charity poetry group, which holds meetings on the last Thursday of every month at Books and Beans, 22 Belmont Street, Aberdeen. The meetings are informal, incorporating a guest reader and open mic. Experienced poets and beginners welcome. 6.30-8.30pm.

Dead Good Poets Society

Everyman Bistro, Third Room, Hope
Street, Liverpool L1 9BH
tel 0151-708 9545 *website*
www.deadgoodpoetssociety.co.uk/
evening.html

Provides monthly Open Floor events and monthly Guest Nights. Currently these take place on the first Wednesday of the month (Open Floor) and the third Wednesday of the month (Guest Night).

Dutchpot

Bush Hall, 310 Uxbridge Road, London
W12
tel 020-8222 6933
email notes@bushhallmusic.co.uk

Last Friday of the month hosted by Noel Mckoy, at 8 pm. An acoustic night where singers, songwriters, musicians, and poets perform their original material (of all genres) in a chilled cafe vibe.

Exiled Writers Ink

Poetry Café, 22 Betterton Street, London
WC2

tel 020-7420 9888
website www.poetrysociety.org.uk

Usually first Monday of the month, at 7.30pm. A blend of featured performers and floorspots of writers exiled from their homelands.

Exploding Alphabets

West Walls, Back Stowell Street, Newcastle upon Tyne
email explodingalphabets@hotmail.co.uk

Prefers no old work and delights in an open stage filled with experimental performance. Nights correspond to the number of the month, i.e. 10/10, 11/11, 12/12, etc.

Express Excess

The Enterprise, 2 Haverstock Hill, London NW3 2BL
tel 020-7485 2659

A mix of comedy, poetry and storytelling every Wednesday at The Enterprise.

The Fitzwilliam Museum

Trumpington Street, Cambridge CB2 1RB
tel (01223) 332900
email fitzmuseum-enquiries@lists.cam.ac.uk

Holds occasional poetry events.

Foakies

1 Infirmary Street, Edinburgh EH1 1LT
email tomf@miscorp.ed.ac.uk
Contact Tom Fairnie

20-minute spots featuring a singer-songwriter and then a poet, followed by a 40-minute spot featuring the main act, usually a singer-songwriter. First Tuesday of every month.

The Foundry

94-96 Great Eastern Road, London EC2A 3JL

email poetry@foundry.tv
website www.foundry.tv

Sundays, 7 pm.

FourCast

Poetry Café, 22 Betterton Street, London WC2H 9BX
tel 020-7420 9888
website www.poetrysociety.org.uk

Monthly readings hosted by Roddy Lumsden, with 4 guest readers.

Fourth Friday: Poetry & Acoustic Music at the Poetry Cafe

Poetry Café, Betterton Street, London WC2H
tel 020-8299 2767
email info@fourthfriday.co.uk
website freespace.virgin.net/mp3.city
Contact Hylda Sims, Liz Simcock

A poetry and music event at the Poetry Café, at the headquarters of the Poetry Society in London's Covent Garden. At 8pm on the fourth Friday of (almost) every month, poets, singers, songwriters and musicians will be featured – known and not so known.

The Garden Café

16 Stony Street, Frome, Somerset
tel (01373) 454178
email jazz@nunneyjazzcafe.org

Regular poetry events.

Hammer and Tongue Poetry Slam

The Zodiac, 190 Cowley Road, Oxford
tel (01865) 200550
email poetry@hammerandtongue.org
website www.hammerandtongue.org
Contact Steve Larkin

Hammer and Tongue is a monthly open poetry slam and showcase that has built up a lively, dynamic performance poetry scene in Oxford. First Tuesday of every month with open poetry slam and some of the best UK and international performers as guest artists.

The Hydrogen Jukebox
Darlington Arts Centre, Vane Terrace D13 7AX
tel (01325) 486555
email jocolley@ntlworld.com
website www.hjbox.co.uk

Cabaret, poetry and music.

Irish Poetry Night
Hammersmith & Fulham Irish Centre, Blacks Road, Hammersmith, London W6
tel 020-8563 8232
email irish.centre@lbhf.gov.uk
Contact Niall McDevitt

A bimonthly gathering.

Kin
Café Royal 19, West Register Street, Edinburgh EH2 2AA
tel 0131-556 1884
website www.kinhead.net

Fortnightly open mic sessions. Last Thursday of each month (excluding August and December), 7.30pm-1am.

The Klinker
107a Culford Road, London N1
email eggpress@eggstore.demon.co.uk
Contact Paul Hill

Thursdays, and the last Friday of the month, at 8.30pm. Poetry performance event.

The Language Club
Plymouth Arts Centre, Looe Street, The Barbican, Plymouth
tel (01752) 206114

Final Saturday of each month, except August and December, at 7.30pm.

Last Thursday at the Dylan Thomas Centre
Somerset Place, Maritime Quarter, Swansea SA1 1RR
tel (01792) 463980
email dylanthomas.lit@ swansea.gov.uk
website www.dylanthomas.org

Popular monthly live music and poetry night. Last Thursday of the month, 8pm.

Liquid Cafe Bar
City Arcade, Coventry, West Midlands CV1 3HX

A poetry night every third Tuesday.

Mac
Cannon Hill Park, Birmingham, West Midlands B12 9QH
tel 0121-440 3838
email info@macarts.co.uk
website www.macarts.co.uk

Mac, the most visited arts centre in the Midlands, offers a huge range of literature events for adults and children. From poetry readings, meet-the-author, courses and workshops, music, literature, and theatre with a strong basis in literature – there is something for everybody!

The Marlborough Theatre
Prince's Street, Brighton, East Sussex
tel (01273) 695294
email paul@stopalltheclocks.co.uk
website www.stopalltheclocks.co.uk
Contact Paul Stones

The only venue run by poets in Brighton, the Marlborough has a regular programme of spoken-word events and is the centre of the fringe literature festival. Under the management of Brighton's foremost promoters, it has garnered a reputation as the best and most accesible venue for poetry in the city.

The Masque
90 Seel Street, Liverpool L1 4BH
tel 0151-708 8708

website www.masquevenue.co.uk

Regular poetry events.

The Morden Tower

West Walls, Back Stowell Street, Newcastle upon Tyne
email conniepickard@btopenworld.com
website www.mordentower.com

One of the oldest poetry venues in England.

Pangari Poetry in Motion

Deluxe Gallery, 2-4 Hoxton Square, London N1
mobile (07957) 267172
email production-team@pangari.com
website www.pangari.com
Contact Fiona McColl

Performance poetry events.

Parasol Unit

14 Wharf Road, London N1 7RW
tel 020-7490 7373
email info@parasol-unit.org
website www.parasol-unit.org

Parasol Unit Foundation for Contemporary Art is a non-profit initiative established to showcase the work of leading international contemporary artists. It stages regular poetry readings.

Perceptive Perspective

Hanger Farm Arts Centre, Aikman Lane, Totton, Southampton SO40 8FT
tel (02380) 667274
email hstanden@totton.ac.uk
website www.hangerfarm.totton.ac.uk
Contact Hannah Standen

An event bringing together local professional poets and London-based performance artists to present poetry to a wide audience of all ages. Also provides a forum for all members of the community to read their poetry, in a professional theatre environment.

Piccadilly Poets

tel (01908) 340379
email piccadillypoets@yahoo.co.uk
website http://dspace.dial.pipex.com/town/park/yaw74/Piccadilly.htm
Contact Leo Aylen

A whole range of poetry events.

Poems, Portcullis and Potation

The Portcullis, Clifton, Sion Hill, Bristol BS8 4LD
tel 0117-973 8955

Second Thursday of the month; 7.30 for 8.00pm.

Poems at the Albert

40 Leymoor Road, Golcar, Huddersfield, West Yorkshire HD3 4SP
tel (01484) 305179
Contact John Bosley

Second Thursday of each month at 8pm.

poetry@brick lane

coffee@brick lane, 154 Brick Lane, London E1 6RU
tel 020-7247 4654

Every 4 weeks on a Thursday; hosted by Ian Joynson. 7 pm. Free event open to all genres of poetry, prose and music.

The Poetry Café

22 Betterton Street, London WC2H 9BX
tel 020-7420 9880
email poetrycafe@ poetrysociety.org.uk
Contact Jess York

In the afternoon, people sit and write; in the evening they may stay to listen to poets perform or read in the basement to a small but informed audience. Sometimes the café is full of exiled writers well known in their own countries but glad of an audience here; at other times people are crowding out of the door to get a seat for a famous poet who has been caught on their way through London. With each event the café mood changes, while the place itself, the delicious vegetarian food offered and the classic dishes like marmite toast and Portuguese custard tarts, remain constant. At the moment there is a series of poets resident in the café who put on new and interesting events, as well as offering their services for poetry surgeries to look at anyone's work who cares to approach them. Customers say: "Lovely staff, peaceful, friendly, aesthetically pleasing," and *The Guardian* included the café in its guide this summer to the "most funky, stylish and interesting cafés".

Poetry@TheRoom

The Room, 33 Holcombe Road, Tottenham N17 9AS
tel 020-8808 9318
email info-theroom@fsmail.net
website www.the-room.org.uk

An Arts Council-funded London poetry event that takes place at 7.30pm on the first Wednesday of every month. Presents a diverse selection of talented poets of all different styles, both new and established, in a salon-type atmosphere. £5 and free wine.

Poetry Unplugged

Poetry Café, 22 Betterton Street, London WC2
tel 020-7420 9888
website www.poetrysociety.org.uk

Tuesdays, hosted by Carl Dhiman, at 7pm. Presents a wide range of material.

Poets Anonymous

Harry's Bar, Nassau Street, Dublin 2
email nedluddtc@yahoo.com

A weekly poetry event which aims to provide a platform for up-and-coming poets to perform their work, to gain insight into the work of 1 featured poet each week, and to bring poetry to a wider audience. Wednesday evenings 7-30-9.30pm.

The Poet's Letter

Poetry Café, 22 Betterton Street, London WC2H 9BX
tel 020-7420 9888
website www.poetrysociety.org.uk

Monthly readings hosted by Munayem Mayenin, with a distinguished stable of poets. Second Monday of month.

Pure Poetry

The Horseshoe, Clerkenwell Close, London EC1
tel 020-7687 6742

Mondays, 8.30pm.

Purple Patch Poetry Evenings

Barlow Theatre, Langley Nr Oldbury, West Midlands
website www.poetrywednesbury.co.uk

Guest poets, open mic and music.

Reading the Leaves

Tchai Ovna House of Tea, 42 Otago Lane, Glasgow G12 8PB
email readingtheleaves@hotmail.com

Monthly readings on first Friday of every month, 8-10pm. An evening of poetry and creative writing, featuring writers from Glasgow and beyond.

Research Centre in Modern and Contemporary Poetry

Oxford Brookes University, Oxford OX3 0BP
email rbuxton@brookes.ac.uk

website http://ah.brookes.ac.uk/index.php/english/poetry
Contact Dr Rachel Buxton

Hosts an annual programme of events whose ambition is to involve academics alongside poets in the discussion of central themes and ideas relating to British, Irish, American and postcolonial poetries in English across the 20th and into the 21st centuries.

Salisbury Poetry Café

Salisbury Arts Centre, Bedwin Street, Salisbury Wiltshire SP1 3UT

Last Thursday of every month at 8pm. The programme includes a different guest poet every month, and an open mic.

Sallis Benney Theatre

University of Brighton, 58-64 Grand Parade, Brighton, East Sussex BN2 2JY
tel (01273) 643010
email c.l.matthews@bton.ac.uk
website www.bton.ac.uk

The University of Brighton theatre; puts on alternative touring plays, spoken-word and musical events.

Sammy Dow's

69 Nithsdale Road, Glasgow G41 2AJ
tel 0141-423 0107

On the first Monday of the month, when the South Side Writers' Group hosts its popular Words and Music events. The Mayfest poetry competition for performance poetry is also be held at this venue during May, in addition to the regular monthly event.

Scavel An Gow

3 Penlee Villas, Playing Place, Truro, Cornwall TR3 6EY
tel (01872) 865176
email paul@a39LM.freeserve.co.uk

Contact Paul Farmer

A group of leading Cornish writers dedicated to the creation of new work for live performance. The stories range around the world, but are often strongly rooted in the Cornish communities that inspire them. Scavel An Gow shows are unique, weaving words and music together to explore new areas in the field of live performance, in a warm and informal environment. Shows take place in village halls and venues throughout Cornwall and beyond.

The Scotia Bar

112 Stockwell Street, Glasgow G1 4LW
tel 0141-552 8681

The best of Glasgow's poetry, literature and music scene. On the last Tuesday of the month at 8.00pm.

Shaftesbury Poetry Group

The Upstairs Parlour, Bell Street Café, Bell Street, Shaftesbury, Dorset
tel (01747) 853703
Contact Krissy Elliot-Foster

First Wednesday of the month, 8-10pm.

The Shed

Brawby, Malton, North Yorkshire YO17 6PY
tel (01653) 668494
website www.theshed.co.uk
Contact Simon Thackray

Music and poetry venue created by Simon Thackray in 1992. The finest modern jazz, blues, folk, country, classical, world and improvised music, comedy, poetry and knitting are all performed in front of an old shed door in one of the smallest venues in the world, with an audience of just over 100 people around candlelit tables.

Shore Poets

The Canons' Gait, 232 Canongate, Edinburgh EH8 8DQ

Readings by mainly Scottish poets on the last Sunday of every month, 7.45pm.

Shortfuse

Camden Head, Camden Walk, Islington, London N1
tel 020-8536 0652
email shortfuse@ morethanwords.co.uk

A mix of performance comedy, stand-up poetry and music. Thursdays, 8.30pm.

Silencio

The Counting House, West Nicolson Street, Edinburgh EH8 9DD
mobile (07969) 163065
email silenciocabaret@yahoo.co.uk
Contact Jennifer Williams

Glamorous and decadent cabaret featuring poetry, experimental music, theatre, spoken word, visuals, comedy and more, with MC Penny Pornstar and DJ Daniel.

Slammers

14 Queens Road, Westbourne, Bournemouth, Dorset BH2 6BE
website www.thepeoplespoet.com
Contact Paula Brown

Centre Stage, venue of Funnybone Comedy Club; second Tuesday of every month, 7.30pm. £2.

The South Bank Centre

The South Bank Centre, Royal Festival Hall, London SE1 8XX
tel 020-7921 0904
email mcolthorpe@rfh.org.uk
website www.rfh.org.uk
Contact Martin Colthorpe

The South Bank Centre has an uninterrupted commitment to presenting poetry. It is home to the Poetry Library; hosts Poetry International, a biennial festival of world poetry; and is constantly looking for opportunities to introduce poetry to new audiences.

Speakeasy

The Quaker Centre, 1 Oakley Gardens, Downhead Park, Milton Keynes, Buckinghamshire MK15 9BH
tel (01908) 663860
email speakeasy@ writerbrock.co.uk
website www.mkweb.co.uk/speakeasy
Contact Martin Brocklebank

Provides a meeting place and encouragement for writers in the Milton Keynes area. Attracts poets, aspiring and published novelists, and writers of short stories, articles and comedy. Regular guest evenings provide an opening for nationally recognised writers, while its poetry forum and critique group enable members to refine and develop their work. The Speakeasy open poetry competitions are now an established part of the annual competition calendar, and attract entries from around the world.

Speakeasy

The Green Room, 54-56 Whitworth Street West, Manchester M1 5WW
tel 0161-236 1261

Open mic nights with guests.

Speakeasy Cafe/Bar

Speakeasy Cafe/Bar, Glasgow Lesbian, Gay, Bisexual & Transpeople Centre, 11 Dixon Street, St Enoch, Glasgow G1 4AL
tel 0141-429 4672
email lgbtart@gglc.org.uk

A celebration of the spoken word and music with poets, writers, comedians, soap-box stars, folk singers, guitarists, opera singers, pop singers, authors, actors, drama queens, cellists. Third Wednesday of the month, from 7.30pm till late.

Spiel

20 Coxwell Street, Cirencester, Glos GL7 2BH

tel (01285) 640470
email spiel@scarum.freeserve.co.uk,
spiel@arbury.freeserve.co.uk
website www.author.co.uk/spiel/index.htm

The Spoken Word Campaign
The Jolly Brewer, Lincoln, Lincolnshire
mobile (07770) 830051
email wilgress@ntlworld.com

Lincoln's premier open poetry slam. The
event takes place on the last Monday of
every month, and is free to audience and
competitors.

Spoken Word Antics
The Red Deer, 18 Pitt Street, Sheffield
S1 4DD
tel (01142) 722890

An open mic without the mic, reliant on
the warmth of human technology. All
forms of spoken word are welcome.
Second Tuesday of the month (usually),
8.30pm.

STAMPS
3 Coronation Road, Crosby, Merseyside
tel 0151-525 0417
email brian@seftonarts.freeserve.co.uk
Contact Brian Wake

This special venue for poetry readings and
music has been active for more than 5
years. It has welcomed guests such as
Adrian Henri, Henry Graham, Levi Tafari,
Pete Morgan, Pete Finch, Richard Hill,
Janine Pinion, and David Bateman. Its
open mic slot has helped to introduce a
whole number of new writers to local
audiences, and is valued by a younger
generation of writers anxious to air their
work in a friendly but competitive
atmosphere.

Subtle Flame
Tiger Inn, Lairgate, Beverley, East
Yorkshire

tel (01262) 601398
email mloz21@hotmail.com
Contact Sue Lozynskyj

Performers produce a varied and balanced
programme of poems, stories and music.

The Tea House
5 Wright's Court, Elm Hill, Norwich,
Norfolk
email Sara@thepoetrycubicle.org.uk
website http://
www.thepoetrycubicle.org.uk

Monthly series of live poetry and music
events, with Norfolk's most innovative
and talented poets and musicians.

Ten Bells
74-78 St Benedicts Street, City Centre,
Norwich NR2
tel (01603) 667833

Open mic meets on the last Sunday of the
month at the Ten Bells pub in St Benedicts
Street, at 8.30pm.

Torriano World Poetry
99 Torriano Avenue, Kentish Town,
London NW5 2RX
tel 020-7281 2867
email philhenrypoole@yahoo.co.uk
Organiser Phil Poole

Meets every Friday.

Uncut Poets
Black Box, Media Centre, Exeter Phoenix,
Gandy Street, Exeter
mobile (07879) 888319
Contact James Bell

Thursdays, 7.30pm. Call to book an open
mic slot.

Vic's Cabaret Corner
The Windmill, Blenheim Gardens, Brixton
Hill, London SW2

email viclambrusco@hotmail.com
website www.urban75.org/brixton/
features/poets.html
Every second Thursday, 9pm.

Voice Box
Level 5, Royal Festival Hall, London
SE1 8XX
tel (08703) 804300

A performance space for readings at the
South Bank Centre.

Wirrall Ode Show
Stork Hotel, Price Street, Birkenhead
tel 015-1638 3648
email jasonrichards69@hotmail.com

Third Thursday each month – open floor
8.30-11pm.

The Writers' Café
Georgian Theatre, Green Dragon Yard,
Stockton-on-Tees, Cleveland TS18 1AT

tel (01642) 674115

One of the biggest and best performance
nights in the North East. The word is
spreading, and the Writers' Café is
growing fast along with a network of other
great performance venues.

The Writing Centre
Liverpool Hope University College,
Liverpool, Merseyside L16 9JD
tel 0151-291 3882
email hurleyu@hope.ac.uk
website www.hope.ac.uk
Contact Ursula Hurley

Has access to a variety of venues within
the Hope campus, including theatres and
conference rooms, in which it runs a
regular programme of poetry readings.
Would be pleased to consider any
suggestions for future events.

A poet's life

John Burnside

When I started writing poetry, I had no idea what I was doing. I was working in the computer industry, and poetry began for me out of a personal need, something I did to balance out my life – numbers and logic by day, words and the imagination by night (either by temperament, or because of time constraints, I usually found myself writing in the small hours). To begin with, I had no intention of publishing my efforts, I just wanted to see if I could write a poem that would satisfy me on my own rather generous terms. Later, though, as I got going, I started sending work out – and that was when the other questions, questions I had not anticipated, came to the fore.

At that point, the poetry I wrote, like the poetry I most admired, was rather unfashionable. I wrote about the world I saw around me and, since I lived at the edge of the suburbs, in a thin headland between town and woods (with the occasional sojourn in Gloucestershire farming country), I wrote a good deal about the sky, the weather, the land, trees, flora and fauna. It's definitely not a term I would use, but other people considered this 'nature poetry' and everybody knew, at the time, that nature poetry wasn't a serious pursuit. It's interesting to think how recently this view was held by intelligent people – and alarming to note that there are still those who think that if a bird flaps through a piece of verse, it's a piece of self-indulgent neo-romanticism, to be condemned as unworthy of enlightened critical attention.

Of course, the deeply unfashionable part is easy to admit: there is even cachet to be gained from being 'misunderstood'. The harder thing to admit is that my first efforts were nowhere near as good as they ought to have been. Sometimes, talking to younger poets, I recollect how many of my early poems I destroyed, more in sorrow than in anger or frustration, but there were many more that should have been cast into the fire. One tendency we have, starting out, is to read the current magazines, and the prize-winning poems, and all the rest, with the growing conviction that we could do better. Couple that with the aforementioned glow of being deeply unfashionable (and with the idea that everything that goes around comes around), and it is easy to settle into a groove of writing brilliant misunderstood poems that will, one day, find the audience they deserve (possibly in the unreal afterlife of posterity). I was working in isolation; I knew no other poets, or even poetry readers, and never went to a workshop, which meant that it was easy to sustain these romantic illusions for some time – until, that is, a (possibly inebriated) editor took some of my poems and I got to see them in print. That was when the romantic bubble burst, and I saw that I had been deceiving myself. I wasn't misunderstood, I was just incompetent.

Or perhaps just lazy. I hadn't taken my vocation seriously enough. In fact, I hadn't taken it seriously at all. All the time I had felt a misunderstood legend in my own living room, I had really just been a dilettante who didn't bother to do the work that any vocation – from poetry to mathematics to gardening – demands. I did not know my craft. I had a poor understanding of poetic traditions and, most important of all, I had no idea what it meant to make poetry. After that first set of publications, I stopped and examined what I was doing: how I made a poem, where and when I made it, and what I did to convince myself that it was finished. At the time, I wrote poetry after some vague model I had in my head from a desultory education in literature; I sat down with a sheet of paper, worked at it, revised, deliberated, stared out of the window. (I did a good deal of staring out of windows, in fact.) Yet this process was entirely unlike my self, unlike the way I operated in any other field. Outside (and sometimes inside) my workaday box, I was – and still am – an intuitive, spontaneous, wu-wei type. (Wu-wei is probably my one guiding principle: a principle that has been called "doing by not doing", though I would describe it as an unceasing vigilance aimed at allowing one's true nature to come forth, spontaneously [yes: it's a paradox].) Another angle on this might be to remember Robert Frost's view that the work of the poet is to avoid getting in the way of the poem.)

Now, over a period of weeks, I changed my working method. I began by destroying everything I wrote, no matter what I thought of it. I never sat down at a desk to write, and I stopped carrying my little notebook around or jotting down striking images that came to me as I went about my business. Whatever was not memorable enough to stay in my head was left by the wayside. I had read about a process that Osip Mandelstam called "writing on the lips"; a process that he had adopted; one that had served Dante, and many others; a process that keeps the poet in touch, both with the oral tradition from which s/he springs and with the song of the earth itself (the rhythm, one might say, of all that surrounds us: earth and sea and sky and living things). I adopted this same process ... and the results surprised me. I found myself writing poems I liked, I went outside my own expectations of poetry (for example, I began to write prose poems, and I didn't consider 'form' until it began to emerge in the poem itself). From that point onwards, I was on what I thought of as an unending journey, a lifelong discipline in making poems according to their own nature, without interference from 'me' (I say 'me', because by this I mean ego, the social self, the educated, deliberating, controlling person).

I hope it is obvious, however, that I am not advocating a freefall into self-expression here. Poetry is work – but it is work in the way that making a garden or being a parent is work: it is, in other words, work, not effort, the work of setting aside the preordained, the resigned, the easy, the conditioned, and allowing the real to emerge and live. The real, not the conditioned, response. A surrender, not a submission. The graceful, as opposed to the merely easy. This probably sounds mystical and, in some ways, it is, but the only advice I have for anybody starting out in this privileged discipline is that success is determined – not by the world, and not by one's own feeling of having expressed something, but by the poem itself. I would never advocate the garrety existence of the deeply misunderstood, unfashionable poet, but I would also say that nothing the world gives us – the published book, the award, the good review – is anything like the blessing of the poem itself, still warm and alive in the little grey cells and ready to be copied down on to the cool, white page. Marianne Moore, paraphrasing *The Baghavad Gita*, said: "If I do well I am blessed, whether anyone bless me or not." This is the true guide to success in poetry: the gut-feel, the intimation, the pure (and fleeting) blessing of the poem itself.

John Burnside has had a number of collections published, including the recent *Selected Poems* (Jonathan Cape). His memoir, *A Lie About My Father*, was published in 2006.

Getting seen
Poetry agents

Congratulations! If you are perusing this page you are, indeed, a rare bird – a poet in need of an agent! Most agents actively discourage submissions from poets: "No poetry" is written in bold capitals in many entries in *Writers' & Artists' Yearbook*. The list below includes a couple who would welcome submissions from poets, but mostly you are going to have to be very persuasive (or enjoy the surname Heaney) to be taken on by a mainstream literary agent. It is, of course, worth considering whether you do in fact require the services of an agent. Most poets do not.

A & B Personal Management Ltd
Suite 330, Linen Hall, 162-168 Regent Street, London W1B 5TD
tel 020-7434 4262 *fax* 020-7038 3699
email billellis@aandb.co.uk

Gillon Aitken Associates Ltd
18-21 Cavaye Place, London SW10 9PT
tel 020-7373 8672 *fax* 020-7373 6002
email reception@gillonaitken.co.uk
website www.gillonaitkenassociates.co.uk

Caroline Davidson Literary Agency
5 Queen Anne's Gardens, London W4 1TU
tel 020-8995 5768 *fax* 020-8994 2770
email cdla@ukgateway.net
website www.cdla.co.uk

Handles novels and non-fiction of high quality, including reference works (12.5%). Send preliminary letter with CV and detailed, well thought-out book proposal/synopsis and/or first 50pp of novel. Large sae with return postage essential. No reading fee. Quick response.

Authors include Andrew Dalby, Emma Donoghue, Cindy Engel, Chris Greenhalgh, Tom Jaine, Huon Mallalieu, Linda Sonntag, Caroline Williams. Founded 1988.

DGA Ltd
55 Monmouth Street, London WC2H 9DG

tel 020-7240 9992 *fax* 020-7395 6110
email assistant@davidgodwinassociates.co.uk
website www.davidgodwinassociates.co.uk
Directors David Godwin, Heather Godwin

Literary fiction and general non-fiction (home 15%, overseas 20%, film 15%). No reading fee; send sae for return of MSS. Founded 1995.

Robert Dudley Agency
8 Abbotstone Road, London SW15 1QR
tel 020-8788 0938 *mobile* (07879) 426574
fax 020-8780 3586
email rdudley@btinternet.com
Proprietor Robert Dudley

Specialises in history, biography, sport, management, politics, militaria, current affairs (home 15%, overseas 20%; film/TV/radio 15–20%). No reading fee. Will suggest revision. All material sent at owner's risk. No MSS returned without sae.

Authors include Steve Biko, Simon Caulkin, Peter Collins, Ali Dizaei, Jim Drury, Paul Gannon, Chris Green, Tim Guest, Mungo Melvin, Brian Holden Reid, Tim Phillips, Nick Rengger, Heather Reynolds, Michael Scott, Dan Wilson. Founded 2000.

Eddison Pearson Ltd
West Hill House, 6 Swains Lane, London N6 6QS

tel 020-7700 7763 *fax* 020-7700 7866
email info@eddisonpearson.com
Contact Clare Pearson

Children's books and scripts, literary fiction and non-fiction, poetry (home 10%, overseas 15–20%). No unsolicited MSS. Email for up-to-date submission guidelines by return, or enquire by letter enclosing brief writing sample and sae. No reading fee. May suggest revision where appropriate.

Authors include Valerie Bloom, Sue Heap, Sally Lloyd-Jones, Robert Muchamore, Ruth Symes.

Edwards Fuglewicz

49 Great Ormond Street, London WC1N 3HZ
tel 020-7405 6725 *fax* 020-7405 6726
Partners Ros Edwards, Helenka Fuglewicz

Literary and commercial fiction (but no children's fiction, science fiction, horror or fantasy); non-fiction: biography, history, popular culture (home 15%, USA/translation 20%). No unsolicited MSS or email submissions. No reading fee. Founded 1996.

Fox & Howard Literary Agency

4 Bramerton Street, London SW3 5JX
tel 020-7352 8691 *fax* 020-7352 8691
Partners Chelsey Fox, Charlotte Howard

General non-fiction: biography, history and popular culture, reference, business, mind, body & spirit, health and fitness (home 15%, overseas 20%). No reading fee, but preliminary letter and synopsis with sae essential for response. Founded 1992.

Barrie James Literary Agency

(including New Authors Showcase)
Rivendell, Kingsgate Close, Torquay, Devon TQ2 8QA
tel (01803) 326617
email mail@newauthors.org.uk
website www.newauthors.org.uk
Contact Barrie James

Internet site for new writers and poets to display their work to publishers. No unsolicited MSS. First contact: send sae or email. Founded 1997.

Lutyens & Rubinstein

231 Westbourne Park Road, London W11 1EB
tel 020-7792 4855 *fax* 020-7792 4833
email name@lutyensrubinstein.co.uk
Directors Sarah Lutyens, Felicity Rubinstein *Submissions* Susannah Godman

Fiction and non-fiction, commercial and literary (home 15%, overseas 20%). Send outline/2 sample chapters and sae. No reading fee. Founded 1993.

Duncan McAra

28 Beresford Gardens, Edinburgh EH5 3ES
tel 0131-552 1558 *fax* 0131-552 1558
email duncanmcara@hotmail.com

Consultancy on all aspects of general trade publishing; editing, re-writing, copy-editing and proof-correcting for publishers, financial companies, academic institutions and other organisations. Main subjects include art, architecture, archaeology, biography, military, Scottish and travel. Founded 1988.

Laura Morris Literary Agency

21 Highshore Road, London SE15 5AA
tel 020-7732 0153 *fax* 020-7732 9022
email laura.morris@btconnect.com
Director Laura Morris

Literary fiction, film studies, biography, media, cookery, culture/art, humour (home 10%, overseas 20%). No unsolicited MSS, no children's books.

Authors include Peter Cowie, Christobel Kent, Laurence Marks and Maurice Gran, the Barbara Pym Estate, David Thomson, John Travolta, Brian Turner, Janni Visman. Founded 1998.

David O'Leary Literary Agency

10 Lansdowne Court, Lansdowne Rise, London W11 2NR
tel/fax 020-7229 1623
email d.o'leary@virgin.net

Popular and literary fiction and non-fiction. Special interests: Ireland, history, popular science (Fees: home 10%, overseas 20%, performance rights 15%). No reading fee. Write, call or email before submitting MSS. Please enclose sae.

Authors include Alexander Cordell, Donald James, Nick Kochan, Jim Lusby, Derek Malcolm, Daniel O'Brien, Ken Russell. Founded 1988.

PVA Management Ltd

Hallow Park, Worcester WR2 6PG
tel (01905) 640663 *fax* (01905) 641842
email pva@pva.co.uk
Managing Director Paul Vaughan

Full-length MSS. Non-fiction only (home 15%, overseas 20%, performance rights 15%). Please send synopsis and sample chapters together with return postage.

Raft

9-10 Jew Street, Brighton BN1 1UT
tel (01273) 730070 *email* info@raftpr.com
website www.raftpr.com
Contact Adrian Weston

Currently looking for authors of narrative non-fiction, history, politics, current affairs, music, self-help, poetry and business projects. Raft also has a significant track record in event management and tour booking which enables it to work creatively with talent

from booking individual performances, and seasons through to whole tours whether spoken word, live music or drama.

Rogers, Coleridge & White Ltd

20 Powis Mews, London W11 1JN
tel 020-7221 3717 *fax* 020-7229 9084
Managing Director Peter Straus, *Directors* Deborah Rogers, Gill Coleridge, Patricia White (USA, children's), David Miller, Laurence Laluyaux, Stephen Edwards, Zoe Waldie

Anthony Sheil in association with Gillon Aitken Associates

18–21 Cavaye Place, London SW10 9PT
tel 020-7373 8672 *fax* 020-7373 6002
email anthony@gillonaitken.co.uk
website www.gillonaitkenassociates.co.uk
Proprietor Anthony Sheil

Quality fiction and non-fiction (home 10%, overseas 20%). No reading fee.

Authors include Caroline Alexander, John Banville, Josephine Cox, John Fowles, John Keegan, Robert Wilson.

Sheil Land Associates Ltd

(incorporating Richard Scott Simon Ltd 1971 and Christy & Moore Ltd 1912)
52 Doughty Street, London WC1N 2LS
tel 020-7405 9351 *fax* 020-7831 2127
email info@sheilland.co.uk
Agents UK & US Sonia Land, Vivien Green, Ben Mason, *Film/theatre/TV* Sophie Janson, Emily Hayward, *Foreign* Gaia Banks

Quality literary and commercial fiction and non-fiction, including: politics, history, military history, gardening, thrillers, crime, romance, drama, biography, travel, cookery, humour, UK and foreign estates (home 15%, USA/translation 20%). Also theatre, film, radio and TV scripts. Welcomes approaches from new clients either to start or to develop their careers. Preliminary letter with sae essential. No reading fee. Overseas associates: Georges Borchardt, Inc. (Richard Scott Simon). US film and TV representation: CAA, APA and others.

Clients include Peter Ackroyd, Pam Ayres, Hugh Bicheno, Melvyn Bragg, Steven Carroll, David Cohen, Anna del Conte, Elizabeth Corley, Seamus Deane, Robert Green, Bonnie Greer, Susan Hill, Richard Holmes, HRH The Prince of Wales, Mark Irving, Ian Johnstone, Simon Kernick, Richard Mabey, Michael Moorcock, Graham Rice, Steve Rider, Martin Riley, Diane Setterfield, Tom Sharpe, Martin Stephen, Jeffrey Tayler, Andrew Taylor, Rose Tremain, Barry Unsworth, Kevin Wells, Prof. Stanley Wells, John Wilsher, Paul Wilson, Chris Woodhead and the Estates of Catherine Cookson, Patrick O'Brian and Jean Rhys. Founded 1962.

Sinclair-Stevenson

3 South Terrace, London SW7 2TB
tel 020-7581 2550 *fax* 020-7581 2550
Directors Christopher Sinclair-Stevenson, Deborah Sinclair-Stevenson

Full-length MSS (home 10%, USA/ translation 20%). General – no children's books. No reading fee; will suggest a revision. Founded 1995.

Jonathan Williams Literary Agency

Rosney Mews, Upper Glenageary Road, Glenageary, Co. Dublin, Republic of Ireland
tel (01) 2803482 *fax* (01) 2803482 *Director* Jonathan Williams

General fiction and non-fiction, preferably by Irish authors (home 10%). Will suggest revision; no reading fee unless a very fast decision is required. Return postage appreciated (no British stamps – please use IRCs). Sub-agents in Holland, Italy, France, Spain, Japan. Founded 1981.

Parapoetry

While you are waiting for that first slim volume to be published, how do you get close to the poetry world? **Julia Bird** calls herself a *parapoet*, working in many areas of poetry.

Sometimes, when I describe my job to people, I call myself a 'parapoet'. Before they get carried away with the idea of someone covered in camouflage paint delivering yomping quatrains about the glories of war, I explain that it's akin to 'paramedic', or 'paralegal'. While I do write myself, the living I make from poetry is not as a writer. As an administrator, I work alongside poets and support their writing and performance.

That first slim volume of our own: an untoppable writerly thrill. But while we're all waiting for that to happen, this parapoetry can strengthen our involvement with the art, while keeping us from bug-eyed obsession about publication prospects. Full-time career or weekend passion? It can be both.

So, where to start? Submitting your own work to poetry magazines is a recognised first step towards formal publication. But setting up your *own* magazine gives you additional poetry-related editorial, design, typesetting, sales and distribution experience. Poetry mags flutter in and out of existence all the time: visit www.poetrylibrary.org.uk/magazines or www.poetrymagazines.org.uk: or study the Magazines section of this Yearbook to find and plug the current gap in the market with your own tone, style and content. If the Photoshop & Quark / Letraset & Tippex approaches don't appeal, try a web or e-zine. Actual or virtual, launch each issue with a reading of featured poets and a knees-up for your existing and potential subscribers. While vanity publishing probably won't do much for either your poetic career or your mortal soul, self-publishing is a very different enterprise. Avoiding the photocopier and the clip-art, it doesn't cost that much to edit, set and print a decent-looking short-run poetry pamphlet. Sell it at readings; distribute it generously to other publishers and poetry advocates to promote yourself as a writer. Self-published pamphlets are currently also eligible for the Poetry Book Society's quarterly Pamphlet Choice scheme – see www.poetrybooks.co.uk for details.

If publishing your own work gives you a taste for the world of font, stock and end-papers, consider establishing your own small press, where you'll enjoy creative freedom over every aspect of book production and marketing. Publishing needn't involve whole books or pamphlets – for example, the Poetry Cubicle offers a platform for writers in Norwich by publishing one poem at a time (www.thepoetrycubicle.org.uk). Look at Lollipop (List of Little Press Publications – www.indigogroup.co.uk/llpp/) for more small-press inspiration.

Develop your own poetry performance skills. You don't have to be an actor or a stand-up comedian to hold a crowd, but audiences expect more than an unprepared set from a mumbler with a mic. Pick up hints from poets whose readings you rate (or don't!). Try out a couple of poems at open mic slots; get to know the event promoters and introduce them to your written and spoken work; and build up to performances where your name is on the bill. *Poetry London* and *Mslexia* magazines both have excellent (national) listings pages with ideas of where you might read.

Setting up your own events or series of readings calls for production and promotion skills – and a certain ringmasterly panache if you want to compere the events yourself. If you live in a place where there is lots of competition from existing poetry events, invent a way of presenting writers and readers that stands out in the listings pages. I've heard of poetry pub quizzes, poetry curry banquets, poetry cabarets – even speed-poetry, a literary equivalent of speed-dating (www.20six.co.uk/shortfuse). A few years ago, the Poetry Society commissioned a promoters' tool kit – there are still some good tips here: www.newaudiences2.org.uk/downloads/poetrytoolkit.pdf. But if there is one golden guarantee of a successful night, it's keeping it short. Attending to poetry demands an intense attention – and more than an hour and a half of it (including the interval) is exhausting. I have worked in poetry and literature development for the last ten years, involved with author tours, writers' residencies, literature festivals, poets' commissions and general organisational support. This last decade has seen a real clarification in the purpose of the individuals and organisations who work in the profession, so if your creative interest in poetry and literature is complemented by promotional, administrative and management skills, there is an increasing range of jobs open to you. Your first stop for advice, contacts, case studies, skill sharing and job adverts should be NALD – the National Association for Literature Development (www.nald.org.uk). A support and advocacy organisation, NALD is the professional body for all involved in developing writers, readers and literature audiences. The National Association of Writers in Education (www.nawe.co.uk) features the Literature Training Bulletin on its website, another excellent source of information about jobs, courses, training and conferences. Subscribe to the Arts Council's ArtsJobs e-mailing list (via www.artscouncil.org.uk) for a wealth of opportunities, especially part-time and short contract work.

You may have heard the grumble that the poetry world is impenetrable, too tightly controlled – some would say policed – and that the circles of publishing, reviewing, mentoring and prize-giving overlap way too closely. Perhaps that's a valid complaint – but in the last ten years I have seen small presses, magazines, new promoters and performers spring from nowhere to prominent positions in that world. You may want to be part of this establishment or you may want to knock the helmets off the poetry police, but enthused, imaginative people and groups of like-minded individuals can find a public platform for their ideas.

Life as a parapoet lets you experience ideas and writing you might not otherwise have encountered. If, after publishing your own magazine, setting up your own small press and running your own month-long haiku festival, you still yearn to see your own name in print, exposure to these good, bad and frankly bananas ideas will only have had a positive effect on your own writing and its promotion.

Julia Bird worked for the Poetry Book Society for eight years. She now works for the Poetry School and as a freelance live literature producer and promoter.

Competitions and awards

There are literally hundreds of poetry competitions in this country alone. Prizes range from publication to hundreds or even thousands of pounds. We cannot hope to cover them all, but this section gives a good representation of what is available. Funding opportunities are also listed.

Aber Valley Arts Festival Annual Literature Competitions

Undercurrents – Aber Valley, 15 Graig y Fedw, Abertridwr, Caerffili CF83 4AQ
tel 029-2083 1668
email eryl893107392@aol.com
website www.academi.org
Prizes 1st prize, £50; 2nd prize, £30; 3rd prize, £15

Usually on a theme.
   Submission details Maximum length, 60 lines.

Academi Poetry Competition

The Welsh Academy, Mount Stuart House, Mount Stuart Square, Cardiff CF10 5YA
tel 029-2047 2266 *fax* 029-2049 2930
email post@acdemi.org
website www.academi.org
Contact Peter Finch
Prizes 1st prize, £5000; 2nd prize, £1000; 3rd prize, £700

An annual competition, offering one of the largest money prizes for a competition of its kind. Judged on poems of any style and on any subject.
   Submission details Poems must be in English and can be submitted by writers of any nationality and from any country. They should be no more than 50 lines in length and typed, printed or clearly written on one side of the paper only. No covering letter or other material should be enclosed with an entry. Any number of poems may be submitted. See website for details and to obtain entry form. Entry fee, £5 per poem.

The Annual British Haiku Society Haibun Anthology

38 Wayside Avenue, Hornchurch, Essex RM12 4LL
website www.britishhaikusociety.org
Contact Dr Doreen King

Specialises in haiku and related poetry. There are usually 2 prizes a year and an award with each issue of the quarterly journal.
   Submission details Entry details can be found on the website.

Arts Council England

The Literature Dept, Arts Council England, 14 Great Peter Street, London SW1P 3NQ
tel 0845-300 6200 *textphone* 020-7973 6564
fax 020-7973 6590
email enquiries@artscouncil.org.uk
website www.artscouncil.org.uk

Arts Council England presents national prizes rewarding creative talent in the arts. These are awarded through the Council's flexible funds and are not necessarily open to application: the Children's Award, the David Cohen Prize for Literature, the *Independent* Foreign Fiction Prize, John Whiting Award, Meyer Whitworth Award and the Raymond Williams Community Publishing Prize.

Arts Council England, London

David Cross, Literature Administrator, Arts Council England, London, 2 Pear Tree Court, London EC1R 0DS
tel 020-7608 6184 *fax* 020-7608 4100
website www.artscouncil.org.uk

Arts Council England, London, is the regional office for the Capital, covering 33 boroughs and the City of London. Grants are available through the 'Grants for the arts' scheme throughout the year to support a variety of literature projects, concentrating particularly on:
• original works of poetry and literary fiction and professional development for individual writers, including writers of children's books;
• touring and live literature;
• small independent literary publishers; and
• literary translation into English.

Contact the Literature Unit for more information, or see website for an application form.

The Arts Council/An Chomhairle Ealaíon

Details 70 Merrion Square, Dublin 2, Republic of Ireland
tel (01) 618 0200 *fax* (01) 676 1302
email artistsservices@artscouncil.ie
website www.artscouncil.ie

Publishes a guide for individuals and organisations to Arts Council bursaries, awards and schemes. It is also available online. This guide is called *Supports for Artists*.

Arvon Foundation International Poetry Competition

The Arvon Foundation, 42a Buckingham Palace Road, London SW1W 0RE
tel 020-7931 7611
email london@arvonfoundation.org
website www.arvonfoundation.org
Prizes £10,000

A prestigious biennial competition (next in 2008). Andrew Motion, Poet Laureate, was the first winner of the prize in 1980.
   Submission details Entry fee, £7 for first poem; £5 thereafter. No line or word limit,

no restrictions on theme.See website for entry form.

Asla Open Poetry Competition

Searle Publications Ltd, PO Box 52, Welshpool, Powys SY21 8WQ
tel (01743) 260960
email asla@searlepublications.com
website www.searlepublications.com
Contact Lydia Searle
Prizes £250

Quarterly competitions on varying topics. See entry form at entries@searlepublications.com. Telephone for details: (01938) 554695.

The Authors' Foundation

The Society of Authors, 84 Drayton Gardens, London SW10 9SB
tel 020-7373 6642
email info@societyofauthors.org
website www.societyofauthors.org

Grants are available to novelists, poets and writers of non-fiction who are published authors working on their next book. The aim is to provide funding (in addition to a proper advance) for research, travel or other necessary expenditure. Closing dates: 30th April and 30th September. Send sae for an information sheet. Founded in 1984 to mark the centenary of the Society of Authors.

Award (Formerly the Haiku Award)

1 Lambolle Place, Belsize Park, London NW3 4PD
website www.into.demon.co.uk

Biannual competition for free-form and conventional haiku (5-7-5) and tanka (5-7-5-7-7).
   Submission details Entry fee, £2 per haiku or tanka, or £10 for a set of 6. For more information and entry forms visit the website, or write to above address.

Closing date, 31st March and 30th September annually.

Bardd Plant Cymru (Children's Poet Laureate)

Welsh Books Council, Castell Brychan, Aberystwyth, Ceredigion SY23 2JB
tel (01970) 624151 *fax* (01970) 625385
website www.cllc.org.uk

A venture established by Planed Plant, S4C, the Welsh Books Council and Urdd Gobaith Cymru, and recently the Academi to raise the profile of poetry among children, and to encourage them to compose and enjoy poetry.

BBC Wildlife Magazine Poet of the Year Awards

Origin Publishing Ltd, 14th Floor, Tower House, Fairfax Street, Bristol BS1 3BN
tel 0117-927 9009 *fax* 0117-934 9008
email sophiestafford@
originpublishing.co.uk
website www.bbcwildlifemagazine.com
Contact Sophie Stafford
Prizes 1st prize, publication in *BBC Wildlife Magazine*, possible broadcast on BBC Radio 4's 'Poetry Please' programme and a wildlife weekend in the UK; runners-up, publication in *BBC Wildlife Magazine*, possible broadcast on BBC Radio 4's 'Poetry Please' programme, and poetry books

Poems must be about the natural world and/or our relationship with it (no domestic plants or animals, please). Don't feel you have to write about 'big issues' – start with your own 'lived experience' and call upon your senses to create fresh images.

Submission details Poems can take any form, in rhyme, free or blank verse but must be no longer than 50 lines. Names must not be on entries.

Bedford Open Poetry Competition

38 Verne Drive, Ampthill, Bedford MK45 2PS
email achisholm@britishlibary.net
website www.interpretershouse.org.uk
Contact Anne Chisholm
Prizes 1st prize, £300; 2 x 2nd prizes, £100 each; 3rd prize (Bedfordshire only), £50

Poems on any subject.

Submission details Submit poems up to 40 lines in length. Entry form from the above address or via the website.

Belmont Poetry Prize

Belmont Arts Centre, 5 Belmont, Shrewesbury SY1 1TE
tel (01743) 243755
email admin@belmontartscentre.org.uk
website www.belmontartscentre.org.uk
Contact Neil Rathmell
Prizes £500

The only national competition for poets writing for children. The final judging is based on votes cast by children in primary schools. The winner is announced on National Poetry Day.

Submission details Only open to poems written for children. Maximum of 40 lines in length. Entry fee £3.

Blinking Eye Publishing Competition

Blinking Eye Publishing, PO Box 549, North Shields, Tyne & Wear NE30 2WT
tel 0191-257 3778
email Jeanne@millview77.freeserve.co.uk
website www.blinking-eye.co.uk
Contact Jeanne MacDonald
Prizes Publication of overall winner's collection and 100 copies given to the winner. Entry into anthology of commended poets

Annual competition for poets over 50 years of age. Closing date, 7th August.

Submission details Entry fee: £10 for 10 poems; £5 for 5 poems.

Bluechrome Award for Poetry

PO Box 109, Portishead, Bristol BS20 7ZJ
tel (07092) 273360
email submissions@ bluechrome.co.uk
website www.bluechrome.co.uk
Contact Anthony Delgrado

Annual competition. See website for details.

The Bridport Prize

Bridport Arts Centre, South Street, Bridport, Dorset DT6 3NR
tel (01308) 485064 *fax* (01308) 485120
email frances@bridportprize.org.uk
website www.bridportprize.org.uk
Contact Frances Everitt
Prizes 1st prize, £5000; 2nd prize, £1000; 3rd prize, £500

Annual prizes are awarded for poetry and short stories. Winning stories are read by a leading London literary agent, without obligation, and an anthology of winning entries is published each autumn.

Submission details Entries should be in English, original work, typed or clearly written, and never published, read on radio/TV/stage. Send sae for entry form or enter online. Closing date: 30th June each year.

The Callum Macdonald Memorial Award

The Callum Macdonald Memorial Fund, National Library of Scotland, George IV Bridge Building, Edinburgh EH1 1EW
website www.nls.uk
Contact The Administrator
Prizes The Callum Macdonald Quaich and a cash prize of £500.

This Award has been created to recognise publishing skill and effort; to validate the practice of poetry publication in pamphlet form; and to encourage the preservation of printed material of this kind in the national collections. It has been created in memory of Callum Macdonald MBE, Scottish literary publisher and founder of Macdonald Publishers and Printers.

Submission details Publishers of Scottish origin, living in Scotland, or engaged with Scottish culture may submit up to 3 pamphlets, which should not be less than 6 pages or more than 30 in length. The original print run will not exceed 300 copies. It is also acceptable for pamphlets to be published by poets themselves.

Cambridge Writers Open Poetry Competition

39 West Street, Over, Cambridgeshire CB4 5PL
email helenculnane@tiscali.co.uk
website www.hphoward.demon.co.uk/campoetry/
Competition Secretary Helen Culnane
Prizes 1st prize, £100; 2nd prize, £60; 3rd prize, £30

Competition for poems in any style and on any theme.

Submission details Poems should not exceed 40 lines in length. Entries should not previously have been published in print. Website publishing is acceptable. Entry fee, £2 per poem. Members of Cambridge Writers are entitled to 3 free entries, but in all other respects are bound by the rules of this competition. Closing date, 30th.

Cardiff International Poetry Competition

Academi, PO Box 438, Cardiff CF10 5YA
tel 029-2047 2266 *fax* 029-2047 0691
email post@academi.org
website www.academi.org
CEO Peter Finch
Prizes 1st prize, £5000; 2nd prize, £750; 3rd Prize, £250

Annual competition, open to all.
Submission details 50 lines maximum on

any subject. Postal submissions only. Must be accompanied by entry form. £5 entry fee per poem.

Carillon Magazine Poetry Competitions.

19 Godric Drive, Brinsworth, Rotherham, South Yorkshire S60 5AN
website www.carillonmag.org.uk
Contact Graham Rippon
Prizes 1st prize, £80; 2nd prize, £40; 3 additonal prizes of £20. Plus an annual subscription to *Carillon*
  Submission details Poetry should be 15-20 lines. No email entries. No entry form required – include a cover sheet with contact details and titles of all entries. Entry fee, £3 first entry; £1 each additional entry.

Cholmondeley Awards

Awards Secretary, The Society of Authors, 84 Drayton Gardens, London SW10 9SB
tel 020-7373 6642
email info@societyofauthors.org
website www.societyofauthors.org

These honorary awards are to recognise the achievement and distinction of individual poets. Submissions are not accepted. Total value of awards about £8000. Established by the then Dowager Marchioness of Cholmondeley in 1965.

Christopher Tower Poetry Competition

Christ Church, Oxford OX1 1DP
tel (01865) 286591
email info@tpwerpoetry.org.uk
website wwwtowerpoetry.org.uk
Contact Lesley Bankes-Hughes
Prizes 1st prize, £3000; 2nd prize, £1000; 3rd prize, £500; Highly Commended prizes, £200
  Submission details Submissions must be no longer than 48 lines on a set theme. 1 entry per person. Email submissions are not accepted.

Cinnamon Press Poetry Collection Award

Meirion House, Glan yr afon, Tanygrisiau, Blaenau Ffestiniog, Gwynedd LL41 3SU
email jan@cinnamonpress.com
website www.cinnamonpress.com
Prizes The winning author will have his/her poetry collection published with Cinnamon Press and receive a commissioning fee of £100. The runners-up and best short-listed poetry will be included in a winners' anthology and receive a complimentary copy (in addition to the copy sent to all entrants)
  Submission details Entry fee, £16. Closing date, 30th June.

CLPE Prize for Poetry

CLPE (Centre for Literacy in Primary Education), Webber Street, London SE1 8QW
tel 020-7401 3382/3 *fax* 020-7928 4624
email info@clpe.co.uk
website www.clpe.co.uk
Contact Ann Lazim (ann@clpe.co.uk)

Annual prize presented in June, for a book of poetry for children or young people first published in the UK or Republic of Ireland during the previous year.
  Submission details Send books to Ann Lazim at the above address.

The Duff Cooper Prize

Details Artemis Cooper, 54 St Maur Road, London SW6 4DP
tel 020-7736 3729 *fax* 020-7731 7638

An annual prize for a literary work in the field of biography, history, politics or poetry published in English or French and submitted by a recognised publisher during the previous 12 months. The prize of £4000 comes from a Trust Fund established by the friends and admirers of Duff Cooper, 1st Viscount Norwich (1890–1954) after his death.

Corneliu Popescu Prize for European Poetry Translation

Translation Prize, The Poetry Society, 22 Betterton Street, London WC2H 9BX
tel 020-7420 9880 *fax* 020-7240 4818
email competition@poetrysociety.org.uk
website www.poetrysociety.org.uk
Prizes £1500

Awarded every 2 years, and open to collections which feature poetry translated from a European language into English. It is named after Corneliu M Popescu, translator of the work of one of Romania's leading poets, Mihai Eminescu, into English. Popescu was tragically killed in the violent earthquake of 4th March 1977, aged 19.

Costa Book Awards

(formerly the Whitbread Book Awards)
The Booksellers Association, Minster House, 272 Vauxhall Bridge Road, London SW1V 1BA
tel 020-7802 0801 *fax* 020-7802 0803
email anna.okane@booksellers.org.uk
website www.costabookawards.co.uk
Contact Anna O'Kane

The awards celebrate and promote the most enjoyable contemporary British writing. Judged in 2 stages and offering a total of £50,000 prize money, there are 5 categories: Novel, First Novel, Biography, Poetry and Children's. They are judged by a panel of 3 judges and the winner in each category receives £5000. 9 final judges then choose the Costa Book of the Year from the 5 category winners. The overall winner receives £25,000. Writers must be resident in Great Britain or Ireland for 3 or more years. Submissions must be received from publishers. Closing date: end of June.

Creating Reality Poetry Competition

8a Womersley Road, London N8 9AE
email mail@creatingreality.co.uk

website www.creatingreality.co.uk
Contact Milly Chapman
Prizes Poetry £1000, £250, £100; Haiku £150, £50, £25; Flash £300, £100, £50

A non-profit-making collective of writers and artists running competitions and providing small bursaries and services, drastically reduced in price for writers and artists.

Submission details See website for up-to-date information on all competitions, as guidelines, dates and prizes may vary from year to year.

Davidian Open Poetry Competition

Norfolk Poets and Writers, 9 Walnut Close, Norwich NR8 6YN
email tipsforwriters@yahoo.co.uk
Contact Wendy Webb

Annual competition to promote poetry in the Davidian form.

Submission details See entry form for length and theme. Entry fee, £2 (5 for £10). Closing date, 7th December.

The Rhys Davies Trust

Details Prof Meic Stephens, The Secretary, The Rhys Davies Trust, 10 Heol Don, Whitchurch, Cardiff CF14 2AU
tel 029-2062 3359 *fax* 029-2052 9202 The Trust aims to foster Welsh writing in English and offers financial assistance to English-language literary projects in Wales, directly or in association with other bodies.

Geoffrey Dearmer Prize

Poetry Society, 22 Betterton Street, London WC2H 9BX
tel 020-7420 9880
email poetryreview@ poetrysociety.org.uk
website www.poetrysociety.org.uk

An annual prize, established in 1997, for the Poetry Review 'new poet of the year' who has not yet published a book.

The City of Derby Short Story and Poetry Competition

PO Pox 7065, Derby DE1 OAD
tel (01332) 725362
email info@
cityofderbywritingcompetition.org.uk
website
www.cityofderbywritingcompetition.
org.uk

Competition for poetry on any theme.
Submission details Maximum of 40 lines.

John Dryden Translation Competition

School of Literature and Creative Writing, University of East Anglia, Norwich NR4 7TJ
tel (01603) 593360
email transcomp@uea.ac.uk
website www.bcla.org
Contact Dr Jean Boase-Beier

Annual competition for translations (prose and drama as well as poetry) from any language into English.
Submission details Entry fee, £5. Up to 25 pages translated into English.Closing date, mid-February.

Earlyworks High Fantasy Challenge

PO Box 258, Hastings TN34 9BB
email earlyworks@tiscali.co.uk
website www.earlyworkspress.co.uk
Contact K Green
Prizes Cash prizes and publication for top 30 entries

Genre poems and stories.
Submission details Closing date, June 30th. Entry fee, £2.50 per poem. Send sae for details, or email.

Envoi International Poetry Competition

44 Rudyard Road, Biddulph Moor, Stoke-on-Trent ST8 7JN
tel (01782) 517892

Prizes 1st prize, £150; 2nd prize, £100; 3rd prize, £50, plus 3 annual subscriptions
Submission details Work must be unpublished and not entered into other competitions. Poems must be 40 lines maximum length.
Name and address on a separate sheet. Send sae. Entry fee, £3 per poem and 5 for £12.

Essex Poetry Festival Open Poetry Competition

website www.essex-poetry-festival
Prizes 1st prize, £500; 2nd prize, £200; 3rd prize, £100; 3 runner-up prizes of £10 book tokens. Winners & runners-up will be invited to read their winning poems at the festival. Winning poems will be published on the website
Submission details For further details, rules and entry form, visit website. Closing date, 31st August.

European Jewish Publication Society Grants

PO Box 19948, London N3 3ZL
tel 020-8346 1668
email cs@ejps.org.uk
website www.ejps.org.uk
Contact Dr Colin Schindler

A charity, which was founded in 1995 and has since assisted in the publication of many books of Jewish interest, including poetry.

Christopher Ewart-Biggs Memorial Prize

The Secretary, Memorial Prize, Flat 3, 149 Hamilton Terrace, London NW8 9QS

This prize of £5000 is awarded once every 2 years to the writer, of any nationality, whose work is judged to contribute most to:
• peace and understanding in Ireland;

• closer ties between the peoples of Britain and Ireland;
• cooperation between the partners of the European Union.

Eligible works must be published during the 2 years to 31st December 2006. Closing date, 15 January 2007.

The Geoffrey Faber Memorial Prize

Faber & Faber, 3 Queen Square, London WC1N 3AU
tel 020-7465 0045 *fax* 020-7465 0034
website www.faber.co.uk

An annual prize of £1000 is awarded in alternate years for a volume of verse and for a volume of prose fiction, first published originally in the UK during the 2 years preceding the year in which the award is given which is, in the opinion of the judges, of the greatest literary merit. Eligible writers must be not more than 40 years old at the date of publication of the book and a citizen of the UK and Colonies, of any other Commonwealth state or of the Republic of Ireland. The 3 judges are reviewers of poetry or fiction who are nominated each year by the literary editors of newspapers and magazines which regularly publish such reviews. Faber and Faber invite nominations from reviewers and literary editors. No submissions for the prize are to be made. Established in 1963 by Faber and Faber Ltd, as a memorial to the founder and first Chairman of the firm.

First Thursday International Poetry Competition

36 Hilbre Court, West Kirby, Wirral CH48 3JU
Contact Peggy Poole
Prizes £500, £250, £125
   Submission details Entry fee, £3. Maximum length, 40 lines. Closing date, June 30th.

firstwriter.com Poetry Competitions

website www.firstwriter.com
Prizes Publication

Has at least 1 poetry competition running at all times.
   Submission details Entry fee, £5.

Forward Prizes For Poetry

Details Forward Poetry Prize Administrator, Colman Getty PR, 28 Windmill Street, London W1T 2JJ
tel 020-7631 2666 *fax* 020-7631 2699
email pr@colmangettypr.co.uk

3 prizes are awarded annually:
• The Forward Prize for best collection of poetry published between 1st October and 30th September (£10,000);
• The Felix Dennis Prize for best first collection of poetry published between 1st October and 30th September (£5000); and
• The Forward Prize for best single poem in memory of Michael Donaghy, published but not as part of a collection between 1st May and 30th April (£1000).
   Submission details All poems entered are also considered for inclusion in the *Forward Book of Poetry*, an annual anthology. Entries must be submitted by book publishers and editors of newspapers, periodicals and magazines in the UK and Eire. Entries from individual poets of their unpublished or self-published work will not be accepted. Established 1992.

Foyle Young Poets Award

Poetry Society, 22 Betterton Street, London WC2H 9BX
tel 020-7420 9892
email fyp@poetrysociety.org.uk
website www.poetrysociety.org.uk
Prizes Include books, posters, membership of the Poetry Society, visits to schools by a leading poet and, for the 15 overall winners, a week-long residential course at

the prestigious Arvon Centre in Lumb Bank, as well as publication in the annual anthology

Britain's most prestigious poetry prize for young writers between the ages of 11 and 17. The closing date each year is 31st July.

The Frogmore Poetry Prize

42 Morehall Avenue, Folkestone, Kent CT19 4EF
mobile (07751) 251689
website www.frogmorepress.co.uk
Prizes 200 guineas plus a subscription to *The Frogmore Papers*

The prize was founded in 1987; previous winners include Ann Alexander, Tobias Hill and Mario Petrucci. Unpublished poetry only.

Submission details 40 lines maximum. Name and address on a separate sheet. Entry fee, £2 per poem.

The Eric Gregory Trust Fund

Awards Secretary, The Society of Authors, 84 Drayton Gardens, London SW10 9SB
tel 020-7373 6642
email info@societyofauthors.org
website www.societyofauthors.org

A number of substantial awards are made annually for the encouragement of young poets who can show that they are likely to benefit from an opportunity to give more time to writing. An eligible candidate must:
• be a British subject by birth, but not a national of Eire or any of the British dominions or colonies, and be ordinarily resident in the UK or Northern Ireland;
• be under the age of 30 on 31st March in the year of the Award (i.e. the year following submission). Send sae for entry form. Closing date, 31st October.

Griffin Poetry Prize

The Griffin Trust for Excellence in Poetry, 6610 Edwards Boulevard, Mississauga, Ontario L5T 2V6, Canada

tel 905-565 5993 *fax* 905-564 3645
website www.griffinpoetryprize.com

2 annual prizes of Can.$50,000 awarded for collections of poetry published in English during the preceding year. One prize to a living Canadian poet, the other to a living poet from any country. Collections of poetry translated into English from other languages are also eligible and will be assessed for their literary quality in English. Submissions only from publishers. Closing date: 31st December. Founded 2000.

The James W Hackett Annual International Award for Haiku

38 Wayside Avenue, Hornchurch, Essex RM12 4LL
website www.haikusoc.ndo.co.uk
Prizes 2 x prizes of £70 and a year's free subscription to The British Haiku Society. Winning and commended haiku will be published in Volume 17 no. 2 of *Blithe Spirit,* and on the BHS website

Administered by the British Haiku Society, this contest was instituted in 1990, using an initial donation from James W Hackett, a well-known pioneer in the field of haiku writing. It has been held annually ever since, with James W Hackett himself choosing the winners.

Submission details Haiku must be original, in English, not previously published nor under consideration for publication or entered in any other competition. Closing date, 30th November 2006.

Haiku Calendar Competition

Snapshot Press, PO Box 132, Waterloo, Liverpool L22 8WZ
email info@snapshotpress.co.uk
website www.snapshotpress.co.uk
Contact John Barlow
Prizes £360 total prize money

The Haiku Calendar Competition has been held annually since 1999. As a result of the contest, 52 haiku are published each year in *The Haiku Calendar*.

Submission details Collections should comprise 50-100 haiku. Poems may have been previously published in magazines, journals or anthologies, but must not have appeared in an individual collection. Any number of manuscripts may be entered, provided each is accompanied by the entry fee. Entry fee, £20 per manuscript.

Haiku Presence Award

90d Fishergate Hill, Preston PR1 8JD
website http://freespace.virgin.net/
haiku.presence
Contact Martin Lucas
Prizes 1st prize, £100; 4 x 2nd prizes, £25 each

An annual competition.

Submission details Send 2 copies of each haiku, adding your name and address to 1 copy. For full details, see website or send an sae to the above address. Closing date, 31st October. Entry fee, £5 for up to 5 haiku; additional haiku £1 each.

Hastings International Poetry Competition

'The Snoring Cat', 194 Downs Road, Hastings, East Sussex TN34 2DZ
Contact Josephine Austin
Prizes 1st prize, £150; 2nd prize, £75; 3rd prize, £50; winners published in *First Time*
Submission details Entry fee, £2. Closing date, 21st October.

Hawthornden Fellowships

The Administrator, International Retreat for Writers, Hawthornden Castle, Lasswade, Midlothian EH18 1EG
tel 013-1440 2180 *fax* 013-1440 1989

Applications are invited from novelists, poets, dramatists and other creative writers whose work has already been published by reputable or recognised presses. Four-week fellowships are offered to those working on a current project. Translators may also apply. Application forms are available from March for Fellowships awarded in the following year.

The Hawthornden Prize

The Administrator, 42a Hays Mews, Berkeley Square, London W1J 5QA

This prize is awarded annually to the author of what, in the opinion of the Committee, is the best work of imaginative literature published during the preceding calendar year by a British author. Books do not have to be specially submitted.

The Felicia Henmans Prize for Lyrical Poetry

The Sub-Dean, Faculty of Arts, The University of Liverpool, Foundation Building, Brownlow Hill, Liverpool L69 7ZX
tel 0151-794 2458
email wildere@lv.ac.uk
Contact The Sub-Dean

An annual prize open to past and present members and students of the University of Liverpool only. It is awarded for a lyrical poem, on any subject.

Submission details Only 1 poem may be submitted, either published or unpublished. The prize will not be awarded more than once to the same competitor. Poems, endorsed 'Henmans Prize', must be submitted by 1st May.

Ilkley Literature Festival Annual Poetry and Short Story Competition

Manor House, 2 Castle Hill, Ilkley LS29 9DT
website www.ilkleyliteraturefestival.org.uk/
competitions.html

Prizes Arvon Foundation Poetry Course
Poems of any length on any subject. See
website for details.

Ilkley Literature Festival Children's and Young People's Poetry Competition

Manor House, 2 Castle Hill, Ilkley LS29
9DT
website www.ilkleyliteraturefestival.org.uk/
competitions.html

A competition for schools and individual
children. Three age-groups – see website
for details.

Indigo Dreams Press Poetry Awards

The Manacles, Predannack, The Lizard,
Cornwall TR12 7AU
email ronnie.g@indigodreams.plus.com
website www.indigodreamspress.co.uk/
competition.html
Contact ronnie.g@indigodreams.plus.com
Prizes 1st prize, £100; 2nd prize, £75; 3rd
prize, £25

Any length, any style.
Submission details Entry fee, £3 per
single poem; £5 per 3 poems; £9 per 5
poems.

The International Poetry Mart Ongoing Competition

51 Leeds Road, Mirfield, West Yorkshire
WF14 OBY
Prizes £300
Submission details Entry: £2 for the first
poem, £1 for subsequent poems.

International Queer Writing Competition

Chroma Writing Competition, PO Box
44655, London N16 OWQ
website www.chromajournal.co.uk
Prizes 1st prize, £300; 2nd prize, £150; 3rd
prize, £75 and publication in *Chroma*

A short story and poetry competition for
lesbian, gay, bisexual and trans writers.

Submission details For poems of up to
50 lines. Entry fee, £5. Closing date, 10th
September.

Irish Times Poetry Now Award

Poetry Now Festival, The Arts Office, Dun
Laoghaire, Rathdown, County Dublic,
Ireland
tel (035312) 054872
email arts@dlrcoco.ie
website www.dlrcoco.ie/ARTS/
festival_pn_2006award.htm
Contact Aisling McLaughlin
Prizes €5000

The only award of its kind, recognising
and rewarding work by Irish poets. It is
given to the author of the best single
volume of poems published by an Irish
poet, or by Irish publisher annually.

Submission details Volumes published in
English by Irish presses or by Irish writers
in the calendar year are eligible.
Translations and anthologies are not
eligible. Only single volumes (and not
selected poems or collected poems) are
eligible. Self-published collections, or
editions of deceased poets, will not be
accepted. Each press (but not individual
poets) should submit 5 copies of each title
eligible for the award, in book, proof or
galley form.

JBWB Poetry Competition

87 Home Orchard, Yate, South
Gloucestershire BS37 5XH
tel (01454) 324717
email competitions@jbwb.co.uk
website www.jbwb.co.uk
Contact Jenny Hewitt, Doug Watts
Prizes 1st prize, 100; 2nd prize, £50; 3rd
prize, £20

Popular quarterly competition that has
been running for 8 years.
Submission details Poems no longer
than 30 lines on any subject. See website
for details.

Jerwood Aldeburgh First Collection Prize

The Poetry Trust, The Cut, 9 New Cut, Halesworth, Suffolk IP19 8BY
tel (01986) 835950 *fax* (01986) 835949
email info@thepoetrytrust.org
website www.thepoetrytrust.org
Prizes £2000 plus a fee-paying invitation to read at the following year's Aldeburgh Festival

Funded by the Jerwood Charity, an annual competition for any first collection of at least 40 pages published in Britain or Eire since 1st September of the previous year.

Submission details Send 3 bound or proof copies with a note of the publication date. Closing date, 31st August.

Keats Shelley Prize

KSMA Competition Secretary, School of English, The University, St Andrews KY16 9AL
website www.keats-shelley.co.uk
Contact Jill Gamble

Sponsored by the Cowley Foundation and The School of English, University of St Andrews.

Submission details Maximum length, 50 lines. Entry fee of £5 sterling for a single entry, £3 for a second entry. Closing date, 30th June.

The Petra Kenney Poetry Competition

Details Morgan Kenney, The Belmoredean Barn, Maplehurst Road, West Grinstead RH13 6RN
email morgan@ petrapoetrycompetition.co.uk
website www.petrapoetrycompetition. co.uk
Editor 1st prize, £1000 and publication in *Writing Magazine*; 2nd prize, £500; 3rd prize, £250; 3 prizes at £125; also an inscribed Royal Brierley crystal vase to the 3 winners

This annual competition is for unpublished poems on any theme and in any style, and is open to everyone. Poems should be no more than 80 lines. Entry fee, £3 per poem. Closing date, 1st December each year. Founded 1995.

Kent & Sussex Poetry Society Open Poetry Competition

website www.kentandsussexpoetrysociety.org
Prizes 1st prize, £500; 2nd prize, £200; 3rd prize, £100; 4th prize, £50
Submission details 40 lines maximum, typed on A4. Name and address on separate sheet. Closing date, 31st January each year.

The Kilkenny International Swift Society Competition

website www.swiftsociety.com/ competition/competition.html
Prizes 1st prize, €1000

For an an unpublished satirical poem, in the spirit and style of Swift, on a topic of current and relevant social/political interest. The competition is both a celebration of Swift as one of Ireland's greatest satirists and a move to promote political and social commentary through satire.

Killie Writing Competition

Details Killie Writing Competition, Kilmarnock College KA3 7AT
tel (01355) 302160
email enquiries@killie.co.uk
website www.killie.co.uk

Annual competition usually with 4 categories: 5–7 year-olds, 8–11 year-olds, 12–16 year-olds, adults. Free expessive writing (poetry or fiction) with no limit on subject, word count, style or format. See website for guidelines. Work submitted must have been previously unpublished. Various prizes with the overall best entry receiving £1000 and a trophy. Closing date: April. Founded 2000.

Leaf Books Short Poetry Competition
website www.leafbooks.co.uk
Prizes All selected poems will be featured in a Leaf Book. The overall winner will receive £200

Competition for short poems (16 lines or fewer) on any theme.
   Submission details £2.50 per entry; cheques made payable to Leaf Books. Entry forms available on the website. Entry fee, £3. Closing date, 31st July.

Ledbury Poetry Festival Competition
Ledbury Poetry Festival, Church Street, Ledbury, Herefordshire HR8 1DH
tel (01531) 634156
email charle@poetry-festival.com
website www.poetry-festival.com
Contact Charles Bennett
Prizes Category 1 (18 and over) 1st prize, Ty Newydd writing course; 2nd prize, £250; 3rd prize, £150. Category 2 (11-17) 1st prize, £100; 2nd prize, £50; 3rd prize, £25. Category 3 (10 and under) 1st prize, £25 book token; 2nd prize, £15 book token; 3rd prize, £10 book token

See website for full details.

Linkway Magazine Open Writing Competition
Linkway Magazine, The Shieling, The Links, Burry Port, Carmarthenshire SA16 0HU
Contact FC Davies
Prizes £50

Competition for poetry on the theme of Animals. For poems of up to 60 lines.
   Submission details Entry fee, £2 per poem.

Literary Review Grand Poetry Prize
44 Lexington Street, London W1F 0LW
tel 020-7437 9392 *fax* 020-7734 1844
website www.literaryreview.co.uk

Literary Review runs a competition each month for poems on a given subject which are no more than 24 lines, rhyme, scan and make sense. The Grand Prize of £5000 is awarded to the best of these each year. Closing date: September. Founded 1990.

Litfest Poetry Competition
26 Castle Park, Lancaster LA1 1YQ
tel (01524) 62166
email all@litfest.org
website www.litfest.org
Contact Jonathan Bear

A biannual competition.
   Submission details Entry forms are available from the Litfest office. See website for details.

Littoral Magazine Poetry Pamphlet competition
Littoral Magazine, 38 Barringtons, 10 Sutton Road, Southend-on-Sea, Essex SS2 5NA
email mervynlinford@aol.com
website http://mysite.wanadoo-members.co.uk/mervyn_linford/comp.htm
Editor Mervyn Linford
Prizes The winner will receive 50 colour-cover pamphlets under the imprint of The Littoral Press

A twice-yearly poetry pamphlet competition.
   Submission details Titled collections consisting of 24 pages (published or not, by 1 author only), any subject or form, arranged in the order you wish the poems to be printed. Send on CD, floppy disk or as an email attachment in Microsoft Word or RTF format. Entry fee, £10 per collection. Closing dates, Feb 21st and Aug 21st.

London Writers Competition
Arts Office, Wandsworth Council, Room 224A, Wandsworth Town Hall, High Street, London SW18 2PU

tel 020-8871 8711
email arts@wandsworth.gov.uk
website www.wandsworth.gov.uk/arts
Prizes 1st prize, £600; 2nd prize, £250; 3rd
prize, £100; 4th prize, £50

Open to writers who live, work or study in
the Greater London area. Awards are
made annually in 4 classes (Poetry, Short
Story, Fiction for Children and Play) and
prizes total £1000 in each class. Entries
must be previously unpublished work.
Judging is under the chairmanship of
Francine Stock.
   Submission details Contact the Arts
Office at the above telephone number to
receive an entry form, or visit the website.

Love and Out of Love
Gti Suite, Valleys Innovation Centre,
Navigation Park, Abercynon, Rhondda
Cynon Taff CF45 4SN
tel (01443) 483341 *fax* (01443) 654278
email leafbooks@yahoo.co.uk
website www.leafbooks.co.uk
Contact Cecile Morreau
Prizes 1st prize, £200 and publication; 2nd
prize, £50 and publication

Entries accepted on any theme.
   Submission details Entry via form
(available on website, or by post with a
covering letter including name and
contact details). Entry fee, £5 (cheques
payable to 'Leaf'.

Manchester Cathedral Poetry Competition
The Religious Poetry Competition, The
Cathedral, Manchester M3 1SX
email albert.radcliffe@dsl.pipex.com
Contact Albert Radcliffe
Prizes 1st prize, £300; 2nd prize, £150; 3rd
prize, £75

The poems submitted should be broadly
religious; that is, spiritual in nature and,
like all good religious poetry, should
appeal to those who would not necessarily
describe themselves as such. 'Religious'
thus includes poems that are Christian, as
well as those from within other faith
traditions. Those struggling to discover
their own sense of the sacred are also
invited to submit entries. Poems are
welcome in any style or form and will be
judged solely on their merits as poetry.
   Submission details Entry fee, £3. Closing
date, 1st July.

Martello Writers Poetry Competition
11 Barcombe Walk, Old Town,
Eastbourne BN20 8HT
Contact Barbara Champion
Prizes 1st prize, £100; 2nd prize, £30; 3rd
prize, £20, plus 3 x £10 prizes

Annual competition founded in 1994,
which has helped many writers and poets
with readings and radio appearances and
publication.
   Submission details Poems should be
original work of not more than 40 lines
and may have already been published.
Should be typed (or well-written) on 1
side of A4 paper. Send sae for details.

The John Masefield Memorial Trust
Awards Secretary, The Society of Authors,
84 Drayton Gardens, London SW10 9SB
tel 020-7373 6642 *fax* 020-7373 5768
email info@societyofauthors.org
website www.societyofauthors.org

This trust makes occasional grants to
professional poets who find themselves
with sudden financial problems. Apply for
an information sheet and application
form.

McLellan Award for Poetry
Corriegills Farm, Corriegills, Isle of Arran
KA27 8BL
email poetry@mclellanfestival.com

website www.mclellanfestival.com
Prizes 1st prize, £1000; 2nd prize, £350;
3rd prize £150

Awarded as part of the McLellan Festival
on the Isle of Arran; celebrates the work of
playwright, poet and short story writer
Robert McLellan, who spent most of his
working life on Arran writing exclusively
in Scots, the living language of the
communities he grew up in. The McLellan
Award for Poetry invites entries in all
varieties of Scots and in English. All the
poems will be judged in 1 category, with
no distinction being made on the basis of
the language used. Poems may be on any
subject and will be judged anonymously.
   Submission details Maximum length of
40 lines. See entry form on website.

Mere Literary Festival Poetry Competition

c/o Lawrences, Old Hollow, Mere,
Wiltshire BA12 6EG
tel (01747) 860475
email merewilts@aol.com
website www.merewilts.org.uk
Editor Adrienne Howell
Prizes Cash prizes and local and junior
categories. Shortlisted poems are
showcased at a festival event

A biannual poetry competition in aid of
charity, The Mere & District Linkscheme.
Awards ansd adjudication form part of the
literary festival in October.
   Submission details Maximum 40 lines
on any theme. Send sae for entry form and
details, which are available from 1st
March, or download from website.

Middlesex University Poetry Competition

The Writing Centre, Middlesex University,
North London Business Park, Oakleigh
Road South, London N11 1QS

tel 020-8411 5000
website www.mdx.ac.uk/subjects/mcc/
cmw/writecen.htm
Prizes 1st prize, £1000; 2nd prize, £250;
3rd prize, £100.

An annual competition.

National Poetry Competition

Competition Organiser, The Poetry
Society, 22 Betterton Street, London
WC2H 9BX
tel 020-7420 9895 *fax* 020-7240 4818
email marketing@poetrysociety.org.uk
website www.poetrysociety.org.uk
Prizes 1st prize, £5000; 2nd prize, £1000;
3rd prize, £500 – plus 10 commendations
of £50

One of Britain's major annual open poetry
competitions. Poems on any theme, up to
40 lines. All poems will be read by a team
of poetry specialists before the final
judging process.
   Submission details For rules and entry
form, send an sae. Entries also accepted
via the website. Closing date, 31st October
each year.

The New Writer Prose and Poetry Prizes

PO Box 60, Cranbrook, Kent TN17 2ZR
tel (01580) 212626 *fax* (01580) 212041
email admin@thenewwriter.com
website www.thenewwriter.com
Prizes Collection, 1st prize £300; 2nd
prize, £200; 3rd prize, £100. Single, 1st
prize, £100; 2nd prize, £75; 3rd prize £50

Short stories up to 5000 words, novellas,
essays and articles; poets may submit
either 1 or a collection of 6-10 previously
unpublished poems. Total prize money
£2500 as well as publication for the prize-
winners in the *New Writer* magazine.
Founded 1997.
   Submission details Poems must be no
more than 40 lines in length. In single-

poem section they must be unpublished. In collection of poems section, work may be previously published and there is no limit as to length. Entry fees: £4 per poem; £10 for a collection of 6-10 poems. Closing date, 31st October each year.

New Writing Ventures
Booktrust, Book House, 45 East Hill, London SW18 2QZ
tel 020-8516 2972
email tarryn@boooktrust.org.uk
website www.boooktrust.org.uk, www.newwritingpartnership.org.uk
Contact Tarryn MacKay

An annual series of major national prizes and awards for emerging writers in poetry, fiction and non-fiction. The winner in each of the 3 categories – fiction, creative non-fiction and poetry – will receive £5000, and 2 shortlisted writers in each category £1000 each. All the winners and shortlisted writers will receive a place on the year-long Ventures Development Programme, which includes individual mentoring, workshops and professional advice. Closing date: end of May.

New Writing Ventures is one of the programmes delivered by the New Writing Partnership, which is supported by Arts Council England East, UEA, Norwich City Council and Norfolk County Council.

The Nobel Prize in Literature
Awarding authority Swedish Academy, Box 2118, S–10313 Stockholm, Sweden
tel (08) 555 12554 *fax* (08) 555 12549
email sekretariat@svenskaakademien.se
website www.svenskaakademien.se

This is one of the awards stipulated in the will of the late Alfred Nobel, the Swedish scientist who invented dynamite. No direct application for a prize will be taken into consideration. For authors writing in English it was bestowed upon Rudyard Kipling in 1907, WB Yeats in 1923, George Bernard Shaw in 1925, Sinclair Lewis in 1930, John Galsworthy in 1932, Eugene O'Neill in 1936, Pearl Buck in 1938, TS Eliot in 1948, William Faulkner in 1949, Bertrand Russell in 1950, Sir Winston Churchill in 1953, Ernest Hemingway in 1954, John Steinbeck in 1962, Samuel Beckett in 1969, Patrick White in 1973, Saul Bellow in 1976, William Golding in 1983, Wole Soyinka in 1986, Joseph Brodsky in 1987, Nadine Gordimer in 1991, Derek Walcott in 1992, Toni Morrison in 1993, Seamus Heaney in 1995, VS Naipaul in 2001 and Harold Pinter in 2005.

Northern Writers' Awards
2 School Lane, Whickham NE16 4SL
tel 0191-488 8580
email mail@newwriting.com
website www.newwritingnorth.com

Awards introduced to support writers, both new and established, who live and work in the North East region. There are now 4 different types of awards, from support for talented new writers to specific support for established writers who are working on new projects. This year, awards up to the value of £25,000 are being made.

Norwich Writers' Circle Open Poetry Competition
25 Wensum Valley Close, Norwich NR6 5DJ
tel (01508) 536912
email Shirley.Collin@mac.com
website www.norwichwriters.org.uk
Contact Mrs Jean Shackleton
Prizes 1st prize, £200; 2nd prize, £100; 3rd prize, £50; Rural theme, £25; Humorous poem, £15 (John Coleridge Prize); Minimalist Poem, £15 (Hilary Mellor Prize)

Annual competition with different adjudicators each year.

Submission details Poems should be a maximum of 40 lines in length. They should be typed on A4, with details of poet and titles of poems on a separate sheet. Closing date, second Tuesday in February.

Nottingham Open Poetry Competition

Jeremy Duffield, Chairman, 71 Saxton Avenue, Heanor, Derbyshire DE75 7PZ
tel (01773) 712282
email info@nottinghampoetrysociety.co.uk
website www.nottinghampoetrysociety.co.uk
Contact Viv Apple (*tel* 0115-914 5838; *email* viv.apple@ntlworld.com)
Prizes 1st prize, £300; 2nd prize, £150; 3rd prize, £75 plus 10 merit prizes of subscriptions to *Poetry Nottingham*

Submission details Entries should be in English, unpublished and not accepted or submitted for publication elsewhere. Poems must be no longer than 40 lines and each poem should be typed on a separate sheet of A4 paper. Poems are judged anonymously. On a separate piece of paper state name and address and provide a list of poems submitted. Entry fee: £3 per poem; £10 for 4 poems.

The Royal Society of Literature Ondaatje Prize

Royal Society of Literature, Somerset House, Strand, London WC2R 1LA
tel 020-7845 4676 *fax* 020-7845 4679
email paulaj@rslit.org
website www.rslit.org
Contact Paula Johnson
Prizes £10,000

Endowed by Sir Christopher Ondaatje and awarded annually to a book of literary merit, fiction or non-fiction, best evoking spirit of place.

Submission details All entries must be published within the calendar year and should be submitted between 1st September and 1st December. The writer must be a citizen of the United Kingdom, Commonwealth or Ireland. Each UK publisher or imprint of a publisher may enter 1 book published or due to be published within the calendar year. An entry form must be completed.

Oxfambooks Poetry Calendar Competition

Oxfam Ireland, 9 Burgh Quay, Dublin 2, Ireland
website www.oxfamireland.org
Contact Sheila Powers
Prizes Winners will join poets John F Deane, Rita Ann Higgins, Nick Laird, Mary O'Donnell, Caitriona O'Reilly and Peter Sirr on Oxfambooks Poetry Calendar

Competition for poems of up to 20 lines. Entry fee, €5.

Partners Writing Group Competitions

289 Elmwood Avenue, Feltham, Middlesex TW13 7QB
email partners_writing_group@ hotmail.com
Contact Ian Deal
Prizes 1st prize, £300; 2nd prize, £100; 3rd prize, £50; 4th prize, entry fee refunded

An annual competition for poems of any style or length.

Submission details Names should not appear on poems, but on separate sheet. Send sae for full guidelines. Entry fee, £2.50 per poem. Closing date, 1st May.

Patrick Kavanagh Poetry Award

Patrick Kavanagh Society, c/o Mrs M Quinn, Lisarolagh, Inishkeen, Dundalk, Co Louth

Prizes €2500

Annual competition, open to poets born in the island of Ireland, or of Irish nationality, or a long-term resident in Ireland, who have not previously published an individual collection of poems.

Submission details Original, not less than 20 and not more than 30 poems, and individual poems to be not more than 40 lines, unpublished. No return of manuscripts. Only Irish nationals eligible.

Peace & Freedom Press Competitions

17 Farrow Road, Whaplode Drove, Spalding, Lincolnshire PE12 0TS
email p-rance@yahoo.co.uk
website http://uk.geocities.com/p-rance/pandf.htm
Contact Paul Rance
Prizes 1st prize, £100; 5 runners-up, £10 each
Submission details Send sae for details.

Peterloo Poets Open Poetry Competition

2 Kelly Gardens, Calstock, Cornwall PL18 9SA
tel (01822) 833473
email info@peterloopoets.com
website www.peterloopoets.com
Prizes 1st prize, £1500; 2nd prize, £1000; 3rd prize, £500; 4th prize, £100; 10 prizes, £50 each

Annual competition. Closing date, 2nd March. Entry fee, £5 per poem. See website for entry form.

Pier Pressure Poetry Competition

Obligations Competition, Pier Pressure, c/o 17 Wilbury Crescent, Hove, Sussex BN3 6FL
website www.pierpressure.org
Prizes £100

Annual short story and poetry competitions.
Submission details See website or write to the address above.

Plough Prize

The Plough Arts Centre, 9-11 Fore Street, Torrington EX38 8HQ
tel (01805) 624624
email sarah.willans@theploughprize.co.uk
website www.theploughprize.co.uk
Contact Sarah Willans
Prizes 1st prize, £200; 2nd prize, £100; 3rd prize, £50

Open category for poems up to 40 lines in length. Short poem category for poems up to 10 lines in length. Poems should be original, unpublished and should not have won a prize in any other competition.

Submission details Work should be typed, single-spaced on a single side of A4. Name, address, telephone number, email address and poem title(s) should be printed clearly on a separate sheet. Mark each poem 'O' or 'S' to indicate category. Entry fee, £3.50 per poem, or £12 for 4 poems. Thereafter, £3 per poem. For an additional fee of £3.50 per poem, entrants will receive a critique of their work. Send a copy, marked 'Critique' and an sae or email address to which it can be sent. Closing date, 30th November, annually.

The Poetry Business Book and Pamphlet Competition

The Poetry Business, The Studio, Byram Arcade, Westgate, Huddersfield HD1 1ND
tel (01484) 434840 *fax* (01484) 426566
email edit@poetrybusiness.co.uk
website www.poetrybusiness.co.uk
Contact Janet Fisher

An annual competition.
Submission details Submit a short manuscript (16-24pp). Entry fee, £18. Full rules and entry form can be found on the website. Closing date, 31st October.

Poetry Can Competition

Poetry Can, Unit 11, 20-22 Hepburn Rd, Bristol BS2 8UD
email info@poetrycan.co.uk
Prizes Publication, plus 500 copies of collection

Submission details Closing date, 30th June. Entry fee, £15. Submit 10 poems.

Poetry London Competition

1a Jewel Road, London E17 4QU
tel 020-8521 0776
website www.poetrylondon.co.uk
Contact Maurice Riordan
Prizes 1st prize, £1000; 2nd prize, £500; 3rd prize, £200

Submission details Entries must be in English, your own unaided work, not a translation of another poet, and unpublished. The maximum length is 80 lines. For *Poetry London* subscribers the entry fee is £3 per poem; for non-subscribers, £4.

Poet's Letter Beowulf Poetry Prize

tel (07931) 357109
email Editor@poetsletter.com
website www.poetsletter.com
Prizes 1st prize, £10,000; 12 x 2nd prizes, a one-year Poet in Residence with a bursary of at least £500; 12 x 3rd prizes, £100 each

Annual competition based on a theme.

Submission details Maximum length, 60 lines. Entry fee, £10 for 1 poem; subsequent entries, £8 each.

Postcode Poetry Competition

108 Deepdale Road, Preston PR1 5AR
tel (07786) 570415 *fax* (01772) 200462
email philipmorris99@hotmail.com; postcode.poetry@hotmail.co.uk
website www.postcode-poetry.co.uk
Contact Philip Morris
Prizes Fame, fortune and food

A web-based poetry competition based around UK postcode areas, open to all poets, with no restrictions other than that of being a UK resident.

Submission details Entry guidelines and details of entry fee can be found on the website. Closing date: 31st August, each year.

Pulsar Poetry Competition

34 Lineacre, Grange Park, Swindon, Wiltshire SN5 6DA
email pulsar.ed@btopenworld.com
website www.pulsarpoetry.com
Contact David Pike
Prizes 1st prize, £100; 2nd prize, £50; 3rd prize, £25

For poems of not more than 40 lines, on any subject.

Submission details Entry fee, £2.50 first poem, subsequent poems £1 each. Minimum entry fee, £2.50.

Quantum Leap Poetry Competitions

York House, 15 Argyle Terrace, Rothesay, Isle of Bute PA20 0BD

Competition for poems not exceeding 36 lines.

Submission details Entry fee, £3 per poem. Closing date, 1st April and 1st October.

Ragged Raven Press Poetry Competition

1 Lodge Farm, Snitterfield, Stratford-on-Avon, Warks CV37 0LR
website www.raggedraven.co.uk
Prizes 1st prize, £300; 4 runners-up prizes of £50. Selected entries published in anthology

For poems of any length and on any subject.

Submission details Entry fee, £3 per poem, £10 for 4 poems. Closing date, October 31st. See website for details.

Susan Rands Memorial Poetry Prize

18 Chequers Lane, Prestwood, Great Missenden, Buckinghamshire HP16 9DW

tel (01494) 866318
email dwoods@hotmail.com
website www.christies.org
Contact David Woods
Prizes 1st prize, £50; 2nd prize, £40; 3rd prize, £25 (all winners are published)

Open to all UK residents aged 16 years and over. All monies are donated to cancer research at Christie's Hospital. The competition was founded in memory of Susan Rands, the British record survivor of the terminal Mesothelioma strain of cancer.

Submission details Entrants may submit as many poems as they wish, provided each is a maximum length of 40 lines. Contact details should be enclosed on a separate sheet of paper, as entries are judged anonymously. Poems must be typed, and cannot be returned. Enclose sae for results. Entry fee: £4 for 1 poem; £2 for each subsequent entry. Closing date: 1st May, October 31st, annually.

The Rise Londonwide Youth Slam Championship

Poetry Society, 22 Betterton, Street, London WC2H 9BX
tel 020-7420 9893
email jtaylor@poetrysociety.org.uk
website www.poetrysociety.org.uk/respect
Prizes All entrants win a year's membership of the Poetry Society, plus books, CDs and the chance to perform alongside professionals at top London venues. Winners will spend a weekend developing their acts with a professional spoken-word artist, record their track at a major London recording studio for a compilation album, and showcase their work at the Mayor's annual anti-racism festival, Rise, before crowds of up to 100,000

Presented by the Mayor of London, in association with the Poetry Society. Open to all aged between 12 and 18. The top 12 who are successful in both the quarter-finals and semi-finals go on to form the Londonwide Slam Championship showcase team, and will represent the capital in the UK Slam Championship.

Tom Roder Memorial Prize for Poetry

Dept. of English Literature, The University, Sheffield S10 2TN
email s.vice@sheffield.ac.uk

Annual poetry prize awarded for a collection of 20-30 individual unpublished poems (around 24 pages). Closing date: 30th Sept.

The Rooney Prize for Irish Literature

Details JA Sherwin, Strathin, Templecarrig, Delgany, Co Wicklow, Republic of Ireland
tel (01) 287 4769 *fax* (01) 287 2595
email rooneyprize@ireland.com

An annual prize of €10,000 is awarded to encourage young Irish writing talent. To be eligible, individuals must be Irish, published and under 40 years of age. The prize is non-competitive and there is no application procedure or entry form. Founded in 1976 by Daniel M Rooney, Pittsburgh, Pennsylvania.

Rubies in the Darkness Poetry Competition

41 Grantham Road, Manor Park, London E12 5LZ
Contact Peter Geoffrey Paul Thompson
Prizes Publication in magazine and appearance on published Honours List

Judged annually by poet and editor Peter Geoffrey Paul Thompson.

Submission details Poems of any length on any theme. Entry fee, £3 per poem. Closing date, 1st November.

Runciman Award

The Anglo-Hellenic League, 16-18 Paddington Street, London W1U 5AS

tel 020-7486 9410
email anglohellenic.league@ virgin.net
website www.hellenicbookservice.com/
ahr.htm
Contact The Administrator
Prizes Prize money of £9000 to be
distributed at the discretion of the judges

Award in honour of the late Sir Steven
Runciman for work wholly or mainly
about some aspect of Greece or the world
of Hellenism, published in English in any
country of the world in its first edition.
   Submission details Closing date, mid-
January every year.

The David St John Thomas Charitable Trust Competitions & Awards

The David St John Thomas Charitable
Trust, PO Box 6055, Nairn IV12 4YB
tel (01667) 453351 *fax* (01667) 452365
email dsjtcharitynairn@fsmail.net
Contact Lorna Edwardson

Programme of writing competitions and
awards totalling £20,000–£30,000. Regular
competitions are the annual ghost story
and annual love story (each 1600–1800
words with £1000 1st prize) and the open
poetry competition (up to 32 lines, total
prize money £1000). Publication of
winning entries is guaranteed, usually in
Writers' News/Writing Magazine. The Self-
Publishing Awards are open to anyone
who has self-published a book during the
preceding calendar year, with 4 categories
each with £250 prize. The overall winner is
declared Self-Publisher of the Year with a
total award of £1000. For full details of
these and other awards, including an
annual writers' groups anthology and
letter-writer of the year send a large sae.

Salisbury House Poets Poetry Competition

Salisbury House Poets, Salisbury House,
Bury Street West, Enfield, Middlesex N9
9LA

website www.chela.co.uk/poetry.php
Contact The Competition Secretary
Prizes 1st prize, £500; 2nd prize, £250; 3rd
prize, £100

For poems in English not over 50 lines.
   Submission details Closing date, 1st
November.

The Saltire Society Awards

Details The Saltire Society, 9 Fountain
Close, 22 High Street, Edinburgh EH1 1TF
tel 0131-556 1836 *fax* 0131-557 1675
email saltire@saltiresociety.org.uk
website www.saltiresociety.org.uk

Scintilla Open Poetry Competition

Little Wentwood Farm, Llantrisant, Usk,
Mon NP15 1ND
email anne.cluysenaar@virgin.net
Contact Anne Cluysenaar
Prizes Prizes in each category, £200, £100,
£50

Competition in 2 sections; short poems
and long poems/sequences.
   Submission details Entry fee, £3 for first
short poem, then £2 per short poem. Long
poems/sequences, £5 for first poem, then
£4.

Scottish Arts Council Book of the Year

Scottish Arts Council, 12 Manor Place,
Edinburgh EH3 7DD
tel 0131-226 6051
website www.scottisharts.org.uk
Prizes £10,000

The biggest prize for Scottish writing.

Second Light Network Poetry Competition

9 Greendale Close, London SE22 8TG
tel 020-8299 0088
email dyliswood@tiscali.co.uk
Contact Dylis Wood
Prizes 1st prize, £250; 2nd prize, £100; 3rd
prize, £50

An annual competition. Second Light Network is a network of older woman poets.

Submission details For women aged 30 years or over. Entry fee, £3 for 1 poem: £7 for 3 poems: £12 for 8 poems.

Snapshot Press Haiku Competitions

website www.snapshotpress.co.uk
Prizes £200/US$300 and publication of collection as a perfect-bound book

Established in 1998 and now an annual event, alternating between haiku and tanka. It provides a rare and equal opportunity for authors to have a collection published in a professional manner, regardless of reputation and publishing history.

Submission details Haiku may be free-form or 5–7–5 and must be the original work of the individual entrant. Entry fee, £20/US$30 per manuscript.

Somerset Maugham Awards

84 Drayton Gardens, London SW10 9SB
tel 020-7373 6642 *fax* 020-7373 5768
email info@societyofauthors.org
website www.societyofauthors.org
Contact Awards Secretary

Granted for a full-length published work of poetry, fiction, belles-lettres by a British author under 35. No dramatic works.

Submission details Entry by publisher only. Apply to the Society for full details and an entry form.

Southport Writers' International Poetry Competition

Poetry Competition, 32 Dover Road, Southport, Merseyside PR8 4TB
tel (01704) 560923
Contact Mrs Hilary Tinsley
Prizes 1st prize, £200; 2nd prize, £100; 3rd prize, £50; £25 Humour prize; £25 Local prize

Open to all subjects and forms.

Submission details 40 lines maximum. Enclose sealed envelope marked with poem titles and containing an sae. Entry fee, £2 per poem. Closing date, 30th April, annually.

Southwark Poets of the Year

Languages and Humanities Dept., Morley Cottage, 61 Westminster Bridge Road, London SE1 7HT
tel 020-7928 1836
website www.southbanklondon.com
Contact Edward Anderson

To enter you must live, work or study in the borough, and poems must be inspired by some aspect of life in Southwark: its people, places or history.

Submission details Poems should be no longer than 50 lines.

Speakeasy – Milton Keynes Writers' Group Open Creative Writing Competition

website www.mkweb.co.uk/speakeasy
Prizes Poetry 1st Prize £100; 2nd Prize £50; 3rd Prize £25.

For poetry and short stories. Poetry maximum of 60 lines.

Submission details No names and addresses, drawings, clip art, or any other marks that will make the entry stand out from the other entries will be allowed. Entries must be accompanied by a signed entry form and the required entry fee. Each entry must have the number of lines printed on the top left hand corner of the first sheet. Entry fee, £3 (£10 for 4 poems). No maximum entries. Closing date, 31st October. Entry forms and further details available from the Speakeasy website,

Spice Box Open Poetry Competition

Aramby Publishing, 1 Alanbrooke, Broadway, Knaphill, Surrey GU21 2RU *email* thespicebox@aol.com

An ongoing poetry competition

Submission details Closing date, 1st June annually.

Strokestown Poetry Prize

Strokestown Poetry Festival Office, Strokestown, County Roscommon, Ireland
tel (07) 1963 3759
email pbushe@eircom.net
website www.strokestownpoetry.org
Director Paddy Bushe
Prizes €4000 (approximay £2500 sterling), €2000 and €1000; in addition there are up to 7 commended poets who will be invited to read at the Strokestown Festival for a reading fee and travelling expenses totalling €450

Prestigious annual competition for an unpublished poem.

Submission details For an unpublished poem in English not exceeding 70 lines. Entry fee, €5 (£4 sterling or $5) per poem.

Dylan Thomas Literary Prize

The Dylan Thomas Centre, Ty Llen, Somerset Place, Swansea SA1 1RR
tel (01792) 474051/463980
website www.dylanthomasprize.com

An award of £60,000 is given to the winner of this prize, which was established to encourage, promote and reward exciting new writing in the English-speaking world and to celebrate the poetry and prose of Dylan Thomas. Entrants should be the author of a published book (in English), under the age of 30, writing within one of the following categories: poetry, novel, collection of short stories by one author, play that has been professionally performed, a broadcast radio play, a professionally produced screenplay that has resulted in a feature-length film. Authors need to be nominated by their publishers, or producers in the case of performance art. Closing date: May.

Times Stephen Spender Prize for Poetry Translation

3 Old Wish Road, Eastbourne, East Sussex BN21 4JX
tel (01323) 452294
email info@stephenspender.org
website www.stephen-spender.org
Contact Robina Pelham Burn
Prizes Open Category: 1st prize, £500; 2nd prize, £250; 3rd prize, £100. 18 and Under: 1st prize, £250; 2nd prize, £100; 3rd prize, £50. 14 and under, £100

An annual competition awarded for the translation into English of a poem in any language, modern or classical.

Submission details Submit with a commentary of no more than 300 words (see website or phone the number above for details and entry form). Maximum length of 60 lines. £3 entry fee for Open Category and free entry for 18 and under. For British residents only.

Torbay Poetry Competition

The Mount, Higher Furzeham, Brixham, Devon TQ5 8QY
tel (01803) 851098
email pwoxley@aol.com
website www.acumen-poetry.co.uk
Contact Patricia and William Oxley

Annual competition.

Submission details For submission form, send sae to above address. Entry fee, £3. Closing date, 15th August.

John Tripp Award for Spoken Poetry

Academi, Mount Stuart House, Mount Stuart Square, Cardiff CF10 5FQ
tel 029-2047 2266 *fax* 029-2049 2930
email post@academi.org

website www.academi.org

A competition for any form of spoken poetry in the English language. There are 5 regional heats around Wales, with the winners from each heat going forward to the Grand Final in Cardiff. Performers have 5 minutes to read their work at each stage of the competition and are judged on the content of their poetry and their performance skills. Anyone either born or currently living in Wales is eligible to enter, and all works must be unpublished. Founded 1990.

TS Eliot Prize

Fourth Floor, 2 Tavistock Place, London WC1H 9RA
tel 020-7833 9247 *fax* 020-7833 5990
email info@poetrybooks.co.uk
website www.poetrybooks.co.uk
Director Chris Holifield

Awarded annually for the best single collection of poetry published during the calendar year.
  Submission details Submissions by publisher only, by sending 4 copies of each eligible title to the Poetry Book Society. Closing date, early August.

Understanding Poetry Competitions

127 Milton Road West, 7 Duddingston House Courtyard, Edinburgh EH15 1JG
tel 0131-661156
Contact Denise Smith
Prizes £150

An annual competition.
  Submission details Guidelines available on request. Entry fee, £2 to £5 per poem, depending on competition.

Ver Poets Open Competition

181 Sandbridge Road, St Albans AL1 4AH
tel (01727) 762601
email gillknibbs@yahoo.co.uk

website www.verpoets.org.uk
Contact Gillian Knibbs
Prizes 1st prize, £500; 2nd prize, £300; 3rd prize, £100

Poems on any theme, up to 30 lines in length. Winning and selected poems are published in an anthology.
  Submission details Send 2 copies of each poem on separate sheets of paper. There should be no identification on poems. Name and address should be typed on accompanying A4 sheet. No translations and only unpublished work.

Wendy Webb Poetry Competitions

email wwbuk@yahoo.co.uk
Contact Wendy Webb

Various poetry competitions for poems on different themes and styles. Email for details.

Wells Festival of Literature International Poetry Competition

The Competitions' Organiser, Chegworth House, Moor Lane, Draycott, Cheddar BS27 3TD
website www.somersite.co.uk/wellsfest.htm
Prizes 1st prize, £500; 2nd prize, £200; 3rd prize, £100; Wyvern prize, £100
  Submission details For poems of up to 40 lines. Poets may submit up to 5 poems. Entry fee, £4. Closing date, 31st July.

Wigtown Poetry Competition

Wigtown Book Town Company, Freepost NAT5359, Wigtown, Newton Stewart DG8 9BR
tel (01988) 402036
website www.wigtown-booktown.co.uk/poetrycomp
Prizes £2000, £1000, £500; Gaelic Prize, £1000

One of Scotland's biggest poetry competitions.

The Raymond Williams Community Publishing Prizes

The Literature Dept, Arts Council England, 14 Great Peter Street, London SW1P 3NQ
tel 020-7973 5325
website www.artscouncil.org.uk

This award commends published works of outstanding creative and imaginative quality that reflect the life, voices and experiences of the people of particular communities. The winning entry will be awarded £3000 and the runner-up £2000.

Winchester Writers' Conference Competitions

Faculty of Arts, University of Winchester, Winchester, Hants SO22 4NR
tel (01962) 827238
email barbara.large@ winchester.ac.uk
website www.writersconference.co.uk
Contact Barbara Large

Fifteen writing competitions are attached to this major international Festival of Writing, which takes place at the end of June. Each entry is adjudicated and 64 sponsored prizes are presented at the Writers' Awards Dinner. Categories are the First Three Pages of the Novel, Short Stories, Shorter Short Stories, Writing for Children, A Page of Prose, Lifewriting, Slim Volume, Small Edition, Poetry, Feature Articles, Retirement, Reaching Out for disabled writers, Local History, and Young Writers' Poetry Competition.

The Writers Bureau Poetry Competition

The Writers Bureau, Sevendale House, 7 Dale Street, Manchester M1 1JB
email studentservices@writersbureau.com
website www.writersbureau.com/ competition
Prizes 1st prize, £1000; 2nd prize, £400; 3rd prize, £200; 4th prize, £100; 6th prize, £50

Submission details Poems must not exceed 40 lines and must be typed. Entry forms can be downloaded from the website.

Writers' Week Poetry Competition

24 The Square, Listowel, Co Kerry, Ireland
tel (0682) 1074 *fax* (0682) 2893
email info@writersweek.ie
website www.writersweek.ie
Contact Eilish Wren, Maire Logue
Prizes Single Poem Category, €900. Poetry Collection Category, €900

In its 36th year; has grown to become one of Ireland's leading literary festivals.

Submission details No entry form required. Entries should be typed and must not have been previously published. Entry fee, £8 for single poem; £25 for collection.

Yorkshire Open Poetry Competition

32 Spey Bank, Acomb Park, York YO24 2UZ
Prizes 1st prize, £500; 2nd prize, £250; 3rd prize, £50

Submission details For poems up to 80 lines. For details, send sae. Entry fee, £4 per poem (£14 for 4 poems). Closing date, 31st July.

Signed, sealed, delivered: self-publishing is nothing to be ashamed of

Poets are increasingly publishing, marketing and distributing their own books. Diminishing opportunities from mainstream publishers, and developments in design and print technology, make this a very viable way to bring your work to the public eye. **Gordon Kerr** has done just that, and shares his experiences.

It arrived in the post, carefully packed in bubblewrap, exotic American stamps decorating the white package. I opened it with trembling hands, carefully snipping the end with scissors. Reaching inside I gripped the corners of a small hardback book, and pulled it out. There it was. I already knew what it looked like, because I had designed it, learning Quark Xpress for just that purpose. But I was stunned, all the same. A book of my very own poetry. All those years of writing – almost 40, in fact – on those pages.

These days, of course, you can publish your poetry in many different ways, but it is quite a feeling seeing your work published for the first time in the old-fashioned way, between the covers of a book. I had never tried to make my poetry public. It was between me and the page in front of me, almost a guilty secret I carried round with me – and I had resigned myself to it staying that way. However, for some reason I cannot recall, I sent a poem to an artist friend of mine who liked it and asked if I had any more. When I said I had hundreds, he suggested that we collaborate. He would respond to each poem with a line drawing, and we could publish and produce a limited-edition run of books. In fact, he said, he knew just the printer – a man called Walt, in Arizona, who produces exquisite chapbooks. 'Walt?' I thought. 'Arizona!' I thought. Now, how is that going to work? It actually worked very well. I selected the poems and got them to my artist friend. He spent a few months working on them and back came a pile of 50 illustrations. I designed the book and sent a disk off to Walt. Walt and I then became email buddies and a couple of months later, there I was, standing in my hallway, clutching a book with tears rolling down my face!

There is nothing to be ashamed of in self-publishing. Very few of the many thousands of people who write poetry actually get published, and, in fact, the opportunities to get picked up by a mainstream (let alone a small) publisher are becoming fewer. Why not do it yourself? You can produce a small run of books and sell them to friends and family to cover costs, or you can just give them away, if you feel so inclined. You can sell them through your website or blog. There are lots of ways to get rid of that pile of books in the corner. Don't expect to get them into your local branch of whatever high street bookseller is in your town, though.

What makes it all so easy, of course, is the new technology available. There are wonderful packages on the market with which you can lay out your work in whatever way you wish. If you have always liked that font – Trebuchet MS – well you can have it, without arguing with some spotty designer at a publishing house who looks at you as if you have about as much visual sense as a plank of wood. Printers will even do it for you, if you feel that a course in Adobe InDesign is beyond you. That brings an added cost, of course.

So what does it involve? You have to consider the following:

Keying in the text, and proofing it
You will probably do this yourself. But make sure another pair of eyes looks through it for embarrassing typos and spelling errors.

Layout/design
Quark Xpress and InDesign are just two of a number of computer programmes that will enable you to lay out your book in whatever way you want.

Cover design
Be adventurous and make your book as attractive as possible, especially if you are going to try to sell it to complete strangers. That particularly fetching photo of you wearing a fedora might not be the best idea!

ISBN
This is the identifying number on the back of every book sold. You may choose not to put an ISBN on your book if it is being sold privately, but without an ISBN the book cannot appear on Amazon, for example. ISBNs in the UK are supplied by the ISBN Agency (www.isbn.nielsenbookdata.co.uk) and cost £94 for a block of ten (they are not available singly).

Print
There are many options. You will undoubtedly have many local printers in your area. Check previous work by them for quality, and shop around to get the best price. There are also print-on-demand printers who can handle small runs very cost-effectively. A search on the Internet will provide you with lots of options.

Marketing/publicity
The local press is usually very sympathetic towards local authors. Also, if you were brought up somewhere else, don't forget the local paper there – or the local library, which will often take a copy of a local author's privately produced book.

Warehousing and distribution
This may, of course, be a corner of the bedroom and delivery by hand. However, if you print 300 books, they will take up a fair amount of space. Make sure you

have it! There are companies who can do all this for you, of course, at a price. The Internet will again provide you with lots of options.

Not vanity publishing ...

Self-publishing is not vanity publishing. You control the process from beginning to end, and are not handing over a wad of cash to an anonymous publisher to produce unsatisfactory product in an uncaring and often fraudulent way. If you do wish to go down the vanity publishing route, it is essential to be careful: there are many unscrupulous publishers out there. Check them out as thoroughly as you can. Ensure that they do, in fact, provide the services they promise – or your book may forever be tainted. For good advice about vanity publishing, see the websites listed below:

www.zyworld.com/alanjulia/Alan/vanitypublish.htm (names and shames some websites it is worth avoiding)

www.poetrykit.org (the ever-useful poetry site with good advice)

http://en.wikipedia.org/wiki/Vanity_publishing (helpful entry)

www.societyofauthors.net (good article about vanity publishing)

www.cultural-alliance.org/pubs/selfpublishing.htm (American; deals with the basics)

www.sff.net/people/VictoriaStrauss/poetbeware.html (helpful advice)

www.publishers.org.uk (the Publishers Association)

www.anotherealm.com/prededitors/pubwarn.htm (really useful tips on how to spot a scam)

And my little book? It was called *You Can't Get to East Kilbride from Here*, and I'm afraid you can't get it, because it sold out. However, if you go to the library in my home town of East Kilbride you will find a copy nestling on the shelves. It was worth it just for that, alone.

Gordon Kerr is a freelance editor, writer and poet.

Poetry festivals

Festivals provide a good opportunity to see successful poets in action, and to learn from them. Many festivals also run workshops and/or seminars, which can be very helpful in taking your work forward.

Aber Valley Arts Festival

Undercurrents – Aber Valley, 15 Graig y Fedw, Abertridwr, Caerffili CF83 4AQ
tel 029-2083 1668
email eryl893107392@aol.com
website www.academi.org.
Takes place October

Annual arts festival with concerts and events in various locations.

Aldeburgh International Poetry Festival

The Poetry Trust, 9 New Cut, Halesworth, Suffolk
OP19 8BY
tel (01986) 835950
email info@thepoetrytrust.org
website www.thepoetrytrust.org
Director Naomi Jaffa
Takes place First weekend in Nov

An annual festival of contemporary poetry with readings, workshops, talks, discussions, public masterclass, children's event. Features leading international and national poets, including a writer-in-residence and the winner of the Jerwood Aldeburgh First Collection Prize.

Ashbourne Festival

Ashbourne Arts, PO Box 5552, Ashbourne DE6 2ZR
tel (01335) 348707
email info@ashbournearts.com
website www.ashbournearts.co.uk
Takes place June

17 days of literary events, including poetry.

Aspects: A Celebration of Irish Writing

North Down Borough Council, North Down Heritage Centre, Town Hall, The Castle, Bangor, County Down BT20 4BT
tel (02891) 278032
email GlynisWatt@ Northdown.gov.uk
website www.northdown.gov.uk
Contact Glynis Watt
Takes place September

Brings a wealth of Irish talent, covering all tastes and age ranges. Has included many established and emerging writers.

Bay Lit

Academi, Mount Stuart House, Mount Stuart Square, Cardiff CF10 5FQ
tel 029-2047 2266 *fax* 029-2049 2930
email post@academi.org
website www.academi.org
Contact Peter Finch, Chief Executive
Takes place autumn

A bilingual (Welsh and English) literature festival, held in Cardiff Bay. It is organised by Academi, the Welsh National Literature Promotion Agency and Society for Writers, and features an array of writers from Wales and beyond.

Beverley Literature Festival

Wordquake, Council Offices, Skirlaugh, East Riding of Yorkshire HU11 5HN
mobile (07870) 584889
email johnwedgwood.clarke3@ eastriding.gov.uk
website www.beverley-literature-festival.org
Contact John W Clarke
Takes place October

A festival of readings and discussions (which, along with readings, continue throughout the year) on contemporary and historic poetry; seeks to magnify the pleasure and understanding of poetry.

Brighton Festival

12A Pavilion Buildings, Castle Square, Brighton BN1 1EE
tel (01273) 700747 *fax* (01273) 707505
email info@brightonfestival.org.uk
website www.brightonfestival.org.uk
Takes place 5–27 May 2007

An annual general arts festival with a large literature programme. Leading guest writers cover a broad range of subjects in a diverse programme of events. Programme published end of February.

The Cambridge Conference of Contemporary Poetry

Trinity College, Cambridge CB2 1TQ
tel (01223) 332922
email lan22@cam.ac.uk
website www.cccp-online.org
Takes place April

A weekend of poetry readings, performances, discussion and other events. Emphasis is on modernist developments in contemporary poetry.

Cambridgewordfest

6 St Edwards Passage, Cambridge CB2 3PJ
tel (01223) 503333
email cam.wordfest@ btinternet.com
website www.cambridgewordfest.co.uk
Festival Director Cathy Moore
Takes place April

An annual literature festival held in the spring in Cambridge and surrounding area. It aims to provide a richly packed weekend of some of the best in contemporary fiction, political debate, workshops and events for children. It is a festival for writers as well as readers.

Camelford Poetry Festival

The Indian King Arts Centre, Camelford, Cornwall PL32 9PG
tel (01840) 212161
email indianking@btconnect.com
Contact Helen Jagger Wood
Takes place April

Formerly the Jon Silkin Memorial Poetry Festival, as a tribute to the support the poet gave to the Indian King Arts Centre. Geared to writers of poetry, with plenty of workshops as well as open mic readings, informal discussion, and performances.

Canterbury Festival

Festival Office, Christ Church Gate, The Precincts, Canterbury, Kent CT1 2EE
tel (01227) 452853 *fax* (01227) 781830
email info@canterburyfestival.co.uk
website www.canterburyfestival.co.uk
Takes place October

An annual general arts festival with a literature programme. Programme published in July.

Cheltenham Literature Festival

Town Hall, Imperial Square, Cheltenham, Glos. GL50 1QA
tel (01242) 227979 (box office), 237377 (brochure), 263494 (festival office) *fax* (01242) 256457
email clair.greenaway@cheltenham.gov.uk
website www.cheltenhamfestivals.com
Artistic Director Sarah Smyth
Takes place October

This annual festival is the largest of its kind in Europe. Events include talks and lectures, poetry readings, novelists in conversation, exhibitions, discussions, workshops and a large bookshop. *Book It!* is a festival for children within the main festival with an extensive programme of events. Brochures are available in August.

Chester Literature Festival

Viscount House, River Lane, Saltney, Chester CH4 8RH

tel (01244) 674020 *fax* (01244) 684060
email info@chesterlitfest.org.uk
website www.chester-literature-
festival.org.uk
Festival Administrator Katherine Seddon
Takes place September/October

An annual festival commencing the first
weekend in October. Events featuring
international, national and local writers
and poets are part of the programme, as
well as a literary lunch and festival dinner.
There is a poetry competition for school
children, events for children and
workshops for adults. A Cheshire Prize for
Literature is awarded each year; only
residents of Cheshire are eligible.

The City Chapter

Library HQ, 1 Markethill Road, Armagh
BT60 1NR
tel (02837) 520754
email gerry.burns@ni-libraries.net
website www. citychapter.org
Contact Gerry Burns
Takes place October

A partnership of the main library
providers in the Armagh City area. Each
year as part of National Poetry Day in
October it organises a Poetry Festival with
readings and workshops held in the
various local libraries.

City of London Festival

12–14 Mason's Avenue, London EC2V
5BB
tel 020-7796 4949 *fax* 020-7796 4959
email admin@colf.org
website www.colf.org
Takes place Last 2 weeks of June and first
week of July 2007

An annual multi-arts festival with a
programme of literary events. Programme
published in April.

Cley Little Festival of Poetry

Cley, Sheringham, Norfolk NR26 8HU
tel (01263) 821012

Contact Helen Birtwell
Takes place Twice a year

Founded by Elsa Martin; organised by the
Cley Poetry Circle. Set up more than 50
years ago, the group and festival provide a
welcome platform for poetry in North
Norfolk.

The Cúirt International Festival of Literature

Galway Arts Centre, 47 Dominick Street,
Galway, Republic of Ireland
tel (091) 565886 *fax* (091) 568642
email info@galwayartscentre.ie
website www.galwayartscentre.ie
Managing Director Tomás Hardiman,
Progamme Director Maura Kennedy
Takes place April

An annual week-long festival to celebrate
writing, bringing together national and
international writers to promote literary
discussion. Events include readings,
performances, workshops, seminars,
lectures, poetry slams and talks. The
festival is renowned for its convivial
atmosphere ('cúirt' means a 'bardic court
or gathering').

Cuisle, Limerick City International Poetry festival

The Belltable Arts Centre, 69 O'Connell
Street, Limerick, County Limerick, Ireland
tel (06) 131 9866
email info@belltable.ie
website www.limerickcity.ie
Takes place October

An annual poetry festival that celebrates
poets and poetry.

Dublin Writers' Festival

c/o Dublin City Council, Arts Office, The
Lab, Foley Street, Dublin 1, Republic of
Ireland
tel (01) 222 7847

email dublinwritersfestival@eircom.net
website www.dublinwritersfestival.com
Takes place June

An annual festival with readings by major Irish and international poets and writers to celebrate the best in contemporary literature.

Dulwich Festival

tel 020-8299 1011
email enquiries@dulwichfestival.co.uk
website www.dulwichfestival.co.uk
Contact Alison Lloyd
Takes place May

A community arts festival that features literary talks and readings, poetry, historical/architectural walks, theatre, music, art and family entertainment.

Durham Literature Festival

c/o Durham City Arts Ltd, 2 The Cottages, Fowlers Yard, Durham DH1 3RA
tel 0191-301 8830 *fax* 0191-301 8821
email alison@durhamcityarts.org
Festival Coordinator Alison Lister
Takes place September/October

Edinburgh International Book Festival

5A Charlotte Square, Edinburgh EH2 4DR
tel 0131-718 5666 *fax* 0131-226 5335
email admin@edbookfest.co.uk
website www.edbookfest.co.uk
Director Catherine Lockerbie
Takes place August

Now established as Europe's largest book event for the public. In addition to a unique independent bookselling operation, more than 600 writers contribute to the programme of events. Programme details available in June.

Essex Poetry Festival

Cramphorn Theatre, Fairfield Road, Chelmsford, Essex CM1 1JG

email derek@essex-poetry-festival.co.uk
website www.essex-poetry-festival.co.uk
Contact Derek Adams
Takes place October

A lively and varied series of poetry events and workshops.

Farrago Festival of the Spoken Word

Farrago Poetry, 108 High Street, West Wickham, Kent BR4 0ND
tel (07905) 078375
email farragopoetry@yahoo.co.uk
website http://London.e-poets.net/
Contact John O'Neill
Takes place May

A festival aimed at children and young people. A selection of poets perform their own work. There are also poetry workshops.

Folkestone Literary Festival

Church Street Studios, 11 Church Street, Folkestone, Kent CT20 1SE
tel (01303) 211300 *fax* (01303) 211883
email info@folkestonelitfest.com
website www.folkestonelitfest.co.uk
Takes place September

This annual festival launches with the announcement of the winner of the Saga Award for Wit, followed by over 40 events. The Children's Day concludes the festival.

The Guardian Hay Festival

Festival Office, The Drill Hall, 25 Lion Street, Hay-on-Wye HR3 5AD
tel (0870) 7872848 (admin)
website www.hayfestival.com
Takes place May/June

This annual festival aims to celebrate the best in writing and performance from around the world, to commission new work, and to promote and encourage young writers of excellence and potential.

More than 200 events over 10 days, with leading guest writers. Programme published April.

Guildford Book Festival

c/o Tourist Information Office, 14 Tunsgate, Guildford GU1 3QT
tel (01483) 444334
email deputy@ guildfordbookfestival.co.uk
website www.guildfordbookfestival.co.uk
Festival Director Glenis Pycraft
Takes place October

An annual festival. Diverse, provocative and entertaining, held throughout the historic town. Author events, poetry, workshops for all age groups from 6 months onwards. Its aim is to further an interest and love of literature by involvement and entertainment. Founded 1990.

Hackney Word Festival

London Borough of Hackney, Hackney Town Hall, Mare Street, London E8 1EA
tel 020-7249 6572
email literature@ centerprisetrust.org.uk
website http://www.hackney.gov.uk/discoverhackney

Brings acclaimed talents to venues and stages throughout Hackney. Also gives new talent a chance to shine, and to learn directly from the stars of the festival. Poetry workshops for all ages plus a poetry competition.

Huddersfield Literature Festival

University of Huddersfield, Queensgate, Huddersfield HD1 3DH
tel (08709) 905025
email enquiry@litfest.org.uk
website www.litfest.org.uk
Takes place March

Organised through the English Division at the University of Huddersfield ,and funded by the University of Huddersfield and Arts Council England, Yorkshire. Works closely with local organisations including The Media Centre, Kirklees Metropolitan Council, Huddersfield Art Gallery, Huddersfield Library and The Poetry Business.

The Humber Mouth

City Arts Unit, Central Library, Kingston upon Hull HU1 3TF
tel (01482) 616961
email Maggie.Hannan@ hullcc.gov.uk
Contact Maggie Hannan
Takes place June

Hull's biggest festival, attracting major writers and artists to the city over a 16-day period.

Isle of Barra International Festival of Poetry and Song

Isle of Barra Hotel, Isle Of Barra, Western Isles HS9 5XW
tel (01871) 890280
email bipas3@yahoo.com
website www.bipas3.co.uk
Contact John Pendrey
Takes place September

Stunningly inspiring venue for an open-stage festival, attracting both new and experienced poets of all ages and nationalities.

King's Lynn Poetry Festival

19 Tuesday Market Place, Kings Lynn, Norfolk PE30 1JW
tel (01553) 617602
email jberrypoet@aol.com
website www.lynnlitfests.co.uk
Contact Robert Davison
Takes place September

A 20-year-old festival featuring writers and poets from all over the world. There are 6 sessions, from Friday afternoon until

Sunday at 5pm. The sessions usually consist of writers and poets reading from their works and holding discussions on a variety of associated subjects.

Laugharne Arts Festival
c/o Corran Bookshop, King Street, Laugharne, Carmarthenshire SA33 4RY
tel (01994) 427444
email janetremlett@btconnect.com
Contact Jane Tremlett
Takes place August

A programme that brings together the local and the international in the unique setting that was home and inspiration to Dylan Thomas. A blend of poetry, art, drama, music, film and literature.

Lewes Live Literature
PO Box 2766, Lewes, East Sussex BN7 2WF
tel (01273) 400560
email info@leweslivelit.co.uk
website www.lewesliveliterature.co.uk
Takes place October/November

Lewes Live Literature aims to create enjoyable, interesting events in a sociable, artistic environment. Working across traditional artform boundaries, LLL festivals bring together the spoken word, performance, creative writing workshops, music, film and visual art. The LLL year revolves around 2 main programmes of work: a variable spring season covering activities from April to June (including events as part of the Brighton Festival), and the intensive 3-day Lewes Live Literature Festival, which takes place at the end of October/beginning of November.

Lincoln Book Festival
c/o City of Lincoln Council, DDES, City Hall, Beaumont Fee, Lincoln, Lincolnshire LN1 1DF
tel (01522) 873844
email arts@lincoln.gov.uk
website www.lincolnbookfestival.co.uk
Contact Sara Bullimore
Takes place May

A celebration of books and all that they inspire. The programme includes poetry competitions and events.

Lincolnshire Literature Development Programme
Community Services, Lincolnshire County Council, County Offices, Lincoln LN1 1YL
tel (01522) 553235 *fax* (01522) 552811
email chris.kirkwood@lincolnshire.gov.uk
County Arts Development Officer David Lambert, *Arts Officer* Chris Kirkwood
Takes place Throughout the year

A series of varied literary events. Occasional festivals, tours, publications in Lincolnshire.

Lit.Com
King Edward Street, Grimsby, North East Lincolnshire DN31 3LU
tel (01472) 323382
email charlotte.bowen@ nelincs.gov.uk
website www.nelincs.gov.uk/leisure/arts
Contact Charlotte Bowen
Takes place October

A celebration of both literature and comedy, including book and poetry readings, writing workshops, open mic and the best in up-and-coming stand up.

Lit Up
Brewery Arts Centre, Kendal, Cumbria
tel (01539) 722833 ext 242
email info@litup.org
website www.litup.org
Takes place September

A brand new event for arts professionals: a showcase of performance poetry, literature and spoken-word events alongside debates and discussions, all designed to explore new ways of developing the role of live literature in performing arts programmes.

Live Poetry at The Cut

The Cut Arts Centre, 9 New Cut, Halesworth, Suffolk IP19 8BY
tel (01986) 835950
website http://www.thepoetrytrust.org/html/cut_poetry.htm
Contact Charlotte Du Cann
Takes place July

Small poetry festival.

Lowdham Book Festival

4th Floor, Arts, County Hall, West Bridgford, Nottingham NG2 7QP
tel 0115-977 4435
email ross.bradshaw@nottscc.gov.uk
website www.lowdhambookfestival.co.uk
Contact Ross Bradshaw, Literature Officer
Takes place June/July

An annual 10-day festival of literature events for adults and children, with a daily programme of high-profile national writers. There is a writer-in-residence during the festival and a book fair on the last Saturday.

Middlesex University Literary Festival

White Hart Lane, Tottenham, London N17 8HR
tel 020-8411 5000
email s.wardle@mdx.ac.uk
Contact Sarah Wardle
Takes place March

Poets, poetry and publishers, performances, readings, music, workshops and discussions in a free festival. Organised by third-year undergraduate writing students, under the supervision of a member of staff.

National Eisteddfod of Wales

40 Parc Ty Glas, Llanisien, Cardiff CF14 5WU
tel 029-2076 3777 *fax* 029-2076 3737
email elfed@eisteddfod.org.uk
website www.eisteddfod.org.uk
Director Elfed Roberts
Takes place August

Wales's largest cultural festival, based on 800 years of tradition. Activities include competitions in all aspects of the arts, fringe performances and majestic ceremonies. In addition to activities held in the main pavilion, it houses over 300 trade stands along with a literary pavilion, a music studio, a movement and dance theatre, a rock pavilion and a purpose-built theatre. The event is set in a different location each year, and will take place on the outskirts of Mold in 2007.

Off the Shelf Literature Festival

Central Library, Surrey Street, Sheffield S1 1XZ
tel 0114-273 4400 *fax* 0114-273 4716
email offtheshelf@sheffield.gov.uk
website www.offtheshelf.org.uk
Contact Maria de Souza, Su Walker, Lesley Webster
Takes place October

The festival comprises a wide range of events for adults and children, including author visits, writing workshops, storytelling, competitions and exhibitions. Programme available in September.

Oundle Festival of Literature

2 Herne Road, Oundle, Peterborough, Northants PE8 4BS
tel (01832) 274960
email liz@oundlelitfest.org.uk
website www.oundlelitfest.org.uk
Contact Liz Dillarstone (Publicity)
Takes place March

Featuring a full programme of author events, poetry, philosophy, politics, story-telling, biography, illustrators and novelists for young and old. Includes events for children.

Poetry-next-the-Sea
Rowans, Warham Road, Wells-next-the-Sea, Norfolk NR23 1NE
tel (01328) 710193
email enquiries@ poetrynextthesea.com
website www.poetrynextthesea.com
Contact Helen Flanagan
Takes place April

An annual festival attracting poets of international standing to perform their work in the beautiful North Norfolk countryside.

Poetry International
Literature Section, Royal Festival Hall, South Bank Centre, London SE1 8XX
tel 020-7921 0906 *fax* 020-7928 2049
email awhitehead@rfh.org.uk
website www.rfh.org.uk
Contact Angela Whitehead
Takes place October 2008 (biennial)

The biggest poetry festival in the British Isles, bringing together a wide range of poets from around the world. Includes readings, workshops and discussions. The Literature + Talks also runs a year-round programme of readings, talks and debates.

Poetry Now Festival
The Arts Office, Dun Laoghaire, Rathdown, County Dublin, Ireland
tel (01) 205 4872
email arts@dlrcoco.ie
website www.dlrcoco.ie/arts
Contact Aisling McLaughlin
Takes place March

Ireland's leading poetry festival.

Poet's Letter London Poetry Books Festival
mobile (07931) 357109

email Editor@poetsletter.com
website www.poetsletter.com
Takes place May

Celebrating the craft of poetry, poetry publications of each and every sort, and poetry books.

ProudWords Festival
mobile (07973) 894912
email pwcwf@hotmail.com
website www.proudwords.org.uk

Promotes all kinds of writing by lesbian, gay and bisexual writers. The organisation was established in 1997 and runs an annual writing festival in Newcastle and Gateshead featuring poets, playwrights, novelists, singer-songwriters and performers.

Redbridge Book and Media Festival
London Borough of Redbridge, Arts & Events Team, 8th Floor, Lynton House, 255–259 High Road, Ilford IG1 1NY
tel 020-8708 3044
email laurence.staig@ redbridge.gov.uk
website www.redbridge.gov.uk/leisure/bkmdfest.cfm
Contact Arts & Events Team
Takes place May 2007

Features author talks, performances, panel debates, Urdu poetry events, an exhibition, workshops, children's activities and events, and a schools outreach programme.

Scottish Book Town Festival
County Buildings, Wigtown, Dumfries & Galloway DG8 9JH
tel (01988) 403222
email jenny@wigtownbookfestival.com
website www.wigtownbookfestival.com
Festival Chair Michael McCreath, *Festival Administrator* Jenny Bradley
Takes place Last 2 weekends in Sept

An annual festival in Scotland's national Book Town, which boasts 23 bookshops and book-related businesses. Readings and talks take place in the County Buildings, bookshops and nearby Bladnoch Distillery.

Sheffield Poetry International
40 Crescent Road, Sheffield S7 1HN
tel 0114-258 6035
email geraldine@ westhousebooks.co.uk

Sheffield Poetry International is a reading series featuring leading poets from Ireland, North America, Australia and Portugal who are partnered by locally based writers. It offers a unique opportunity for Yorkshire audiences to hear and meet poets of international reputation whose readings in England are usually restricted to London and Cambridge.

Snape
The Poetry Trust, The Cut, 9 New Cut, Halesworth, Suffolk IP9 8BY
tel (01986) 835950
email info@thepoetrytrust.org
website www.aldeburghpoetryfestival.org/ html/the_trust1.htm
Takes place August

Annual poetry prom at Snape Maltings Concert Hall.

Southwell Poetry Festival
Nottinghamshire County Council 4th Floor, Arts Nottingham NG2 7QP
tel 0115-977 4435
email http:// www.southwellpoetryfestival.co.uk
Literature Officer Ross Bradshaw
Takes place March

Poetry events based at the historic Southwell Minster.

Split the Lark Poetry Festival
1 King Edward Road, Deal, Kent CT14 6QL

tel (01304) 367625
Contact Liz Turner
Takes place June

Festival organised by the Split the Lark Poets in Deal, Kent

StAnza: Scotland's Poetry Festival
57 Lade Braes, St Andrews, Fife KY16 9DA
email info@stanzapoetry.org
website www.stanzapoetry.org
Contact Brian Johnstone
Takes place March

The only regular festival dedicated to poetry in Scotland, StAnza is catholic and international in outlook. Held annually in the ancient university town of St Andrews, it is an opportunity to engage with all forms of poetry and to hear world-class poets reading in exciting and atmospheric venues.

Stoke Newington Festival
tel 020-8356 6410
email info@stokenewingtonfestival.co.uk
website www.stokenewingtonfestival.co.uk
Contact Fiona Fieber
Takes place June

A 10-day multi-arts programme, including 'WordontheStreet', which focuses on literature, spoken work, performance, texts and readers.

Stop All The Clocks at The Marlborough
The Marlborough, Prince's Street, Brighton, East Sussex
tel (01273) 207562
email simon@stopalltheclocks.co.uk
website www.stopalltheclocks.co.uk
Contact Simon Clayton
Takes place May

The highlight of Brighton's poetry year, including more traditional readings, performance events and 'fringe of the fringe' nights like 'All Mouth No Trousers' – a combined poetry/striptease performance.

Stratford-upon-Avon Poetry Festival

Shakespeare Centre, Henley Street, Stratford-upon-Avon CV37 6QW
tel (01789) 204016 *fax* (01789) 296083
email info@shakespeare.org.uk
website www.shakespeare.org.uk
Director Roger Pringle
Takes place June–August, mainly on Sunday evenings

This annual festival opens with a reading by Andrew Motion. Recitals feature well-known actors presenting poetry of the past as well as contemporary poets.

The Sunday Times Oxford Literary Festival

301 Woodstock Road, Oxford OX2 7NY
tel (01865) 514149 *fax* (01865) 514804
email oxford.literary.festival@ntlworld.com
website www.sundaytimes-oxfordliteraryfestival.co.uk
Festival Directors Angela Prysor-Jones, Sally Dunsmore
Takes place 2 weeks prior to Easter

An annual 8-day festival for both adults and children. Presents topical debates, fiction and non-fiction discussion panels, and adult and children's authors who have recently published books. Topics range from contemporary fiction to discussions on politics, history, science, gardening, food, poetry, philosophy, art and crime fiction. An additional 2 days of events for schools.

Swindon Festival of Literature

Lower Shaw Farm, Shaw, Swindon, Wiltsshire SN5 5PJ
tel (01793) 771080 *fax* (01793) 771080
email swindonlitfest@lowershawfarm.co.uk
website www.swindonfestivalofliterature.co.uk
Festival Director Matt Holland
Takes place Starts at dawn on 1 May for 15 days

An annual celebration of literature – prose, poetry, drama and storytelling – by readings, discussions, performances, talks, etc, indoors and out.

Tears in the Fence Festival

38 Hod View, Stourpaine, Blandford Forum, Dorset DT11 8TN
tel (01258) 456803
email david@davidcaddy.wanadoo.co.uk
website www.wanderingdog.co.uk
Contact David Caddy
Takes place July

A themed international poetry festival that includes readings, talks, writing workshops, art exhibits, music, children's workshops and events, bookstalls and signings.

Text Festival

Exeter Phoenix, Bradninch Place, Gandy Street, Exeter EX4 3LS
tel (01392) 667080
email director@exeterphoenix.org.uk
website www.textfestival.org
Takes place April/May

Exeter-based writing festival.

Dylan Thomas Festival: A Refusal To Mourn

Dylan Thomas Centre, Somerset Place, Maritime Quarter, Swansea SA1 1RR
tel (01792) 463980
email dylanthomas.lit@swansea.gov.uk
website www.dylanthomas.org
Contact David Woolley
Takes place October/November

Annual festival of contemporary writing and art.

Torbay Weekend Festival of Poetry

The Mount, Higher Furzeham Road,
Brixham, Devon TQ5 8QY
tel (01803) 851098
Contact Patricia Oxley
Takes place October

Audience participation is actively
encouraged, with 8 events having space for
the audience to join in.

Ty Newydd Festival

3rd Floor, Mount Stuart House, Mount
Stuart Square, Cardiff CF10 5FQ
tel (02920) 472266 *fax* (02920) 492930
email post@academi.org
website www.academi.org
Contact Peter Finch, Chief Executive
Takes place April 2008 (biennial)

Events are centred on the writing centre at
Llanystumdwy in Gwynedd, and feature a
mix of Welsh and English events including
Poetry Stomps and guest readers. The
Academi, the Welsh National Literature
Promotion Agency, supports Ty Newydd
to create this festival.

Warwick International Festival

Northgate, Warwick CV34 4JL
tel (01926) 410747 *fax* (01926) 409050
email richardp@warwickarts.org.uk
Festival Director Richard Phillips
Takes place June–July

A music festival which includes some
literature and poetry events: readings,
performances and workshops.

Wells Festival of Literature

25 Chamberlain Street, Wells, Somerset
BA5 2PQ
tel (01749) 670929
website www.somersite.co.uk/wellsfest.htm
Takes place Mid-October

An annual week-long festival featuring
leading writers and poets. It includes

theatre and cinema events, writing
workshops and short story and poetry
competitions. Events take place in the
historic Bishop's Palace and other venues
around the historic city of Wells.

Wonderful Words Book Festival

Penzance Library, Morrab Road, Penzance
TR18 4EY
tel (01736) 363954
email agunderson@ cornwall.gov.uk
website www.cornwall.gov.uk/library
*Library Outreach Officer & Festival
Organiser* Alison Gunderson
Takes place September/October

A biennial festival organised by the
Cornwall Library Service. Events take
place throughout the county, including
talks, discussions, workshops, poetry and
storytelling. The festival attracts high-
profile authors.

Word – University of Aberdeen Writers Festival

University of Aberdeen, Office of External
Affairs, University of Aberdeen, King's
College, Aberdeen AB24 3FX
tel (01224) 274444 *fax* (01224) 272086
website www.abdn.ac.uk/word
Artistic Director Alan Spence, *Festival
Producer* Elly Rothnie, *Festival Co-
ordinator* Fiona Christie
Takes place May

Over 50 of the world's finest writers and
artists take part in a packed weekend of
readings, music, art exhibitions and film
screenings. The Word Kid's Programme
hosts some of the UK's best-loved
children's writers as well as some of the
richest talents in Gaelic literature.

Word About Town

The Foresters Arms, 2 Shepherd Street, St
Leonards-on-Sea, East Sussex TN38 0ET

tel (01424) 436513
email info@dontfeedthepoets.co.uk
website www.dontfeedthepoets.co.uk
Contact John Knowles
Takes place November

Live literature, poetry, music, comedy, film, workshops and competitions.

Wordfringe
email info@wordfringe.co.uk
website www.wordfringe.co.uk
Director Haworth Hodgkinson
Takes place May

A new community-based festival showcasing writers and writing in the North East of Scotland. The festival takes place both before and after the weekend of Word 06, the University of Aberdeen Writers' Festival. The 2 festivals complement each other, with Word bringing some highly respected writers to Aberdeen, and Wordfringe providing opportunities for many more new writers to appear alongside some more established names. Events range from poetry readings and storytelling sessions to events combining the spoken word with music, dance and video. Many of the writers taking part live and work in the North East of Scotland, but visiting guests from Shetland, Lewis, Northumberland and Devon also feature.

Wordsworth Trust Poetry Season
The Waterside Ho, Keswick Road, Grasmere, Cumbria LA22 9PR
tel (01539) 435544
email R.Stanton@wordsworth.org.uk
website www.wordsworth.org.uk
Contact R Stanton
Takes place May–October

A programme of readings by major poets.

World Book Day
c/o The Booksellers Association, 272 Vauxhall Bridge Road, London SW1V 1BA
tel 020-8987 9370
email cathy.schofield@blueyonder.co.uk
website www.worldbookday.com
Contact Cathy Schofield
Takes place 1 March 2007

An annual celebration of books and reading aimed at promoting their value and creating the readers of the future. Every schoolchild in full-time education receives a £1 book token. Events take place all over the UK in schools, bookshops, libraries and arts centres.

Writers' Week
24 The Square, Listowel, Co. Kerry, Republic of Ireland
tel (068) 21074 *fax* (068) 22893
email info@writersweek.ie
website www.writersweek.ie
Administrators Eilish Wren, Máire Logue
Takes place 30 May–3 June 2007

Aims to promote the work of Irish writers in both the English and Irish language, and to provide a platform for new and established writers to discuss their works. Events include readings, seminars, lectures and book launches.

Writing On the Wall
60 Duke Street, Liverpool L1 5AA
tel 015-1707 4313
email info@writingonthewall.org.uk
website www.writingonthewall.org.uk
Contact Janette Stowell
Takes place May

An annual programme of events culminating in an annual festival, which – with schools, young people, local communities and broader audiences – celebrates writing, diversity, tolerance, storytelling and humour through controversy, inquiry and debate.

Supporting your work
The Poetry Book Society

The Poetry Book Society (PBS) is both book club and poetry promotion agency, doing fine work – in these days of invisibility for poetry titles in bookshops – in getting poetry to its readership. **Chris Holifield** explains the work of the Society.

When TS Eliot and friends set up the Poetry Book Society in 1953, its remit was to support and develop the sales of poetry books. To this day the organisation, now regularly funded by the Arts Council, is focused on maximising poetry book sales, although it has also taken on the task of promoting the reading of poetry. The PBS functions as a book club for poetry lovers, and *Bulletin* magazine provides its members with an overview of the best newly published poetry.

Four times a year the PBS requests submissions from poetry publishers, in accordance with PBS eligibility criteria. Books are submitted by publishers and the PBS's Poet Selectors choose the best new single-author poetry collection of the quarter. This title is then ordered from the publisher (with the words 'Poetry Book Society Choice' proudly emblazoned on the cover) and sent to all PBS full members.

The Selectors also make four Recommendations, and choose a Special Commendation, which need not be a single-author collection and is sometimes a non-fiction book. The *Bulletin,* which is sent to members quarterly with their books, is in effect a review of the best new poetry. It also features the Translation Choice, chosen by the Translation Selector. The fairly newly established Pamphlet Choice, which has proved a successful way of bringing interesting new work to a wider audience, is chosen by two Pamphlet Selectors: this is the only category for which self-published work is eligible. Other new books are featured in the *Bulletin,* which also lists every poetry book submitted by publishers for that quarter.

The Poetry Book Society members are knowledgeable and enthusiastic about poetry; they are extremely loyal and many of them have been with the PBS for many years. As well as full membership, the PBS offers Associate membership: associates receive only the *Bulletin* each quarter, but can still buy books at the members' discount of 25 per cent off. Then there is the Charter membership for libraries. Charter members receive the Choice and all the Recommendations, i.e. five books a quarter. Finally, there is the Education membership, which is designed for secondary school teachers and includes teaching tips on poems from the books chosen. The PBS also has special expertise in finding poetry titles from smaller presses, and can often track down a hard-to-find title.

The PBS website is at www.poetrybooks.co.uk; here members get their 25 per cent discount on all the poetry books in print in the UK.

The PBS also runs the Children's Poetry Bookshelf, offering poetry written for children in the 7- to 11-year-old age group. The CPB was relaunched in 2005, with a lively child-friendly website at www.childrenspoetrybookshelf.co.uk, providing quizzes and poetry puzzles for children, as well as the chance for children to send their own poems and reviews to go on the site. The adult part of the site recruits new members, including teachers, parents and grandparents, and libraries. Members receive books every term and teaching tips are freely available to all members. The new gift membership allows the member to send the books straight to the child they nominate, making it possible for any poetry lover to give the gift of poetry to a child throughout the year. Members can buy all the children's poetry titles available in the UK through the website at a discount of 25 per cent, with a further discount for class sets.

In 2004 the PBS launched www.poetrybookshoponline.com, a niche online bookselling site which offers all the poetry titles in print in the UK. This new website was launched in response to the difficulty many readers have experienced with locating a good selection of poetry in bookshops. We intend to develop the website into a poetry portal, with reviews, news and events – a wide range of information of interest to poetry readers – as well as a strong emphasis on books. Every January, the PBS awards the annual TS Eliot Prize for the best new single-author poetry collection published in the previous year. Titles are entered by the publishers, and there is keen interest in the winner. The Prize is sponsored by the broadcaster Five, and Mrs Valerie Eliot provides the winner's cheque for £10,000. The evening before the award ceremony, the ten shortlisted poets are invited to take part in the annual TS Eliot Readings in London – an electrifying evening of superb poetry.

In 2004 the PBS also ran the Next Generation Poets promotion. The judging panel – chaired by Poet Laureate Andrew Motion – chose, from among the poets whose first collections were published in the previous decade, the 20 poets who in their opinion were the most exhilarating new voices.

In 2005 the PBS took on the exclusive sales of the CDs from the Poetry Archive, featuring 60-minute recordings from 80 poets. The Archive is dedicated to making recordings of living poets, so that their voices will not be lost to posterity. It has produced superb new digital recordings, which enable everyone to have the luxury of being able to listen to their favourite poets.

There is great concern in the poetry world about the poor sales of poetry books. In the current retail climate, many bookshops struggle to maintain a reasonable stockholding of poetry titles, and all too often there is only a small selection of poetry available. Faced with this problem, the Poetry Book Society's mission to serve readers and support poets by maximising the sales of poetry books becomes even more important. The Society is also unique in a global context, as is the Children's Poetry Bookshelf, as they are the only poetry book clubs in existence. With this in mind, future plans will involve growing the PBS membership internationally, and selling as many poetry books as possible both in the UK and all over the world.

For more information contact: The Poetry Book Society, Fourth floor, 2 Tavistock Place, London WC1H 9RA
tel 020-7833 9247
email info@poetrybooks.co.uk
website www.poetrybooks.co.uk.

Chris Holifield is Director of the Poetry Book Society.

The Poetry Society

The Poetry Society was founded in London almost a hundred years ago, as a small membership organisation to promote "a more general recognition and appreciation of poetry". Since then, it has grown into one of Britain's most high-profile arts organisations representing British poetry both nationally and internationally. Today, it has more than 3000 members around the world. If you read, write or enjoy poetry, the Poetry Society can help open up the world of contemporary poetry for you.

Membership benefits include a subscription to *Poetry Review* magazine, a free information directory, a discount on entry to the National Poetry Competition, 'partner' discounts at bookshops and events around the UK, and *Poetry News*, a members' newsletter that explores the contemporary landscape of poetry. Membership is open to all, with special categories of membership for libraries, schools and young poets.

Poetry Review

The place in which to get published, and the place to find out about the best in contemporary poetry, *Poetry Review* has been a part of the Poetry Society's membership benefits since 1912. Ripped eagerly from the envelope each quarter by readers and writers of good poetry, *Poetry Review* puts you at the heart of what's happening, with a diverse selection of poems by contemporary writers – from the famous and established to promising newcomers; from the formally traditional to the modernist and avant-garde. It's a literary magazine with authority and vision, and a forum for intelligent reviews. One feature of the magazine is the annual Geoffrey Dearmer Prize, which was established to enable *Poetry Review* to award £400 to the "new poet of the year". This goes to the best poem published in the *Review* by a poet who has not yet published a book.

Poetry News

Poetry News is our quarterly newsletter. Members are invited to send in poems on a particular theme each quarter, and six of the best are included on a regular dedicated members' page as well as on the Poetry Society's website. There is also a 'close-up' on the nuts and bolts of poetic craft; a Q&A on the route to a first collection; interviews with rising stars; profiles of poetry publishers and magazines; features on poetry overseas; news of prize-winners; and details of current activities at the Poetry Society. Each year the Hamish Canham Poetry Prize awards £300 for the best member's poem to appear in *Poetry News* during the year.

Poetry Directory

When you join the Poetry Society, you'll receive the indispensable *Poetry Directory* absolutely free of charge. This is packed with information on everything from copyright law to courses, reference books to residential workshops. In it you'll find the answers to many of the questions an interest in poetry raises.

The website

For poetry events and activities around the country, visit the Poetry Society website at www.poetrysociety.org.uk. Have the poetry world at your fingertips; look up specific poetry locations (more than 500 and growing) on 'Poetry Landmarks of Great Britain'; explore how to celebrate National Poetry Day; keep in touch with what's been happening with poetry in the news; find out who UK publishers are publishing in 'Forthcoming Publications'; discover an ever-changing range of lively poetry links; enter the National Poetry Competition; and of course, keep up to date with everything the Poetry Society is doing. The members' page on the website provides a guide to Poetry Society Stanzas, listings of members' books, discounts for Poetry Society members at bookshops, and special offers on tickets to poetry events nationwide.

Stanzas

In these days of virtual communication, the local poetry group still thrives. Years ago we had the nationwide Poetry Secretariat; today we have the nationwide (potentially worldwide) Poetry Society Stanzas. We're committed to developing local links between Poetry Society members on a voluntary basis, whereby the members constitute themselves a Poetry Society 'Stanza' so that they can exchange information, meet, and contribute to the local poetry scene more effectively. Our aim is to connect members with what is happening in their locality – our local 'stanzas' can circulate news and 'happenings' from groups, competitions, journals, publishers and readings in your area.

The Poetry Café

The Poetry Café (22 Betterton Street, Covent Garden) is the public face of the Poetry Society. It's a great place to meet other poetry-lovers and to pick up news and information. The range of events at the Café gives you the opportunity to try out a number of different poetry activities to see which suits your interests best. You can hear both complete beginners and internationally renowned poets. As a Poetry Society member you'll enjoy a discount on all events.

The Café has different moods: from quiet in the morning and mid-afternoon, when members come to write and talk to friends, to busy lunches with excellent, reasonably priced, freshly cooked food, culminating in buzzing evenings that might feature a visit by 15 poets from Birmingham, an open mic evening, a book launch, or an opportunity to catch one of the leading lights of the poetry world as they pass through London.

Poetry Prescription

For an honest, unbiased critical appraisal of your poetry, you can have your work looked at by our team of published poets. The Poetry Prescription service is an invaluable opportunity to get constructive advice from a professional poet; and as a member you will get a 20 per cent discount.

National Poetry Competition

Since it was established in 1978 by the Poetry Society, the National Poetry Competition has become the biggest and most prestigious poetry competition of its kind. It offers the chance to get your poetry read by some of the most distinguished writers of our time. The entry fee is £5 for the first poem submitted, and £3 for subsequent entries. Poetry Society members get a *free* second entry. All entries are judged anonymously. Past winners have been both well known and previously unpublished poets.

The Foyle Young Poets Award

This is one of the leading competitions for writers between 11 and 17 years old. Funded by the Foyle Foundation, and commonly referred to as the 'Young National', the award stands out for not only recognising but also nurturing talented young poets. The 15 overall winners are invited to attend a residential writing course at the Arvon Lumb Bank centre, where they are tutored by the very same poets who judged the competition. Previous winners have enjoyed the long-term benefits from this extraordinary opportunity to form a tightly knit writing community, and some have gone on to be published by Carcanet Press, in established poetry journals, and as part of Young Poets on the Underground. The competition is free to enter, with entries accepted from February to July each year.

Poems on the Underground

Travellers on London's Underground don't have to open a book to enjoy poetry: Poems on the Underground is Britain's most popular public art project. And the Poetry Society is happy to announce that you don't have to be a traveller on the London Underground to enjoy these wonderful posters displaying the history of English and world poetry, and featuring poets from William Blake to Don Paterson, from Carol Rumens to anonymous medieval scribes. With our special 'Underground Membership' we'll send you six new Poems on the Underground posters three times a year. NB: If you are affiliated with a school, Poems on the Underground is a benefit of school membership.

Slam

The 'respect slam' is aimed at young people in Greater London, aged between 12 and 18. Slam is the competitive art of performance poetry, and the Poetry Society's respect slam showcase team is chosen from over a hundred participants. The showcase team of young poets shares the stage with professional performance poets in a spectacular finale of original work on the theme of 'respect' at the Mayor of London's annual anti-racism festival. Out of this project we now have a team of 'Poetry Slambassadors' who are available to travel to communities across the UK to perform and discuss their work.

The Poetry Society, 22 Betterton Street, London WC2H 9BX
tel 020-7420 9881 *fax* 020-7240 4818
email info@poetrysociety.org.uk
website www.poetrysociety.org.uk
Director Jules Mann

Poetry organisations

Academi – The Welsh National Literature Promotion Agency and Society for Writers

Mount Stuart House, Mount Stuart Square, Cardiff CF10 5FQ
tel (02920) 472266
email post@academi.org
website www.academi.org
Contact Peter Finch

The Welsh Academi is the Welsh National Literature Promotion and Society of Writers. The Academi runs events, courses, competitions, conferences, tours by authors, events for schools, readings, literary performances and festivals. Has responsibility for offering financial bursaries and critical advice, and administers the annual Book of the Year award. Publishes a number of magazines including *A470*, *What's On In Literary Wales*, and *Taliesin*, a literary journal in the Welsh language.

Academy of American Poets

The Academy of American Poets, 584 Broadway, Suite 604, New York, NY 10012-5243
tel (001212) 2740343 *fax* (001212) 2749427
email academy@poets.org
website www.poets.org

The Academy of American Poets was founded in 1934 to support American poets at all stages of their careers, and to foster the appreciation of contemporary poetry. To fulfill this mission, the Academy administers a wide variety of programmes, including National Poetry Month (April), the largest literary celebration in the world; online educational resources providing free poetry lesson plans for high school teachers; the Poetry Audio Archive, a collection of nearly 500 recordings dating back to the 1960s; and Poets.org, an award-winning website which provides a wealth of content on contemporary American poetry and receives an average of 400,000 unique users each month.

Apples & Snakes

Battersea Arts Centre, Lavender Hill, London SW11 5TN
tel 020-7924 3410
email info@applesandsnakes.org
website www.applesandsnakes.org
Contact Geraldine Collinge

Promotes live, spoken-word, performance poetry, through shows/performances and educational workshops.

Arts Council England

The Literature Dept, Arts Council England, 14 Great Peter Street, London SW1P 3NQ
tel 0845-300 6200 *textphone* 020-7973 6564
fax 020-7973 6590
email enquiries@artscouncil.org.uk
website www.artscouncil.org.uk

Arts Council England is the national development agency for the arts in England, providing funding for a range of arts activities. (see Gary McKeone's article, page 191, for details of ACE's involvement with poetry).

Arts Council England, East

Eden House, 48-49 Bateman Street, Cambridge CB2 1LR
tel 0845-300 6200 *fax* 0870-242 1271
textphone (01223) 306893

Area covered: Bedfordshire, Cambridgeshire, Essex, Hertfordshire, Norfolk, Suffolk; and unitary authorities of Luton, Peterborough, Southend-on-Sea, Thurrock.

Arts Council England, East Midlands

St Nicholas Court, 25-27 Castle Gate, Nottingham NG1 7AR
tel 0845-300 6200 *fax* 0115-950 2467

Area covered: Derbyshire, Leicestershire, Lincolnshire (excluding North and North East Lincolnshire), Northamptonshire, Nottinghamshire; and unitary authorities of Derby, Leicester, Nottingham, Rutland.

Arts Council England, London

Details David Cross, Literature Administrator, Arts Council England, London, 2 Pear Tree Court, London EC1R 0DS
tel 020-7608 6184 *fax* 020-7608 4100
website www.artscouncil.org.uk

Arts Council England, London, is the regional office for the Capital, covering 33 boroughs and the City of London.

Arts Council England, North East

Central Square, Forth Street, Newcastle upon Tyne NE1 3PJ
tel 0845-300 6200 *fax* 0191-230 1020
textphone 0191-255 8585

Area covered: Durham, Northumberland; metropolitan authorities of Gateshead, Newcastle upon Tyne, North Tyneside, South Tyneside, Sunderland; and unitary authorities of Darlington, Hartlepool, Middlesbrough, Redcar and Cleveland, Stockton-on-Tees.

Arts Council England, North West

Manchester House, 22 Bridge Street, Manchester M3 3AB
tel 0845-300 6200 *fax* 0161-834 6969
textphone 0161-834 9131

Area covered: Cheshire, Cumbria, Lancashire; metropolitan authorities of Bolton, Bury, Knowsley, Liverpool, Manchester, Oldham, Rochdale, St Helens, Salford, Sefton, Stockport, Tameside, Trafford, Wigan, Wirral; and unitary authorities of Blackburn with Darwen, Blackpool, Halton, Warrington.

Arts Council England, South East

Sovereign House, Church Street, Brighton BN1 1RA
tel 0845-300 6200 *fax* 0870-242 1257
textphone (01273) 710659

Area covered: Buckinghamshire, East Sussex, Hampshire, Isle of Wight, Kent, Oxfordshire, Surrey, West Sussex; and unitary authorities of Bracknell Forest, Brighton & Hove, Medway Towns, Milton Keynes, Portsmouth, Reading, Slough, Southampton, West Berkshire, Windsor and Maidenhead, Wokingham.

Arts Council England, South West

Senate Court, Southernhay Gardens, Exeter EX1 1UG
tel 0845-300 6200 *fax* (01392) 229229
textphone (01392) 433503

Area covered: Cornwall, Devon, Dorset, Gloucestershire, Somerset, Wiltshire; unitary authorities of Bath and North East Somerset, Bournemouth, Bristol, North Somerset, Plymouth, Poole, South Gloucestershire, Swindon, Torbay.

Arts Council England, West Midlands

82 Granville Street, Birmingham B1 2LH
tel 0845-300 6200 *fax* 0121-643 7239
textphone 0121-643 2815
website www.artscouncil.org.uk
Literature Officer Adrian Johnson
Literature Assistant Maeve Haughey

Area covered: Shropshire, Staffordshire, Warwickshire, Worcestershire;

metropolitan authorities of Birmingham, Coventry, Dudley, Sandwell, Solihull, Walsall, Wolverhampton; and unitary authorities of Herefordshire, Stoke-on-Trent, Telford and Wrekin.

Arts Council England, Yorkshire
21 Bond Street, Dewsbury, West Yorkshire WF13 1AX
tel 0845-300 6200 *fax* (01924) 466522
textphone (01924) 438585

Area covered: North Yorkshire; metropolitan authorities of Barnsley, Bradford, Calderdale, Doncaster, Kirklees, Leeds, Rotherham, Sheffield, Wakefield; and unitary authorities of East Riding of Yorkshire, Kingston upon Hull, North Lincolnshire, North East Lincolnshire, York.

Arts Council/An Chomhairle Ealaíon
Literature Officer, 70 Merrion Square, Dublin 2, Republic of Ireland
tel (01) 6180200 *fax* (01) 6761302
website www.artscouncil.ie
Arts Programme Director John O'Kane

The national development agency for the arts in Ireland. Founded 1951.

Arts Council of Northern Ireland
MacNeice House, 77 Malone Road, Belfast BT9 5JW
tel 028-9038 5200 *fax* 028-90661715
website www.artscouncil-ni.org
Chief Executive Roisín McDonough,
Literature Officer Damian Smyth, *Visual Arts Officers* Iain Davidson, Suzanne Lyle

Promotes and encourages the arts throughout Northern Ireland. Artists in drama, dance, music and jazz, literature, the visual arts, traditional arts and community arts can apply for support for specific schemes and projects. The value of the grant will be set according to the aims

of the application. Applicants must have contributed regularly to the artistic activities of the community, and been resident for at least 1 year in Northern Ireland.

The Arts Council of Wales
9 Museum Place, Cardiff CF10 3NX
tel 029-2037 6500 *minicom* 029-2039 0027
fax 029-2022 1447
email info@artswales.org.uk
website www.artswales.org.uk
Chairman Prof. Dai Smith, *Arts Director* David Alston, *Head of Communications* Sian Phipps, *Wales Arts International* Chris Richetts, *Director of South Wales* David Newland, *Director of North Wales* Simon Lovell Jones, *Director of Mid & West Wales* Sian Tomos

National organisation with specific responsibility for the funding and development of the arts in Wales. ACW receives funding from the National Assembly for Wales and also distributes the National Lottery funds in Wales to the arts. From these resources, ACW makes grants to support arts activities and facilities. Some of the funds are allocated in the form of annual revenue grants to full-time arts organisations. It also operates schemes which provide financial and other forms of support for individual activities or projects. ACW undertakes this work in both the English and Welsh languages.

The Arvon Foundation
Lumb Bank, Heptonstall, Hebden Bridge, West Yorkshire HX7 6DF
tel (01422) 843714 *fax* (01422) 843714
email l-bank@arvonfoundation.org
website www.arvonfoundation.org
Contact Ilona Jones
Moniack Mhor, Teavarran, Kiltarlity, Beauly, Inverness-shire IV4 7HT

tel (01463) 741675 *fax* (01463) 741733
email m-mhor@arvonfoundation.org
Contact Chris Aldridge
The Arvon Foundation, Totleigh Barton,
Sheepwash, Beaworthy, Devon EX21 5NS
tel (01409) 231338 *fax* (01409) 231144
email t-barton@arvonfoundation.org
Contact Julia Wheadon
The Hurst – The John Osborne Arvon
Centre
Clunton, Craven Arms, Shropshire SY7
0JA
tel (01588) 640658 *fax* (01588) 640509
email hurst@arvonfoundation.org

Founded in 1968, the Arvon Foundation
run 5-day residential courses throughout
the year for anyone over the age of 16,
providing the opportunity to live and
work with professional writers. Writing
genres explored include poetry, narrative,
drama, writing for children, song-writing
and the performing arts. Bursaries are
available.

Association for Scottish Literary Studies (ASLS)

c/o Dept of Scottish History, 9 University
Gardens, University of Glasgow G12 8QH
tel 0141-330 5309
email office@asls.org.uk
website www.asls.org.uk
Hon. President Alan MacGillivray, *Hon.
Secretary* Lorna Borrowman Smith,
Publishing Manager Duncan Jones
Membership £38 p.a. individuals, £10 UK
students, £67 corporate

Promotes the study, teaching and writing
of Scottish literature and furthers the
study of the languages of Scotland.
Publishes annually an edited text of
Scottish literature, an anthology of new
Scottish writing, a series of academic
journals and a Newsletter (2 p.a.). Also
publishes *Scotnotes* (comprehensive study
guides to major Scottish writers), literary

texts and commentary CDs designed to
assist the classroom teacher, and a series of
occasional papers. Organises 3 conferences
a year. Founded 1970.

Australia Council for the Arts

PO Box 788, Strawberry Hills, NSW 2012,
Australia
tel (02) 9215 9000 *fax* (02) 9215 9111
email mail@ozco.gov.au
website www.ozco.gov.au
Chairperson David Gonski

Provides a broad range of support for the
arts in Australia, embracing music,
theatre, literature, visual arts, crafts,
Aboriginal arts, community and new
media arts. It has 8 major Boards:
Literature, Visual Arts/Craft, Music,
Theatre, Dance, New Media, Community
Cultural Development, Major Performing
Arts, as well as the Aboriginal and Torres
Strait Islander Arts Board.

The Literature Board's chief objective is to
support the writing of all forms of creative
literature – novels, short stories, poetry,
plays and literary non-fiction. It also
assists with the publication of literary
magazines, has a book publishing
subsidies programme, and initiates and
supports projects of many kinds designed
to promote Australian literature both
within Australia and abroad.

Big Mouth

18 Allington Road, Southville, Bristol
BS3 1PS
mobile (07771) 546919
email rosemary.dun@virgin.net
website www.rosemarydun.co.uk
Contact Rosemary Dun

Has been promoting poetry, poets and
poetry events in Bristol for 5 years.
Regular Big Mouth Cabaret nights see
poetry mixed with music, comedy, visuals –

anything. Big Mouth has an ethos of bringing on new poets, and has run master classes with top international poets as well as slams. It organises the Big Mouth poetry tent at Bristol's Ashton Court Festival, with audiences of between 200 and 400. Also supports education in schools projects, which can and often do include football poetry.

Big Word Performance Poetry

72 Roseburn Street, Edinburgh EH12 5PL
tel 0131-476 3822
email jemrolls@bigword.fsnet.co.uk
Co-ordinator Jem Rolls

Organises regular poetry performances and competitive 'slams' around Scotland, as well as undertaking international tours, including yearly visits to fringe festivals in Canada. Its aim is to aid the development of a vibrant and diverse live poetry scene in Edinburgh and beyond, by presenting high-quality work at accessible prices.

Blue Nose Poets

204 Horsenden Lane South, Perivale, Greenford UB6 7NU
email bluenose@athelstan.netkonect.co.uk
website www.netkonect.net/~athelstan/who.html

National poetry organisation based in London. Provides workshops, cross-artform events, residential courses, platforms for new writing, correspondence workshops, poetry competitions, and services to schools. Aims to bring new audiences to poetry by forming collaborations with groups working in other fields, especially the visual arts.

Booktrust

(formerly the National Book League, founded 1925)
Book House, 45 East Hill, London SW18 2QZ
tel 020-8516 2977 *fax* 020-8516 2998
email info@booktrust.org.uk
website www.booktrust.org.uk
www.booktrusted.com
Chairman Trevor Glover, *Executive Director* Chris Meade

Booktrust is an independent charity bringing books and people together. It exists to open up the world of books and reading to people of all ages and cultures. Its services and activities include the Book Information Service, a unique specialist information service for all queries on books and reading (business callers are charged at £1.50 per minute on 0906-516 1193, weekdays 10am–1pm). Booktrust administers a number of literary prizes, including the Orange, Commonwealth, Nestlé Children's and the Booktrust Teenage, and runs a series of reader development projects.

The Children's Literature Team at Booktrust offers advice and information on all aspects of children's reading and books. The 'booktrusted' website is dedicated to children's books and resources for professionals working with young readers, including annotated book lists, information about organisations concerned with children's books, publishers, children's book news and much more. Booktrust also produces a range of publications, including *Best Book Guide for Children and Young Adults*, and resource materials for National Children's Book Week. It also coordinates the national Bookstart (books for babies) programme which gives free advice and books to parents/carers attending their baby's health checks.

The Bridlington Heritage Poets

c/o Spindrift, 7 George Street, Kingsgate , Bridlington, East Yorkshire YO15 3PH
Contact J. Sykes

Promotes poetry throughout the region, including involvement with schools and societies, runs poetry competitions and works with established poets and musicians in concert and raises funds for many worthwhile charities.

Brightside
33 Churchill Street, Leicester LE2 1FH
website www.brightside.mcmail.com

Opened in April 1996 as a poetry cabaret event in Leicester, the Brightside is now a performance poetry organisation made up of professional performance poets who have backgrounds in teaching, youth work, theatre, mental health and stand-up comedy.

The British Council
10 Spring Gardens, London SW1A 2BN
tel 020-7930 8466 *fax* 020-7839 6347
website www.britishcouncil.org
Chair The Rt Hon. Lord Kinnock,
Director-General Sir David Green, *Director of Literature* Susanna Nicklin, *Director of Arts* Leigh Gibson

The British Council connects people worldwide with learning opportunities and creative ideas from the UK, and builds lasting relationships between the UK and other countries. It works in 110 countries, where it has over 180 libraries and information centres, each catering to the needs of the local community with print and electronic resources. In 2005–6, 300,000 library members borrowed over 7.5 million books and videos. British Council libraries not only provide information and materials to users, but also promote the latest UK publications.

Working in close collaboration with book trade associations, British Council offices organise book and electronic publishing exhibitions ranging from small, specialist displays to participation in major international book fairs. Other projects include Global Publishing Information, a collection of online publishing market reports on international markets compiled in collaboration with the Publishers Association. It also provides various resources on its website for those interested in finding out more about UK publishing.

Details of the British Council's many publications are available online (www.britishcouncil.org/publications/index.htm). The British Council is the agent for the Department for International Development (DFID) for book aid projects in developing countries, and is an authority on teaching English as a second or foreign language. It also gives advice and information on curriculum, methodology, materials and testing.

The British Council promotes British literature overseas through writers' tours, academic visits, seminars and exhibitions. It publishes *New Writing*, an annual anthology of unpublished short stories, poems, extracts from works in progress and essays; and a series of literary bibliographies, including *Eyes Wide Open: New Fiction from the UK 1999–2001*, *Hunting Down the Universe: A Bibliography of Popular Science and Literature*, and *Teaching Management Principles Using Literature*. Through its Literature Department, the British Council provides an overview of UK literature and a range of online resources on its literature website, www.britishcouncil.org/arts/literature. This includes a literary portal (www.literature.britishcouncil.org), directories of postgraduate and short courses in literature and creative writing, a directory of literary conferences, information about UK and Commonwealth authors on www.contemporarywriters.com and www.literarytranslation.com, including translation workshops. A worldwide online book club and reading group for adults, teenagers and children (www.encompassculture.com) was launched in 2003, and also www.youngtranslators.com for young European translators.

The Visual Arts Department, part of the British Council's Arts Group, develops and enlarges overseas knowledge and appreciation of British achievement in the fields of painting, sculpture, printmaking, design, photography, the crafts and architecture, working closely with the British Council's overseas offices and with professional colleagues in the UK and abroad.

Further information about the work of the British Council is available from Press and Public Relations at the above address, or from British Council offices overseas.

The British Haiku Society

38 Wayside Avenue, Hornchurch, Essex RM12 4LL
tel (01772) 251827
website www.britishhaikusociety.org
General Secretary Doreen King *President* Martin Lucas

Promotes the appreciation and writing of haiku, senyru, tanka, haibun and renku. It provides tutorials, workshops, readings, critical comment and information. It also runs a haiku library, administers a haiku and a haibun contest, and produces the journal *Blithe Spirit* (quarterly) and a regular newsletter. The Society has active local groups but welcomes overseas members. See website for membership details. Founded 1990.

The Browning Society

52 Esmond Road, Bedford Park, London W4 1JQ

tel 020-8995 4900
email b.chev@virgin.net
website www.browningsociety.org
Contact Dr Berry Chevasco
Membership £15 p.a.

Aims to widen the appreciation and understanding of the lives and poetry of Robert Browning (1812–89) and Elizabeth Barrett Browning (1806–61), and other Victorian writers and poets. Founded 1881; refounded 1969.

Byron Society (International)

Byron House, 6 Gertrude Street, London SW10 0JN
website www.internationalbyronsociety.org
Hon. Director Mrs Elma Dangerfield CBE
Membership £20 p.a.

Aims to promote research into the life and works of Lord Byron (1788–1824) by seminars, discussions, lectures and readings. Publishes *The Byron Journal* (annual, £6.50 plus postage). Founded 1971.

Canadian Poetry Association

331 Elmwood Drive, Suite 4-212, Moncton NB E1A 1X6, Canada
website www.canadianpoetryassoc.com

The main aims of the Canadian Poetry Association are: to promote the reading, writing, publishing and preservation of poetry in Canada, through the individual efforts of members; to promote communication among poets, publishers and the general public; to encourage leadership and participation from members; and to encourage the formation and development of autonomous local chapters.

Centerprise Literature Development Project

Centerprise Literature Development Project, Centreprise, 136–138 Kingsland High Street, London E8 2NS

tel 020-7249 6572
email literature@centerprisetrust.org.uk
Contact Eva Lewin, Sharon Duggal, Susan Yearwood

Runs courses and workshops in creative writing, organises poetry and book readings, discussions and debates on literary and relevant issues, writers' surgeries, and telephone information on resources for writers in London. Publishes *Calabash* newsletter for writers of Black and Asian origin. Funded by ACE London. Founded 1995.

Commonword
6 Mount Street, Manchester M2 5NS
tel 0161-832 3777
website www.commonword.org.uk

Along with its sister organisation, Cultureword, co-ordinates a range of Writing Development and Publishing Projects, often in collaboration with other organisations. The aim of these projects is to encourage specific sections of the community to engage in creative writing and reading activities.

Creative Arts East
Wymondham, Norfolk
tel (01603) 774789
email lisa.d'onofrio@cae.norfolk.gov.uk
website www.creativeartseast.co.uk
Contact Lisa D'Onofrio

A fast-growing arts development agency, which provides practical support to the arts community in Norfolk; directly promotes tours, exhibitions, and one-off performances and readings by professional artists and companies; and develops community-based arts projects which address social issues around isolation and disadvantage. The agency was formally launched in 2002, and was set up to combine the collective expertise and

energy of 4 smaller arts organisations: Rural Arts East, Norfolk Arts Marketing, Norfolk Literature Development, and Create!. Whether you are a writer or a reader, join the Norfolk Literature Network newsletter for information, news, events listings and competitions.

Dead Good Poets Society
96 Bould Street, Liverpool, Merseyside L1 4HY
tel 0151-709 5221
email dgps@blueyonder.co.uk
Contact Cath Nichols

Organises Open Floors for new writers to try out their material, as well as Guest Nights for audiences to hear established poets. Also arranges workshops plus various projects to increase everyone's enjoyment of poetry.

Disability Writes
Just Services Ltd, Beaumont Enterprise Centre, 72 Boston Road, Beaumont Leys, Leicester LE4 1HB
tel 0116-229 3102
email www.disabilitywrites.org.uk
website info@disabilitywrites.org.uk.

A website where disabled writers and would-be writers can get support and feedback, specific to them, from people who recognise the barriers faced by disabled people. Actively supports and encourages disabled writers, whatever their previous writing experience. Promotes the work of disabled writers to a wide audience of disabled and non-disabled people, through the website and printed publications.

Don't Feed the Poets Productions
The Foresters Arms, 2 Shepherd Street, St Leonards-on-Sea, East Sussex TN38 0ET
tel (01424) 436513
website www.dontfeedthepoets.co.uk

Contact John Knowles

Organises year-round poetry events, open mics and theatrical readings as well as the Word About Town Festival, which runs in Hastings from late April to early May.

Driftwood Publications

5 Timms Lane, Formby, Merseyside
L37 7DW
tel 0151-525 0417
email janet.speedy@btinternet.com
Contact Janet Speedy

One of the most active poetry organisations in Merseyside. First registered as a poetry publishing press in the 1970s, it began by publishing booklets by (then) new and neglected poets. It has recently been revived to include promotions (poetry readings at The Freshfield Ho) and has just announced its new programme of events. The organisation also produces spoken-word CDs by many of the poets whose work is published in its book series. Driftwood works closely with Sefton Arts Development and is involved in its annual poetry competition and in many of the promotions, including the recent visits/ readings in Southport and Crosby, Merseyside by Andrew Motion, Brendan Kennelly, Paul Durcan, UA Fanthorpe, John Cooper Clarke and the late Miroslav Holub, among others.

The Dylan Thomas Society of Great Britain

Fernhill, 24 Chapel Street, Mumbles, Swansea SA3 4NH
tel (01792) 363875
Chair Mrs Cecily Hughes

The society aims to foster an interest in Dylan Thomas's writings, and those of other Welsh writers in English.

Dylan Thomas Centre

Somerset Place, Swansea SA1 1RR
tel (01792) 463980
email dylanthomas.lit@ swansea.gov.uk
website dylanthomas.centre@swansea.gov.uk
Contact David Woolley/Jo Furber

Opened by former US President Jimmy Carter in 1995, the Dylan Thomas Centre is home to a permanent exhibition on Dylan Thomas and a year-round programme of literary events. It also hosts the annual Dylan Thomas Celebration, from 27th October to 9th November.

English Association

University of Leicester, University Road, Leicester LE1 7RH
tel 0116-252 3982 *fax* 0116-252 2301
email engassoc@le.ac.uk
website www.le.ac.uk/engassoc/
Chair Peter J Kitson, *Chief Executive* Helen Lucas

Aims to further knowledge, understanding and enjoyment of English literature and the English language, by working towards a fuller recognition of English as an essential element in education and in the community at large; by encouraging the study of English literature and language by means of conferences, lectures and publications; and by fostering the discussion of methods of teaching English of all kinds.

Exiled Writers Ink

31 Hallswelle Road, London NW11 0DH
tel 020-8458 1910
email jennifer@ exiledwriters.fsnet.co.uk
website www.exiledwriters.co.uk
Director Jennifer Langer

Provides a platform for the work of artists living in exile in the UK and Mainland Europe through performance, publishing and training activities.

Farrago Poetry

108 High Street, West Wickham, Kent BR4 OND

mobile (07905) 078376
email farragopoetry@yahoo.co.uk
website http://london.e-poets.net
Contact John O'Neill

A spoken-word and performance poetry organisation based in London. Runs a range of different events, from Spanish language poetry nights to events for elders, but is best known for pioneering slam poetry in the UK and for its links to the international performance poetry scene.

Guernsey Arts Council

La Fontaine, Courtil de la Fontaine, Kings Road, St Peter Port, Guernsey GY1 1QB
tel (01481) 254144
email tdguernsey@cwgsy.net
Chairman Mrs Terry Domrille, *Secretary* Ann Wilkes-Green

Dedicated to promoting the arts in Guernsey.

Hammer and Tongue

16b Cherwell Street, Oxford OX4 1BG
tel (01865) 200550
email poetry@ hammerandtongue.org
website www.hammerandtongue.org
Contact Steve Larkin

Oxford's live literature community. Runs a regular monthly poetry slam and showcase (first Tuesday of the month) and stages larger performance poetry events. Also organises workshops and training for individual poets, schools and community groups.

Seamus Heaney Centre for Poetry

46-48 University Road, Belfast BT7 1NN
tel (02890) 273319
email shc@qub.ac.uk
website www.qub.ac.uk/heaneycentre

Designed to celebrate, and to build upon, Seamus Heaney's enormous contribution to contemporary poetry, as well as the achievements of poets from Northern Ireland more generally. The centre will house an extensive library of contemporary poetry volumes and journals, which will be open to the public. It will host regular creative writing workshops, a fortnightly poetry reading group, and an ongoing series of readings and lectures by visiting poets and critics from all over the world.

Independent Northern Publishers

Aidan House, Sunderland Road, Gateshead NE8 3HU
tel 0191-478 8431
email info@northernpublishers.co.uk
website www.northernpublishers.co.uk
and www.literaturenortheast.co.uk

A collective of poetry and fiction publishers, including magazines based in the North East of England. Members include: *Mslexia*, *Other Poetry* and *Bullet* magazines; Arrowhead Press, Biscuit Publishing, Blinking Eye, Diamond Twig, Dogeater, Flambard, Iron Press, Ek Zuban (including *Kenaz* magazine), Mudfog, Morning Star, Sand, Smokestack, Vane Women Press and Zebra Publishing.

Independent Publishers Guild

PO Box 93, Royston, Herts SG8 5GH
tel (01763) 247014 *fax* (01763) 246293
website www.ipg.uk.com
Membership £150 + VAT p.a. Open to new and established publishers and book packagers; supplier membership is available to specialists in fields allied to publishing (but not printers and binders)

Provides an information and contact network for independent publishers. The IPG also voices the concerns of member companies with the book trade. Founded 1962.

Inpress

Northumberland House, 11 The Pavement, Popes Lane, Ealing, London W5 4NG

tel 020-8832 7464
email info@inpressbooks.co.uk
website www.inpressbooks.co.uk

Provides sales, marketing and technical support for independent publishers in the UK. Funded by Arts Council England, Inpress offers practical support and gives members a strong collective voice, helping small presses to achieve healthy sales and wider exposure for their published output each year. This is achieved by providing sales representation through Troika, distribution via Central Books Ltd, attendance at fairs and events across the UK, and by offering secure transactions for purchasers, via the Inpress Books website, which allows purchasers to deal directly with independent publishers.

Irish Writers' Centre
19 Parnell Square, Dublin 1, Republic of Ireland
tel (01) 8721302 *fax* (01) 8726282
email info@writerscentre.ie
website www.writerscentre.ie
Director Cathal McCabe

National organisation for the promotion of writers and writing in Ireland. Runs an extensive programme of events at its headquarters; operates the Writer in Community Scheme, which funds events throughout Ireland; runs an education programme offering courses and workshops in writing; and operates an International Writers' Exchange Programme. See website for further details. Founded 1991.

Keats-Shelley Memorial Association
1 Satchwell Walk, Leamington Spa, Warks CV32 4QE
tel (01926) 427400 *fax* (01926) 335133
Chairman Hon. Mrs H Cullen
Membership £12 p.a. minimum

Owns and supports the house in Rome where John Keats (1795–1821) died, as a museum open to the public; celebrates the poets Keats, Shelley (1792–1822) and Leigh Hunt (1784–1859). Regular meetings; poetry competitions; annual *Review;* 2 literary awards; and progress reports. Founded 1903.

League of Canadian Poets
920 Yonge Street, Suite 608, Toronto, Ontario M4W 3C7, Canada
tel 416-504-1657 *fax* 416-504 0096
email info@poets.ca
website www.poets.ca
Executive Director Joann Poblocka
Membership $175 p.a.

Aims to promote the interests of poets and to advance Canadian poetry in Canada and abroad. Administers 3 annual awards; operates the 'Poetry Spoken Here' webstore; runs National Poetry Month; publishes a newsletter and *Poetry Markets for Canadians, Who's Who in The League of Canadian Poets*, and *Poets in the Classroom* (teaching guide). Promotes and sells members' poetry books. Founded 1966.

The Literary Consultancy
Diorama Arts, No 1 Euston Centre, London NW1 3JG
tel 020-7813 4330
email info@literaryconsultancy.co.uk
website www.literaryconsultancy.co.uk
Contact Rebecca Swift

While working as an editorial assistant in her early years at Virago Press, Rebecca Swift, founder of TLC, realised that there was no professional, trustworthy body for authors to send work to before they approached publishers and agents. TLC provides detailed critiques and invaluable advice to writers, including poets.

Litfest
PO Box 751, Lancaster, Lancashire LA1 9AJ

tel (0152) 462166
email all@litfest.org
website www.litfest.org
Contact Steve Lewis, Sarah Hymas

The literature festival and development agency for Lancashire. Litfest also develops literature through projects across the county.

Mini Mushaira

c/o 11 Donnington Road, Sheffield, South Yorkshire S2 2RF
tel (01743) 245004
email simon@shrews1.fsnet.co.uk
Contact Simon Fletcher, Debjani Chatterjee

Mushaira is the Arabic word for 'a gathering of poets', and the Mini Mushaira writers (Debjani Chatterjee in Sheffield, Simon Fletcher in Shrewsbury, Basir Sultan Kazmi in Manchester and Brian G D'Arcy in Sheffield) are a group of multicultural poets and storytellers who seek to build cultural bridges through their work with both children and adults. Mini Mushaira have given excellent multilingual poetry performances and run poetry workshops throughout the country.

Moose Foundation for the Arts

PO Box 34388, London NW6 1WJ
tel 020-7794 8510
email paul@moosefoundation.org.uk
website www.moosefoundation.org.uk
Contact Paul Hobson

A charitable foundation which supports a range of art forms and organisations in London, with a particular interest in poetry.

National Association of Writers' Groups

The Arts Centre, Biddick Lane, Washington, Tyne and Wear NE38 2AB
tel (01262) 609228
email nawg@tesco.net
Secretary Mike Wilson, 40 Burstall Hill, Bridlington, East Yorkshire YO16 7GA
website www.nawg.co.uk
Membership £30 p.a. plus £5 registration per group; £12 Associate individuals

Aims "to advance the education of the general public throughout the UK, including the Channel Islands, by promoting the study and art of writing in all its aspects". Publishes *Link* bimonthly magazine. Annual Festival of Writing held in Durham in September. Annual Creative Writing Competition. Founded 1995.

National Literacy Trust

Swire House, 59 Buckingham Gate, London SW1E 6AJ
tel 020-7828 2435 *fax* 020-7931 9986
email contact@literacytrust.org.uk
website www.literacytrust.org.uk, www.rif.org.uk, www.readon.org.uk
Director Neil McClelland, *PA* Jacky Taylor

Independent registered charity dedicated to building a literate nation in which everyone enjoys the skills, self-esteem and pleasures that literacy can bring. The only organisation concerned with raising literacy standards for all age groups throughout the UK. Maintains an extensive website with literacy news, summaries of key issues, research and examples of practice nationwide; organises an annual conference, courses and training events, and runs a range of initiatives to turn promising ideas into effective action. Initiatives include the National Reading Campaign, funded by the government; Reading is Fundamental, UK, which provides free books to children; Reading The Game, involving the professional football community; the Talk To Your Baby campaign; and the Literacy and Social Inclusion Project, a partnership with the Basic Skills Agency. Founded 1993.

National Poetry Day

Poetry Society, 22 Betterton Street, London WC2H 9BX
tel 020-7420 9880
email npd@poetrysociety.org.uk
website www.poetrysociety.org.uk

Takes place in October of each year. A day of poetry events and performances all over the country at venues and in schools.

New Forest Poetry Society

Forest Arts, New Milton, Hants BH25 6DS
tel (01590) 675409
email keithbennett532@hotmail.com
Contact Keith Bennett

Forest Arts, an arts centre in the New Forest, hosts the monthly Poems and Pints evenings organised by the New Forest Poetry Society, and runs an ambitious literary programme of book groups, readings, performances, workshops and literary happenings.

New Writing North

2 School Lane, Whickham NE16 4SL
tel 0191-488 8580 *fax* 0191-488 8576
email mail@newwritingnorth.com
website www.newwritingnorth.com

The writing development agency for the north east of England (the area covered by Arts Council England, North East). It aims to create an environment in the north east of England in which new writing in all genres can flourish and develop. It is a unique organisation within the UK, merging individual development work with writers across all media with educational work and the production of creative projects. It works with writers from different genres and forms to develop career opportunities, new commissions, projects, residencies, publications and live events.

New Writing Partnership

4-6 Netherconesford, 93-95 King Street, Norwich NR1 1PW
tel (01603) 877177
email info@newwritingpartnership.org.uk
website www.newwritingpartnership.org.uk
Contact Trevor Davies

Aims to advance the education of the public by the promotion, encouragement and development of creative writing and the appreciation of the written word in all its forms.

New Zealand Poetry Society

PO Box 5283, Lambton Quay, Wellington
email info@poetrysociety.org.nz
website www.poetrysociety.org.nz
President James Norcliffe

For more than 30 years the New Zealand Poetry Society has been supporting New Zealand poets and poetry in its many forms.

Outlook

Mount View Cottage, Mousehole Lane, Paul, Penzance, Cornwall TR19 6TY
tel (01736) 732508
email outlook@easynet.co.uk
Contact Roger Butts

An agency for artists who work in education; also organises cross-curricular and language-based projects through Outlook, which are inspired by the out-of-doors and in which schools (mainly Cornish Primary) can take part.

Wilfred Owen Association

17 Belmont, Shrewsbury SY1 1TE
website www.1914-18.co.uk/owen
Membership £6 p.a. (£10 overseas), £15 groups/institutions, £4 concessions

Aims to commemorate the life and work of Wilfred Owen (1893–1918), and to encourage and enhance appreciation of his work through visits, public events, a newsletter and journal. Founded 1989.

Oxford University Poetry Society

Magdalen College, Oxford OX1 4AU
mobile (07973) 249419
email jonathan.taylor@magd.ox.ac.uk
website users.ox.ac.uk/~magd1931
Contact Jonathan Taylor

Society run for, and by, students of Oxford interested in the reading and writing of poetry. The Society meets once a week for readings, workshops and other events, and produces *The Reader* – a biannual poetry pamphlet.

Pass on a Poem

112 Elgin Crescent, London W11 2JL
tel 020-7229 9152
email enquiries@passonapoem.com
website www.passonapoem.com

Exists to provide entertainment and to create enthusiasm for poetry, by bringing people together to read out loud poems which have a special personal significance and to explain, briefly, why. Some readings take place in private homes, with group membership being by invitation. Others are organised at regular intervals in public venues, so that anybody who enjoys or who would like to try reading or simply listening to poetry can be included. No previous experience of reading out loud is necessary. Anybody is welcome to submit a poem they would like to share. The adminstration of the project is based in London, but the idea is to promote local live readings nationwide, using them as a resource and support.

PEN, International

Brownlow House, 50–51 High Holborn, London EC1V 6EK
tel 020-7405 0338 *fax* 020-7405 0339
email intpen@dircon.co.uk
website www.internationalpen.org.uk
Executive Director Caroline McCormick
Membership Apply to Centres

A world association of writers. PEN was founded in 1921 by C.A. Dawson Scott under the presidency of John Galsworthy, to promote friendship and understanding between writers and to defend freedom of expression within and between all nations. The initials PEN stand for Poets, Playwrights, Editors, Essayists, Novelists – but membership is open to all writers of standing (including translators), whether men or women, without distinction of creed or race, who subscribe to these fundamental principles. PEN takes no part in state or party politics. The International PEN Writers in Prison Committee works on behalf of writers imprisoned for exercising their right to freedom of expression, a right implicit in the PEN Charter to which all members subscribe. The International PEN Translations and Linguistic Rights Committee strives to promote the translations of works by writers in the lesser-known languages and to defend those languages. The Writers for Peace Committee exists to find ways in which writers can work for peaceful co-existence in the world. The Women Writers' Committee works to promote women's writing and publishing in developing countries. The Writers in Exile Network helps exiled writers. International Congresses are held annually.

Membership of any one Centre implies membership of all Centres; at present 144 autonomous Centres exist throughout the world. Associate membership is available for writers not yet eligible for full membership and for persons connected with literature. The English Centre has a programme of literary lectures, discussion, dinners and parties.

Penned in the Margins

53 Arcadia Court, 45 Old Castle Street,
London E1 7NY
tel 020-7375 0258
email info@pennedinthemargins.co.uk
website www.pennedinthemargins.co.uk
Contact Tom Chivers

Celebrates the power of words in
performance and on the page with live
poetry events. Also manages spoken-word
artists, publishes new work by emerging
writers, creates innovative projects, and
provides research and consultancy services
to the live literature sector.

Performing Right Society Ltd (PRS)

Copyright House, 29–33 Berners Street,
London W1T 3AB
tel 020-7580 5544 *fax* 020-7306 4455
website www.prs.co.uk
Chief Executive Adam Singer

Pirandello

9 Jew Street, Brighton, East Sussex BN1
1UT
tel (01273) 735353
email pirandello@newwritingsouth.com
website www.pirandello.org.uk

A database of writers, all published and/or
performed. They cover all genres – novels,
biography, poetry and playwrighting, with
books published by major mainstream
publishers as well as cutting-edge small
presses like Two Rivers Press and Arc.
Their work has been broadcast on radio
and television and played on national
stages. From a writing workshop for
youngsters to a commissioned poem, from
a reading to a live literature performance,
you can find the writer that could be
invaluable to your workshop, workplace,
school or event.

Poems on the Underground

22 Betterton Street, London WC2H 9BX
tel 020-7420 9880 *fax* 020-7240 4818
email info@poetrysociety.org.uk

website www.poetrysociety.org.uk
Contact Carl Dhiman

Poems on the Underground was launched
in 1986. The programme was the
brainchild of American writer Judith
Chernaik, whose aim was to bring poetry
to the wide-ranging audience of
passengers on the Underground. In 2000,
more than 3.5 million journeys were made
each day. Judith Chernaik, together with
poets Cicely Herbert and Gerard Benson,
continue to select poems for inclusion in
the programme.

Poeticize

PO Box 2147, Bristol BS99 7SF
email base@poeticize.co.uk
website www.poeticize.co.uk

The UK's first interactive performance
forum, fusing cutting-edge spoken word,
new media and live beats from a black
perspective. Since the organisation was
founded in 1999, Poeticize has developed
a reputation for pushing back the
boundaries of 'performance poetry' by
introducing progressive, high-profile
cross-arts platforms that project emerging
and established live black artists to new
audiences.

Poetry Australia Foundation

School of Creative Arts, University of
Melbourne, Parkville VIC 3010 Australia
email rpretty@unimelb.edu.au
website www.poetryaustraliafoundation.org.au

The Poetry Australia Foundation was
established in 2002 to promote the
reading, writing, reviewing and
appreciation of poetry in all its forms. It is
a not-for-profit, community-based
organisation.

The Poetry Book Society – see page 163

The Poetry Business

Byram Arcade, Huddersfield, Yorkshire
HD1 1ND

tel (01484) 434840
email edit@poetrybusiness.co.uk
website www.poetrybusiness.co.uk/
Contact Peter Sansom

Publishes contemporary poetry books, pamphlets and cassettes under the Smith/ Doorstop imprint; also publishes a literary magazine known as *The North*. As well as running an annual Book & Pamphlet Competition, The Poetry Business holds monthly Writing Days (Saturday, 10.15am to 4.15pm at its premises in Huddersfield).

The Poetry Can

20-22 Hepburn Road, Bristol BS2 8UD
tel 0117-942 6976
email info@poetrycan.co.uk
website www.poetrycan.co.uk
Contact Colin Brown

A poetry development agency based in Bristol. Provides advice and support in matters relating to poets and poetry, organises events such as the Bristol Poetry Festival, and runs a lifelong learning programme.

The Poetry Cubicle

28 Burton Stone Lane, York YO30 6BU
email sara@thepoetrycubicle.org.uk
website www.thepoetrycubicle.org.uk
Contact Sara Wingate Gray

A not-for-profit educational resource base, shop, library and interactive performance centre, dedicated to making poetry more accessible.

The Poetry House

The Scores, St Andrews, Fife KY16 9AL
tel (01334) 462666
email english@st-andrews.ac.uk
website www.thepoetryhouse.org
Contact Lilias Fraser

The Poetry House is based in the School of English at the University of St Andrews,

and promotes a programme of public readings and events with Scottish and international poets throughout the year. It is also home to a leading MLitt in Creative Writing, and publishes *Scores*, *The Red Wheelbarrow* and the international poetry magazine, *Verse*. Some of Scotland's major poets work at the Poetry House, including John Burnside, Robert Crawford, Douglas Dunn, Kathleen Jamie and Don Paterson. The Poetry House website is designed to be the most authoritative guide to information about poetry across the English-speaking world. Its coverage is both historical (from Old English to the present) and geographical, taking in all the world's major English-speaking areas. Its authority derives from the acumen of its international team of editors, each an expert in his or her subject area. The Poetry House may not be the largest site on the web devoted to poetry, but it aims to be one of the most helpful and easy to use.

Poetry International Foundation

William Boothlaan 4, 3012 VJ Rotterdam, The Netherlands
tel (00311) 0282 2777
email poetry@luna.nl
Editor www.poetry.nl

Poetry International is a Dutch government-sponsored foundation working to promote interest in and foster love for the art of poetry, and to encourage contacts between poets, poetry translators, poetry lovers and publishers from all countries. It does so by organising the annual Poetry International Festival, the Children's Poetry Festival, a National Poetry Day and various international exchange projects. Poetry International also tries to bring poetry to a wider public by posting poems in public areas, on building, in railway carriages, even on garbage trucks.

Poetry Ireland/Éigse Éireann

2 Prouds Lane, off St Stephen's Green, Dublin 2
tel (01) 478 9974 *fax* (01) 478 0205
email poetry@iol.ie
website www.poetryireland.ie
Director Joseph Woods

Poetry Ireland is the national organisation dedicated to developing, supporting and promoting poetry throughout Ireland. A resource and information point for any member of the public with an interest in poetry; works towards creating opportunities for poets working or living in Ireland.

The Poetry Society – see page 166

The Poetry Society (India)

L-67 A, Malviyar Nagar, New Delhi-110017, India
email hkkaul@delnet.ren.nic.in
website www.indianpoetry.org
Secretary-General Dr HK Kaul

Promotes poetry in India written in the Indian languages. Organises workshops, readings, lectures, conferences and competitions.

The Poetry Society of America

15 Gramercy Park, New York, NY 10003
tel (212) 254-9628
email anita@poetrysociety.org
website www.poetrysociety.org
Executive Officer Alice Quinn

WH Auden, Robert Frost, Langston Hughes, Edna St Vincent Millay, Marianne Moore and Wallace Stevens were among the original members, who envisioned a society that would not only be a local meeting place for poets, but also a centre from which a national poetry renaissance would emerge. Current members, such as John Ashbery, Rita Dove, Kimiko Hahn, Brenda Hillman, Yusef Komunyakaa, Stanley Kunitz, Sharon Olds, Robert Pinsky and Adrienne Rich, carry on their great tradition.

Poetry Translation Centre

Room 404, School of Oriental & African Studies, Thornhaugh Street, London WC1H 0XG
tel 020-7898 4367
email ptc@soas.ac.uk
website www.poetrytranslation.soas.ac.uk

The Poetry Translation Centre at the School of Oriental & African Studies was established in February 2004. Concentrates on translating contemporary poetry from non-European languages into English to the highest literary standards, through a series of innovative collaborations between leading international poets and poets based in the UK. Visitors to the Centre's website will be able to read translations of contemporary poets in a wide variety of languages, and to take part in lively debates about poetry and translation with people from all over the world.

The Poetry Trust

The Cut, 9 New Cut, Halesworth, Suffolk IP19 8BY
tel (01986) 835950
email info@thepoetrytrust.org
website www.aldeburghpoetryfestival.org/html/the_trust1.htm

An arts organisation which runs the UK's leading annual festival of international contemporary poetry at Aldeburgh on the Suffolk coast (established 1989), and promotes the reading, writing and enjoyment of poetry to a wide variety of children and adults. Delivers a year-round programme of events, creative education opportunities, prizes and publications.

ProudWords

mobile (07973) 894912
email pwcwf@hotmail.com
website www.proudwords.org.uk

Promotes all kinds of writing by lesbian, gay and bisexual writers. The organisation was established in 1997.

Renaissance One

PO Box 22004, London SW2 5ZS
tel 020-7326 0048
email info@renaissanceone.com
website www.renaissanceone.com

Provides literature and spoken-word promotion; artist management; tours and events; arts consultancy, education and outreach.

Royal Society of Literature

Somerset House, Strand, London WC2R 1LA
tel 020-7845 4676 *fax* 020-7845 4679
email info@rslit.org
Chairman of Council Maggie Gee, FRSL, *Secretary* Maggie Fergusson
Membership £30 p.a.

For the promotion of literature and encouragement of writers by way of lectures, discussions, readings, and by publications. Administers the VS Pritchett Memorial Prize, the Royal Society of Literature Ondaatje Prize, and the Royal Society of Literature/Jerwood Awards. Founded 1820.

Scottish Book Trust (SBT)

Sandeman House, 55 High Street, Edinburgh EH1 1SR
tel 0131-524 0160 *fax* 0131-524 0161
email info@scottishbooktrust.com
website www.scottishbooktrust.com

With a particular responsibility towards Scottish writing, SBT exists to promote literature and reading, and aims to reach (and create) a wider reading public than has existed before. It also organises exhibitions, readings and storytellings, national author tours, administers the Live Literature Scotland Scheme, operates an extensive children's reference library and provides a book information service for writers and readers. SBT has a range of publications and advises other relevant art organisations. Its latest initiative, BRAW (Books, Reading and Writing), the Network for the Scottish Children's Book, aims to promote books, reading and writing, by authors and illustrators living in Scotland and for young people across Scotland. Founded 1960.

Sentinel Poetry Movement

60 Titmuss Avenue, Thamesmead, London SE28 8DJ
tel (07940) 249812
email info@sentinelpoetry.org.uk
www.sentinelpoetry.org.uk
Administrator Nnorom Azuonye

Sentinel Poetry Movement is a non-profit free-to-join poetry society open to writers of all levels of accomplishment, regardless of racial or religious background.

The Society of Authors

84 Drayton Gardens, London SW10 9SB
tel 020-7373 6642 *fax* 020-7373 5768
website www.societyofauthors.net

A non-profit organisation, founded in 1884 "to protect the rights and further the interests of authors". The Society represents the writing profession by campaigning for improved terms and changes in legislation, such as copyright and libel laws. It also manages literary estates and administers a number of prizes, grants and awards.

The South

PO Box 145, Brighton, East Sussex BN1 6YU

tel (01273) 242850
email info@thesouth.org.uk
website www.thesouth.org.uk
Contact John Davies

An independent, not-for-profit, literary arts development group and promoter which has emerged from the 'grass roots' of poets and writers in Brighton and along the south coast. Through its readings and presentations, writers' workshops, hosting international poets, building links with publishers, cross art-form collaborations, promoting networks and commissioning special projects, the South has quickly established itself as an organisation which makes things happen. In addition to supporting the production of new high-quality work, it has successfully sought to build new audiences and to respond to their interests through its programming, communication and other activities. The South has stimulated a dramatic renaissance in poetry activity in the south of England.

Speak-a-Poem

5 South Vale, London SE19 3BA
tel 020-8771 1980
email kate.welbourne@speak-a-poem.co.uk
website www.speak-a-poem.co.uk
Contact Kate Welbourne

A national organisation dedicated to the art of speaking poetry. The website has articles, poets' views on reading poetry aloud, and full information on regional workshops and the Lockwood West Award held annually in London.

Speaking Volumes

Ground Floor, Marshall Court, 1 Marshall Street, Leeds LS11 9YP
tel 0113-394 4840
email info@
speakingvolumesonline.org.uk

website
www.speakingvolumesonline.org.uk

Aims to bring the enjoyment of reading and involvement in reading activities to people with a visual impairment, through the public libraries in all 15 local authorities throughout the Yorkshire and Humber region.

Stop All the Clocks

The Marlborough Theatre, Prince's Street, Brighton, East Sussex
tel (01273) 207562
email simon@stopalltheclocks.co.uk
website www.stopalltheclocks.co.uk
Contact Simon Clayton

Formed as an amalgamation of the 3 best poetry-promotion stables in Brighton: Don't Feed The Poets, Holy! Holy! Holy! Holy!, and Wanderlust Wonderlust. Organises year-round, genuinely grass-roots events as well as the Brighton fringe literature festival every May.

Survivors' Poetry

Studio 11, Bickerton House, 25-27 Bickerton Road, London N19 5JT
tel 020-7281 4654
email info@survivorspoetry.org.uk
website www.survivorspoetry.com
Contact Dr Simon Jenner

Promotes poetry for survivors of mental distress, through a programme of workshops, performances, readings, training and publications. There is a free subscription to the quarterly magazine, *Poetry Express*.

The Tennyson Society

Central Library, Free School lane, Lincoln LN2 1EZ
tel (01522) 552851 *fax* (01522) 552858
email jeffersk@lincolnshire.gov.uk
website www.tennysonsociety.org.uk

Membership £10 p.a., £12 family, £15 institutions

Promotes the study and understanding of the life and work of the poet Alfred, Lord Tennyson (1809–92) and supports the Tennyson Research Centre in Lincoln. Holds lectures, visits and seminars; publishes the *Tennyson Research Bulletin* (annual), Monographs and Occasional Papers; tapes/recordings available. Founded 1960.

Time Haiku

Basho-An, 105 King's Head Hill, London E4 7JG

Contact Doreen King

Promotes haiku and haiku-related forms. Aims to increase accessibility through education, and encourages school and college activities as well as providing a biannual journal and newsletter.

The Windows Project

Liver House, 96 Bold Street, Liverpool L1 4HY

tel 015-1709 3688 *fax* 015-1707 8722
email windows@windowsproject.demon.co.uk
website www.windowsproject.demon.co.uk

Since 1976 the Windows Project has been making poetry fun – helping children to start writing, and providing support and advice for poetry-writing by and with all ages and abilities. Over the years, the Project has been involved in most aspects of poetry.

Word Market

PO Box 150, Barrow in Furness, Cumbria LA14 3WF

mobile (07812) 172193
email janice@word-market.co.uk
website www.word-market.co.uk
Contact Janice Benson

Supports literary events in South Cumbria; organises a wide range of events

aimed at encouraging the development of aspiring writers in the region; is committed to increasing employment opportunities for local writers, professional or amateur; organises workshops and training for writers.

Write Out Loud

11 Palace Court, Bolton, Lancs BL1 2DR
tel (01204) 398148
email julianjordon@clara.co.uk
Contact Julian Jordan

Aims to increase the opportunities for the widest range of the public to express themselves through the medium of poetry, in its broadest sense. Holds informal poetry open-floor nights on the third Sunday of every month at the Howcroft Inn, Bolton, and more formal readings bimonthly at the Octagon Theatre Bolton. Currently developing a strategy to take performance poetry to new audiences, as well as providing workshops for new poets.

Write Together

18 Penshaw View, Hebburn on Tyne, Tyne & Wear
tel 0191-483 7071
Contact Mrs P Brown (Secretary)

A voluntary community group aiming to promote creative writing (including poetry) and to provide support, advice and benefit of experience to writers in the borough of South Tyneside.

The Writing Centre

Liverpool Hope University College, Liverpool, Merseyside L16 9JD
tel 0151-291 3882
email hurleyu@hope.ac.uk
website www.hope.ac.uk
Contact Ursula Hurley

The Writing Centre's role is to celebrate and promote writing of all kinds, including poetry. There are a variety of venues within the Hope campus, including theatres and conference rooms. Runs a regular programme of poetry readings and would be pleased to consider any suggestions for future events.

Writing Together

Booktrust, Book House, 45 East Hill, London SW18 2QZ
tel 020-8516 2976
email writingtogether@booktrust.org.uk
website www.booktrust.org.uk
Contact Nikki Marsh

Works to establish links with other organisations in the field of literature development; to devise models for writers and teachers to work together out of school; to pilot a new form of professional development for teachers based on The Poetry Society's Poetry Class course, but using writers of different genres – drama, journalism and science writing; to sponsor training for writers organised on our behalf by the National Association of Writers in Education; to organise conferences for local authority staff, to help them promote the idea of working with writers to their schools; and to fund 8 residencies in schools that will be written up as case studies and will include teaching materials.

Poetry and Arts Council England

Poetry is heavily dependent on the work and funding of Arts Council England; without it, many publishers would find it hard to exist. **Gary McKeone** explains the work of ACE in relation to poetry.

Poet Laureate, Poetry Society, Poetry Library, Poems on the Underground, Poems in the Waiting Room, poetry in schools, hospitals and prisons; poetry publishers, poetry magazines, poetry competitions; slam poetry, performance poetry. Enough. Poetry is not an invisible literary genre, yet its status, impact and reach are constantly debated. Who buys it? Do we publish too much? Who reads it? Why? Why not? Does poetry matter any more? Has it been buried in the avalanche of other demands on our time, its heartbeat hardly perceptible beneath the noise of contemporary life?

Yet, we still reach for it *in extremis*; for weddings, births and funerals, in grief and in wonder, in public and in private, as if we retain some residual, instinctive belief in its talismanic, perhaps sacred qualities. Why? A definitive answer to that question would be reductive. There are some things in this age of outputs and outcomes that rightly remain beyond scrutiny. That doesn't, of course, deter the scrutinisers.

Perhaps the essence of poetry is simply, "the best words in the best order" as Samuel Taylor Coleridge has it. Andrew Motion eloquently suggests that, "Poetry is sanctified by a sense that it helps us to enjoy and endure our existence." We needn't probe too deeply. Poetry can move us and amuse us; it can illuminate and confound; it can shout out loud in the public domain or whisper to us privately in that unique communion between writer and reader. A single, all-embracing definition eludes us, but no matter. We might just as well try to 'define' the blood that runs in our veins. Impossible, but without it, where would we be?

Arts Council England's role in all this is to nurture and develop an environment in which poetry, in its many shapes, can find its way in the world. There was a time when this would simply have meant supporting poetry publishers. We continue to do this, of course. Presses like Carcanet, Bloodaxe and Enitharmon, Anvil and Arc, magazines such as *Modern Poetry in Translation, Rialto, Agenda* and *Poetry Review* use Arts Council investment to bring new poets and new poetries to the notice of the reading world. Our support enables editors to take risks with new work, often poetry in translation, that the purely commercial sector might not countenance.

But there is more to poetry in the 21st century than words on a page. Any listings magazine worth the name advertises events that are happening in all sorts of places right across the country. This might mean a poetry festival in Ledbury or a Poetry Prom in Aldeburgh; a poetry tour, or National Poetry Day. In most cases, Arts Council support will have provided the necessary financial backing.

And if heading out to enjoy poetry is not your thing, the Internet can keep you up to speed with its e-magazines and ever-increasing number of poetry websites. Click on www.poetryarchive.org and listen to poets reading their own work. Explore the site further and you'll find resources for teachers, students, librarians and children – in fact anyone with an interest in poetry. While you're surfing, try www.poetrybooks.co.uk, home of the Poetry Book Society. With a couple of clicks you can become a member and receive discounted poetry books all year round by post: poetry for adults and poetry for young people.

The Arts Council is both a funding agency and a development agency. What does that mean? In short, we make resources available through our open application programme, Grants for the Arts. This enables individuals, organisations and touring organisations to seek funding for a truly wide range of artistic programmes and initiatives. For a poet, that might mean buying time to write, funding for a period of research or travel, or support for a residency, to name but a few options; for an organisation, Grants for the Arts can support a programme of work, e.g. a series of poetry translations, set-up money for a literary magazine, or finance for organisational development that will help an organisation evolve and make it fit for purpose in a constantly changing environment. Support for touring does what it says on the tin, by making resources available for literature touring initiatives.

We also make good use of strategic budgets, i.e. resources not open to application that we invest in Arts Council-generated programmes of work. Often our financial input will lever resources from other partners, the commercial world, government departments, the education or library sectors, essentially any group or organisation that can help make literature a prominent and effective part of all our lives. This might mean work around children and young people, or arts and health; it might mean an international dimension or work on distribution. We rightly keep an eye on the cultural weather to identify those areas that need our intervention. In this way, we can function properly as a development agency.

The Arts Council, a national office and nine regional offices, has, of course, more strings to its bow than budgets. There is a wealth of experience and expertise in the organisation, people who are knowledgeable and passionate about the arts, people who work with individuals and organisations to maximise all opportunities and towards securing the long-term future of the sector with which we are involved. It is when we work *with* the sector that we work best.

The details can be found on our website, www.artscouncil.org.uk ... but let me finish, not with strategies or policies, not with funding programmes or priorities, but with a poem. It's by Jackie Kay. She once worked as a Literature Officer at the Arts Council. It's called *Promise*.

Remember, the time of year
when the future appears
like a blank sheet of paper

a clean calendar, a new chance.
You vow fresh footprints
then watch them go
with the wind's hearty gust.
Fill your glass. Here's tae us. Promises
made to be broken, made to last.

Gary McKeone is Literature Director for Arts Council England.

A poetry tutor's experience

Poets are increasingly turning to teaching to supplement their income. An explosion of writing courses and summer schools has opened up many opportunities. **Myra Schneider** has a great deal of experience in teaching poetry, both on a one-to-one basis and in a classroom set-up; she provides here some useful methods and tips for those wanting to teach poetry.

It is true that it isn't possible to *teach* someone to be a poet. Nevertheless I believe profoundly in the value of poetry courses and workshops, especially those run by practising poets who like teaching. Good tutors may play a key role in helping a gifted participant develop his/her talent. They can also offer everyone the opportunity to learn about the craft of poetry, to use words more effectively and to share in the enjoyment of writing and reading poems. I love generating an enthusiasm for poetry and I find it immensely satisfying when I see a student's work flowering.

I began running poetry and creative writing workshops for local education authorities in 1988. At that time I had had three collections of poetry published, as well as a novel for children and two for teenagers. I had also had experience of teaching in comprehensive schools and had been a member of a poetry society. The former had taught me something about teaching and managing people. The latter I'd found very frustrating, because in meetings to workshop poems, members commented on a poem the moment it had been read, often referring to minor points. Sometimes there were arguments; only rarely, in-depth feedback. I left the group and started a much smaller one with a poet friend, Colin Rowbotham, who suggested that after a poem was read we should spend some minutes in silence re-reading it and writing our comments on the script before we began to discuss it.

This idea worked so well that I adopted it for my teaching. The method was very successful and I still use it. What participants in workshop classes want most is a focused response to their work, and they find it valuable to have everyone's considered points written on their poem. Moreover, asking students to crystallise their reactions to each piece of work discussed is a useful way to help them develop critical faculties to apply to their own writing. It's crucial, of course, to give rigorous and explanatory criticism, but important too that comments should be positive and constructive (and I impress this on groups). I also try to ensure that I offer feedback that is appropriate to the stage the writer is at and I try to remember there is always an ability range in any workshop. In the main I find members of a group are very supportive to one another

I think it is essential that a poetry class should open doors. Whatever a group's terms of reference I think the relationship between reading and writing should always be stressed. I introduce published poets, look at their poems and the techniques they use, discuss possible approaches to material and the writing process.

In some of my groups the setting of exercises, which encourage students to write in new ways, has been an important element.

When I began running poetry workshops, I realised that I must try to combine informality with management. Controlling a group of adults is trickier than controlling a class in a school. Unlike children, they cannot be *told*. Sometimes there is a workshop member who wants to utter his/her views or feelings about everything, or who is quickly on the defensive, however tactfully feedback is given. Quite soon I decided that I would not have a free-for-all even after a piece of work had been considered in silence. Instead I asked one person to make the opening comments, added my own and then invited general discussion. This structure has worked well. It means that everyone, not just the most articulate or dominating, has the opportunity to express their views. When problems have arisen, this framework has made it easier to deal with them.

After a few years I stopped working for local authorities, mainly because they wanted to make all courses accredited which I felt was inappropriate for creative work. For a while I ran monthly groups privately; I also gave one-to-one tutorials with detailed comments on about six pages of poetry, together with a general assessment and suggestions for developing work. When my friend, Mimi Khalvati, started The Poetry School in 1997 I was keen to be part of it, as I very much agreed with her vision. I currently run monthly workshops and a small seminar group for the School. In the main I now work with poets who have moved beyond the very early stages of writing. One of my workshops begins with an in-depth focus on an aspect of the writing process. The other is open to writers of serious prose as well as poetry.

For the last 15 years I have also run one-off poetry courses for poetry groups, colleges, literature departments and the Second Light Network of Women Poets. I have also co-tutored many residential weekends with poet John Killick (who has done a wide range of writing residencies, and for several years has used writing as a way to communicate with people suffering from dementia). The main aim in all these courses has been to help poets and sometimes prose writers develop their work by offering exercises and ideas which will stretch them. Longer workshops give participants space to try out different ideas and to exchange views with other aspiring writers.

To become a poetry tutor it is crucial to have a catholic taste, an ability to communicate, and a feeling of sympathy with people who are trying to develop their work. Ideally one should have had at least one collection published and a track record in good magazines. The best way of finding work is to approach adult education authorities which run or are willing to set up poetry workshops, or universities offering courses in creative writing. It may also be worth looking at education websites for information, or contacting The Poetry Society. The number of poetry workshops and courses is growing; poets interested in this field will probably be able to find work in it.

Myra Schneider's most recent books are *Multiplying The Moon* (Enitharmon 2004), *Insisting on Yellow*, new and selected poems (Enitharmon 2000), and *Writing My Way Through Cancer*, a journal with poem notes and poems (Jessica Kingsley 2003). She has also co-edited four anthologies of poetry by contemporary women poets.

Creative writing courses

Poets have realised that they can make a good living from teaching, while passing on some of their hard-earned experience. Many are now involved in creative writing courses, the venues for which range from community centres to the Greek Islands. However, there are also (literally) hundreds of university and college courses in creative writing, most of which will provide a poetry module or option. The website of the National Association of Writers in Education (nawe.co.uk) provides a comprehensive list of creative writing courses available throughout the country.

Alston Hall College

Alston Lane, Longridge, Preston PR3 3BP
tel (01772) 784661 *fax* (01772) 785835
email alston.hall@ed.lancscc.gov.uk
website www.alstonhall.com

The Arvon Foundation

Lumb Bank, Heptonstall, Hebden Bridge, West Yorkshire HX7 6DF
tel (01422) 843714 *fax* (01422) 843714
email l-bank@arvonfoundation.org
website www.arvonfoundation.org
Contact Ilona Jones
Moniack Mhor, Teavarran, Kiltarlity, Beauly, Inverness-shire IV4 7HT
tel (01463) 741675 *fax* (01463) 741733
email m-mhor@arvonfoundation.org
Contact Chris Aldridge
The Arvon Foundation, Totleigh Barton, Sheepwash, Beaworthy, Devon EX21 5NS
tel (01409) 231338 *fax* (01409) 231144
email t-barton@arvonfoundation.org
Contact Julia Wheadon
The Hurst – The John Osborne Arvon Centre
Clunton, Craven Arms, Shropshire SY7 0JA
tel (01588) 640658 *fax* (01588) 640509
email hurst@arvonfoundation.org

Founded in 1968, the Arvon Foundation run 5-day residential courses throughout the year for anyone over the age of 16, providing the opportunity to live and work with professional writers. Writing genres explored include poetry, narrative, drama, writing for children, song-writing and the performing arts. Bursries are available.

The Ashburton Centre

A Taste of Travel Ltd, The Ashburton Centre, 79 East Street, Ashburton, South Devon TQ13 7AL
tel (01364) 652784
email stella@ ashburtoncentre.co.uk
website www.a-taste-of.com

Runs a range of creative writing holiday courses in Italy and Spain.

Blaze Online Writing Courses

University of Strathclyde, Livingstone Tower, 26 Richmond Street, Glasgow G1 1XH
tel 0141-552 3493
email alix.mcdonald@strath.ac.uk
website www.strath.ac.uk

The Centre for Lifelong Learning has been championing creative writing classes for a number of years. Due to demand, the Centre has launched 'Blaze' – a collection of online creative writing classes, developed to suit writers at all levels.

Bridgewater College

Bridgewater Arts Centre, Castle Street, Bridgewater, Somerset TA6 3DD
tel (01278) 422700
email info@bridgewaterartscentre.co.uk
or gwmailbox@yahoo.co.uk

website www.bridgewaterartscentre.co.uk
Contact Genista Wheatley

A creative writing workshop – fiction/non-fiction, poetry, playwriting. All abilities welcome. £50 for a 10-week term.

Burton Manor
Burton, Neston, Cheshire CH64 5SJ
tel 0151-336 5172 *fax* 0151-336 6586
email enquiry@burtonmanor.com
website www.burtonmanor.com
Principal Keith Chandler

College offering a wide range of residential courses.

Centerprise Literature Development Project
Centerprise Literature Development Project, Centreprise, 136–138 Kingsland High Street, London E8 2NS
tel 020-7249 6572
email literature@centerprisetrust.org.uk
Contact Eva Lewin, Sharon Duggal, Susan Yearwood

Runs courses and workshops in creative writing, organises poetry and book readings, discussions and debates on literary and relevant issues, writers' surgeries, and telephone information on resources for writers in London. Publishes *Calabash* newsletter for writers of Black and Asian origin. Funded by ACE London. Founded 1995.

Cinnamon Press Writing Courses
Meirion House, Glan yr afon, Tanygrisiau, Blaenau Ffestiniog, Gwynedd LL41 3SU
email jan@cinnamonpress.com
website www.cinnamonpress.com

Bespoke tuition for writers – from young people to adults – both beginning writers and those who want to develop skills further, or who want specific input on a work-in-progress. Tailor-made study can include an introduction to writing skills across a range of genres, such as journaling, non-fiction, poetry and fiction, or a more specialist focus on novel-writing, a work of non-fiction or poetry. At more advanced levels students can also be referred to other practising experts.

Creative in Calvados
1 Ormelie Terrace, Joppa, Edinburgh EH15 2EX
tel 0131-669 5330
email steveharvey@creativeincalvados.co.uk
website www.creativeincalvados.co.uk
Contact Stephen Harvey

Midweek and long weekend courses in poetry, songwriting/music, scriptwriting, drama and prose. Courses take place in Normandy. Founded 2001.

Dingle Writing Courses
Ballintlea, Ventry, Co. Kerry, Republic of Ireland
tel (066) 9159815 *fax* (066) 9159815
email info@dinglewritingcourses.ie
website www.dinglewritingcourses.ie
Contact Nicholas McLachlan

Residential writing weekends combining group work, individual tutorials, lectures, kick-start exercises and a critique of your work. The fee of €350 includes all tuition, meals and shared accommodation, normally twin.

Dorset East Street Poets
Garden Cottage, The Down House, Blandford Forum, Dorset DT11 9AD
tel (01258) 454026
email westrow@cooper.co.uk
website www.theworldtravels.com
Contact Westrow Cooper

Organises weekend writing courses tutored by established national and international poets and writers, at hotels and other venues linked to the literary landscape. See website for current and forthcoming events and courses.

Far West
23 Chapel Street, Penzance, Cornwall TR18 4AP
tel (01736) 363146
email angela@farwest.co.uk
website www.farwest.co.uk
Contact Angela Stoner

Offers a range of creative writing courses.

Fire in the Head
PO Box 17, Yelverton, Devon PL20 6YF
tel (01822) 841081
email roselle.angwin@internet-today.co.uk
website www.fire-in-the-head.co.uk
Contact Roselle Angwin

Poetry and prose; journaling and personal development; retreats and short courses; correspondence courses.

Highgreen Arts
Highgreen, Tarset, Northumberland NE48 1RP
tel 020-7602 1363
email highgreenarts@aol.com
website www.highgreen-arts.co.uk
Contact William & Cynthia Morrison-Bell

Highgreen Arts runs residential writing and arts courses with a strong emphasis on poetry. Highgreen is in the heart of the Northumberland National Park, and is also home to Bloodaxe Books. Course tutors to date have included Brendan Kennelly and David Constantine, both Bloodaxe poets. Good teachers, friendly hosts, great food and accommodation.

Indian King Arts
Garmoe Cottage, 2 Trefrew Road, Camelford, Cornwall PL32 9TP
tel (01840) 212161
email indianking@btconnect.com
website www.indianking.org.uk
Contact Helen Jagger Wood

Weekly poetry group, the Indian King Poets; bi-monthly novel-writing surgery led by Karen Hayes; annual poetry festival led by 1 poet as series of writing workshops, with readings and performances by participating poets (2006 led by John Greening with participants including Penelope Shuttle, Caroline Carver, Lyn Moir and Rob Evans). Numbers at all courses limited to 18, but usually 12. Price £30 per day minimum; non-residential.

La Muse
1 Rue de la Place, Labastide Esparbairenque, France
tel ++33 (0)4 68 26 33 93
email getaway@lamuseinn.com
website www.lamuseinn.com
Contact Kerry Eielson, John Fanning

Provides a peaceful space where artists and writers can work in a peaceful, isolated and inspiring setting. La Muse is a self-service establishment. The house is informal and comfortable, but a structure exists with the purpose of vigorous work and focus on a creative project. That structure consists of the house guidelines, which each guest is asked to consult before applying. The purpose is to support a true retreat from life back home.

National Association of Writers in Education
PO Box 1, Sheriff Hutton, York YO60 7YU
tel (01653) 618429
email paul@nawe.co.uk
website www.nawe.co.uk
Director Paul Munden

The only organisation supporting the development of creative writing of all genres and in all educational and community settings throughout the UK.

NorthCourt Manor

Shorwell, Isle of Wight
tel (01983) 740980
email lydia_fulleylove@lineone.net
website www.shorewomen.org.uk
Contact Lydia Fulleylove

This ancient manor house with its beautiful garden has inspired many writers and artists, including the poet Swinburne who often stayed there. Now, writing weekends are run at the house, Arvon style, for keen young writers – an opportunity to work alongside professional writers (for example, Philip Gross, Mimi Khalvati, Jane Draycott) and artists intensively for 2 days. Each year a publication, often with a strong cross arts-emphasis(poetry and artwork), is produced. These weekends are organised by Literature Development Worker & Writer in Healthcare, Lydia Fulleylove. Lydia also runs poetry days to refresh and restore teachers' creative energies, writing days for able writers in primary schools, and independent writing days for adults and for Healing Arts clients. Northcourt is, as one young writer commented, "A world of its own, a writer's paradise."

Old Olive Press

Old Olive Press, C/ de la Mare de Deu del Miracle, 56 Relleu 03578, Spain
tel (00349) 66 856 003
email oldolivepress@tiscali.es
website www.oldolivepress.com/

Designed as a home and as a centre for residential writing, art and other cultural courses. Runs a variety of workshops, activities and creative writing courses.

The Open College of the Arts

Registration Department, OCA, The Michael Young Arts Centre, Unit 1B

Redbrook Business Park, Wilthorpe Road, Barnsley S75 1JN
email open.arts@ukonline.co.uk
website www.oca-uk.com

An open-access college dedicated to artistic development. No formal qualifications are required, there are no age limits and students can enrol at any time of the year. The poetry course explains and illustrates the essential elements of the art and craft of poetry; and a tutor, who is a poet with a good record of publication, will assess students' poems and help them to develop their skills.

Open Studies – Part-time Courses for Adults: Office of Lifelong Learning

University of Edinburgh, 11 Buccleuch Place, Edinburgh EH8 9LW
tel 0131-650 4400 *fax* 0131-667 6097
email oll@ed.ac.uk
website www.lifelong.ed.ac.uk

Open University

PO Box 197, Milton Keynes MK7 6BJ
tel (08703) 334340
email general-enquiries@open.ac.uk
website www.open.ac.uk

Start Writing Poetry course. This course will introduce students in a gradual and accessible way to the basic 'tools of the trade'. Through examples, exercises, and games, they will practise poetic devices and methods, get ideas for subject matter, and learn how to edit their work. They will eventually write in a variety of forms from the haiku to the sonnet and in a range of styles including satire and parody. The course will also enhance reading skills and increase the ability to appreciate contemporary poetry. This is a 12-week course.

Poetry: Writing Our Lives

Missenden Abbey, Great Missenden HP16 0BD

tel (08450) 454040
Contact Gerard Benson

A writing course with tutor Gerard Benson. Residential or tuition-only.

Poetry & Writing

World Spirit, 12 Vale Road, Bowden, Cheshire WA14 3AQ
tel 0161-928 5768
email worldspirit99@aol.com
website www.worldspirit.org.uk/writers.html

Exploring artistic creativity within the inspiring natural resource of South West Crete. Courses take place over 5 days. Short private tutorials may be offered. Each course offers short course summaries upon application and, unless stated otherwise, takes place irrespective of numbers.

Poetry Class

Poetry Society, 22 Betterton, Street, London WC2H 9BX
tel 020-7420 9889
email poetryclasss@poetrysociety.org.uk
website www.poetryclass.org
Contact Andrew Bailey

An online poetry classroom and unique INSET training provides teachers with a 'nuts and bolts' insight into how poetry works. A training team of poets – all of whom are highly experienced with work in schools, and have between them hundreds of tried and tested ideas – is available to work with teachers to overcome their problems and concerns with teaching poetry.

Poetry Dorchester

Toller Mill, Toller Pocorum, Dorchester DT2 0DQ
tel (01305) 320826
email pamzhope@tolmill.freeserve.co.uk

Contact Pam Zinnemann-Hope, Zenobia Venner

Workshop for writing and reading poetry.

Poetry Otherwise

Emerson College, Forest Row, East Sussex RH18 5JX
tel (01342) 822238
email mail@emerson.org.uk
website http://www.poetryotherwise.org
Contact Paul Matthews

A creative summer gathering for poets, creative writers and lovers of language.

The Poetry School

1a Jewel Road, Walthamstow, London E17 4QU
tel 0845-223 5274 *fax* 020-8223 0439
email programme@poetryschool.com
website www.poetryschool.com

The Poetry School was founded in 1997 and now offers a comprehensive programme of courses, workshops and tutorials. The tutors are celebrated poets. Courses, workshops and Special Events take place at various venues in London, Manchester, York, Exeter and Lewes. In 2006, Poetry School Online will offer seminars and tutorials over the Internet. Fees vary. A generous Bursary Scheme is available for all UK courses and workshops.

Poetry Surgery with Carole Satyamurti at the Poetry Café

Poetry Society, 22 Betterton, Street, London WC2H 9BX
tel 020-7420 9887
email poetrycafe@poetrysociety.org.uk
website www.poetrysociety.org.uk/cafe
Contact Jessica Yorke

One-to-one surgeries for anyone writing poetry who wants to talk to an experienced poet about their work. For

£20 (£15 for Poetry Society members) you will be able to talk to Carole for 30 minutes about your work. Surgeries happen quarterly. When enough people have asked to see her, Carole comes in to the Café for an afternoon.

The Poets' House
Clonbarra, Falcarrash, Co. Donegal, Republic of Ireland
tel (07) 465 470 *fax* (07) 465 471 *Contact* John Fitzsimmons

Residential writing courses, weekends and week-long or two-week workshops; also MA programme in Creative Writing in English and Irish.

Salmon Poetry Courses
Cliffs of Moher, County Clare, Ireland
tel (06) 5708 1941
email jessie@salmonpoetry.com
website www.salmonpoetry.com

Runs regular weekend creative writing workshops at the Salmon premises. The workshops include all aspects of writing and publishing. Creative writing residencies lasting 1-4 weeks are also available.

School of English, University of Newcastle upon Tyne
Percy Building, Newcastle upon Tyne NE1 7RU
tel 0191-222 7619
email melanie.birch@ncl.ac.uk
website www.ncl.ac.uk/elll/creative
Contact Melanie Birch

The School of English hosts poetry readings and book launches. Offers various creative writing courses – short evening classes, one-week intensive spring and summer schools, and Postgraduate Certificate, MA and PhD degrees.

South Hill Park Poetry Workshop
South Hill Park Arts Centre, Ringmead, Birch Hill, Bracknell, Berks RG12 7PA

tel (01344) 416206
email gail.babb@southhillpark.org.uk
website www.southhillpark.org.uk
Contact Gail Babb

Regularly hosts day-long poetry and creative writing workshops; has started 5-week courses for adults and young people with published poets.

Swanwick, The Writers' Summer School
10 Stag Road, Lake, Sandown, Isle of Wight PO36 8PE
website www.wss.org.uk
Contact Jean Sutton

Trinity College, Carmarthen
Trinity College, Carmarthen SA31 3EP
tel (01267) 676721 *fax* (01267) 676863
email p.wright@trinity-cm.ac.uk
website www.trinity-cm.ac.uk
Contact Dr Paul Wright

Trinity College offers University of Wales degrees in creative writing at undergraduate and postgraduate level, with a particular emphasis on poetry. The writing director is Menna Elfyn, and the course has a growing relationship with a number of publishers, including Parthian. Applications to MA course on request.

Ty Newydd
Llanystumdwy, Criccieth, Gwynedd LL52 0LW
tel (01766) 522811 *fax* (01766) 523095
email post@tynewydd.org
website www.tynewydd.org
Contact Sally Baker

Residential 5-day poetry courses for all levels of expertise and experience, tutored by poets of the highest calibre. Ty Newydd is a beautiful, historic house, situated in stunning surroundings overlooking the sea in North West Wales. Has run residential creative writing courses for the past 16 years and has recently re-opened, with greatly improved facilities including disabled access. There are a variety of courses in all genres – poetry, fiction, scriptwriting and drama; courses suitable for writers of all levels of ability and experience. The maximum number on any course is 16. Students work with 2 tutors who are experienced writers in their field. Nearly all courses run from Monday evening to Saturday morning and are a combination of workshops, individual tutorials and readings, with time in between for writing. A bursary fund exists and it is the aim to enable everybody who would benefit from a course at Ty Newydd to do so. Ty Newydd also offers courses with a similar format to groups of young writers from schools and colleges. Details of all the courses are available on the website. Course cost is approximately £425.

University of St Andrews Creative Summer Writing Programme

St Katharine's West, 16, The Scores, St Andrews, Fife KY16 9AX
tel (01334) 462238 *fax* (01334) 462158
email crsp@st-andrews.ac.uk
website www.st-andrews.ac.uk/admissions/CWSPweb.htm
Director Dr MIS Hunter

Now well established, the Creative Writing Summer Programme has proved as popular as the successful Scottish Studies Summer Programme, and incorporates many of its features. A series of master classes and workshops with leading Scottish writers allow students to develop skills of authoring, oral presentation, editing and analysis. In addition to the stimulating environment of St Andrews, there is a full programme of excursions and social and cultural activities to provide additional inspiration for students' poetry and prose. You can experience what it is like to live and study in one of the most atmospheric and beautiful universities in the world, while honing your writing skills.

The Virtual Writing School

Manchester Metropolitan University Writing School, Geoffrey Manton Building, Oxford Road, Manchester M15 6LL
tel (01612) 471735
email h.beck@mmn.ac.uk
website www.hlss.mmn.ac.uk/english/writingschool/
Contact Heather Beck

Campus or online MA/PGDip in Poetry or Novel-Writing, full- or part-time. Practitioners include Simon Armitage, Heather Beck, Andrew Biswell, Carol Ann Duffy, Michael Symmons Roberts, Jeffrey Wainwright.

Write Away

Arts Training Central (Arts Council, East Midlands), 16 New Street, Leicester LE1 5NR
tel 0116-242 5202
email sapna@artstrainingcentral.co.uk
website www.artstrainingcentral.co.uk
Contact Sapna Chandihok

The ATC programme of Write Away courses runs each summer. The programme consists of 4 residential writing courses for writers of all levels, which run from Friday afternoon to Sunday afternoon. Each course offers workshops, surgeries and individual writing time to a small and informal group. The fee for each course is £145, which includes all meals, accommodation and tuition. The exact course topics vary each year. Previous courses have included Writing for Children, Poetry, Writing for

Life, Writing for Theatre and Writing for Magazines. Register to receive details of the next programme.

Write Away in Tuscany

99 Via Della Fonte, Monticiano 53015, Siena, Italy
tel (0039) 3334149837
website wwwthewordworks.org.uk
Contact Sandra Stevens

Flexible week-long courses by special appointment only. For small groups or individuals who want to stretch themselves as writers and have a holiday in the hills of Tuscany, mentored by a professional and experienced tutor. A real retreat – and a stimulating retreat. The focus is usually on the local environment, nature, and art and language.

The Writers Bureau

Sevendale House, 7 Dale Street, Manchester M1 1JB
tel (08008) 562008
email studentservices@writersbureau.com
website www.writersbureau.com

Home-study courses in Creative Writing, Journalism, Poetry and Writing Biographies, Memoirs and Family Histories.

Poets in schools

Many poets take their poetry, and the poetry of others, into our schools. Not only does this provide welcome income for the poet; it also helps, if the poet does a good job, to create a future audience for poetry. **Mandy Coe** tells us how it works, and provides some handy resources.

Every week in the UK a poet is invited into a school to deliver workshops, answer questions or give a reading. The schools benefit by gaining new teaching ideas and having their pupils work alongside a published writer. Poets benefit by supplementing their income and – if they write for young people – having instant feedback on their work. That's the bare bones of it. But there is more … If there weren't, most poets would have thrown away their copies of the A to Z years ago (I'm partial to spending my time writing, not setting the alarm for 6am so I can get to a school three counties away). But having enjoyed working with young people for many years, I am fascinated by what draws poets to this unpredictable formula of poet and school; poem and child.

The curriculum (for secondary schools in particular) leaves little room to explore the writing of poetry in any depth. Pupils study set forms and texts, but looking at the recipe is not the same as eating the food, and dissecting verse without placing it firmly in the context of mystery or pleasure can immunise a child against the enjoyment of poetry for life. A poet's visit, on the other hand, creates time 'out of school' – within the school, where teacher, writer and pupils have space to explore poetry in a more dynamic way. A time where literacy outcomes are secondary. When this happens, pupils develop not just their language skills and confidence levels; they also learn to think differently. They discuss, they ask questions. They take up their pens and paper and go away inside themselves to formulate thoughts and ideas. This act of *doing* is a very powerful one, and the feedback universal: *We learned to use our imagination.*

There is real pleasure to be found in this process – witnessing young people discovering a voice through poetry. Fortunately for poets, schools know that it's pleasure, not SATs, that keeps children plugged in to literacy. Poetry has mystery, narrative and humour and can be *about* anything. It has both a visual and an oral dynamic, it's short, re-readable and – with children taking turns to compose and listen – utterly democratic. I believe that poetry is one of the most child-centred, literacy-friendly artforms there is.

Readers of the future

It's hard to read a newspaper or listen to the BBC without being told that poetry exists in a small world inhabited by a handful of academics and the ghosts of dead writers. This is puzzling, especially when we recognise the long tradition of poets working in schools, and the vibrant relationship this builds with the readers and writers of tomorrow. When he was the Children's Laureate, Michael Morpurgo said he believed an author's visit could "help a child become a reader for life". He is not alone in believing this. Many of the best-known poets in the UK know that there is no better way to encourage a child to read than to let them meet the author.

Residencies and visits

So how does it work? The one-day visit will always remain a staple for schools and poets, but through organisations such as Writing Together (writingtogether@booktrust.org.uk) the shape and breadth of this work is evolving in exciting ways: year-long residencies; projects based in museums; poets working across the curriculum; poets working with writers in other genres. Through residencies with schools I have collaborated with photographers, dancers and musicians in venues such as the Tate Gallery, the Royal Festival Hall, Mersey Ferries and of course, the classroom.

Making it work

When asked what three things would make her work in schools more rewarding, Jackie Kay said: "Small workshop groups; teacher participation and students reading at least one poem of mine before I get there," (www.poetryclass.net). This is sound advice. The poet's role is different from that of the teacher – the passion s/he brings as a practising writer is both contagious and slightly dangerous. The poet should always be presented in the context of their poetry.

In his keynote address to Writing Together, Andrew Motion said: "It's vital for us to be prepared to look for 'relevance', or even 'irrelevance', in the widest possible array of talents. Not that we should begin to look on writers merely as passive collaborators, who might be co-opted to shore up existing ambitions and intentions. We should look at them instead as people who can help to change the landscape. The fact of their difference in the classroom is crucial – however complementary it might be to teachers' own efforts."

Partnerships

- In addition to local projects and Arts Council regional offices, the following national organisations can offer information on partnership and employment options, training and good practice:
- The National Association of Writers in Education (www.nawe.co.uk);
- The National Association for Literature Development (www.nald.org);
- The Poetry Society (www.poetrysociety.org);
- Live Literature Scotland (www.scottishbooktrust.com);
- Poetry Ireland/Éigse Éireann (www.poetryireland.ie);
- Apples and Snakes (www.aplesandsnakes.org).

Resources

A comprehensive guide for writers is *Our thoughts are bees: Writers Working with Schools* (Wordplay Press, www.wordplaypress.com). This handbook covers subjects such as writers finding work in schools, fees, planning and project ideas. For an introduction to poetry workshops in the classroom, try *Jumpstart Poetry in the Secondary School* (Poetry Society): edited by Cliff Yates, this book is full of insight on how to encourage young people to read and write poetry. For primary years, *The Poetry Book for Primary Schools* (Poetry Society), edited by Anthony Wilson and Siân Hughes, provides a wonderful selection of poems, interviews, games and lesson ideas.

If you are interested in other ways of encouraging poetry in the classroom (books, worksheets, lesson plans), take a look at the Poetry Society's *Poetryclass* (www.poetryclass.net); The Poetry Archive (www.poetryarchive.org); the Children's Poetry Bookshelf (www.childrenspoetrybookshelf.co.uk) and the Barbican's award-winning *Can I Have A Word* e-learning site (www.canihaveaword.org.uk).

Mandy Coe writes poetry for children and adults. She works for Poetryclass, Writing Together, NAWE and the Children's Poetry Bookshelf. Her work has been widely published and broadcast on radio and television, and her latest collection is *The Weight of Cows* (Shoestring Press). She received a Hawthornden Fellowship in 2005.

Poetry writers' groups

It is all very well to scribble away in your lonely garret, but there comes a point at which you need to share your work with others. Writers' groups are ideal for this: they not only provide a wonderful support group, but will also help you to improve the quality of your work. A number of these groups also publish books or magazines, providing you with a printed outlet for your work. The list below is made up mainly of groups with a particular interest in poetry, but most writers' groups welcome all kinds of writing. To find out where your nearest writing group is, visit the website of the National Association of Writers' Groups, where you will find a comprehensive, countrywide list. It also provides information about how to set up and run your own writers' group.

4th Monday Poets
tel (07834) 150523
Contact Linda Graham

Meets at the new venue of The King's Arms Upstairs, King Street, Ulverston, at 7.30pm. Anyone who is serious about pursuing the craft of poetry writing, in any style – whether a beginner or experienced – is welcome to join. Please bring 10 copies of your poem and be prepared for critical feedback.

Aberdeen Writers' Circle
c/o Aberdeen Arts Centre, 33 King Street, Aberdeen AB24 5AA

Meets every Wednesday morning from 10am to 12pm (summer and Christmas/ New Year holidays excepted).

Aberystwyth Arts Centre Writing and Poetry Group
Penglais, Aberystwyth, Ceredigion SY23 3DE
tel (01970) 621512
email ggo@aber.ac.uk
website www.aber.ac.uk
Contact Gill Ogden, Performing Arts Officer

An informal group that meets every month to discuss and share each other's poetry and writing. Open to all adults and led by a professional tutor.

Airedale Writers' Circle
20 Glenhurst Avenue, Park Lane, Keighley BD21 4RJ
tel (01535) 607946
email lesley@annelesley.freeserve.co.uk
Contact Maureen O'Hara

Meets on the second Tuesday of every month, at the Social Centre for the Association for the Blind in Keighley (7.30pm) for a meeting with speakers; also on the last Thursday of the month at 15 Manor Road, Utley, Keighley, for a manuscript evening.

Alford Writers Group
Badgers, Hodgetoft Lane, Maltby Le Marsh, Alford, Lincolnshire LN13 0JR
tel (01507) 450630
email hazelbogg@aol.com
Secretary Hazel Bogg

Founded in 2000. Meetings are held in the Alford Library on the first Wednesday evening of every month. Average attendance is 12-15 people per month. A list of topics is distributed for each month and members usually write on the selected theme. The group is informal and aims to get writers together and share one another's creations, with critiques on request. A guest speaker attends once or twice a year and there are occasional workshops, either in-house or with a paid speaker or workshop leader. Members have enjoyed successes in various competitions and the group produces small anthologies.

Alsager Writers' Circle

35 Fields Road, Alsager, Stoke-on-Trent, Staffs ST7 2NA
email inkspot@tiscali.co.uk
Contact John Statham

Meets alternate Thursday evenings to share and evaluate members' work. Writing in any genre is welcome. Meetings include a writing workshop. Evenings are friendly, sociable events.

Angus Writers' Circle

email kfarrow@mateng.co.uk

Meets on the evenings of the first and third Wednesday of each month. The venue is the Viewfield Hotel, Viewfield Road, Arbroath, Angus.

Ayr Writers Club

16 Yorke Road, Troon, Ayrshire KA10 6LB
tel (01292) 316009
email awc@rowenamlove.co.uk
website www.ayrwriters.co.uk
Contact Rowena M Love

Founded in 1970, this well-established group is strong on encouraging its members towards achieving success in various genres; many of them have been published. Meetings are held every Wednesday from September to May at 7pm at Kyle Academy. There are at least 2 poetry workshops and 1 poetry speaker per year.

Back Room Poets

6 Princes Street, Oxford
email enquiries@brpoets.org
website www.brpoets.org

Ballycastle Writers

45a Drumavoley Road, Ballycastle BT54 6PQ
Contact Heather Newcombe

Meets at the Sheskburn Recreation Centre, Ballycastle.

Bank Street Writers

c/o R Riesco, 22 Longworth Road, Horwich, Bolton BL6 7BA
tel (01204) 669858
email bswscribe@aol.com
website http://hometown.aol.co.uk/bswscribe/myhomepage/writing.html
Secretary Rod Riesco

An independent writers' group for those living in the Bolton area. Meets monthly, covering writing of all kinds but mostly poetry and short stories. All interested writers are invited to attend on a free-trial basis.

Bards in the Park

Winter Gardens, Tollcross Park, Glasgow
email mail@poets-writers.co.uk
Contact R Sherland

Meets to read work and to encourage participation in the spoken word. Poetry, short stories and comment always welcome. On the first Saturday of the month, 1-3pm.

Bassetlaw Writers' Group

149 Galway Crescent, Retford, Notts DN22 7YR
tel (01777) 700307
Secretary Mrs P Mann

Meeting of like-minded people with an interest in writing – any type, any level. Poetry competition annually, around September/October.

Battle Writers' Group

21 Oxshott Court, Sutton Place, Bexhill TN40 1PH

Contact Geoffrey Hume

A friendly group that has been in existence since 1979. Members have had several publications in various forms, many with poetry. The biggest group effort was *The Tapestry of Battle*, which is still on sale. All members are from Battle, Hastings and Bexhill.

The Beehive Poets/Bradford Poetry Workshop

The New Beehive, Westgate, Bradford, West Yorks
tel (01274) 490561
Contact John Sugden

The Beehive Poets meet in the back room of the last gas-lit pub in the UK – the New Beehive, Westgate, Bradford, on a Monday night. The sessions are either read-arounds, or invited poets from almost anywhere, but somehow they have a Yorkshire connection. On every fourth Monday Bradford Poetry Workshop offers a critical and constructive forum for poets wishing to get feedback on their work.

Berwick-upon-Tweed Writers' Group

6 The Glebe, Gavinton TD11 3QU
tel 013-188 3297
Contact Francis Blacklock

Meets fortnightly, Wednesdays, 7pm at The Maltings, Berwick-upon-Tweed.

Bexley Poets

Civic Centre, Bexleyheath, Kent
tel (01322) 431997
email bexleypoets@ukf.net
Contact Paul Seymour

A great 'meeting place' for local poets and poetry enthusiasts. The group meets up once a month (normally on the first Monday of each month) and is both popular and entertaining.

The Black Horse Poets

25 Wyecliffe Street, Ossett, Wakefield, West Yorkshire WF5 9ER

email blackhorsepoets@hotmail.com

A group based in the city of Wakefield. Meets twice-monthly at Henry Boons Pub, Westgate, to workshop, perform and promote new poetry. Twice-yearly magazine and annual competition. New members welcome.

Bracknell: Poetry Workshop at South Hill Park Arts Centre

Ringmead, Bracknell, Berkshire RG12 7PA
tel (01344) 484858
website www.southhillpark.org.uk

Meets on the third Wednesday of the month.

Bracknell Library Writers' Group

Bracknell Library, Town Square, Bracknell RG12 1BH
tel (01344) 423149
email jill.harvey-brown@bracknwell-forest.gov.uk
website www.bracknell-forest.gov.uk/learning/learn-libraries.htm
Contact Jill harvey-Brown, Community Services Librarian

Meets once a month on a Friday lunchtime. Both poets and writers of prose are welcome to receive feedback on work in progress, and to find support and inspiration from like-minded people.

Brewery Poets

Brewery Arts Centre, Highgate, Kendal, Cumbria LA9 4HE
tel (01539) 821304
Contact Patricia Pogson

Bridlington Writers' Group

24 Belgrave Mansions, South Marine Drive, Bridlington, East Yorkshire YO15 3JL
tel (01262) 605914
email Anne.Mullender@tesco.net

Contact Anne Mullender

Meets on Tuesdays at 7.30pm at the Jamroz Centre, North Street, Bridlington. A mixed group, always willing to welcome new members.

Bristol Black Writers' Group

Kuumba Project, 20-22 Hepburn Road, St Pauls, Bristol BS2 8QT
website www.discoverybristol.org.uk
Contact Bertle Martin

For black writers in the Bristol area. Monthly newsletter and active performance groups and workshops.

Burton Poets' and Writers' Group

86 Beamhill Road, Burton-on-Trent, Staffordshire DE13 0AD
email bpws2001@yahoo.com

BWSG Book Project

c/o 11 Donnington Road, Sheffield S2 2RF
tel (01142) 723906
email debjani@chatterjee.freeserve.co.uk
Contact Dr Debjani Chatterjee

Part of the Bengali Women's Support Group in South Yorkshire. Its members are very friendly and meet on the first Saturday of the month at the Space Centre above Park Library, Duke Street, Sheffield S2, for workshops and readings. BWSG Book Project is also an exciting community publisher and publishes bilingual poetry in Bengali and English. Any woman who is interested in Bengali culture and is living, studying or working in South Yorkshire is welcome to join.

Café Writers, Norwich

tom@cafewriters.org.uk
Contact Tom Corbett

Meets on the second Monday of each month from 7.15pm at Jurnet's Bar, Wensum Lodge, King Street, Norwich. All welcome. Free entry (voluntary collection). Presents a wide range of writers performing a variety of styles – poetry, drama, prose – in an atmosphere that both welcomes new work and invites professional polish. There are opportunities to read from the floor.

Cambridge Writers Poetry Group

48 Bishop's Road, Cambridge CB2 2NH
tel (01223) 512133
email tpl@eng.cam.ac.org
website www.cambridgewrites.org
Contact Tim Love

Cambridge Writers is a fairly large writing group with a poetry sub-section. This meets monthly on the evening of the third Tuesday in the month. The Cambridge Writers' website has a poetry anthology and the group holds an annual open poetry competition.

Camden Poetry Group

64 Lilyville Road, London SW6
Contact Hannah Kelly

Meets on Saturdays, once a month.

Cannon Poets

22 Margaret Grove, Harborne, Birmingham B17 9JH
tel (01384) 354228
Contact Nicholas Paton Philip

Meets at MAC (Midlands Arts Centre), Hexagon Room, on the first Sunday in the month (2-5.30pm), except August.

Century Poets

Century House, 99-101 Sutton House, Birmingham B23 5XA
tel 0121-382 0109
Contact Prof Kopan Mahadeva

Meets on the last Sunday in the month (2-6pm).

Circle in the Square

45 Totterdown Road, Weston-Super-Mare, Somerset BS23 4LJ

tel (01934) 628994 (for details of meetings)
Contact Bill Pickard

Meets on alternate Thursdays, from 7.45pm until 10.30pm. Over-18s only; admission 50p. No meetings in August or over Christmas. Has been running for 46 years and held more than 2000 meetings. Ex-members now live worldwide.

Cootehill Writers' Group
Station Road, Cootehill, County Cavan, Ireland
tel (00353) 495552321
email kphelan04@eircom.net
Contact Kay Phelan

A small group that meets occasionally to discuss poetry and prose.

Coventry Live Poets Society
Earlsdon Library, Earlsdon Avenue North, Coventry CV5 6FZ
tel (02476) 675359
email info.follib@covnet.co.uk
Contact C Jones

Meets on the first Wednesday of the month.

Cumbria Poets Workshop
Keswick Library, Heads Lane, Keswick CA12 5HD
tel (01768) 772656
email workington.library@cumbriacc.gov.uk
Contact Chris Pilling

Meets at Keswick Library.

Dean Clough Writers Group
227 Stirling Street, Halifax, West Yorkshire HX3 5AZ
Contact Gaia Hughes

Dialstone Writers
90 Hillcrest Road, Offerton, Stockport, Cheshire SK2 5SE

tel (01614) 835958
email cliffjim7@aol.com

A creative writing group meeting in a room in the local church. Encourages all types of writing, and takes its work out into the local community.

Dorset East Street Poets
38 Hod View, Blandford Forum, Dorset DT11 8TN
Contact David Caddy

Monthly meetings with workshops and talks from visiting poets and writers.

Dublin Writers' Workshop
email dubwriter@indigo.ie
website www.dublinwriters.org

Dublin's longest-running writers' group.

East Anglian Writers
email chair@eastanglianwriters.org.uk
Chairman Benjamin Scott

Aims to bring together – and help promote the work of – professional writers working or living in Norfolk, Suffolk, Essex, Cambridgeshire and Bedfordshire. Runs a number of social events throughout the year to help break the isolation of writing and to share experiences; also organises a number of speaker events. To join the EAW you must be a professional writer living, or planning to live, in Norfolk, Suffolk, Essex, Cambridgeshire, or Bedfordshire. You must have had a work published, performed or broadcast, but not vanity-published. Illustrators, self-published and retired writers are also welcome.

East Coker Poetry Group
The Helyar Arms, East Coker, Yeovil, Somerset BA22 9JR
tel (01935) 863573
email info@eastcokerpoetry.org.uk

website www.eastcokerpoetry.org.uk
Contact Sue McKerracher

The village of East Coker, home to TS Eliot's ancestors, was immortalised in his *Four Quartets*; the poet's ashes are buried in the churchyard of St Michael's. This heritage prompted the formation of the East Coker Poetry Group, meeting 6 times a year to share favourite verse in the informal, relaxed environment of the village inn, the Helyar Arms.

Eastwood Writers' Group

c/o Eastwood Library, Wellington Place, Nottingham Road, Eastwood, Nottingham NG16 3GB
tel (01773) 788752
email gorbutler@hotmail.com
website www.eastwoodwriters.co.uk/eastwho.htm
Contact Gordon Butler

Meets every Tuesday at the Catholic Social Centre, Nottingham Road, Hilltop, Eastwood, Nottingham, from 1.30 to 3.30pm, to share and appraise each other's short stories, novels and poetry.

Erewash Writers' Group

631 Tamworth Road, Long Eaton, Nottingham NG10 3AB
tel 0115-849 8519
Secretary Janet Devereux

The group's main aim is to promote the art of creative writing, including poetry. Most members write some poetry.

Falmouth Poetry Group

Falmouth Library, Municipal Offices, The Moor, Falmouth TR11 3QA
tel (01736) 763803
email tozer.jane@virgin.net
website www.falmouthpoetrygroup.org.uk
Contact Jane Tozer

Falmouth Poetry Group was founded 30 years ago, by the later Peter Redgrove. It meets fortnightly at Falmouth Library, for critical workshops; also acts as a discussion forum for work-in-progress. It still follows the method used by The Group, founded by Philip Hobsbaum, of which Redgrove was a founder member. FPG endures as a dynamic and influential source of inspiration and encouragement to poets in Cornwall, and has an excellent record of achievement. When funds allow, it runs readings, creative workshops and other poetry events, and publishes a quarterly newsletter featuring poems by members.

Fareham WordWrights

20 Laurel Gardens, Locks Heath SO31 6QH
tel (01329) 846480
email liza@look828.fsnet.co.uk
Contact Rosa Johnson, Sylvie Whitaker (Secretary)

A group for budding writers in Hampshire. Help, discussion and constructive criticism always available. Meets at Litchfield Community Centre, Litchfield, Hants.

Fire River Poets

2 Deane View, Bishops Hull Road, Bishops Hull, Taunton, Somerset TA1 5EG
tel (01823) 252486
email enquiry@fireriverpoets.org.uk
website www.fireriverpoets.org.uk
Contact John Stuart

A group of poets who meet about 20 times a year to read their own poetry, and sometimes other people's. Criticism is invited. All forms of poetry are welcomed, from light to serious; formal to informal. Membership is not open to complete beginners, however, and meetings are not completed as an evening class.

Flint Creative Writers

10 Hillcourt Avenue, Bagillt, Flintshire CH6 6DW

tel (01352) 735302
Contact EM Hudson

Group includes several members who write poetry and enter competitions.

Flowerfield Arts Centre
185 Coleraine Road, Portstewart, County Derry, Northern Ireland
tel 028-7083 1400
email info@flowerfield.org
Contact Bernie McGill

Meets once a week on a 10-week term basis, October-December and January-March, with a short 6-week term after Easter each year. Enrol at Flowerfield Arts Centre at the start of each new term. The group tackles short writing exercises in-session, and each member produces a piece at home for the following week's meeting. 12 members write poetry and fiction. New members welcome.

Footwork
Flat 1, 30 Pembroke Avenue, Hove, East Sussex BN3 5DB
email info@footwork.org.uk
Contact Robert Walton

A collective of Sussex poets.

Fosseway Writers
Ashleigh, 5 Main Street, Upton, Notts NG23 5ST
tel (01636) 812484
Contact Kirsty Adlard

Galway Writers' Workshop
Galway Language Centre, Bridge Mills, Galway, Ireland
website www.crannogmagazine.com/gww.htm

Meets each Saturday in The Bridge Mills building. It is a peer-led workshop, i.e. does not use a facilitator. Members bring copies (usually 10-12) of their work

(poetry, fiction, drama), read it aloud and have it critiqued by the other members. Usually about 15 minutes allotted to each reader. New members to the workshop must be nominated in advance by an existing member. Also publishes *Crannog Magazine*.

Hereford Poetry Group
tel (01684) 576445
Contact Amanda Attfield

Herga Poets
10 Runnelfield, Harrow on the Hill, Middx HA1 3NY
tel 020-8864 3149
Contact Dorothy Pope

Meets on the third Sunday of every month (second Sunday in December), 2-5.15pm in the Library of Orley Farm School, South Hill Avenue, Harrow on the Hill. (Please call before attending.)

Highgate Poets
9 Western Road, London N2 9JB
tel 020-8883 8095
Contact Jill Bamber

Meets on the first Sunday of the month, in members' homes in the North London area. Would-be joiners must submit a sample of work with an sae. The group offers common ground for exchange, criticism and help for poets keen to find a platform for their work.

Indian King Arts Centre Poets Writing Group
Fore Street, Camelford, Cornwall PL23 9PG
tel (01840) 212161
email indianking@btconnect.com
website www.indianking.org.uk
Contact Helen Wood

Meets weekly.

Islington Poetry Workshops
FPHC, 12 Pine Grove, London N4 3LL
tel 020-7272 9023/020-8340 5974
Contact Brian Docherty

Offers opportunities to present and
discuss poetry in a supportive and friendly
group.

Keele Writers
23 The Bridle Path, Madeley, Cheshire
CW3 9EL
tel (01782) 750029
email rog.bradleythefirst@ tiscali.co.uk
Contact Roger Bradley

Based on a poetry writing group at Keele
University, with the assistance of Harry
Owen, Cheshire's first Poet Laureate, the
group meets out of term time at other
venues. It consists of about 16 poets at
present, many having contributed to
poetry magazines, both local and national.

Kelso Writers' Group
Lammercote, 7 Hadden Farm Cottages,
Sprouston, nearr Kelso TD5 8HU
tel (01890) 830364
Contact Maureen Still

Meets Mondays, fortnightly, at the Abbey
Road Centre, Kelso.

Kent & Sussex Poetry Society
The Camden Centre, Market Square,
Tunbridge Wells, Kent TN1 2SW
email info@KentAndSussexPoetrySociety.org
website
www.kentandsussexpoetrysociety.org

Established for 60 years in Tunbridge
Wells. Activities include: monthly open
poetry readings from a wide range of
contemporary poets, including a short
open mic slot for readings from the floor;
monthly poetry workshops; biannual
Saturday all-day 'master poet' workshops
for igniting new inspiration; annual

writing retreat for members, which is
highly subsidised by the Society; annual
open poetry competition, with £1000 in
prizes.

Kick Start Poets
c/o 'Corydon', Pennings Drove, Coombe
Bissett, Salisbury SP5 4NA
tel (01722) 329687
website www.kickstartpoets.freeuk.com
Contact Ruth Marden

An independent group of poets, founded
in 1997 and sponsored by The Arts
Council of England, South West. Regular
meetings are normally on the third
Thursday of every month, at Sarum
College in Salisbury Cathedral Close.
Non-members are welcome at all regular
meetings. Membership fee, £15 p.a.

King's Lynn Writers
The Friends' Meeting House, 38 Bridge
Street, King's Lynn, Norfolk PE30 5AB
tel (01553) 67563

Meets on the second Thursday of every
month.

Lampeter Writers' Workshop
tel (01570) 422351 ext 297
email writersworkshop@lamp.ac.uk

Meets on Tuesday nights, 7pm (term time
only) in Lecture Room 7, Canterbury
Building, University of Wales Lampeter.

The Larkfield Writers
The Larkfield Centre, 39 Inglefield Street,
Glasgow G42
email larkfieldwriters@hotmail.com

Meets every Monday afternoon from 1-
3pm.

Leicester Poetry Society
tel (01162) 567074
email e.lee@bssgroup.com

Contact Emma Lee

Runs workshops at the Leicester Adult Education College, Friday evenings at 7-9.30pm.

Leigh and Atherton Writers

54 Orchard Close, Leigh, Lancs WN7 1NY
tel (01942) 678454 or (01942) 876279
email nopampen@supanet.com
Joint Secretaries H Wellings, P Button

A group of writers interested in poetry, drama, short stories, articles and novels.

Lichfield Poetry Writers' Group

Lichfield Library, The Friary, Lichfield, Staffordshire WS13 6QG
tel (01543) 510700
email valerie.lovatt@ staffordshire.gov.uk
Contact Val Lovatt

A venture in writing that is at the forefront of a poetry revival in the city of Lichfield. The group promotes opportunities for writers of all ages and experience to develop their craft through workshops, events, performances, readings and publication. Thus a natural part of this work is to reach out to a wider audience, and to turn the joy of verse into a more mainstream attraction. LPWG's monthly meetings are hosted at, and generously supported by, Lichfield Library. All are welcome to attend. Admission is free of charge, with refreshments provided.

Llanelli Writers' Circle

20 Rectory Close, Loughor, Swansea SA4 6JU
tel (01792) 891679
email cazleucarum@tesco.net
Secretary Carole Ann Smith

Aims to stimulate and encourage the craft of writing, including poetry. Several members of the group are published poets. Welcomes beginners and more experienced writers, providing a network of support.

London Voices Poetry Workshop

70 Holden Road, London N12 7DY
tel 020-8445 0090 *fax* 020-8445 6663

Friendly discussion of members' poetry and prose; produces an annual anthology. The group encourages young people and all ages; meets on the second-last Friday of the month (except December and July) at the Sekforde Arms, Sekforde Street, London EC1 (Farringdon tube). A collection is taken.

Longford Writers

Norwood House, 2 Bowling Green Road, Gainsborough, Lincolnshire DN21 2QA
tel (01427) 612414
email john_silkstone@yahoo.co.uk
website http://groups.yahoo.com/group/longfordwriters
Contact John A Silkstone

A poetry group that publishes an A5 quarterly magazine of members' work (£16, €25, $30 p.a.).

Ludlow Poetry Cafe

Ludlow Library, 10 Old Street, Ludlow, Shropshire SY8 1NP
tel (01584) 872619
Contact Gill Mortimer

Meets on the first Wednesday each month at the Assembly Rooms, Ludlow.

Magnetic North Writers

email magneticnorthse10@yahoo.co.uk
website www.geocities.com/magnorth_writing

An open writers' group, based in South London and covering poetry, short fiction and non-fiction.

Manchester Poets

Chorlton Library, Manchester Road, Chorlton, Manchester M21 9PN

tel 0161-429 6385
Contact Dave Tarrant

Meets 1 Friday (usually the first) each month, for a workshop. Meetings are held from 7.30 to 10pm at Chorlton Library, Manchester Road, Chorlton, Manchester.

Manky Poets

Chorlton Library, Manchester Road, Chorlton, Manchester M21 9PN
tel 0161-1881 3179
email manky@toucansurf.com
Contact Copland Smith

Has met since 1978, on the third Friday of every month. Floor spots and a guest. 7.30 to 9.30pm. £2/£1. All welcome.

Market Rasen Writers' Group

'Cobwebs', Middlefield Lane, Glenthm, Market Rasen LN8 2ET
tel (01673) 878633
email cobwebs1@tiscali.co.uk
Contact CF Green

A group of local writers who meet monthly to discuss each other's work.

Mendip and Somerton Writers

11 Chapman's Close, Wookey, Wells, Somerset BA5 1LU
email jmthom@tiscali.co.uk
Contact Judith Thomas

Classes are for Somerset County Council's Learning and Leisure groups. Poetry is included; some learners write nothing else.

Metroland Poets

Pucks Paigles, Burtons Lane, Little Chalfont, Bucks
tel (01494) 762290

Contact Christopher North

A poetry appreciation group with workshop elements for members' original work.

National Association of Writers' Groups

Headquarters The Arts Centre, Biddick Lane, Washington, Tyne and Wear NE38 2AB
tel (01262) 609228
email nawg@tesco.net
Secretary Mike Wilson, 40 Burstall Hill, Bridlington, East Yorkshire YO16 7GA
website www.nawg.co.uk
Membership £30 p.a. plus £5 registration per group; £12 Associate individuals

Aims "to advance the education of the general public throughout the UK, including the Channel Islands, by promoting the study and art of writing in all its aspects". Publishes *Link* bimonthly magazine. Annual Festival of Writing held in Durham in September. Annual Creative Writing Competition. Founded 1995.

New Rivers Writers Group

The Wenlock Arms, 26 Wenlock Road, Islington, London N1 7TA
tel (07949) 621288
email Dffusjjg@hotmail.com
website www.foxglove.co.uk/newrivers
Contact Julian Duffus

A workshop-based group that meet weekly (Thursday evenings, 8.30-11pm) to read out work-in-progress of any type and give each other supportive feedback. Also runs a programme of social events during the summer in and around London. Particularly welcomes visitors passing through London. No fee is charged.

Newquay Library Poetry group

Newquay Library, Marcus Hill, Newquay, Cornwall
tel (01872) 241106
Contact Zeeba Ansari

Meets on the second Friday of the month from 11-1 in Newquay Library.

Norwich Writers' Circle

1 Osbert Close, Lakenham, Norwich NR1 2NL
tel (01603) 479342
Contact Sean Hindle

Established in 1943, to serve a growing need for writers and would-be writers in the City of Norwich. Since then it has enjoyed the support of many individuals with varying involvements in the art, craft and hard-nosed business of writing. Today, membership is widely dispersed, throughout the region of East Anglia and beyond. Membership fee, £20.

OU Poets

email adrian@greenad.co.uk
website www.oupoets.org.uk
Contact Adrian Green

A poetry group for students and staff, past or present, of the Open University, Milton Keynes. Currently has about 120 members. Like other poetry groups, members submit poems for others to read and comment on; unlike most other poetry groups, they do this by post and not face-to-face, because they are scattered all across the country, with some in Ireland and in other parts of Europe. The magazine (strictly for members only) contains poems, criticisms and comments, and is issued 5 times a year.

Peebles and Innerleithen Writers' Group

Craig View, 4 Ballantyre Street, Innerleithen, Peeblesshire EH44 6LN
tel (01896) 830396
Contact Joan Hailstones

Meets Thursdays, fortnightly, 7:30pm at Walkerhaugh Community Centre, Peebles.

Pennine Ink Writers' Workshop

The Gallery, Mid-Pennine Arts, Yorke Street, Burnley, Lancs BB11 1HD

Established in 1983. Meets every Monday night from 8-10pm at the Woodman Inn, Todmorden Road, Burnley. Programme is stimulating and varied and includes workshops on articles, short stories, poetry and plays.

Pentland Writers' Group

Amulree, Carlops, Penicuik EH26 9NF
tel (01968) 660727
email annamulree@cs.com
Contact Ann Smith

Meets in the Carlops area.

Penwith Poets and Writers Group

Newburn, Cockwells, Penzance, Cornwall TR20 8DB
Contact Patricia Bishop

Meets on the third Wednesday of every month from 11.30-3.30pm. One-to-one help for beginners is possible.

Penzance Poetry Group

tel (01872) 241106
Contact Zeeba Ansari

Meets on the first Monday and third Thursday of each month at Trevelyan House, Chapel Street, Penzance, Cornwall.

Pitshanger Poets

Questors Theatre, Mattock Lane, Ealing, London W5 5BQ
tel 020-8567 7234 or 020-8567 0011
email nala.ques@virgin.net or pitshangerpoets@virgin.net
website pitshangerpoets.co.uk
Contact Alan Chambers/Nigel Lawrence

A weekly workshop-cum-discussion evening at Questor Theatre, every Tuesday except during August. Runs special events and readings with guest poets. Also runs a national poetry competition.

Poetry I.D.

The Place, 18-20 Leys Avenue, Letchworth Garden City, Hertfordshire SG6 4UB

tel (01438) 217614
Contact Richard Copeland

A group of poets who meet every Thursday at The Place in Letchworth Garden City for regular workshop sessions and, occasionally, 'surgeries', where members can submit work for criticism and analysis. Also holds occasional members' performance evenings; recently, guest poets have performed their work.

Poetry Ireland
2 Prouds Lane, off St Stephen's Green, Dublin 2
tel (00353) 1478 9974
email poetry@iol.ie
website www.poetryireland.ie

Provides a comprehensive list of writers' groups and workshops throughout Ireland.

Poetry Round
Finborough Arms PH, Finborough Road, London SW10
email info@poetryround.8m.com
website http://poetryround.8m.com

Meets Mondays at 7.30pm.

Poetry Society Stanzas
22 Betterton Street, London WC2H 9BX
tel 020-7420 9880
email membership@ poetrysociety.org.uk
website www.poetrysociety.org.uk/
members/stanzas.htm

The Poetry Society has introduced Poetry Society Stanzas, an opportunity to meet other Poetry Society members. Any Poetry Society member is welcome to volunteer their contact details in order to form a local Stanza. A section of *Poetry News* will be dedicated to publicising all Stanza locations and contact details around the UK.

Poetry Wednesbury
25 Griffiths Road, West Bromwich, West Midlands B71 2EH

tel (07950) 591455
email geoff@poetrywednesbury.co.uk
website www.poetrywednesbury.co.uk
Contact Geoff Stevens

A group of poets who meet at The George in Wednesbury on the last Wednesday of each month.

Poets Anonymous
70 Aveling Close, Purley, Surrey CR8 4DW
tel 020-8645 9956
email poets@poetsanon.org.uk
website www.poetsanon.org.uk
Contact Peter Evans

Holds 2 meetings a month: on the first Friday of the month at the Dog and Bull, Surrey Street, Croydon from 8pm; and on the second Saturday of the month in the Primary Room, United Reformed Church, Addiscombe Grove, Croydon, 2.30-4pm.

Poets of London
PO Box 4YP, London W1A 4YP
email sallycrawford@poetsoflondon.com
website www.poetsoflondon.com

A workshop and collegiate base for poets visiting London. Open to poets and those interested in poetry and the built environment. Monthly 'Creating Poetic Space' meetings on the first Saturday of the month at Waterstone's Gower Street. Ongoing Poetry of City project to encourage more poetry of place and places of poetry in cities.

Rathmines Writers' Workshop
8 Brighton Gardens, Rathgar, Dublin 8, Ireland
tel 08 6402 5578 (08 6492 6980, evenings and weekends) *email*
rathmineswritersworkshop@eircom.net
website
www.rathmineswritersworkshop.com

Contact James Conway

Meets every second Thursday at 7.30pm; reviews original work by writers who attend. Established in 1990, membership numbers around 40. Fee of €5 per workshop.

Reddich Poetry Workshops
41 Buckleys Green, Alvechurch, Birmingham B48 7NG
tel 0121-445 2110
Contact Charles Johnson

A welcoming mutual-criticism group of poets, meeting on the second Tuesday of every month.

Saint Johns Library Poetry Workshops
41 Buckleys Green, Alvechurch, Birmingham B48 7NG
tel 0121-445 2110
Contact Charles Johnson

Meets Saturdays, 1pm, bi-monthly.

Salisbury New Writers
4 Rosedale, Cholderton Road, Newton Tony, Salisbury, Wilts SP4 0EU
tel (01980) 629440
email Susandown5@aol.com
Contact Susan Down

Many members write poetry, free verse, rhymed and traditional forms; holds readings and enables group criticism of work-in-progress. Currently working on a group anthology, which also includes short stories and novels. Meetings are monthly on the first Thursday of each month at 6.30pm in the United Reform Church, Salisbury.

Scarborough Poetry Workshop
19 Trinity Road, Scarborough, North Yorkshire YO11 2TD
tel (01723) 365562
email ritasherriff-hammond@tiscali.co.uk

Contact Rita Sherriff-Hammond

A group that promotes all aspects of poetry and its performance, and encourages new and experienced poets to develop their existing talent and discover their hidden talents.

Scriveners
The Secretary, Ty Beirdd, 53 Church Street, Ebbw Vale NP23 6BG
tel (01495) 305463
email scriveners@lycos.co.uk
website www.scriveners.co.uk
Contact The Secretary

A group of published and unpublished writers who meet fortnightly on Wednesday evening, to give constructive criticism on work-in-progress. Work is circulated before meetings to enable in-depth criticism. 50-75% is poetry, but other genres are also welcome.

Southend Poetry Group
c/o Adrian Green (secretary), Railway Hotel, Clifftown Road, Southend-on-Sea
email turnedor029@yahoo.co.uk
website http://welcome.to/southendpoetry
Contact Aidan Green

Meets at 8pm on the first Wednesday of each month, upstairs in the Railway Ho, Clifftown Road, Southend. Meetings usually take the form of a presentation and discussion of a poet or topic, followed, if time allows, by a brief workshop session at which members can read their own work. At least 3 times a year, a whole evening is devoted to workshops. There is no formal membership; anyone is welcome to the meetings and the first time is free!

Southwest Writers
Shortlees Community Centre, Blacksyke Avenue, Kilmarnock KA1 4SR

Contact Alan J Dixon

Meets every second Monday throughout the year to discuss all sorts of literature, including books, short stories, poems and articles.

Speakeasy: Milton Keynes Writers' Group

c/o 46 Wealdstone Place, Springfield, Milton Keynes MK6 3JG
tel (01908) 663860
email speakeasy@writerbrock.co.uk
website www.mkweb.co.uk/speakeasy
Contact Martin Brocklebank

Welcomes writers of all genres. See website for further details.

Suffolk Poetry Society

9 Gainsborough Road, Felixstowe IP11 7HT
email suffolkpoetry@aol.com
website www.blythweb.co.uk/sps
Secretary Maureen Butler

During the summer, occasional meetings are held on Sunday afternoons at various places in Suffolk. Speakers include foremost poets and critical writers of the day (see website for details of the 2006 programme). From November to March inclusive, local groups meet in members' homes to read and discuss poetry. Further details from the Membership Secretary. Membership, £10 p.a.

Survivor Poets Leeds

94 Cherry Tree Walk, East Ardsley, Wakefield WF3 2AJ
website www.survivorspoetry.com
Contact Tom Ireland

Leeds Survivors' Poetry has been running workshops and staging performances since 1994.

Survivor Poets Manchester

Manchester Survivors, Commonword, 6 Mount Street, Manchester M2 5NS

website www.survivorspoetry.com
Contact Rosie Garland

Runs 2 groups that meet for writing workshops and performances. The mixed group meets every Monday from 2-4pm, and the women's group meets on Thursdays from 1-3pm. Workshops are either run by guest facilitators or are a time for the group to receive positive feedback in 'open' writing/reading sessions.

Survivors' Poetry Bristol

26 Bradley Avenue, Shirehampton, Bristol BS11 9SL
tel 0117-983 2790
email steve.hy@blueyonder.co.uk
website www.steppingouttheatre.co.uk
Contact Steve Hennessy

Runs creative writing and drama groups for mental-health-service users.

Survivors' Poetry Scotland

4C4 Templeton Centre, 62 Templeton Street, Glasgow G40 1DA
tel 0141-556 4554
email www.spscot.co.uk
website www.spscot.co.uk

Sutton Coldfield Poetry Society

Sutton Coldfield Library, Lower Parade, Sutton Coldfield B72 1XX
tel 0121-354 3860
Contact Mrs WM Mottram

Meets on the third Tuesday in the month, from 10am onwards.

Thin Raft

Reading International Solidarity Centre, 35-39 London Street, Reading RG1 4PS
tel (01189) 786678
website www.centrepoint.ch/ThinRaft
Contact Susan Utting

Regular poetry workshop sessions are open to anyone looking for structured feedback from a supportive, eclectic poetry group. Poets at all levels of experience are welcome – from absolute beginner to bestsellers. Also arranges dayschools led by visiting poets, as well as public poetry readings.

Tigh Fili Writers Group

Tigh Fili Art Centre, Thompson House, McCurtain St, Cork, Ireland
website www.tighfili.com/literature.asp
Contact Eoin Ryan

Meets once a month at Tigh Filí Arts Centre from 6.30-8.30.

Toddington Poetry Society

82 Marston Gardens, Luton LU2 7DY
tel (01582) 723500
website
www.toddingtonpoetrysociety.co.uk
Contact Jean Janes

Open to all who enjoy reading, writing or hearing poetry. Meets on the second and fourth Tuesdays of the month, in Luton. Meetings usually alternate between a visiting poet or an informal evening, with impromptu contributions of members' and other poems.

Torquay Writers' Group

18 Cedar Road, Preston, Paignton, Devon TQ3 2DD
tel (01803) 520165
Coordinator Danny Pyle

Weekly group meeting at St Marychurch Precinct Centre, Torquay, on Thursdays, 2-4pm, covering short stories, articles and poems which make up 75%. No age bar, but mainly middle-age to senior.

Tottington Writers

30 Beryl Avenue, Tottington, Bury, Lancashire BL8 3NF
tel (01204) 882950

Contact Bettina Jones

A small, tutor-led group; tackles all kinds of creative writing, including poetry, which is the special interest of the tutor.

Truro Library Poetry Group

Truro Library, Union Place, Truro, Cornwall TR1 1EP
email mtwose@cornwall.gov.uk
website www.cornwall.gov.uk
Contact Maureen Twose

Meets on the second Thursday of the month to read, discuss and enjoy their own work and that of other poets.

Tynesidepoets

189 Stamfordham Road, Newcastle upon Tyne NE5 3JL
tel 019-1242 1565
email alantynepoet80@aol.com
Contact Alan C Brown

Has been in existence since 1960; has had cultural exchange with poets from the US, Germany, Bulgaria, Sweden, Norway, Iceland, Russia and elsewhere. Helps writers in all fields of literature and most European languages to learn, discuss and share ideas, and those who do not write but like English poetry or prose. Meets on the second and last Tuesdays of the month at 7.30pm at The Old George, Cloth Market, Newcastle upon Tyne.

Ulverston Writers

tel (01229) 582399
email maggie@townbank1.fsnet.co.uk
Contact Maggie Norton

Short story writers, novelists, poets and playwrights meet to discuss work each fortnight, on Wednesdays, at Owl Barn, Back Lane (first left off Church Walk), Ulverston, at 10.30-1pm.

Ver Poets

15 Brampton Road, St Albans, Herts AL1 4PP

email daphne.schiller@virgin.net
Contact Daphne Schiller, Secretary
Membership £15 p.a. UK, £20 overseas,
£10 students

Was founded in 1996 by May Badman
and has both local and postal members.
Encourages the writing and study of
poetry. Holds evening meetings and
daytime workshops in the St Albans area.
Local and postal members. Holds
members' competitions and the annual
Open Competition.

Ware Poets

c/o David Perman, 11 Musley Lane, Ware,
Herts SG12 7EN
email david@rockpress.freeserve.co.uk
website www.rockingham-press.co.uk
Contact David Perman

Ware Poets meet on the first Friday of
each month in the Ware Arts Centre.
There is a guest poet and readings from
the floor. For further information, see
www.rockingham-press.co.uk.

Westway Writers' Workshop

1 Thorpe Close, Ladbroke Grove, London
W10 5XL
tel 020-8964 1900
email mail@openage.co.uk
website www.openage.co.uk
Contact Mary Callaghan

Poetry, prose, playwriting; a group that is
open to new ideas and new members.

Wimbledon and Merton Poetry Group

tel (07969) 597967
email zznsh@yahoo.co.uk
Contact Russell Thompson

Workshop/group with no fixed house
style. Open to anyone who wishes to
discuss their work, share some
constructive criticism, or simply lend an
ear and meet other poets.

Worcester Writers' Circle

4 Nixon Court, Callow End, Worcester
WR2 4UU
tel (01905) 830660
email phyllathandley6@ wanadeoo.co.uk
Contact Phyllis Handley

Welcomes all kind of writing.

Word for Word

Hornsey Library, Haringey Park, Crouch
End, London N8 9JA
website www.wforw.org.uk
Contact Laurence Scott, c/o Hornsey
Library

A friendly, mixed group of poets, prose
writers, filmmakers and musicians who
meet in Hornsey Library to write. Tuesday
is poetry; Wednesday is poetry and prose.
Word for Word, Wood Green meets on
Saturday morning. See website for details.

Write Direction

Bedford Central Library, Harpur Street,
Bedford MK40 1PG
tel (01234) 269519
Contact Peter Salt

Writers' and Poets' Circle

tel 020-8763 2692
email veronicaspaintbox@ yahoo.co.uk
Contact Veronica Aldous

Meets on the second Friday of each month
at 7pm at the Friends Meeting House.

Writers' Group

6 The Innings, Observatory Lane, Lr.
Rathmines Road, Dublin 6, Ireland
tel (01) 4910034
email phylherbert@hotmail.com
Contact Phyl Herbert

A group comprising people who write in
all genres.

Resources
Getting there

Poet, **Jeremy Reed**, writes about how he became a poet, and pleads for poets to follow their own voices.

My initiation into being a published poet, soon after I left school in Jersey at the age of 18, came about in events as extraordinary as those that have continued to characterise my life as a prolific poet, novelist and non-fiction writer, who is proud never to have worked in any other capacity than that of a writer.

After unsuccessfully attempting to overdose on tranquillisers on a beach in the pouring September rain, the slow-moving bottle-green sea slowly encroaching on my comatose body, I was, after being discovered by a dog-walker, resuscitated in hospital and appointed a Samaritan who visited me twice a week. By some felicitous accident it turned out that my Samaritan, Michael Armstrong, not only wrote poetry, but was in the process of setting up Andium Press, a small self-financed project devoted to publishing poetry. After reading my juvenilia, Michael, who wore chunky Pringle lambswool jumpers in ivory, oatmeal and navy blue, decided to make the poems I was writing at the time the first book to be published by Andium. It was called *Target*, and as a jacket image had a red, white and blue roundel silk-screened on its white covers, like the one popularised by the Mods as their parka logo as they burned through the West End in a raft of chrome and mirror-stacked Vespa and Lambretta scooters in the 1960s.

My first little book sunk without trace, but was picked up on by Asa Benveniste who ran the cutting-edge Trigram Press, a poetry publisher which gravitated towards innovative work that was more American-influenced than British, and who published the likes of Tom Raworth, Jim Dine, Anselm Hollo and Nathaniel Tarn. The spin-off from my first book was the collection *The Isthmus of Samuel Greenberg*, a book typically distinguished by Asa's superb eye for typography, good paper and a smudgy green, grey and purple cover design of the New York harbours hazed into cloudy sea fog.

I was still living in Jersey at the time and took little or no interest in circulating poems to small magazines, except on the rare occasions when I was contacted for contributions. One such magazine, *Joe DiMaggio*, published by John Robinson on an old mimeograph from his bedroom, and stapled together with silk-screened covers, proved not only to be a home for my poetry, but was, through the resulting correspondence, to instigate a lifelong friendship that persists to this day. John proved that a devotion to poetry matched by a practical economic way of producing it could affect wonders, and soon poets like Barry MacSweeney, Lee Harwood and Tom Raworth were regular contributors to the magazine.

At the same time I was publishing small press booklets, which have today become collectors' items, amazed at the ingenuity of the individuals who published work in this form, the money usually being put up by friends to facilitate the costs of production. Today the process has been simplified by desktop publishing and Internet distribution. The problem here is saturation – anyone can publish their own book now – but how do you get anything to stand out, good from bad, in the surfeit of self-published poetry that floods the net?

I suppose the only method of attempting to get published in a way that attracts a small readership is instinctual. Go to somewhere like Borders, or the Poetry Library at the South Bank, and just browse through the magazines on display to see if anything appears to fit with your own style and sympathies in poetry. If it seems to, then chance a submission. Don't be drawn to the idea of being published in a particular journal because it has a reputable name; it may not be the right place for your work at all. My sympathies are always with the underground and not the mainstream milieu, so take your talent where it belongs. You'll find that writers like William Burroughs often published work in the most obscure places. Poetry appeals to a minority, and if its readership comprises a microcosm, then the magnitude of its expression transforms it into a macrocosm in terms of cultural significance. I tend to agree with Oscar Wilde when he wrote, "a man can exist three days without water but not one without poetry".

But don't expect instant feedback when you are published. If work is good it travels slowly through a sort of subterranean network. And it's a fallacy to think that success in your chosen field is dependent on publishing with large houses. The Cambridge poet, JH Prynne, considered in certain circles to be the most important poet writing in Britain today, has remained so consistently hermetic in his approach to publishing his work that his poetry has to be assiduously searched for in often small, self-published booklets, excepting his *Collected Poems* published by Bloodaxe, and is rarely if ever to be discovered in magazines like *Poetry Review*. Prynne is just one example of a writer who has established a reputation through doing his own thing, and consistently avoiding all notions of celebrity, including readings – relying on the work itself to generate a slow but unstoppable momentum.

My advice is always to place the work before the idea of recognition. It's the doing of course, the engagement with creativity that is important; and if there's a small payback later, then that's a bonus. But poetry's essentially a solitary engagement, so before anything else you need to get used to your own company, and to working regularly and with discipline at your writing. Because of his demanding job at New York's Metropolitan Museum of Modern Art, and his recklessly excessive social life, the American poet, Frank O'Hara used to write his poems in every available free moment, often standing up at parties, in taxis gunning across town, and of course in his lunch hours. O'Hara's *Lunch Poems*, published by City Lights in 1964, are precisely that, the marvellous synthesis of his sensory perceptions of fragmented New York life put into the fast visual imagery takes permitted him in his lunchtime strolls around the city. Like Bob Dylan, who rarely bothers with a second take of a song, O'Hara seldom rewrote, trusting his instincts as having got it right first time.

Poets can be too over-precious about letting a poem go. To my mind, writing workshops serve little purpose unless it's the sharing of group energies as a positive instructor to work that you are seeking. I feel if a poem is going to come out right it does so independent of commentary or academic analysis as the dissection of the living organism. Reading your work to sympathetic friends is probably the best criterion as to whether the poem you have written works or not. Try it on your own pulses first and then on people you trust. Somewhere between the two you'll find the poem's natural resting point.

I write poetry every day. To me it's an addiction like a drug, the rush of adrenalin I experience each time I fire-up imagery promoting a dopamine high. I write always by hand in exercise books. That way, rather like Frank O'Hara, I can write any-where: on buses across London, in cafes, sitting outside in squares; and always, because of that, be directly in the moment. The idea of writing at a desk seems to me to be so formal as to be inhibitive. Better to take your laptop or notebook with you anywhere and write when the moment comes up almost as a providential accident. Imagination needs to be open to all experience and kept very separate from any received notions of what literature comprises. You should be able to write a poem about anything if you have the imaginative capacity. And in this respect it's important if you are thinking about magazine publication to look at the editorial policy. There is in mainstream British poetry the constrictive belief that the subject matter of poetry should be confined to a self-limiting radius of domestic issues, nature and socially realist commentary, a circumscribed ethic that in Thom Gunn's words subscribes to a "total lack of ambition". Don't be dragged into the obligatory grey post-Larkin undertow. There are many other outlets. Pete Doherty for instance sometimes publishes his poetry in online magazines. Look for broader horizons. You wouldn't have imagined William Burroughs bothering to submit work to the *TLS*. Choose your canvas, and like the artist Francis Bacon, throw your paint at it in a detonation of colour. Sooner or later you'll find the metier in which you feel most comfortable.

Follow your own voice and you'll find that in time it comes through, and that it makes a little mark with someone. We all need to feel that we have shared the experience of writing a poem and that it has communicated to the reader, so research a prospective outlet and go for it. I tend to write poetry, principally because little I read in British poetry excites me, so I have to create it for myself. That's one reason for writing; but you'll have your own. Whatever it is, value the impulse as central to your life and nurture it. It's up to you to react against Auden's negative belief that "poetry makes nothing happen", and to prove the opposite – that it changes the world every single moment with the tang of biting into a ripe orange.

Jeremy Reed has written a number of books of poetry and prose. *Orange Sunshine: The Party That Lasted a Decade* is published by SAF.

Poetry bookshops

It is increasingly difficult to find a good selection of poetry in many of our high-street booksellers. EPOS, the technology that keeps retailers up to date on what they are selling, has never been kind to poetry and the range of books sold has suffered terribly as a result. Thankfully, most of the shops listed here provide a wider selection of poetry titles than the average bookseller. The Internet, of course, provides an ideal solution, but most bookshops can now get their hands on any book in print. So, if you wish to keep your local bookshop going, you may wish to order through them. At least you will not have the added cost of postage and packing to consider.

Any Amount of Books

56 Charing Cross Road, London WC2H 0BB
tel 020-7836 3697 *fax* 020-7240 1769
email charingx@anyamountofbooks.com
website www.anyamountofbooks.com
Contact Nigel Burwood

Traditional Charing Cross Road bookshop with a wide-ranging stock, including a bargain basement and an antequarian section. The shop has a very high turnover with new books added every day. There is a yearly catalogue and a website with many unusual items.

Arnolfini Bookshop

16 Narrow Quay, Bristol BS1 4QA
tel 0117-917 2313
email bookshop@arnolfini.org.uk
website www.arnolfini.org.uk
Contact Katie Teasdale

Arnolfini is home to one of the best specialist arts bookshops in the country. Has more than 100 magazines and periodicals on art, design, literature and film, as well as an exceptional range of books on contemporary art and culture. The bookshop showcases books by independent publishers.

Blackwell's, Broad Street, Oxford

8-51 Broad Street, Oxford OX1 3BQ
tel (01865) 792792 *fax* (01865) 794143
email oxford@blackwell.co.uk

Vast selection of poetry titles as well as a comprehensive range of poetry magazines, and spoken word. Second-hand titles are also available. Poetry and other readings take place throughout the year.

Blackwell's, Charing Cross Road

100 Charing Cross Road, London WC2H 0JG
tel 020-7292 5100 *fax* 020-7240 9665
email orders.London@blackwell.co.uk
Manager Andrew Chart

Situated in the heart of bookland. Although the focus of the shop is academic, being in the middle of the West End of London, it also stocks a good range of poetry titles as well as a good range of poetry magazines.

The Bookshop, Launceston

10 Church Street, Launceston, Cornwall PL15 8AP
tel (01566) 774107
website www.launceston-bookshop.co.uk

Bookshop at Queens

91 University Road, Belfast BT7 1NL
tel (028) 90 666 302
email info@queensbookshop.co.uk
website www.queensbookshop.co.uk

The oldest independent academic and general bookseller in Belfast. Specialises in history, politics and literature. The bookshop is also proud of its extensive collection of British and Irish poetry. Signed editions of local poets such as Michael Longley, Adrian Rice, etc. frequently in stock. A mail order service is available.

Borders Books, Music, Video and Cafe, Oxford Street

203-207 Oxford Street, London W1D 2LE
tel 020-7292 1600

Borders' flagship store in the heart of London's West End, with a large selection of poetry titles and a varied and interesting events programme. Stocks a good range of literary and poetry magazines.

Centreprise Bookshop

136-138 Kingsland High Street, Dalston, London E8 2NS
tel 020-7254 9632

Specialises in Black writing, contemporary fiction and books for children, plus cards, giftwraps and book tokens. Orders accepted for any book in print; the bookshop can supply books on invoice to schools and libraries.

Children's Poetry Bookshop

tel 020-7833 9247
website
www.childrenspoetrybookshelf.co.uk

Website set up by the Poetry Book Society to support poetry written for children. Its aim is to encourage children to read and enjoy poetry, and it operates as a book club. The books offered are chosen by a panel of expert Selectors, whose task is to find the very best children's poetry.

Cogito Books

5 St Mary's Chare, Hexham, Northumberland NE46 1NQ
tel (01434) 602555

email alan.grint@btinternet.com
Contact Alan and Julia Grint

An independent bookshop run by poetry-loving owners, Alan and Julia Grint. Their poetry section is exceptionally well stocked and has many volumes and anthologies with which the bigger stores no longer bother.

David's Bookshop

14 Eastcheap, Letchworth Garden City, Hertfordshire SG6 3DE
tel (01462) 684631
website www.davids-bookshops.co.uk

Open since 1963, David's Bookshop, Music Shop and Gift Shop are all located in 3 shops in Eastcheap, Letchworth Garden City. Comprehensive range of books of all kinds.

The Derwent Bookshop

10 Finkle Street, Workington, Cumbria CA14 2BB
website www.cumbriabooks.com/product.cfm
Contact John Bailey

The Derwent Bookshop is the largest independent bookseller in West Cumbria, serving a huge geographical area between Barrow in the South and Carlisle in the North – a distance of some 100 miles.

Diehard Books

91-93 Main Street, Callander FK17 8BQ
tel (01877) 339449
email sally.king4@btinternet.com
website www.zen39641.zen.co.uk/ps/diehard.htm

Bookshop and publisher of books and the magazine, *Poetry Scotland*.

Ellwood Books

38 Winchester Street, Salisbury, Wiltshire SP1 1HG

tel (01722) 322975
email info@ellwoodbooks.com
website www.ellwoodbooks.com
Contact Marc Harrison

Large selection of poetry and plays, from fine first editions to paperback reading copies.

Foyles

113-119 Charing Cross Road, London WC2H 0EB
tel 020-7434 1580
email webmaster@foyles.co.uk
website www.foyles.co.uk

The famous London bookshop has a large selection of poetry titles and hosts a large, year-round events programme.

G David

16 St Edward's Passage, Cambridge CB2 3PJ
tel (01223) 354619

Poetry lovers are particularly well-served with an extensive section that covers hard-to-find small press editions as well as the usual sets of complete works and anthologies.

Hatchards

187 Piccadilly, London W1
tel 020-7439 9921 *fax* 020-7494 1313
email books@hatchards.co.uk
website www.hatchards.co.uk
Manager Gavin Pilgrim

Stocks a broad range of poetry titles. The emphasis is on the classic, but also keeps a good selection of contemporary writing. A Mail Order Department sends books to destinations worldwide.

Heffers Booksellers

20 Trinity Street, Cambridge CB2 1TY
tel (01223) 568568
email heffers@heffers.co.uk

Manager David Robinson

Extensive book range, including over 1000 titles covering contemporary poetry from all over the world, along with criticism and biographies. Also offers a comprehensive range of anthologies.

Hellenic Bookservice

91 Fortess Road, London NW5 1AG
tel 020-7627 9499
email info@hellenicbookservice.com
website www.hellenicbookservice.com

Specialises in the poetry of 3 distinguished cultures: Greek, ancient and modern, including 2 Nobel Prize winners, Seferis and Elytis; and Roman. Runs a mail-order service.

John Sandoe (Books) Ltd

10 Blacklands Terrace, Chelsea, London SW3 2SR
tel 020-7589 9473
email sales@johnsandoe.com
website www.johnsandoe.com/

One of London's leading independent bookshops, with books crammed into every bit of available space.

Joseph's Bookstore

2 Ashbourne Parade, 1257 Finchley Road, Temple Fortune, London NW11 0AD
tel 020-8731 7575
email info@josephsbookstore.com
website www.josephsbookstore.com

One of North London's leading independents, offering an events programme, a good range of magazines and a wide selection of books.

Loch Croispol Bookshop and Restaurant

17c Balnakeil, Durness, Sutherland IV27 4PT
tel (01971) 511777

email lochcroispol@ btopenworld.com
website www.scottish-books.net
Contact Kevin Crowe

The most north-westerly bookshop on the British mainland, selling a wide range of poetry titles, from classic texts to contemporary work. There is a large selection of Scottish poets writing in English, Gaelic and Scots. Customers can browse the shelves while enjoying food and drink. Car parking, disabled access and facilities for children.

London Review Bookshop

14 Bury Place, London WC1A 2JL
email books@lrbshop.co.uk
website www.lrb.co.uk
Contact Andrew Stillwell

Situated round the corner from the British Museum, offering a wide range of contemporary and classic poetry, with particular strengths in contemporary European and American verse. Also hosts regular poetry readings and other events.

News From Nowhere

96 Bold Street, Liverpool L1 4HY
tel 0151-708 7270
email nfn@pop3.pop.org.uk
website www.newsfromnowhere.org.uk

A women's co-operative committed to social change. Apart from poetry, a wide range of books are stocked. Subjects include: Black Britain and America, Children, Course books, Fiction, Ireland, Politics, Self-Help, Sexuality and Women. There is also a fast, friendly ordering service.

Owl Bookshop

209 Kentish Town Road, London NW5
tel 020-7485 7793
email owlbookshop1@btconnect.com

Organises regular literary events. Poetry readings have included Margaret Atwood,

John Hegley and Tobias Hill. Can supply books by mail order. As well as any British book in print, can also order American books.

The Palmers Green Bookshop

379 Green Lanes, London
tel 020-8882 2088
email pgreenbooks@aol.com

Stocks an extensive range of adult and children's books. Regular poetry readings and children's storytelling events.

The Poetry Bookshop

The Ice House, Brook Street, Hay-on-Wye, Powys HR3 5BQ
tel (01497) 821812
email info@poetrybookshop.co.uk
website www.poetrybookshop.co.uk
Contact Melanie Prince

The only bookshop in the UK devoted entirely to poetry; covers every aspect, from the antiquarian and the scholarly to contemporary work, and supplies rare, out-of-print and now new books (to order or via the website). Also stocks criticism, biography, small and fine press, Beat, war, illustrated, poetry in translation and much more. Booksearch, Postal Service and Books Bought.

Poetry Bookshop Online

Poetry Book Society, Fourth Floor, 2 Tavistock Place, London WC1H 9RA
tel 020-7833 9247 *fax* 020-7833 5990
email customerservice@ poetrybookshoponline.com
website www.poetrybookshoponline.com
Director Chris Holifield

A book club run by the Poetry Book Society. Not only does it sell poetry books and books about poets and poetry, it also offers reviews and news from the world of poetry as well as biographies of major poets.

Roundstone Books

29 Moor Lane, Clitheroe, Lancashire BB7
1BE
tel (01200) 444242
email joharbooks@aol.com
website www.roundstonebooks.co.uk
Contact Jo Harding

A town centre shop which specialises in all
the Arts (including poetry, fiction and
literary studies) but has books in most
categories. Described as "a haven of
peace" and has friendly, helpful staff.

Sharston Books

Unit 15, Wearlee Works, Longley Lane,
Sharston, Manchester M22 4WT
tel 0161-945 8604
website www.sharstonbooks.com

Bookshop with a large range, situated on
modern warehouse premises.

Soma Books

38 Kennington Lane, London SE11 4LS
tel 020-7735 2101
email books@somabooks.co.uk
website www.somabooks.co.uk

Specialises in books from Asia (including
Urdu poetry with English translations),
Africa and the Caribbean. Selection of
poetry for children and adults. Imports
from USA, Indian subcontinent, etc.

Subterranean Books

270 Hackney Road, London E2 7SJ
email eddie@subterraneanbooks.com
website www.subterraneanbooks.com

Shop selling only poetry. Has great
selection; informative content on its
website and in its newsletter.

Sweetens of Bolton

86 Deansgate, Bolton, Lancashire BL1
1BD
tel (01204) 528457

Supports the work of local writers, and
offers a good stock of poetry titles.

Talking Book Shop

11 Wigmore Street, London W1H 9LB
tel 020-7491 4117
email support@talkingbooks.co.uk
website www.talkingbooks.co.uk

Has the most comprehensive stock of
poetry available on tape and CD. Famous
poets reading their work, e.g. Betjeman,
Eliot, Hughes, Auden, and celebrated
readers giving their own individual
interpretations of favourite poems.
Publishes a yearly catalogue, has an
efficient mail-order service and offers an
exciting Internet site with sound bites!

Truro Bookshop

18 Frances Street, Truro TR1 3DW
tel (01872) 272185
website www.cornwallbooks.com

Stocks more than 20,000 titles crammed
into 2 floors of a grade II listed building.
The range of poetry, plays and literary
criticism is the most extensive in the South
West, and includes works by Cornish
writers and in the Cornish Language.

Ulysses Bookshop

40 Museum Street, London WC1A 1LT
tel 020-7831 1600
email ulyssesbooks@FSBDial.co.uk
Contact Peter Jolliffe

Independent bookshop, dedicated to
keeping important copies of major British
poets in stock.

Waterstone's, Brighton

71-74 North Street, Brighton, East Sussex
BN1 1ZA
tel (01273) 206017

A good selection of poetry books and
magazines.

Waterstone's, Deansgate, Manchester
91 Deansgate, Manchester M3 2BW
tel 016-1832 1992

Extensive range of poetry titles, and exciting programme of events and readings.

Waterstone's, Gower Street
82 Gower Street, London WC1E 6EQ
tel 020-7636 1577 *fax* 020-7580 7680
email enquiries@
gowerstreet.waterstones.co.uk

Stocks work by outstanding contemporary and classical poets, men and women, from every continent, in tranlation, bilingual editions, and original English. The anthologies section ranges from African to Zen School. Also stocks Poetry Journals, Audiobooks, Secondhand/Out of Print, Poetry Criticism and Creative Writing. Full mail-order service.

Waterstone's, Hampstead
68/69 Hampstead High Street, London NW3 1QP

tel 020-7794 1098

Has a very successful, wide-ranging section carrying the classic and the modern, the well known and the less familiar. A growing range of imports and translations, especially by European poets.

Waterstone's, Sauchiehall Street
154/160 Sauchiehall Street, Glasgow G2 3EW
tel 014-1353 2484

A large poetry section including a wide range of Scottish poetry.

Word Power Books
43 West Nicholson Street, Edinburgh EH8 9DB
tel 013-1662 9112
email books@word-power.co.uk
website www.word-power.co.uk
Contact Elaine Henry

An independent bookshop, with a comprehensive range of books of all sorts.

Poetry libraries

The services available from our libraries are quite staggering. Often they are also so understated that we are not fully aware of what is on offer – and it is well worth investigating. Many of the libaries below provide a wonderful resource for poets, whether it be in the form of a collection of small magazines or, simply, in reference material with a specific connection to poetry.

Bangor Library

80 Hamilton Road, Bangor, Down BT20 4LH
tel (02891) 270591
email bangor.library@ni-libraries.net
Contact Stephen Hanson

Has a well-stocked poetry collection concentrating mainly on post 1950 poetry and Irish poets. They run poetry events nearly every month, with readings, workshops, and a poetry reading group. One poet has described it as 'the best poetry library in Northern Ireland'. Also has Poetry Unlimited, a Children's Poetry library with masses of poetry books and tapes of poems for young people. There are competitions, readings and workshops, even producing poems on computers to put on the library walls.

Barbican Library

Barbican Centre, Silk Street, London EC2Y 8DS
tel 020-7382 7098
email barbicanlib@cityoflondon.gov.uk
website www.cityoflondon.gov.uk/ barbicanlibrary
Contact John Lake

Excellent collection of poetry books for loan. Also runs poetry readings and workshops throughout the year.

Birmingham Central Library

Chamberlain Square, Birmingham, West Midlands B3 3HQ
tel 0121-303 4227
Contact Paul Woodward

Large library with an extensive poetry collection.

The British Library

96 Euston Road, London NW1 2DB
tel 0870-444 1500 (Switchboard), 020-7412 7676 (Advance Reservations, St Pancras Reading Rooms and Humanities enquiries), 020-7412 7702 (Maps), 020-7412 7513 (Manuscripts), 020-7412 7772 (Music), 020-7412 7873 (Asia, Pacific & Africa Collections)
website www.bl.uk

The national library of the UK and a legal deposit library. The collection includes in excess of 150 million items, in most known languages. Online catalogues.

Chesterfield Library

New Beetwell Street, Chesterfield, Derbyshire S40 1QN
tel (01246) 209292
email ann.ainsworth@ derbyshire.gov.uk
Contact Ann Ainsworth

Runs regular poetry events.

Halifax Central Library

Northgate, Halifax, Yorkshire HX1 1UN
tel (01422) 392628
email shymas@one.com
website www.calderdale.gov.uk
Contact Sarah Hymas

Runs a poetry book of the month promotion, bringing national and international contemporary poets to users' attention. Also runs poetry reading groups at Central Library, and at branch libraries in Sowerby Bridge and Brighouse. Committed to highlighting the value poetry and poets have to everyday life.

Hall Green Library, Birmingham

Hall Green Library, 1221 Stratford Road, Birmingham, West Midlands B28 9AD
tel 0121-464 6633
email hall.green.library@ birmingham.gov.uk
website www.birmingham.gov.uk/ hallgreenlibrary
Contact Mike Reed

A large selection of poetry books for loan; also runs a poetry group on the first Monday evening of each month.

The Little Magazines, Alternative Press and Poetry Store Collections

The Library, University College London, Gower Street, London WC1E 6BT
tel 020-7380 7796
website www.ucl.ac.uk/Library/special-coll/ litmags.shtml

Extensive holdings from mid-1960s of UK little magazines, small press and underground publications in particular, and large but less comprehensive holdings of US publications. There is also a selection of magazines and books from the Commonwealth, Europe and other countries and a small collection of reference material either about little-magazine and small-press activities or of a more general critical or background nature. The library currently subscribes to around 200 little magazine titles. Over 3500 little magazine and alternative press titles are held in all.

Manchester Central Library

St Peters Square, Manchester M2 5PD
tel 0161-234 1981

email libbtt@ libraries.manchester.gov.uk
Contact Libby Tempest

Has been organising poetry readings and events for a number of years, and has seen a growing audience for live poetry. Extensive collection of poetry books.

Mitchell Library

North Street, Glasgow G3 7DN
tel 0141-287 2838
email catherine.mcinerney@ cls.glasgow.gov.uk
Contact Caherine McInerney

Houses the largest available collection of Burns poetry and songs, as well as an extensive collection of Scottish poetry.

Norfolk and Norwich Millennium Library

The Forum, Millennium Plain, Norwich, Norfolk NR2 1AW
tel (01603) 774774
email millennium.lib@ norfolk.gov.uk
website www.norfolk.gov.uk

A huge range of poetry books available to borrow. Numerous poetry-related events, bringing poetry alive in the heart of Norwich.

Northern Poetry Library

Morpeth Library, Gas House Lane, Morpeth, Northumberland NE61 1TA
tel (01670) 534524
email pahallam@ northumberland.gov.uk
Contact Pat Hallam

The largest collection of contemporary poetry in England outside London, consisting of 17,000 volumes plus magazines covering English-language poetry published since 1968. Adult and children's poetry available. All items are available for loan.

Partick Library

306 Dumbarton Road, Glasgow G11 6AB
tel 0141-287 2838

email catherine.mcinerney@
cls.glasgow.gov.uk
Contact Catherine McInerney

Home to Scotland's very first poetry discussion group. Meetings take place on the first Thursday of every month. There is a regular series of visiting poets.

The Poetry Archive

PO Box 286, Stroud, Gloucestershire GL6 1AL
website www.poetryarchive.org
Editor Esther Morgan, Andrew Bailey

The world's premier online collection of recordings of poets reading their work. here you can enjoy listening, free of charge, to the voices of contemporary English-language poets and of poets from the past. The Archive is growing all the time.

The Poetry Cubicle Library

5 Wrights Court, Elm Hill, Norwich NR2 2RA
tel (07789) 514655
email Sara@ thepoetrycubicle.org.uk
website www.thepoetrycubicle.org.uk
Contact Sara Wingate Gray

The Poetry Cubicle is a not-for-profit organisation dedicated to making poetry more accessible. As part of its remit it has established an independent poetry library, with the aid of a Millennium Award, in Norwich. Specialises in stocking the mad, bad, deranged, denounced poet, the lost, forgotten and renounced poet, and has a wealth of poetical material veering from a William Burroughs APO-33 pamphlet to a Linton Kwesi Johnson spoken-word vinyl LP to *The Illustrated Ape* magazine to Bob Cobbing concrete poetry prints, plus the unusual gamut of pamphlets, books and DIY poetry booklets from the 1960s onwards. Also has a small children's

poetry library and is beginning to convert some of its collection into braille and large print format. Almost free to join, and hopes to provide access to under-supported and under-funded poetry and poets.

The Poetry Library

Royal Festival Hall, Level 5, London SE1 8XX
tel 020-7921 0943 *fax* 020-7921 0939
email info@poetrylibrary.org.uk
website www.poetrylibrary.org.uk;
www.poetrymagazines.org.uk

Comprehensive collection of poetry written in or translated into English since 1912. The biggest collection of its type with over 80,000 volumes and periodicals. An information service relating to all aspects of modern and contemporary poetry is also provided. The library is closed to the public until June 2007; however, a first-rate information service is still available via email, the website, and by letter. The poetry Library provides up-to-date listings of competitions, publications, magazines and workshops, either on its excellent website or if you send an sae to the postal address.

Scottish Poetry Library

5 Crichton's Close, Canongate, Edinburgh EH8 8DT
email inquiries@spl.org.uk
website www.spl.org.uk

The Scottish Poetry Library is a unique national resource, funded by the Scottish Arts Council, offering around 27,000 volumes of poetry, mainly Scottish and contemporary, but with a range of other languages and centuries, as well as a selection of journals, audio tapes, CDs, videos and Braille collections. There are free borrowing facilities, disabled access and postal borrowing as well as an indexed cuttings reference archive and an extensive children's section. The Scottish Poetry Library provides poet-led workshops for schools and other institutions plus resources and CPD worrkshops for teachers. There is a programme of readings and events.

Shirley Library

Church Road, Shirley, Solihull, West Midlands B90 2AX
tel 0121-744 1076
email libraryarts@solihull.gov.uk
Contact Joyce Workman, Barbara Clarke

A poetry-friendly library which hosts regular Poetry Coffee Mornings for its readers. At these sessions poetry lovers can hear contemporary poetry by published poets and can also read some of their own work.

Solihull Central Library

Homer Road, Solihull, West Midlands, B91 3RG
tel 0121-704 6965
website www.solihull.gov.uk/wwwlib
Contact Nickie Thomas

Hosts poetry readings, performances, slams and workshops as part of the Live Literature Programme. Runs a contemporary Poetry Reading Group, which meets every other month, and a new Young People's Poetry writing Group (also meets every other month). Committed to the promotion of contemporary poetry.

South Yardley Library

Yardley Road, Birmingham, West Midlands B25 8LT
tel 0121-464 1944
email south.yardley.library@ birmingham.gov.uk

website www.birmingham.gov.uk/ southyardleylibrary
Contact Pat Gisbourne

Committed to providing a wide range of poetry, particularly modern poetry. A member of both the Poetry Society and the Poetry Book Society.

Walsall Central Library

Lichfield Street, Walsall, West Midlands WS1 1TR
tel (01922) 653121
email CentralLendingLibrary@ walsall.gov.uk
website www.walsall.gov.uk/libraries
Contact Annie Wood

Committed to promoting poetry to a wide audience.

Warwick Library

Barrack Street, Warwick, Warwickshire CV34 4TH
tel (01926) 742744
email warwicklibrary@ warwickshire.gov.uk
website www.warwickshire.gov.uk/libraries
Contact Kate Mackie

Has a wide selection of poetry books for loan.

Wolverhampton Central Library

Snow Hill, Wolverhampton WV1 3AX
tel (01902) 552061
email simon.fletcher@ dial.pipex.com
website www.wolverhampton.gov.uk/ leisureculture/libraries/centrallibrary
Contact Simon Fletcher

The focus of much poetic activity in the city. The Poetry Readers' Group meets regularly, and poetry events are held.

Useful books

There are many books that will help you to write better poetry. Here are just a few:

An Introduction to English Poetry by James Fenton (Penguin)

A Poetry Handbook by Mary Oliver (Harcourt)

Getting into Poetry: A Readers' and Writers' Guide to the Poetry Scene by Paul Hyland (Bloodaxe Poetry Handbooks)

How Poetry Works by Philip Davies Roberts (Penguin)

How to be Well-Versed in Poetry edited by EO Parrott (Penguin)

How to Publish Your Poetry by Peter Finch (Allison & Busby)

Poets' Handbook – A Guide to Building Great Poems by Kenneth C Steven (Writers' Bookshop)

Taking Your Poetry Further – The Poetry Society's guide for the novice poet, available free by sending an sae to The Poetry Society, 22 Betterton Street, London WC2H 9BU

The Art and Craft of Poetry by Michael J Bugela (Writer's Digest Books)

The Art of Haiku 2000 by Gerald England, Jean M Kahler (Illustrator)

The Creative Writing Coursebook: Forty Authors Share Advice and Exercises for Fiction and Poetry by Andrew Motion (Pan)

Ode Less Travelled: Unlocking the Poet Within by Stephen Fry (Hutchinson)

Our Thoughts Are Bees: Working with Writers and Schools by Mandy Coe (Wordplay Press)

Strong Words: Modern Poets on Modern Poetry by WN Herbert (Bloodaxe)

The Practice of Poetry: Writing Exercises from Poets Who Teach by Robin Behn (HarperCollins)

The Way to Write – A complete guide to the basic skills of good writing by John Fairfax & John Moat (Elm Tree Books)

Writing Poems by Peter Sansom (Bloodaxe Poetry Handbooks)

Writing Poetry by John Whitworth (A & C Black)

Writing Poetry by Matthew Sweeney & John Hartley Williams (Teach Yourself)

Writing the Bright Moment: Inspiration and Guidance for Writers by Roselle Angwin (Fire in the Head)

Poetry websites

The Internet was made for poetry, whether to publish e-magazines or create communities where poets can gather virtually to discuss mutual interests or just share their work. It also provides invaluable resources. Below are some of the websites the poet may turn to for information about the world of poetry.

57 Productions
www.57productions.com

57 presents an extensive and diverse programme of promotional events, and an expanding catalogue of productions – CDs and cassettes, videos and specials for the Internet – featuring popular poets and performers. It offers agency and advisory services to venues and festivals, educational institutions and the general media on a wide range of popular poetic activity.

Askaboutwriting.net
www.askaboutwriting.net

A news and resource site for writers of all abilities everywhere. It updates on Saturdays. A free update notice is emailed on Mondays.

Britain In Print
www.britaininprint.net

Set up to promote the wealth of pre-1700 printed materials that exists within some of Britain's major libraries. A core part of the site is an e-learning project based on Robert Henryson's medieval Scot's poem, *The Testament of Cresseid*. The materials have been piloted in Queen Anne High School in Dunfermline, Fife (birthplace of Henryson), and the innovative online support tools have helped bring the poem alive for school students. Through visits to major libraries, the project has also introduced school students to primary source materials, ranging from first editions of Shaespeare, to early works of Chaucer, Gavin Douglas and other writers.

Cambridgepoetry
www.cambridgepoetry.org

A website for presses and events running in Cambridge, including the poetry summit and Cambridge series readings, featuring new and innovative poetry by young writers.

Can I Have A Word?
www.barbican.org.uk/canihaveaword

Provides teachers with new ideas and resources to inspire creative writing in the classroom.

Contemporary Writers
www.contemporarywriters.com

UK and Commonwealth poet biographies, bibliographies, critical reviews, prizes and photographs. A British Council/Booktrust Initiative.

Everypoet
www.everypoet.com

Poems and poetry resources.

Guardian Poetry Workshop
books.guardian.co.uk/poetryworkshop/

Hosted every month by a different poet who sets an exercise, chooses the most interesting responses and offers an appraisal of them.

hEar4Words
uk.groups.yahoo.com/group/hEar4Words

Online poets meet. News and dates of events.

Lines On the Map
www.cheshire.gov.uk/ReadersAndWriters/Writers/linesonthemap/home.htm

A local project set up by Andrew Rudd, the Cheshire Poet Laureate for 2006. It is a clickable map of Cheshire: each place-name leads to a poem, gradually building into a poetry map of the County. People have been asked to submit poems; more are added each month – currently (June) the total is about 75 poems and the project has been running since March. This gives people a chance to write about the places they know best, and share that work with others.

Lit-Net
www.lit-net.org

A virtual literature centre for the West Midlands with stacks of poetry landmarks, including Poetry of Place with poems about places in the West Midlands, and poetry on loan in public libraries.

New Hope International
www.geraldengland.co.uk

Reviews of hard-copy poetry-related publications, and much more.

Poeticize
www.poeticize.co.uk

The world's first collective black arts, education and media platform.

Poetry International Web
www.poetryinternationalweb.org

A worldwide forum for poetry on the Internet. PIW offers news, reviews, essays, interviews and discussions as well as hundreds of poems by acclaimed modern poets from all around the world, both in the original language and in English translation. In keeping with the spirit of the Web, it is a truly international collaboration of 12 editors in 12 different countries. Each of these countries maintains its own national domain within PIW, with its chosen 'Poet of the Quarter', news and other articles.

Poetry Jukebox
www.poetryjukebox.com

A unique production for the Internet from the 57 organisation. The jukebox features more than 40 poets – and expands in time. It features exclusive works from artists such as Benjamin Zephaniah, Zena Edwards & Brian Patten ... including works-in-progress and those that can only be understood in terms of recent events in the Middle East and the USA (for instance from Moniza Alvi and Michael Rosen). The jukebox also offers rare archive material from poets including Kamau Brathwaite and Christopher Logue, dating from the 60s.

Poetry Landmarks
www.poetrysociety.org.uk/landmark

The Poetry Society's extremely useful Landmarks project – a database of poetry organisations, venues, writing groups, publishers, magazines, etc.

poetrymagazines.org
www.poetrymagazines.org.uk

A full text digital library of British 20th-century and contemporary poetry magazines from the Poetry Library's collection based in London's Royal Festival Hall. New issues and new titles are added all the time.

Poetry On Loan
www.poetryonloan.org.uk

A virtual gateway to over 20 public libraries in the West Midlands, which specialise in poetry – from books on the shelves to poets in between them.

Poetry pf
www.poetrypf.co.uk

The site is principally intended to be a showcase of modern poets, and to provide a focused point for members to take advantage of the visibility and searchable presence the Internet provides. Each member has his/her own pages within the site, and feature articles and reviews (of others' books) are invited. There is a members' events listing, including competitions advised by members associated with them.

Poetry Portal
www.poetry-portal.com

A directory of worldwide poetry online; a simple-to-use and detailed overview of the fascinating variety of literary productions on the Internet.

Poets' Graves
www.poetsgraves.co.uk

An online guide to the graves of famous poets, with photographs!

Poet's Letter
www.poetsletter.com

Website offering lots of poetry material.

Poets On Fire
http://poetsonfire.blogspot.com

A website filled with news and discussion about poetry in performance across the UK.

Spoiled Ink
www.spoiledink.com

Designed to help writers get more readers, improve their craft, get published and promote any already-published work.

The British Electronic Poetry Centre
www.soton.ac.uk/~bepc

A reference guide to the work of contemporary British poets from the parallel tradition. Launched in May 2002, it provides information on poets and their publications, and audio files to accompany examples of their work. The site is particularly dedicated to increasing the understanding of the role of oral performance in poetry, and will be supported by research projects on the history and theory of performance. Its development was supported by an AHRB small grant for the study of the history of poetry readings in post-war Britain.

The Staffordshire Learning Net for Geography
www.sln.org.uk/geography/poem.htm

An award-winning initiative to celebrate geography for young people and to celebrate good practice between teachers. Using poetry in geography-teaching helps by developing a sense of place – through descriptive vocabulary of sights, sounds, smells and even tastes, relating the emotions of experiences, relaying polemic opinions about issues, and illustrating in words, geographical shapes and patterns.

The Poetry Kit
www.poetrykit.org

Incredibly useful and comprehensive website set up in 1997 to provide an information resource for poets. Lists courses, competitions, events, festivals, venues, magazines, poetry organisations, publishers, workshop groups and more. Coverage is full and international. There is also a magazine section that provides an outlet for poetry, reviews, articles and interviews.

The South
www.thesouth.org.uk

Poetry in the south of England, and especially Brighton.

UK Authors
www.ukauthors.com

A writers' showcase and resource site, which has grown hugely over the past three years, and now has almost 2000 members. The resource pages contain thousands of resources for writers of all levels, and the site regularly runs (prose and poetry) competitions and publishes an annual anthology. There are also flourishing forums, poetry workshops and prose and poetry discussions.

writersartists.net
www.writersartists.net

A collaborative of globally and socially minded poets, writers and artists, many of whom specialise in cross-arts work, and who perform, teach and work internationally, especially in the UK, Europe and in the US.

WritersServices
www.writersservices.com

A website for writers, including invaluable resources and help, as well as a self-publishing service.

Index

If you like poetry, you'll **LOVE** what the **Poetry Book Society** has to offer!

Logue's Homer War Music

Receive **Christopher Logue's** *War Music* (worth £12.99) absolutely **FREE!**

Founded by T S Eliot and friends in 1953, the PBS is a unique poetry society. Four times a year, PBS Members receive the Choice book and the *Bulletin*, a 28-page magazine packed with reviews, poems, special offers, and articles by the selected poets. A one-year membership costs only £35.

Call now
to receive your **FREE** book, with no further obligation to buy. Plus, reply before 30 September 2006 and receive a **FREE** book voucher worth £10.

Five great reasons
why **you** should join today!

1. Receive Christopher Logue's *War Music* (worth £12.99) absolutely **FREE**, no strings attached.

2. **FREE** postage and packing on your introductory offer.

3. Receive a **FREE** Book Voucher worth £10 if you reply by 31 October 2006.

4. Receive four **FREE** poetry books (one each quarter) included in the price of your membership – from only £35 for one year!

5. Receive a **FREE** discount of 25% on every poetry book published in the UK.

Call **020 7833 9247** and quote 'PWY06' to take advantage of this offer now, or visit **www.poetrybooks.co.uk**. To find out about our other membership schemes (for schools, libraries and younger children) please call, or email us at **info@poetrybooks.co.uk**.

pbs poetry book society

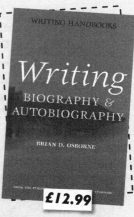
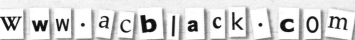

WRITING ESSENTIALS

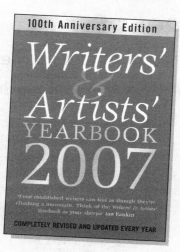
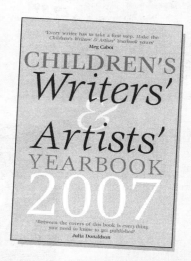